Albania in Crisis

To another rising, shining star, little Arthur, who also often falls . . .

Albania in Crisis

The Predictable Fall of the Shining Star

Daniel Vaughan-Whitehead

Senior Adviser, Central and Eastern European Team,
International Labour Office, Budapest, Hungary

Edward Elgar
Cheltenham, UK • Northampton, MA, USA

Published by
Edward Elgar Publishing Limited
Glensanda House
Montpellier Parade
Cheltenham
Glos GL50 1UA
UK

Edward Elgar Publishing, Inc.
6 Market Street
Northampton
Massachusetts 01060
USA

A catalogue record for this book
is available from the British Library
Library of Congress Cataloguing in Publication Data
Vaughan-Whitehead, Daniel.
    Albania in crisis : the predictable fall of the shining star /
Daniel Vaughan-Whitehead
    Includes bibliographical references and index.
    1. Albania—Economic conditions—1992– 2. Albania—Economic
policy. I. Title.
HC402.V38 1999
338.94965—dc21   98–53764
                                                            CIP
ISBN 1 84064 070 7

Printed and bound in Great Britain by Bookcraft (Bath) Ltd.

Contents

List of Tables and Figures

Tables

Boxes

Figures

Foreword

In early 1997, Albania was paralysed by a crisis without precedent: a major rebellion in the south of the country expanded to other regions in a general rejection of the authorities, characterised by acts of destruction against enterprises and public buildings. The calm was restored only after the intervention of a multinational military force and new elections in June, when the current socialist-led government came to power. After this return to democratic life, the international community rallied round to help to reconstruct the country. An important donors' conference was organised in Brussels in October 1997—involving all the relevant international organisations and bilateral donors—with the aim of mobilising funds and launching the necessary projects to ensure the economic recovery of the country. Thanks to this solidarity movement, large amounts of money have been provided, and new and essential technical co-operation projects have been launched in different fields and regions of Albania.

Paradoxically—probably because of the urgent need to start Albania on the road to recovery as quickly as possible—no comprehensive assessment has yet been provided concerning the causes of the crisis. This book is a contribution to filling this gap.

The explanation most often given for the Albanian crisis is the collapse of the pyramid schemes in which perhaps the majority of the population had invested their life savings. The main thesis of this book is that such an analysis is far from exhaustive, and even misleading. The violent uprising had its roots in a range of other economic, social, and political developments, many of which are documented here for the first time: fragile economic growth, characterised by the collapse of industrial activity, the absence of substituting activities from an emerging and still weak service sector, and a banking system still unable to assume its role of financial intermediary; the absence of efficient corporate governance at the enterprise level, particularly in respect of the inadequacies of foreign investment and the failure of the mass privatisation programme; on the social side, the growth of unemployment and the fall in real wages and living standards which combined to condemn a growing proportion of the people to total destitution; finally, the fragility of public authority and institutions (for example, in terms of public order, tax collection, and so on), combined with the lack of responsibility inherited from the previous regime. Since 1992, the ILO has been particularly active in Albania, attempting to highlight such adverse economic and social trends, and to create the necessary legislative framework, but also tripartite social dialogue at the national level which is likely to prove useful in addressing these issues and possible solutions.

The second major aim of this book is to paint a first picture of the consequences of the 1997 crisis, in terms of destroyed enterprises, interrupted activities, economic results, and social protection. This is also needed to identify the most promising sectors of the economy, and to define some of the policy priorities that could lead to a more sustained economic recovery, that is, one generated by production forces. Beyond this, one of the main conclusions of this book is that the social dimension has been too much neglected in the first years of transition, so much so that it has contributed to block economic and political progress. Against this background, it is now not enough to direct efforts towards the recovery of the economy unless they are accompanied by a revitalised social policy. At the same time, the sacrifices that the new economic policies will require will not be understood or accepted by the people without the full involvement of the trade unions, employers' representatives, and other social actors, and without a range of measures designed to rebuild social cohesion in Albania. It is to this that the ILO has been trying to attract the attention of the international community since the crisis, notably through its report *Albania: Social Dimension of Recovery—Assessment and Proposals for Action* (ILO, 1997).

What marks out this book above all is the direct results and possible policy routes it outlines based on a rich data set collected in the course of three comprehensive surveys of more than 1,000 enterprises carried out by the author with the help of the Albanian statistical institute INSTAT at the end of 1994, 1996, and 1997. We hope these results will be directly useful to other international organisations and bilateral donors, but also to all Albanians involved in the reconstruction process. All efforts should be combined, from different organisations and actors, and covering different angles, to ensure more balanced and sustainable economic growth, the best way of guaranteeing social peace in Albania.

Oscar de Vries Reilingh

Director of ILO–CEET
International Labour Office
Central and Eastern European Team, Budapest

Preface

"Rising shining star", "Balkan tiger", "economic miracle", "fastest transition economy": no terms were positive enough for external experts and the international media to describe the progress made by Albania during its first years of transition. No other country in Central and Eastern Europe had received such compliments about its economic transformation. Characterised by rapid GDP growth and considered the "most obedient IMF student", from 1993 Albania was put forward as one of the best examples to follow in the region.

It is against this background that we must seek to understand the profound shock which resulted when this seemingly model economy was suddenly plunged into a terrible internal conflict in early 1997, after the Albanian people suddenly rebelled following the collapse of the pyramid schemes in which the majority of them had placed their life savings.

This unexpected turn of events seemed likely to compromise what should have been continued and exemplary economic growth. At the time, the Albanian people appeared—and were often presented—as irresponsible and immature, principally to blame for interrupting the virtuous circle pursued so far, and despite all the good advice given them by external experts: everything would have gone on as before if only they had not been so foolish as to invest all their savings in obviously dodgy pyramid schemes, deluding themselves that they could make quick money without having to work for it. Statements of this kind were usually made in ignorance of the realities of the Albanian economy and of the Albanian people. It is largely a desire to set the record straight which motivated the present book: to provide another view of the crisis, to determine its real causes, and to discuss respective responsibilities. With this end in view, we are often compelled to present arguments that are at odds with what one might call "mainstream economics".

In the first place, the frequently presented economic indicators did not reflect the real economic situation. Not only were the national figures, especially on GDP growth, unreliable because based on debatable data and methodology; they were misleading, because they neglected an important part of the economy, the production sphere, while ignoring social developments altogether (Chapter 1). We argue that during the supposed "golden period" of the Albanian economy, there were already increasing signs of its extreme fragility. Industrial production was registering its worst figures so far—and the worst in Central and Eastern Europe—without any attention being paid to the fact in experts' reports and the international press (Chapter 2). It was also clear that the development of services would not be able to compensate the fall in industrial output: their rapid development and promising growth were based mainly on very small enterprises, often precarious, and concentrated in too narrow a range of activities—this was the so-called "kiosk economy" (Chapter 3). The banking sector was known to be totally dysfunctional, and in particular unable to operate as a reliable financial intermediary between the increasing demands for credit from emerging private businesses and the substantial remittances coming from Albanians working abroad, another distinctive feature of the "Albanian miracle". This resulted in the development of an informal credit market, or a credit market 'by default', originally aimed at channelling funds towards investments in new production activities, before progressively giving way to a range of pyramid schemes (Chapter 4).

The systematic presentation of successful macroeconomic indicators also obscured developments at the enterprise level, where significant adjustments were taking place in terms of the labour force and restructuring. These led to a large number of dismissals, another feature of the Albanian transition that was never reflected in the official unemployment statistics which were in fact artificially depressed by the imposition of new eligibility criteria (Chapter 5). At the same time, the strict incomes policy and wage controls, adopted as a basic condition of the macroeconomic stabilisation package implemented by the government on the advice of international monetary institutions alongside price liberalisation, led to a rapid fall in real wages, already the lowest in Europe. This not only plunged an increasing number of workers and their families below any possible measure of the subsistence minimum or poverty line, but contributed to deepen even further the productivity crisis at the enterprise level, with growing worker demotivation, and increasing recourse to the informal economy as the only means of survival (Chapter 6).

The involvement of all citizens in the mass privatisation programme was originally intended to compensate for the heavy burden of transition; it turned out to be a total failure, the price of the distributed vouchers falling to a mere 1 per cent of face value. The privatisation process was also marked by multiple examples of corruption and of compromised corporate governance in newly privatised enterprises (Chapter 7). The privatisation process, combined with the emergence of a growing number of small private businesses, was accompanied by worrying social trends at the enterprise level: trade union recognition—and indeed any form of worker participation—was systematically avoided, collective agreements were not concluded, and individual labour contracts were not signed, denoting a growing social deficit (Chapter 8). Nevertheless, both the local and the international press continued to praise Albania for its GDP figures.

The attraction of massive foreign investment was supposed to solve most economic problems by providing the missing fresh capital, developing local markets, and importing economic and social models that had proven successful in more developed countries. In the event, foreign investment in the first years of transition was at best a mixed blessing, and in many cases an unhappy experience for the Albanian partners (Chapter 9).

It is one of the principal arguments of this book that in many ways the pyramid schemes emerged as a result of these social and economic developments. We argue in particular that the schemes were not the product of "dirty Albanian minds" but were motivated originally by practical economic reasons, to support newly emerging economic activities and to supplement a defective banking sector unable or unwilling to provide the necessary credit to the production sector. The schemes were further advanced by the strict monetary and fiscal policy which—for the same macroeconomic reasons behind the strict incomes policy—only served to further limit the credit available to the production sector (Chapter 10). We also argue that the pyramid schemes did not "interrupt virtuous economic growth", but on the contrary, and paradoxically, contributed to sustain 'short-term' economic growth, providing the government with more 'presentable' economic indicators. We also argue that the pyramid schemes did not call a premature halt to a well-developing economic performance, but instead that, again paradoxically, the systematic presentation of positive economic indicators—economic growth becoming more and more clearly sustained by the money circulating within these schemes—helped to provide them with the political and economic legitimacy they needed to survive a number of years and to grow astronomically.

For all these reasons, the crisis should not have come as a surprise. The collapse of the pyramid schemes was clearly only a catalytic event—the mere tip of the iceberg—and the popular discontent and subsequent uprising were the sudden and violent rejection of a combination of adverse economic and social developments which had finally become too hard to bear. A detailed analysis of the destruction process confirms the complexity and wide extent of the crisis, which seems also to have been generated by a series of factors at the enterprise level. In particular, the fact that in some cases—for instance, in the southern city of Vlora— the rebel movement also took the form of strike committees composed of elected delegates shows that the workers played an important role. The fact that not only government offices and buildings were destroyed, but thousands of enterprises all over the country is another clear sign that the rebellion was partly directed against management, or at least against a particular form of management characteristic of the transition period. Our survey results allow us to better understand the main types of management and enterprise against which this movement arose: by providing systematic results on the destruction process and consequent physical damage by region, property form, and activity, we can also identify more precisely what may have led to such an abrupt eruption of popular anger (Chapter 11).

At the same time, it is important to look to the future, particularly the implications of the crisis for economic activity, allowing us to determine the more substantial sectors and potential pillars of the Albanian economy (Chapter 12). We emphasise, for example, a number of promising industrial activities. Furthermore, while analysis of Albanian macroeconomic indicators clearly shows the direct effects of the crisis—the whole country as it were moving backwards—it also reveals the structural nature of most economic imbalances and deficiencies, many of which were visible before the crisis (Chapter 13).

The crisis and its effects will again hit hardest the poorest categories: the unemployed, smallholders, the recipients of social assistance benefits, public employees, and many others. By the end of 1997, poverty had engulfed more than one million people, that is, more than one-third of the population. The Albanian people, already impoverished during the first years of transition, as a result of the crisis experienced even darker times: the destruction of workplaces, the interruption of economic activity, a new unemployment shock, a sudden surge of inflation, and a general fall in real wages and other incomes, all on top of their severe losses in the pyramid schemes (Chapter 14). As if that were not enough, the conflict in Kosovo has now added a worrying crescendo of social tensions to the situation in the north of Albania.

The present book will if nothing else contribute to the avoidance of similar mistakes or misjudgements on economic growth in Albania. Analysis of the causes and extent of the crisis seems to indicate the central importance of enterprise-related factors, chiefly those affecting individuals, such as wages, employment, and social policies, at a time when only macroeconomic indicators were being monitored by domestic and foreign experts. We would hope to encourage a reconsideration of this approach, not only in Albania but in other transition countries. In this regard, the concentration on dubious GDP growth figures in 1993–96 in the knowledge that the industrial sector had collapsed was perhaps the worst example of intellectual bad faith in the short history of Albania's economic transition. It drew attention and resources away from the most urgent problems, and led to the almost total asphyxia of Albania's productive forces.

However, when we were finalising the book, some initial promising results for 1998 were already generating a new euphoria, although the basic social problems remained unsolved, most enterprises still being in limbo. Overoptimism began once more to dominate all economic reporting, as if the crisis had never taken place. The star had begun to shine again. Furthermore, despite its debatable effects before the crisis, a similar restrictive monetary policy was introduced, allowing the government to conclude a second standard agreement with the IMF. The economic debate focused once again on only four main indicators: inflation, GDP growth, the budget deficit, and the external deficit. Industrial activity was once again forgotten: no credits were being provided to the production sector. Social transfers, such as pensions and unemployment benefits, continued their downward course. At the same time, Albania put itself in the hands of international donors and resumed its attempts to attract foreign investors, as if a solution to the crisis could only come from abroad, totally neglecting the potential of local actors and domestic development.

Whatever the benefits of international assistance—which we fervently hope will continue—and without underestimating the importance of keeping macroeconomic trends under control, we are convinced that Albania would benefit greatly from a new approach. It is in this spirit that we have ventured to propose a number of policy alternatives. First, on the economic side, it might be better to try to regenerate local production forces rather than to count exclusively and systematically on foreign investment: to help enterprises, in the wake of the crisis, to adopt specialisations that could help to ensure their long-term development, and more generally to create a new virtuous circle based on mutually sustaining higher consumption and local production (Chapter 15). Control of inflation and the budget deficit should by no means be deprioritised, but it must also be clear that the development of an economy can come only from internal developments, from production forces which in Albania will never re-emerge unless a more flexible approach is taken to credit delivery and a strategic industrial policy formulated. It must also be clear that the economy will never be able to overcome the crisis in the face of a domestic demand which is seemingly being allowed to die.

Secondly, on the social side it is essential to insist that adverse developments are never again neglected as they were in the past: this seems to have played an important part in the 1997 explosion, particularly in respect of employment, social assistance, and wages and incomes policy. This is particularly important in a situation of continuing political instability: in mid-September 1998 the Democratic Party, led by former president Sali Berisha, attempted a coup, and on 28 September Prime Minister Fatos Nano hastily resigned. The newly nominated Premier Pandelo Majko, Secretary General of the ruling Socialist Party, after announcing his new government, in an interview given to the Italian daily *Corriere della Sera* (30 September, p. 14) stated its willingness to give priority to economic reconstruction, boost investment and employment, and adopt a new constitution, which was approved in a referendum held on 23 November 1998. But an ambitious programme to eradicate poverty should also be urgently designed. We believe the main task of Albanian policy-makers over the next few years will be to generate development better balanced between economic growth and the needs of Albanian society.

This book should be seen not as a provocation, but as the testimony of a labour economist who, after more than five years of intensive work on Albania, has been unable to find any convincing—only misleading—overall explanations of the recent crisis. The book was also inspired by discussions with Albanian experts who, trying with difficulty to return to normal life after the crisis, often repeat the same sentences, in the interest of historical accuracy: "It would be important one day to point out that it happened like this and not like that . . . ", or, "the situation was never as rosy as they said it was", and so on. I hope that the present book is not too far from what they would have liked to say, and that this first attempt will motivate many more of them to tackle and investigate more deeply some of the issues presented.

During the long period of preparation for this volume, I gained much from working with Albanian experts, to whom I would like to express my warm thanks for their constant availability and friendship. Above all, deep gratitude is due to Milva Ikonomi, Director of the National Statistical Office INSTAT, without whose friendly and efficient co-operation and great professionalism our enterprise surveys could never have been completed. I am also grateful to her colleagues, in particular Vojsava Progri, who played a central role in fieldwork, always with great enthusiasm, but also Dhimiter Tolle, Arjan Meni, and their teams of enumerators. I hope that their Institute will receive the recognition it is due—not to mention unconditional public support and funding—as the only independent source of information in Albania. I would also like to thank Filloreta Kodra, who has been the ideal companion at the Ministry of Labour over the years, together with Diana Metohu for our always stimulating discussions and activities. Among many others, thanks are also due to (in alphabetical order) Theodor Bej, Ahmet Ceni, Vangjel Godroli, Gazhmend Haxhia, Imir Kamba, Kristofor Kondi, Halil Laze, Stavri Liko, Xhevdet Llubani, Kastriot Muço, Marta Muço, Rustan Petrela, Baskim Sala, Illir Shmilli, Alfred Topi, and Daut Vata. We are grateful to UNDP Albania, especially Jan Wahlberg, for their kind co-operation. My thanks also go to my colleagues at the ILO, to Rino di Bernardo, Rene Dehee, Maurizio Sacconi, and especially to Oscar de Vries Reilingh for his continuous support. Let me also thank James Patterson for the editing and the typesetting, Marton Kovács for the statistical work, Borocka Gergely for the cover artwork, Tibor Lusztig for preparing the index, and Katalin Hárskuti and Eszter Szabó for their help in finalising the work.

Finally, I hope that this book will be useful to all those currently involved in providing technical assistance in Albania, so urgently needed for reconstructing the country and relieving the sufferings of the people. My aim is not to criticise, but rather, through the provision of new information, to help to make their work more efficient and more effective.

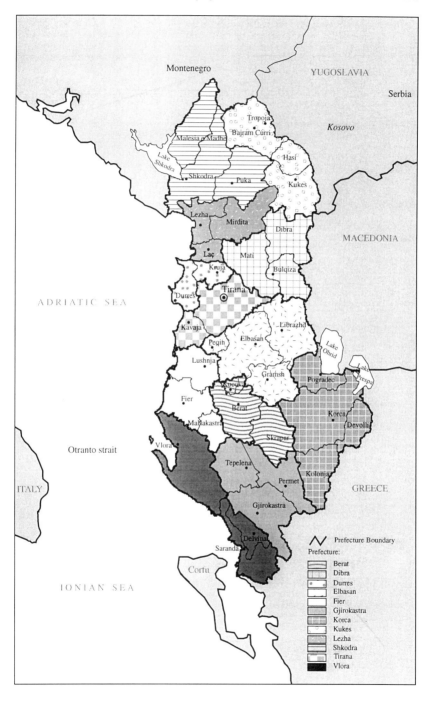

Part One
Assessment: The Reasons for the Crisis

1. The Apparent Rapid Success of the Balkan Tiger

1 INTRODUCTION

Prior to the reforms of the 1990s, Albania had been governed by an extremely severe Stalinist regime since 1945. Increasingly, this system became unsustainable, and the country descended into an economic and social crisis, in the first instance for the reasons common to all ex-communist countries: the reliance on central planning and centralisation, and the rejection of private ownership of the means of production. What set the "Albanian socialist model" apart from its neighbours, however, was the ideal of "self-reliance", not only for the national economy, but for each of the regions. This policy resulted in the development of a form of autarky in the 1980s.

Throughout most of the state-socialist period Albania was able to draw on substantial external resources, first from the USSR in the 1950s, and then from China in the 1960s and 1970s. The late 1970s represent a turning point in this respect, however: in 1976, the new Constitution set the country on a path that would lead to the prohibition of all forms of foreign financial support, most notably in the form of a ban on foreign borrowing. Albania's close relations with China were broken off in 1978. Moreover, Albania disrupted its non-market trading and financial relations with Eastern European countries.

This new situation generated a different kind of economic development. While before 1980 the country had managed to maintain slow but steady growth, and to accumulate significant foreign exchange reserves due to the substantial external subsidies already mentioned, from the 1980s the economy began to suffer a decline in productivity as the government remained committed to providing full employment for a rapidly increasing labour force, and the extreme isolation of the country prevented any accumulation of resources to finance capital investments and to replace basic machinery.

Albanian economic policy was also based on a system of rigidly fixed prices (unrelated to prices abroad) and constant exchange rates that played no allocative role and were used only for accounting purposes. Product markets were characterised by excess demand, as evidenced by long queues for basic goods. Import shortages led to major production losses, even in key export industries. At the same time, the government continued to subsidise losses in inefficient enterprises, mainly by means of an uncontrolled monetary surplus. As a result, in 1990 the budget deficit amounted to over 16 per cent of GDP and monetary expansion exceeded 20 per cent. These policies led to distortions in economic mechanisms and accelerated the total collapse of production. The annual average rate of growth fell to 1 per cent compared to 5 per cent over the previous decade. GDP growth was negative in 1990. All Albania's other macroeconomic indicators also deteriorated towards the end of the 1980s (IMF, 1994).

Since a few key exports (basic minerals and some agricultural products) were called upon to sustain the heavily import-dependent industrial and agricultural sectors, the trade balance deficit increased from USD 36 million in 1985 to USD 150 million in 1990, the most essential imports being financed by a balance of payments deficit and the accumulation of foreign debt.[1] By the end of 1991, official reserves were virtually exhausted (see *Table 1.1*). It was under these circumstances that the transition to a market economy became a necessity.

2 RAPID GDP GROWTH: ALBANIA A SUCCESS STORY?

The first serious economic reform measures were initiated in 1991, notably the liberalisation of trade and prices, followed in 1992 by the introduction of tight monetary, fiscal, and incomes policies. On the advice of the IMF,[2] greater budget discipline and a tightening of the money supply were introduced and, from July 1992, a floating exchange rate. Incomes policy has also been considered as an important nominal anchor under the reform programme. Structural reforms included the privatisation of agricultural land and of many small and medium-sized state-owned enterprises.

The Payment Crisis of 1991–92

During the first years of transition, however, the economic situation was further exacerbated by a major crisis in 1991–92. The fall in industrial output

---

1. See IMF (1994), and in particular Table 37, p. 72.

2. These steps towards fiscal and monetary control paved the way for approval of a 12-month IMF stand-by arrangement in the amount of SDR 20 million (57 per cent of Albania's quota, equivalent to approximately USD 29 million). After almost a year of successful implementation, the stand-by arrangement was replaced by a three-year arrangement in the amount of SDR 42.4 million (120 per cent of the quota, equivalent to about USD 60 million) under the enhanced structural adjustment facility (ESAF) in July 1993.

(70 per cent) was particularly dramatic, due mainly to the disintegration of the CMEA markets, which absorbed more than 50 per cent of Albanian exports, and the sudden removal of state subsidies to enterprises. At the end of 1991, trade with the former CMEA countries had fallen to less than 5 per cent of total commercial trade, from more than 60 per cent in the mid-1980s (IMF, 1994). Output declined by nearly 50 per cent between 1990 and 1992. The break-up of co-operative farms also led to a dramatic decline in agricultural production and widespread food shortages.

Albania's external situation started to deteriorate in the late 1980s, leading to a severe payment crisis in 1990–91. In 1991, exports in convertible currencies declined by nearly 40 per cent (to USD 72 million), reflecting a decline in nearly all major export activities. On the other hand, imports rose by 22 per cent (to USD 250 million). Consequently, the current account deficit (excluding official transfers) widened to USD 213 million (26 per cent of GDP), compared to USD 122 million (6 per cent) in 1990 (see *Table 1.1*). The situation deteriorated even further in 1992, the external deficit reaching more than 60 per cent of GDP (USD 434 million).

The external payment positions became critical and Albania defaulted on large short-term obligations to foreign banks. The fiscal deficit widened to more than 50 per cent of GDP between the second half of 1991 and the first half of 1992 (*Table 1.1*).

Stabilisation and Economic Recovery from 1993

Albania did have some success in stabilising macroeconomic conditions, however: by the end of 1992, Albania began to register positive results. As shown in *Table 1.1*, the decline in GDP was halted in early 1993 and grew by about 9.6 per cent over the year as a whole; GDP continued to increase, by 9.4 per cent in 1994 and by 8.9 per cent in 1995.[3] Overall, during the period 1993–95 GDP grew at an annual average rate of about 9 per cent.

Inflation was also reduced from triple digits in 1992 to single digits in 1995. The average annual inflation rate fell from 226 per cent in 1992 to 7.8 per cent in 1995, a reduction which has been presented as one of the government's notable successes.

The domestically financed budget deficit was reduced from 44 per cent of GDP in 1991 to below 7 per cent in 1995, the external current account deficit from 61 per cent of GDP in 1992 to less than 8 per cent in 1995, and official reserves rose to USD 240 million in 1995 from zero in 1991 (see *Table 1.1*).

---

3. Until 1996, the GDP growth figures published in all IMF and World Bank documents—and so in those of all other economic organisations and reviews—were 11 per cent in 1993, 7 per cent in 1994, and 11 per cent in 1995. In 1997, these figures were revised to 9.6, 9.4, and 8.9 per cent respectively.

Table 1.1 *Main Economic Indicators, 1990–96*

	1990	1991	1992	1993	1994	1995	1996
Economy							
GDP*	−10.0	−28.0	−7.2	9.6	9.4	8.9	8.2
Industrial output*	−14.2	−42.0	−51.2	−10.0	−2.0	1.0	13.6
Agricultural output*	−5.4	−17.4	18.5	10.4	10.3	10.6	3.0
Inflation (end-of-year percentage)	0	104.1	236.6	30.9	15.8	6.0	17.4
Inflation (annual average in percentage terms)	0	36.0	226.0	85.0	22.6	7.8	12.7
Fiscal Sector							
Domestically financed deficit (% of GDP)	4.0	44.0	20.0	9.1	7.0	6.7	10.5
Overall government budget deficit (cash-based; % of GDP)	4.0	44.0	20.3	14.4	12.4	10.4	11.4
External Sector							
External current account balance (excluding official transfers; USD million)	−122.0	−213.0	−434.0	−365.0	−283.0	−181.0	−201.0
External current account balance (excluding official transfers; % of GDP)	−6.0	−26.0	−61.1	−29.7	−14.3	−7.5	−7.7
Trade balance (USD million)	−150.0	−308.0	−454.0	−490.0	−460.0	−474.0	−676.8
Trade balance (% of GDP)	–	–	−64.0	−39.9	−23.2	−19.6	−25.0
Gross international reserves (USD million)	–	11.0	72.0	147.0	204.0	240.0	280.0
Exchange Rate							
Lek/USD	8.9	24.2	75.0	102.1	94.7	92.8	104.5

* Percentage change over previous period at constant 1990 prices.

Note: Government figures for GDP in 1994, 1995, and 1996 were 8.3, 13.3, and 9.1 per cent.

Sources: IMF (1994, 1997b).

GDP growth figures above all led most external experts to rapidly qualify the transition in Albania as a "success story", and to explain it as the natural result of successful reforms implemented under the guidance of international monetary institutions; these institutions started to praise—with some self-satisfaction—Albania's economic record: "Albania has made impressive progress since the overthrow of Communism in 1991" (IMF, 1997b, p. 3); "[s]trong adjustment policies have been the key to Albania's success" (IMF, 1997b, p. 3); "Albania has made tremendous progress . . . The three successive years of high economic growth attest to the major progress made in stabilisation and structural adjustment" (World Bank, 1996b, p. iii).

Similarly for the Economist Intelligence Unit: "As a result of the firm commitment to the IMF and World Bank programme by the Government, measured economic growth has been rapid . . ." and, "since the implementation of the stabilisation of adjustment programme in 1992, the country has made substantial progress in achieving macroeconomic stability". "Albania was Europe's fastest growing economy in 1995, with real GDP growth of 11%" (EIU, 1996, p. 32). "Further strong growth is expected in the next two years, on the back of the dynamic expansion of small and medium-sized private enterprises in the trade and service sector. The private sector now accounts for around 75% of GDP. These trends are expected to continue, with real GDP rising by around 8% this year and in 1997 and 1998."

The European Bank for Reconstruction and Development (EBRD) in its 1995 *Transition Report* also presented Albania on the basis of its GDP as the country with the highest growth in Central and Eastern Europe and placed it without hesitation in the group of countries in which economic reform was being pursued most extensively and most rapidly. The EBRD also predicted similar growth in 1996 (EBRD, 1995). Furthermore, on the basis of the same indicators for the OECD, "Albania was the fastest growing European country in 1993 and 1994" (OECD–CCET, 1995, p. 21). This optimism was largely echoed in the domestic and international press.[4]

As he emphasised at a number of press conferences, President Berisha attached particular importance to these positive economic indicators and optimistic reports from foreign experts. At a press conference in late 1995, he stated that Albania's economic recovery was among the fastest in the region, that the country ranked fourth in the region in respect of low inflation, and that it was the only country to have doubled internal investment between 1991 and 1994.[5]

While Albania undoubtedly showed genuine signs of economic recovery between 1992 and 1995, it was not clear whether this growth was artificial or signalled a real improvement in the economy.

---

4. See, for instance, *The Economist* (8 March 1997).

5. See, for instance, "Significant Economic and Financial Achievements", in the *Albanian Observer*, Vol. 1, No. 12 (1995), p. 10.

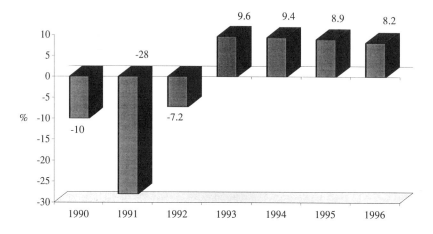

Figure 1.1 *Real GDP Growth (% change on previous year), 1990–96*

Note: Until 1996, the GDP growth figures published in all IMF and World Bank documents—and so in the publications of all other economic organisations and in reviews—were 11 per cent in 1993, 7 per cent in 1994, and 11 per cent in 1995. In 1997, these figures were revised to 9.5, 9.4, and 8.9 per cent respectively. Government figures for 1994–96 were 8.3, 13.3, and 9.1 per cent. *Source*: IMF (1997b).

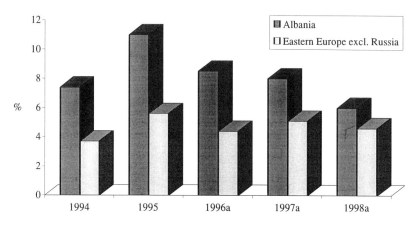

Figure 1.2 *Change in Albania's GDP Compared to Eastern Europe as a Whole, 1994–96 (% change on previous year; (a) EIU forecasts)*

Source: EIU (1996), p. 32.

3 UNRELIABLE DATA AND QUESTIONABLE METHODOLOGY

The first step towards the resolution of these issues was taken when important questions began to be posed in Albania concerning the methodology being used to calculate GDP growth.[6] For some, the methodology employed by the World Bank and the IMF was inappropriate because it calculated GDP growth on the basis of investment and income rather than on real production, so leading to an overestimation of output growth. This method clearly did not take into account the collapse of industrial output. The miscalculation of agricultural output was also mentioned by a few experts from INSTAT.[7]

Even the World Bank itself recognises that there are possible sources of error in such calculations: "there is also a risk of overstating annual growth, due to improvements in data collection by Albanian statistical agencies and government ministries, especially in categories such as private industry and services", concluding that "substantial scope for error remains, given still evolving data collection procedures in Albania" (IMF, 1997b, p. 6).

The fact that these same GDP figures had to be recalculated, most of them downward (from 11 per cent in 1993 and 1995 to 9.5 and 8.9 per cent respectively), shows how this measure of GDP growth could have been only approximate. The systematic presentation of higher figures by the Government in 1995–96 (13.3 and 9.1 per cent respectively) is another illustration of the problems—most notably, political considerations—surrounding GDP figures.

Many analysts have attempted to show how unreliable GDP figures are in Central and Eastern Europe (see, for instance, Jackson and Repkin, 1997), particularly emphasising how important it is, in a region and during a period characterised by a fall in industrial output as a result of the collapse of external markets and outdated industrial enterprises, to take industrial output as an important criterion for the assessment of economic growth and structural changes in transition economies. Furthermore, they emphasise the need to study not only industrial output but more sophisticated measures such as value added, which also takes into account intermediary consumption— and increasing prices—of raw materials and energy. We will see in section 6 how different the assessment of Albania's economic growth in 1993–95 would have been if calculated on the basis of industrial production or other measures of industrial activity rather than on the basis of GDP growth alone.

6. By decision of the Council of Ministers in 1993, this has been left to a new body, the DEDAC (Department for Economic Development and Co-ordination) rather than placed under the responsibility of the official statistical institute INSTAT. In practice, as related by several experts, it was calculated by the IMF.

7. First results from a census on agriculture carried out in the first half of 1998 seem to show that agricultural output has been systematically overestimated (by at least one-third) in the first years of transition.

4 A VERY LOW STARTING BASE

Another important feature of the optimistic evaluations in question is the fact that absolute rather than relative figures were emphasised. In particular, it is important to note that the data indicating spectacular GDP growth were collected immediately after a period of continuous and dramatic decline. GDP growth in 1993 must be measured against the background of a serious collapse in production the year before, together with negative GDP growth which took it to very low levels: between 1990 and 1992, GDP had fallen by more than 50 per cent from its peak in 1989. Work stoppages, a lack of inputs, and distributional problems affected industrial production most severely. The restrictive monetary and credit policies might also have played a role, constraining industrial enterprises' access to credit and their ability to continue with previous industrial activities. Moreover, in the wake of a communist regime under which, from the mid-1960s to 1990, private trade had been forbidden and state and collective enterprises had conducted cashless transactions through balances at the state bank, it is not surprising that the liberalisation of domestic and foreign trade led swiftly to a business euphoria, with sudden and rapid growth rates.

GDP growth in such a context—particularly its very low starting point—should have been interpreted with more caution and not presented as a significant achievement, especially in comparison with other countries in the region that had registered more stable GDP growth in earlier years. It is also significant that the transition in Albania had started much later (in 1991–92) than in the rest of Central and Eastern Europe.

5 GDP STILL BELOW ITS PRE-TRANSITION LEVEL

Despite the favourable trends in economic activity in 1993–95, the level of GDP remained below its pre-transition level: at the end of 1996, recorded GDP stood at only 85 per cent of its 1989 level.

Moreover, despite the GDP growth registered in 1993–96, the level of GDP in Albania was still the lowest in Europe: its 3.2 million inhabitants had an average annual income of USD 560 in 1995 (World Bank Atlas Methodology, as quoted in World Bank, 1996a, p. 1), and of USD 650 in 1996 (World Bank, 1996b, p. 1).

According to the IMF, "Albania remains the poorest country in Europe, and years of isolation have left it with a crumbling infrastructure and institutions ill-adapted to the needs of a modern market economy" (IMF, 1997b, p. 3).

Similarly, for the World Bank, "Albania will need many years of high economic growth to raise the standard of living of the people to approximate

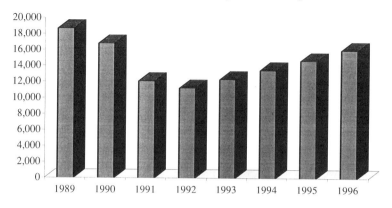

Figure 1.3 *GDP, 1989–96 (million leks at 1990 constant prices)*

Source: IMF (1997b).

that of neighbouring countries" (World Bank, 1996b, p. 1). We may wonder, therefore, what had been the point of identifying Albania as one of the most successful transition economies, merely on the basis of GDP.

6 COLLAPSE OF INDUSTRIAL OUTPUT BY MORE THAN 80 PER CENT

Furthermore, industrial output continued to decline over the period: between 1990 and 1992, it fell by more than 70 per cent, mainly due to work stoppages, lack of material inputs, distributional problems, and confusion concerning property rights. Although it accounted for 80 per cent of total exports in 1990, the industrial sector was particularly hard hit by a weakening of foreign demand, which was initially attributable to the break-up of the CMEA and more recently to UN sanctions against the Federal Republic of Yugoslavia (Serbia and Montenegro). At the same time, the imposition of hard budget constraints on public enterprises and the reduction in state subsidies might have contributed to the sudden collapse of industrial activities. Industrial output in value-added terms contracted further in 1993 (by a further 10 per cent) and 1994 (by 2 per cent), resulting in a cumulative decline in production of more than 80 per cent since 1990.

Industrial production (mostly state-owned) clearly did not contribute to GDP growth in 1993–96, continuing to decline as an increasing number of enterprises closed down and nearly all the others continued to operate far below their capacity. The decline in heavy industries such as mining and metallurgy has been precipitous.

In 1995, an increase in industrial output was announced as another clear sign of Albania's economic recovery: for instance, "industrial output rose for the first time since the transition began, as new private industries, especially textiles and shoe manufacturing, began to take the place of still-declining state industries" (IMF, 1997b, p. 6) or "by 1995, there was an upturn in industrial output" (EIU, 1998a, p. 6).

This increase was only of a single percentage point, however (IMF, 1997b, p. 44), and in any case seems to have been revised in 1997 to a negative figure—the EIU, for instance, presents a -7 per cent figure (EIU, 1998a, p. 24). Similarly, some signs of growth have been reported for 1996 (for instance, a rate of 13.6 per cent by the Government). We believe, however, that this was in no way a turning point for Albanian industry (confirmed by our survey results at the end of 1996): the increase was marginal given the very low starting level of industrial output, which had fallen sharply over the preceding few years.

The survey results on Albanian industry which we present in Chapter 2 vividly portray the profundity of the crisis faced by industry at that time. This was confirmed in particular by the continuous decline of industry's share of GDP, from 40 per cent in 1990 to 11 per cent in 1995 (*Figure 1.6*). At the same time, the share of agriculture in GDP increased from 40.2 per cent to 55.5 per cent.

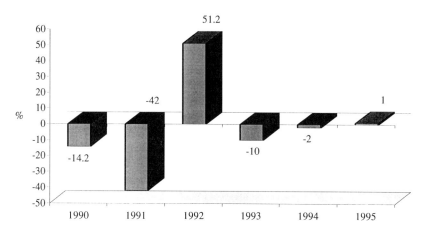

Figure 1.4 *Industrial Output, 1990–95 (percentage of previous year at constant prices)*

Source: IMF (1997b), p. 44.

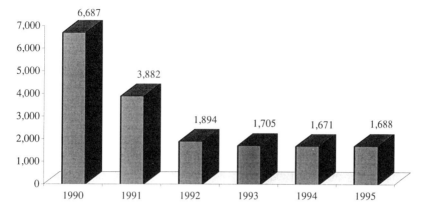

Figure 1.5 *Industrial Output, 1990–95 (million leks at 1990 constant prices)*
Source: IMF (1997b), p. 44.

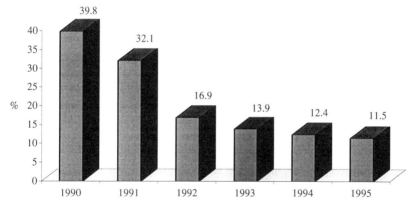

Figure 1.6 *Industrial Output, 1990–95 (share of total GDP at 1990 constant prices)*
Source: IMF (1997b), p. 44.

This low industrial output contributed to the worsening foreign trade deficit, a trend which continued in 1996: part of the increase in the 1996 deficit, for instance, was attributable to a falling-off in mineral production during the second quarter (EIU, 1996, p. 42).

The absence of domestic production also explains the growth of imported goods. In 1996, imports increased by more than 50 per cent, totalling 95 billion leks, compared to 60 billion leks in 1995. The poor state of industrial policy also made it difficult for enterprises to finance the restructuring and diversification strategies they needed to be able to access external markets. In

1996, for instance, export growth was mainly concentrated in textiles and shoes, and was not sufficient (from 4.7 to 5.5 billion leks) to compensate import growth.

As a number of experts have pointed out, growth was mainly led by agriculture: for example, for the OECD, "GDP growth was mainly led by the development of private activity in agriculture"; similarly, for the IMF, recovery "is largely attributable to continued strong growth in agriculture . . . Over 1991–95 as a whole, agricultural output increased by 63 per cent" (IMF, 1997b, p. 5).

To conclude, with the exception of agriculture, reform in Albania so far appears to have been rather superficial. According to one observer, "the political propaganda downplayed the fact that industrial production levels were consistently low, and nearing zero".[8]

7 GROWTH PARTLY SUSTAINED BY EMIGRANTS' REMITTANCES

A distinctive feature of the Albanian economy is the extent to which part of its labour force has been emigrating to neighbouring countries, mainly Italy and Greece. This large exodus took place mainly in 1989–92 and involved young unemployed workers: on average, nearly 400,000 Albanians were working abroad in 1993,[9] representing about 12 per cent of the total population. This emigration flow may be considered as the first step in the Albanian economic transition, and was motivated by the poorest living standards in Europe and a lack of employment prospects. In many cases, the emigration is of short duration, though in some cases it is permanent. Although it is difficult to estimate precisely what percentage of the population is working abroad—because emigration takes place across the whole population, and not just among those of working age (defined as 15–59 for men and 15–54 for women),[10] the IMF (1994) estimated that in 1993 around 15 per cent of the labour force (25 per cent of the male labour force) was working abroad.

The large size of Albania's emigration flows appears to be unique among the former socialist countries of Central and Eastern Europe. Albanian emigrants supported their families and friends, providing an important source

8. See the article, "After Resounding Success, the Economy Slips Back to 1991", in the *Albanian Observer*, Vol. 4, No. 1 (1998), p. 34.

9. Nearly 90 per cent of them were working in Greece, according to Mancellari, Papapanagos, and Sanfey (1996).

10. The World Bank, however, estimated that emigration is heavily concentrated—75 per cent of the total—among males in the age group 15–35. For women, it is concentrated in the 20–35 age range. Approximately 30 per cent of all males in the 15–35 age group are working abroad. See World Bank (1996b), p. 3.

of disposable income, spending, and investment for the country as a whole. According to the IMF (1994, p. 30), "The Albanian economy has been sustained throughout the difficult transition in part by large inflows of private remittances from expatriates."

Given the poor state of the banking system, these transfers are largely effected in cash and in kind (especially consumer durables and electronics). Emigrants' remittances in cash were estimated by the IMF to amount to USD 200 million (IMF, 1994, p. 30), around 20 per cent of GDP, and implying remittances of USD 40–55 per *émigré* per month. Unofficial estimates suggest that the correct figure may be closer to USD 500 million.[11] Remittances sent back from migrant workers have become Albania's largest source of foreign exchange.

These funds from emigrants seem to have represented a key factor in the development of the economy, in two ways (see, for instance, Mancellari, Papapanagos, and Sanfey, 1996): (i) as an alternative to unemployment, and (ii) as a positive force for job creation within the country, particularly in the private sector: "[p]rivate trade and construction have been fuelled in part by transfers from abroad" (IMF, 1994, p. 5); they have helped to create new businesses and stimulate investment projects. As a result, comparison of replacement ratios with other Central and Eastern European countries shows that Albania is one of the few countries in the region in which employment growth in the private sector exceeds the decline in employment in the state sector (Mancellari, Papapanagos, and Sanfey, 1996, p. 485).

However, whatever positive economic effects emigration might have had, it should not be considered as a panacea. On the contrary, it seems to confirm the absence of the internal growth and capital formation necessary to revitalise domestic production. Its contribution to GDP growth is therefore unstable. Moreover, to the extent that they represent the loss of highly skilled people, large emigration flows can have considerable economic and social costs, so undermining long-term economic development.

The fact that most of these remittances came to be placed in pyramid schemes offering high interest rates, rather than in new private economic activities, also shows their unsuitability as a sustainable and permanent pillar of economic recovery (as mentioned by the IMF, 1997b, p. 22).

11. See, for instance, the estimate by Wortman (1995, p. 5) for the International Finance Corporation.

8 CONCLUSION

To summarise, all reservations listed above concerning the calculation method selected for GDP growth, the possible errors due to sometimes unreliable or badly reported data, and the reliability of GDP as a criterion of economic growth in Central and Eastern Europe should undoubtedly have led experienced analysts to adopt more caution in their interpretation of the figures. Comparisons with the economic growth shown by other Central and Eastern European countries were particularly hazardous given the fact that Albania's GDP had still not recovered its 1989 level by 1996. We may wonder why such figures were so strongly emphasised and systematically presented as a clear sign of rapid economic growth, placing Albania all of a sudden as one of the most successful transition economies in the region. At the same time, every indicator related to industrial activities was showing a dramatic decline, reflecting the failure of real forces of production to take off, a state of affairs dealt with in Chapter 2.

The willingness of the Berisha Government to implement reforms and to comply with IMF and World Bank requirements, coupled with the not unrelated willingness of external experts to present Albania as a success story, seems to have masked a reality in which apparent economic success depended in large part on remittances from foreign workers, large-scale smuggling and money-laundering, and illusory short-term profits from pyramid schemes.

In fact, the economic crisis started as early as 1996 as progress in fiscal consolidation was drastically reversed. By the end of that year, the domestically financed fiscal deficit had reached over 10 per cent of GDP, undoing all the progress made on the fiscal side since the beginning of the transition. This uncontrolled fiscal deficit contributed to inflationary pressures and undermined confidence in the lek. Inflation reached nearly 20 per cent by the end of 1996, although this was also due to the liberalisation of bread and domestic fuel prices, and the introduction of VAT.[12] At the same time, the trade balance was ever worsening, probably reflecting the lack of industrial capacity.

These negative trends seem in hindsight to reveal the weaknesses of the Albanian recovery—or the "diseases of the tiger"—all too clearly and to have constituted important premonitory signs of the subsequent crisis. The alleged economic success was quickly overshadowed by the rapid growth of the pyramid schemes in 1996 and their inevitable collapse in 1997.

---

12. After a long-anticipated introduction, the collection of the new value-added tax (VAT) was finally implemented in July 1996, with the expectation that it would reduce the budget deficit.

2. The Profound Crisis in Industry

1 INTRODUCTION

Chapters 2 to 9 constitute an examination of the pattern of production, employment, wages, incomes, and social dialogue in Albanian enterprises at the end of 1996 by means of an analysis of statistical data collected from the majority of enterprises in industry, services, and banking in all regions of Albania. The survey was carried out in October and November 1996 on the basis of extensive interviews with senior management: preparatory and field-work was performed in co-operation with INSTAT, the Albanian Statistical Institute. A similar survey was undertaken in October 1994 in all industrial enterprises: this allows us to compare the development of individual industries between 1993 and 1996 and to identify a number of trends in Albanian industry. The extension of the enterprise survey to services and banking has enabled us to widen our analysis, making possible at least a provisional overview of the future prospects of the Albanian economy as a whole. The sheer size of the survey—involving a total of 1,005 enterprises—346 in industry, 581 in services, and 78 in banking—renders the data fully representative of the Albanian economy.[1]

Since the survey, however, Albania has been rocked by serious economic and financial difficulties as a result of the collapse of the pyramid funds in which a large number of people had for years been investing most of their savings, and which resulted in a terrible crisis in the first half of 1997.

The results of our survey, which was carried out a few months before the crisis, thus represent an invaluable insight into the economic and social situation which gave rise to these events and go a long way towards explaining the depth of the current crisis, of which the alarming situation in industry constitutes a first important element.

---

1. In fact, they represent all industrial enterprises with more than 10 employees and all service enterprises and banks with more than 5 employees.

2 THE EVOLVING STRUCTURE OF ALBANIAN INDUSTRY

The most significant characteristics of the Albanian economy under the communist regime were its extreme isolation from the rest of the world, not only from Western countries but also from the Soviet bloc, and its efforts to implement a self-sufficient economy. Accordingly, the distribution of industrial enterprises in September 1996 showed a rather diversified configuration.[2]

The largest number of industrial establishments was in the food industry (22 per cent of all industrial establishments), followed by textiles and clothing (which increased its share from 14 per cent in 1994 to 20 per cent in 1996), wood and paper (which also increased its share from 11 to 14 per cent), mining (13 per cent), and minerals (12 per cent).

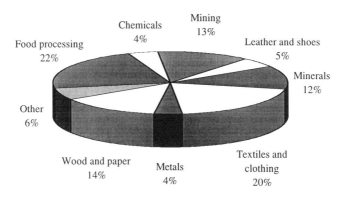

Figure 2.1 *Distribution of Establishments, by Industry, Sept. 1996*

Source: Albanian Labour Flexibility Survey 2 (ALFS2).

Concentration of Employment in Large Labour-Intensive Enterprises

In terms of employment, however, the industrial distribution data showed the continuing predominance of mining, which accounted for 32 per cent of all industrial employees, followed by textiles and clothing (15 per cent), leather and shoes (10 per cent), and food (10 per cent). It should be noted, however, that the share of enterprises in leather and shoes decreased from 18 per cent in 1994 to 10 per cent in 1996.

2. This was very similar to the one prevailing in 1994; see ILO–UNDP–Ministry of Labour of Albania (1995).

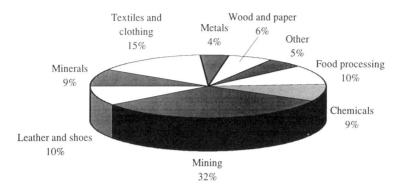

Figure 2.2 *Distribution of Employment, by Industry, Sept. 1996*

Source: ALFS2.

Similarly to mining, such traditional and labour-intensive industries as minerals and chemicals operate on the basis of large, generally still state-owned enterprises of over 200 employees. The importance in employment terms of these traditional and extremely labour-intensive industries underlines the need to restructure them as soon as possible in order to avoid future bankruptcies and massive lay-offs. As shown in the following figures, while there is a similar number of enterprises for each employment size (*Figure 2.3*), this is not the case as far as employment is concerned, with nearly 70 per cent of industrial employees working in enterprises with a workforce of over 200 (*Figure 2.4*).

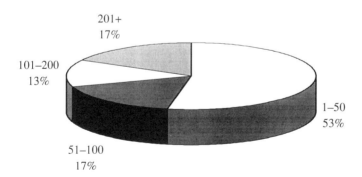

Figure 2.3 *Distribution of Establishments by Number of Employees, Sept. 1996, Industrial Sector*

Source: ALFS2.

Albania in Crisis

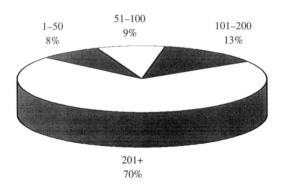

Figure 2.4 *Distribution of Employment by Number of Employees, 1996, Industrial Sector*
Source: ALFS2.

Explosion in the Number of Small Enterprises

At the same time, the proportion of large companies of more than 200 employees has already begun to fall (from 24 per cent in 1994 to 17 per cent in 1996), with rapid growth in the number of new small enterprises of less than 50 employees: at the end of 1996 more than half of all Albanian industrial establishments (53 per cent) came into this category, compared to 5 per cent at the end of 1994. Nevertheless, they still represent only 8 per cent of the total industrial labour force.

The number of medium-sized enterprises of between 50 and 200 employees also fell between 1994 and 1996 (from 35 to 30 per cent), though they continue to employ 22 per cent of industrial workers.

Industrial Changes Reflected at the Regional Level

Enterprises seemed to be equally represented in the different regions of Albania. Industrial employment, however, was found to show some variations, the number of employees being higher in Dibra, Fier, Elbasan and Berat, and lower in Kukes, Tirana, and Vlora, probably reflecting the industrial configuration of those regions (Vlora, for instance, being characterised by a significant number of very small textile enterprises, and Elbasan and Berat by large chemical enterprises).

Some significant changes were also observed between 1994 and 1996. The proportion of industrial enterprises in Tirana fell sharply (from 30 to 19 per cent), with a consequent reduction in industrial employment (from 21 to 8 per cent). In contrast, the percentage of industrial establishments increased in Korca (from 9 to 15 per cent), Durres (from 9 to 14 per cent), and Fier (from 11 to 15 per cent), reflecting a rise in the level of industrial employment in these regions, with the possible exception of Korca, where, despite the emergence of a great number of small enterprises, redundancies in large enterprises could not be compensated: industrial employment here fell from 18 per cent in 1994 to 10 per cent in 1996. The most positive trend was registered in Fier, where employment in industry increased considerably, from 6 per cent of total industrial employment in 1994 to 22 per cent in 1996.

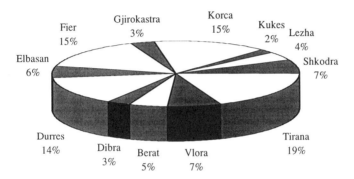

Figure 2.5 *Distribution of Establishments, by Region, Sept. 1996, Industrial Sector*

Source: ALFS2.

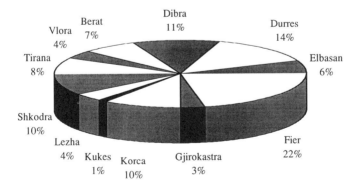

Figure 2.6 *Distribution of Employment, by Region, Sept. 1996, Industrial Sector*

Source: ALFS2.

Development of the Private Sector

The enterprise survey also provided a unique opportunity to examine the distribution of establishments by property form. Impressive changes took place in this regard between 1994 and 1996: while in 1994 state-owned enterprises represented 64 per cent of all industrial enterprises, by the end of 1996 their share had fallen to only 26 per cent. Over the same period, the share of private enterprises increased from 33 to 47 per cent. Leaseholding and co-operative forms progressively disappeared, while new property forms, such as joint ventures and joint-stock companies, emerged. In 1994, the absence of open and closed joint-stock enterprises was striking. Afterwards, they emerged as a standard property form. At the end of 1996, 6 per cent of industrial enterprises were joint-stock companies and 18 per cent were joint ventures.

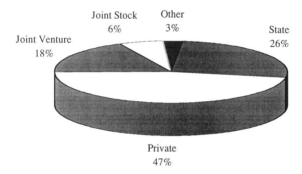

Figure 2.7 *Distribution of Establishments, by Property Form, Sept. 1996, Industrial Sector*
Source: ALFS2.

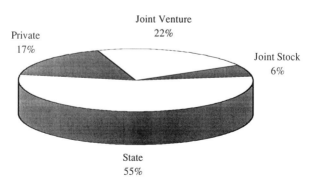

Figure 2.8 *Distribution of Employment, by Property Form, Sept. 1996, Industrial Sector*
Source: ALFS2.

This impressive change was due more to the emergence of private enterprises than to the privatisation process, which has been very slow: most significant was the failure of mass privatisation through the distribution of vouchers to all Albanian citizens (see Chapter 8). The distribution of employees confirmed the predominance of large state-owned enterprises, which still accounted for 55 per cent of industrial employment, while the private sector, dominated by the new small businesses, employed only 17 per cent of the total labour force in industry. Particularly encouraging, however, is the growing employment in joint ventures, which accounted for 22 per cent of the industrial labour force.

It is worth taking a closer look at the cross-distribution of enterprises by industry, property form, and region. While some industries are clearly dominated by one property form—such as mining in the state sector, and food, and textiles and clothing in the private sector—other industries benefit from a balanced combination of different property forms, such as wood and paper, where public, private, and foreign capital seem to be equally represented. Similarly, some regions are often dominated by one industry, for example, mining in Gjirokastra and chemicals in Berat. Other regions have taken the lead in one activity: Korca and Vlora in textiles, Dibra in leather and shoes, and Kukes in food, though leather and shoes also has a significant presence here. Other regions have been traditionally dominated by heavy industry, such as Elbasan, Berat, and Fier, which have had to face closures and the difficult restructuring of large state and outdated enterprises.

3 THE COLLAPSE OF INDUSTRIAL PRODUCTION

Since the beginning of the transition in 1992 Albania has been fraught with a deep economic and social crisis, with shrinking output and sales, numerous bankruptcies, and growing unemployment. During the survey field work in 1994, in the course of only six months, one-third of all industrial enterprises declared themselves bankrupt and ceased operating. This trend continued between the two surveys.

Dramatic Fall in Sales

The economic crisis, which was confirmed from all sides by our first enterprise survey results in 1994, had not been overcome by 1996: it had, if anything, become more profound. This was reflected in the second survey in many ways. Most fundamentally, the value of sales in real terms had shrunk: 33 per cent of all firms had experienced declining sales in 1995–96. On the other hand, the crisis appeared to have become more unevenly distributed by sector, property form, and region. The enterprise survey in 1996 confirmed the industrial differentials of 1994: mining sales continued to fall in 1995–96, although less dramatically than in chemicals, in which sales fell by nearly 70 million leks on average by firm; at the same time, sales growth was registered in textiles and clothing, leather and shoes, and—though to a lesser extent— metals. Textile and clothes and leather and shoes are the only sectors that registered positive sales growth both in 1993–94 and 1995–96. A number of other promising developments were also recorded: for example, food processing returned to positive sales growth in 1996 after several years of deficit (it registered—with mining—the worst sales decline in 1993–94). Private companies alone registered continuous sales growth, while the sales of large state-owned enterprises maintained their downward course, which was perhaps even worse in 1995–96 compared to 1993–94. Even joint ventures did not manage, on average, to register positive sales growth in 1995–96.

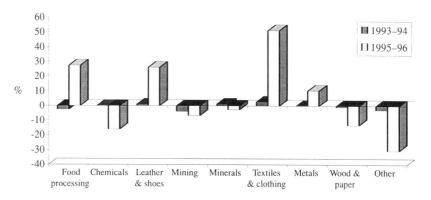

Figure 2.9 *Percentage of Sales Change, by Industry, 1993–96, Industrial Sector* *Sources*: ALFS1, ALFS2.

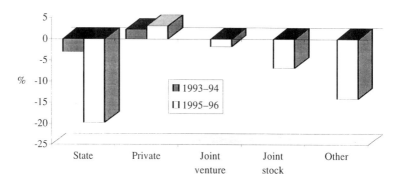

Figure 2.10 *Percentage of Sales Change, by Property Form, 1993–96, Industrial Sector* *Sources*: ALFS1, ALFS2.

The most striking conclusion to be drawn from *Figures 2.9* and *2.10*, however, is the worsening of the fall in sales between 1993–94 and 1995–96. While most sectors in 1993–94 had experienced on average a range of sales changes between 5 and –5 per cent, the range became much greater in 1995–96, stretching from +50 to –30 per cent. This directly increased the gap between industries. The fall in chemicals and in wood and paper was well above 10 per cent, while sales growth in textiles and clothing was close to 50 per cent, mainly due to new emerging small private enterprises that experienced high sales growth in the first years of their existence. The difference between the two periods is also large in state enterprises, which experienced a 3 per cent decline in sales in 1993–94 compared to a larger fall in 1995–96 of 20 per cent, thus confirming their accelerated decline. These figures are another sign of the worsening of the situation in industry, with larger falls in output and also growing differences between enterprises and sectors.

Our survey results were confirmed by data on the volume of industrial production (INSTAT, 1997). In *Figure 2.11*, we show industrial production only from 1993, a year of apparent economic recovery (after an 80 per cent decline in 1991–92) and GDP growth. We can see that, even taking 1993 as a base, industrial production by volume had fallen 40 per cent by the first quarter of 1996. This figure seems to contradict the optimistic figures of industrial recovery in 1995 (by 1 per cent) and in 1996 (by 13.6 per cent) presented by many organisations (see Chapter 1).

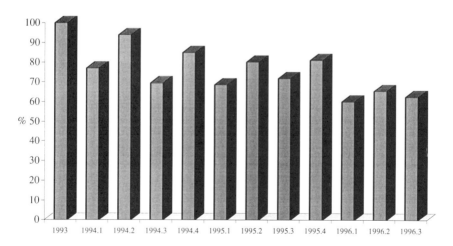

Figure 2.11 *Volume of Industrial Production, 1993–96 (1993 = index 100)*

* Data for last quarter of 1996 not available because of a lack of information on the private sector.
Source: INSTAT (1997).

Poor Results on External Markets

These depressing sales figures can be explained by the collapse of the
domestic market and the poor performance of Albanian enterprises abroad: at
the end of 1996 managers reported exports of less than 11 per cent of total
industrial output, confirming the magnitude of the problems encountered by
Albanian enterprises on external markets. This might be explained in turn by
the former industrial policy (already alluded to in Chapter 1) which aimed at
creating a self-sufficient economy, entailing the poor development of commercial activities and delaying industrial specialisation. Prior to 1990, foreign
trade was carried out by only three or four state enterprises. Non-processed
raw materials comprised 62 per cent of exports in 1990 (UNDP, 1996, p. 10).

In fact, at the end of 1996 most sectors were found to be producing
exclusively for the domestic market, particularly food (96 per cent) and
minerals (95 per cent). The only significant exporting sectors were textiles
and clothing, and leather and shoes—also at the forefront in 1994—which
exported 80 per cent of their output. They are also the most profitable and
promising industries, and are characterised by a larger proportion of private
enterprises, which were also found to be particularly well-performing in
export terms. While textiles and clothing was already exporting 80 per cent of
its production in 1994, leather and shoes increased its exports from 65 per
cent of production in 1994 to 80 per cent in 1996.

Two other sectors improved their export performance significantly: the
wood and paper industry progressed rapidly, increasing its export production

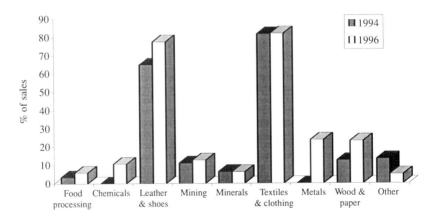

Figure 2.12 *Percentage of Production Exported, by Industry, Sept. 1994 and 1996*

Note: Chemicals and metals included under "Other" in 1994.
Sources: ALFS1, ALFS2.

from 11 per cent in 1994 to 21 per cent in 1996, as did the metals industry, with more than 22 per cent of its sales registered on external markets.

Great differences by property form were also observed. At the end of 1996 joint ventures were found to be the most export-oriented of all enterprises, with more than 50 per cent of production being sold on external markets. A further significant difference was observed between joint ventures in majority and those in minority foreign ownership, the former being considerably more export-oriented. Private firms were also found to be performing better and better on external markets, underlining their dynamism compared to other property forms: state-owned enterprises devoted nearly 90 per cent of production to the domestic market, and joint-stock companies 96 per cent.

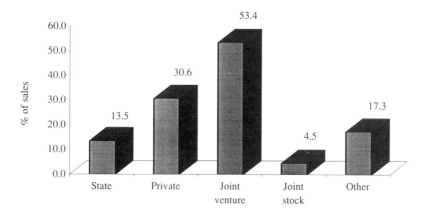

Figure 2.13 *Percentage of Production Exported, by Property Form, Sept. 1996, Industrial Sector*

Source: ALFS2.

The premier exporting regions were found to be Elbasan (with 24 per cent of output going for export), Lezha (22 per cent), and Korca (17 per cent). Particularly poor results were registered in Tirana (9 per cent) and Durres (8 per cent).

A direct correlation was observed between export performance and the employment situation: the most export-oriented sectors enjoyed a more favourable employment situation, with fewer lay-offs and even the occasional employment increase. In stark contrast, sectors concentrating on the domestic market had to implement severe redundancy programmes, accounting for more than 20 per cent of the workforce in a single year.

Our survey results were confirmed by official statistics on imports, exports, and the trade balance. Data for the fourth quarter of 1996 facilitate comparison with our survey data. The most export-oriented industries were clearly footwear and textiles, accounting for more than 50 per cent of Albanian exports. Food and construction materials and metals followed, with 17 and 11 per cent of exports respectively. Albania also exports minerals, mainly chromium.

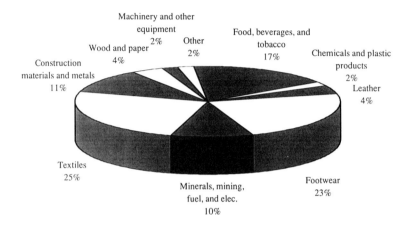

Figure 2.14 *Distribution of Exports, by Sector, Fourth Quarter 1996*

Source: INSTAT (1997).

It is worth noting the countries of destination of Albanian products: 92 per cent of exports at the end of 1996 were to OECD countries, and 85 per cent to EU countries. Italy (with 58 per cent of Albanian exports), Greece (13 per cent), and Germany (7 per cent) are the main destinations of Albanian products. A number of other countries share what is left: Macedonia (3 per cent of exports), Turkey (3 per cent), The Netherlands (3 per cent), and France (2 per cent), which are developing into alternative partners (*Table 2.1*).

Although food exports in 1996 had increased over the previous year (17 per cent of total exports), allowing this sector to become more profitable, these exports were not sufficient to compensate for the considerable food imports (35 per cent of the total), mainly vegetable products (18 per cent), processed foods, beverages, and tobacco (10 per cent), and live animals and animal products (5 per cent). By contrast, textiles and footwear have largely positive trade balances, despite significant raw material imports: textiles are imported by enterprises—generally joint ventures—which then export the finished product to the country of origin at a considerable profit due to the much cheaper labour costs. After food, machinery and transportation equipment are the most imported goods (*Figure 2.15*), a sector in which Albania exports little.

Table 2.1 *Distribution of Exports, by Country of Destination, Fourth Quarter 1996*

Country	Percentage
Italy	58
Greece	13
Germany	7
Macedonia	3
Turkey	3
Netherlands	3
France	2
Belgium	1.5
Venezuela	1.5
Slovenia	1.5
USA	1
Austria	1
Croatia	0.5
Other	4

Source: INSTAT (1997).

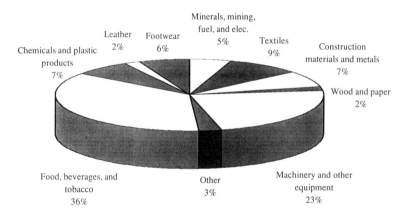

Figure 2.15 *Distribution of Imports, by Sector, Fourth Quarter 1996*

Source: INSTAT (1997).

Imports are also mainly from OECD countries (83 per cent), especially EU countries (76 per cent). Again, Italy and Greece (42 and 21 per cent of imports respectively) are the main partners.

Table 2.2 *Distribution of Imports, by Country of Origin, Fourth Quarter 1996*

Country	Percentage
Italy	42.0
Greece	21.0
Turkey	4.5
Germany	4.0
Bulgaria	4.0
France	3.0
Belgium	2.5
Romania	2.5
Macedonia	2.0
Switzerland	1.7
Croatia	1.5
USA	1.3
Slovenia	1.2
Austria	1.0
Netherlands	0.8
Others	7.0

Source: INSTAT (1997).

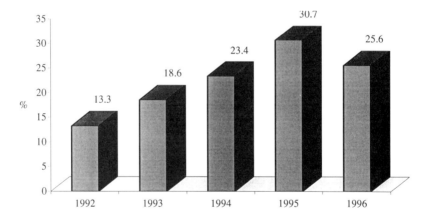

Figure 2.16 *Ratio of Export/Import Coverage, 1992–96 (%)*

Sources: IMF (1997b), INSTAT (1997).

This poor export performance, combined with high import levels in many industrial sectors, has led to a chronic imbalance, partly explaining the sharp deterioration in the trade balance (see *Table 1.1* in Chapter 1).[3] As shown in

3. See "Trade Deficit Deepens: 41 Billion Leks", in the *Albanian Observer*, Vol. 2, No. 3 (1996), p. 9.

Figure 2.16 (which shows the rate of coverage of the value of imports by exports), exports are insufficient to cover more than one-quarter of imports. This contrasts with the 1970s when Albania could easily cover its imports with its exported goods. It is a familiar saying that "imports can only be afforded thanks to foreign aid and Albanians residing abroad".[4]

Production Well Below Full Capacity

Industrial enterprises were found to be operating at an average of 66 per cent of full capacity, confirming the profundity of the production crisis. Nevertheless, this did represent an improvement on 1994, when these enterprises were found to be operating at only 55 per cent of full capacity.

Output was highest in the two export-oriented sectors: textiles and clothing (operating at 83 per cent of full capacity) and leather and shoes (82 per cent). Between 1994 and 1996 the situation had greatly improved in the mining sector, whose output figures had risen from 52 per cent of full capacity to 72 per cent. The food industry also slightly improved its production performance, from 40 per cent of full capacity in 1994 to 67 per cent in 1996. The situation remained grave in metals and in chemicals, however: in 1996 they were operating at only 56 per cent and 57 per cent of full capacity respectively.

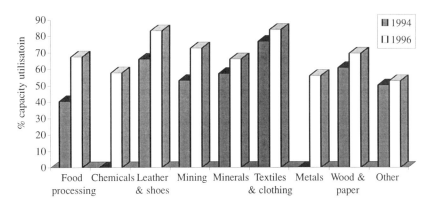

Figure 2.17 *Capacity Utilisation, by Industry, 1994–96, Industrial Sector*

Note: Chemicals and metals included under "Other" in 1994.
Sources: ALFS1, ALFS2.

4. See for instance, "Balkan Tiger", in the *Albanian Observer*, Vol. 2, No. 8 (1996), p. 21.

As far as property form is concerned, the crisis was found to be particularly dramatic in joint-stock enterprises, which were working at only 41 per cent of full capacity, compared to 77 per cent in joint ventures and 75 per cent in private enterprises. The state sector was still operating at only 65 per cent of full production, though this was something of an improvement on 1994, when the figure was only 50 per cent (*Figure 2.18*). Among joint ventures, enterprises in majority foreign ownership again outperformed their minoritarian fellows, with a figure of 79 per cent as compared to only 57 per cent; indeed, enterprises in minority foreign ownership seem to be facing serious production problems, which might be related to their greater export difficulties.

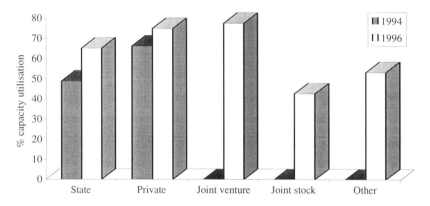

Figure 2.18 *Capacity Utilisation, by Property Form, 1994–96, Industrial Sector*
Sources: ALFS1, ALFS2.

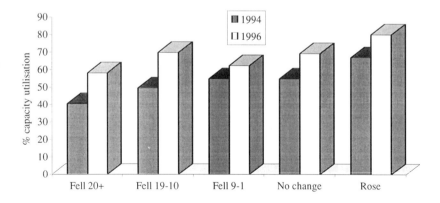

Figure 2.19 *Capacity Utilisation, by Employment Change, 1994–96, Industrial Sector*
Sources: ALFS1, ALFS2.

As expected, there was a clear and direct relationship between employment changes and production: employment cuts were a reflection of economic problems; conversely, firms operating closer to full capacity had more positive employment prospects, reducing their labour force the least or even increasing it (*Figure 2.19*).

Compared to 1994, when the regions operating furthest from full capacity were Berat and Elbasan—which were restructuring their large traditional industries—the worst-hit regions at the end of 1996 were Kukes, where enterprises were operating below 45 per cent of full production capacity, and—surprisingly—Tirana (below 65 per cent). In contrast, production in Berat increased from 46 per cent in 1994 to 65 per cent in 1996, and in Elbasan from 49 to 66 per cent. The best performances were registered in Dibra (86 per cent), Vlora (81 per cent), Korca (75 per cent), and Fier (72 per cent).

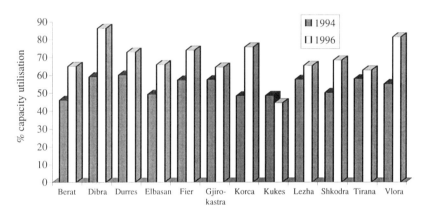

Figure 2.20 *Capacity Utilisation, by Region, 1994–96, Industrial Sector*
Sources: ALFS1, ALFS2.

Increased Risk of Bankruptcy

As a result of the production crisis, the lack of demand, and difficulties finding external markets, the number of bankruptcies multiplied rapidly. In the two years which separated our two surveys, more than 20 per cent of all industrial enterprises declared themselves bankrupt and ceased operating. In November 1996, 30 per cent of the managers questioned reported that their enterprise was threatened with bankruptcy over the next 12 months: the threat was particularly severe in metals (in 50 per cent of them), food (39 per cent), and minerals (36 per cent). More than 20 copper mines were also closed down by the Government in 1995–96.

Surprisingly, small enterprises seemed at the greatest risk of bankruptcy, indicating a need for specific policies targeted on this sector (related to credit, taxes, and so on), in addition to the urgent action clearly required in the case

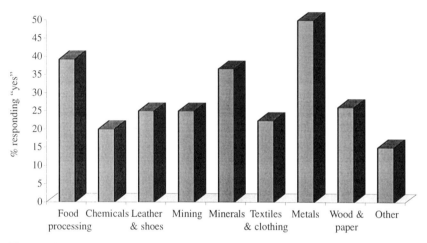

Figure 2.21 *Bankruptcy Likely Within the Next 12 Months, by Industry, Sept. 1996*
Source: ALFS2.

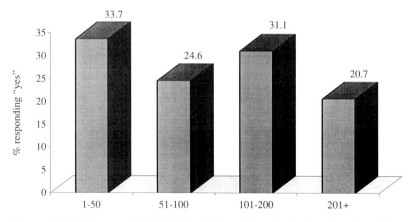

Figure 2.22 *Bankruptcy Likely Within the Next 12 Months, by Number of Employees, Sept. 1996, Industrial Sector*

Source: ALFS2.

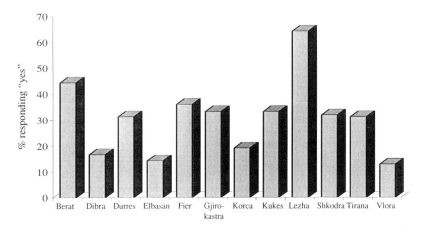

Figure 2.23 *Bankruptcy Likely Within the Next 12 Months, by Region, Sept. 1996, Industrial Sector*

Source: ALFS2.

of large companies. Risk of bankruptcy was reported mainly in Lezha (64 per cent of enterprises), Berat (44 per cent), and Fier (36 per cent), although no region was free of it. This also has implications for regional industrial policy.

4 CONCLUSION

Our survey results for 1996 painted a dramatic picture, which contrasts quite strongly with the overoptimism which prevailed in 1994–96 with regard to the growth and potential of the Albanian economy, an overoptimism which resulted in the systematic underestimation of the real economic problems and the level of social discontent. In many cases, the situation of industries had worsened between 1994 and 1996, generating a growing number of warning signals: further falls in sales and profits in most industries, lower levels of exports, rapid deterioration of the trade balance, and an increasing risk of enterprise bankruptcy. In such a context, a clear strategic policy should have been designed to help industry in a number of ways. It would have been important first to identify the most promising sectors in respect of economic growth and employment generation, and to channel policy action towards them. We have seen, for example, good results in a few dynamic, export-oriented industries, such as textiles and clothing, leather and shoes, and wood and paper. Second, the emergence of small private enterprises should have been more systematically promoted—for example, by relieving them of such burdens as over-taxation, scarce credit, and export difficulties. At the same time, industrial policy could have motivated large state enterprises to press ahead with restructuring, particularly in the light of the good diversification results observed in such traditional industrial regions as Elbasan and Berat. There were also some promising signs in such traditional sectors as minerals, dominated hitherto by large state-owned enterprises, in which new private firms—including joint ventures—were developing. As far as foreign capital is concerned—which remained concentrated in a few sectors and regions—it would have been worth developing the conditions necessary to attract foreign investors in other activities and in regions where restructuring was taking place and where there were comparative advantages. A particular effort was also needed to widen credit channels for the benefit of manufacturing.

By contrast, instead of action on the basis of this comprehensive set of priorities, neglect of the problems of declining Albanian industry seems to have been a necessary condition of retaining consensus on the spectacular recovery of Albania in a climate of generalised self-satisfaction on the part of both the Government and most eminent external experts. This inaction will only serve to delay the expected problems in restructuring and render even more painful the unavoidable reforms in the industrial sector.

As we shall see in Chapters 5 and 6, this generalised crisis in industry has had dramatic consequences, particularly in terms of employment and wages, leading to growing unemployment and falling living standards.

3. Difficulties in Emerging Services

1 INTRODUCTION

The transition in Albania has led to rapid growth in the service sector, with very small enterprises playing a particularly important role. According to the IMF, "strong growth was witnessed in construction, transportation, and other services, reflecting the continued development of shops and restaurants and the beginnings of a tourist industry . . . There is no question that there was a significant increase in these sectors in 1995" (IMF, 1997b, pp. 6–7). At the same time, large state enterprises in traditional services, such as the public utilities, remain in place. Privatisation has started to change the distribution of services among different property forms, but has so far progressed only very slowly. Moreover, despite a very promising performance, the emerging service sector has encountered a number of difficulties which have impeded its progress.

2 TOO NARROW CONCENTRATION OF SERVICES

In our survey carried out at the end of 1996, we were able to cover 581 enterprises in services: these are all the service enterprises in Albania with more than 5 employees. Service activities were found to be concentrated in a very small number of sectors: by far the largest number of service establishments were in trade (more than 25 per cent), followed by hotels and restaurants (16 per cent), gas, water, and electricity (15 per cent), and security and insurance (14 per cent), this last accounting for an amazing 77 firms. Transport and telecoms were also significant. So-called "Other Services" is also a significant sector, with small numbers of firms representing a wide range of services, such as car repairs, construction, research and development, computers, hire of tools and equipment, and sports. Construction is the only sector we did not cover in our survey, although we will try to provide some information.

Although it includes the largest proportion of service enterprises "Trade" involves a rather limited number of activities, as confirmed by INSTAT (1996): in 1995, 39 per cent of turnover in trade was realised in food products, 22 per cent in construction materials, and 12 per cent in appliances. Other products included pharmaceuticals and other non-food items.

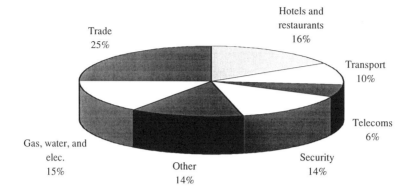

Figure 3.1 *Distribution of Establishments, by Service, Sept. 1996*

Source: ALFS2.

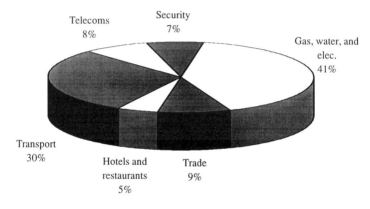

Figure 3.2 *Distribution of Employment, by Service, Sept. 1996*

Source: ALFS2.

3 A SECTOR STILL DOMINATED BY THE STATE

Property forms in services were much less diverse than in industry. By the end of 1996 the majority of establishments (57 per cent) were private, although the state sector remained important (38 per cent), especially in transport, telecommunications, and public utilities. There were only a few joint ventures (16 in all, two-thirds in majority foreign ownership, and representing 3 per cent of the whole sample), and even fewer joint-stock companies. It is interesting that, while no shares had been distributed or sold to employees in industry, in services employee share ownership was fairly widespread as a result of the privatisation programme of small and medium-sized enterprises: it had been developed on a large scale in nearly 10 per cent of enterprises. Management share ownership was even more frequent, being observed in 20 per cent of enterprises, with an average of 83 per cent of the shares in management hands.

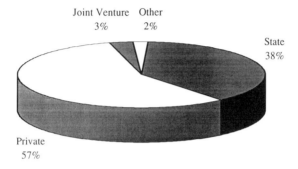

Figure 3.3 *Distribution of Establishments, by Property Form, Sept. 1996*

Source: ALFS2.

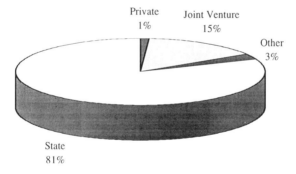

Figure 3.4 *Distribution of Employment, by Property Form, Sept. 1996*

Source: ALFS2.

Most service employment (81 per cent) at the end of 1996 was still concentrated in the state sector, with a low percentage of service employees in the private sector (1 per cent). The public utilities account for more than 40 per cent of total employment in services, and transport for 30 per cent (*Figure 3.2*). The increasing share of the labour force employed in joint ventures is significant (*Figure 3.4*).

Moreover, only 15 per cent of service enterprises reported that they were planning a change in property form in the next 12 months, although this percentage was much higher among state-owned enterprises (37 per cent).

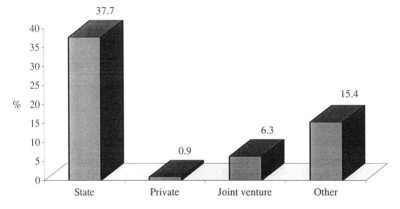

Figure 3.5 *Plans to Change Property Form, by Current Property Form, Sept. 1996, Service Sector*

Source: ALFS2.

This state dominance of the public utilities has often been criticised, particularly in respect of governance and management: for example, bills have not been paid for a number of years by a relatively large share of the public sector (not to mention the general public). In many cases, the termination or suspension of services to non-paying public sector entities and companies was forbidden, while legal action taken by the utility companies proved unsuccessful. The utility companies have requested that the Government make every effort to ensure that the public sector pays its bills on time and that the regulations are properly enforced, while maintaining a certain level of protection for the most vulnerable sections of the population. On the other hand, although it has been claimed that better governance in the public utilities could be achieved only by means of privatisation, this has not always been the best solution, since in this way services essential to all become difficult for the state to monitor. Alternatives include reaching a management arrangement with experienced international firms and combining majority public capital with potential strategic investors.

4 LARGE ENTERPRISES STILL THE MAJOR EMPLOYERS

The average size of service establishments in our sample was very small—54 employees—in marked contrast to the large industrial enterprises. In fact, the majority of service enterprises (more than 70 per cent) had fewer than 50 employees, while only a minority (6 per cent) had more than 200 (*Figure 3.6*). These large firms continue to employ nearly 50 per cent of service employees, however, confirming their importance in terms of employment. In contrast, enterprises of fewer than 50 employees concentrate only 16 per cent of the labour force in services (*Figure 3.7*).

Important size differences existed between property forms—the average number of employees in private enterprises was 16, compared to 131 in state-owned enterprises—and between sectors: services in trade, hotels, and security are delivered by very small private firms (of under 25 employees), while in transport and the public utilities, enterprises—generally state-owned—are much larger. These sectors also employ the majority of workers.

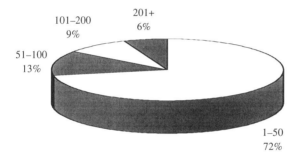

Figure 3.6 *Distribution of Establishments, by Number of Employees, Sept. 1996, Service Sector*

Source: ALFS2.

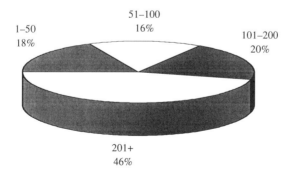

Figure 3.7 *Distribution of Employment, by Number of Employees, Sept. 1996, Service Sector*

Source: ALFS2.

5 THE "KIOSK ECONOMY": THE GROWTH OF MICRO-ENTERPRISES

We did not cover service enterprises with fewer than 5 employees in our survey. However, official statistics show that the number of small businesses increased enormously between 1992 and 1996. There were more than 40,000 private enterprises outside the agricultural sector in 1996, officially employing more than 120,000 workers. This means that the average private firm had 2.2 employees; only 3 per cent of such firms employed more than 10 workers. In these terms, this appears to be largely a "survivalist" sector, with most firms standing little chance of expanding or of improving their market share. Due to their lack of financial resources, most firms operate in less capital-intensive sectors, such as trade (51 per cent of registered firms in 1996), or transport (15 per cent) and other services (19 per cent). In transport and services taken together, the number of registered businesses rose to about 17,000 (IMF, 1997b), 10 per cent of which are in manufacturing, 2 per cent in construction, and 3 per cent in agricultural processing. The statistical office has confirmed that in most businesses (90 per cent) only one or two people are involved.

The majority of enterprises in services and trade are registered as physical entities (a total of 31,740 in the private sector in December 1996) rather than legal ones (9,094). In trade and cafés 97 per cent of enterprises are registered as physical entities, and 91 per cent of restaurants, with the legal form of limited liability company. The growth of these small cafés or retail shops, often known as "kiosks", has led to critical doubts concerning the ability of the Albanian service sector to generate real economic growth, grounded as it is on such simple activities and generally funded from emigrants' remittances. The growth of security services, such as the provision of bodyguards, may also be seen as precarious activities, very much dependent on the general security climate.[1]

6 CONCENTRATION OF SERVICES IN THE LARGER TOWNS

Establishments and employees in services seem to be equally distributed in the different regions, though with a slightly higher concentration in Tirana, Fier, and Durres. This concentration is even more visible in terms of employment (*Figure 3.9*).

1. See "Money for Nothing", in the *Albanian Observer*, Vol. 2, No. 10 (1996), p. 20. As we shall see, however, these activities had their "golden age" during the growth of the pyramid schemes (protecting their leaders) and during the crisis of spring 1997 (see Chapter 12).

Some regions have specialised in one or two services—for instance, Shkodra and Vlora (close to the sea) specialise in trade and hotels, and Durres (due to its harbour) in transport and trade—while other regions have diversified their services, such as Gjirokastra, Fier, and Elbasan. Security services are concentrated in Berat and Elbasan. Other activities—such as public utilities and telecommunications—are disseminated throughout Albania because their services are local in character.

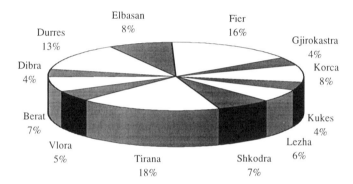

Figure 3.8 *Distribution of Establishments, by Region, Sept. 1996, Service Sector*
Source: ALFS2.

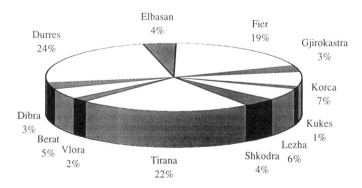

Figure 3.9 *Distribution of Employment, by Region, Sept. 1996, Service Sector*
Source: ALFS2.

7 PROMISING ECONOMIC GROWTH

In contrast to industry, services were found to have undergone rapid expansion. On average, sales growth in services increased by 32 per cent in 1994–95 and by more than 50 per cent in 1995–96. Furthermore, all service sectors registered a positive performance (see *Figure 3.10*).

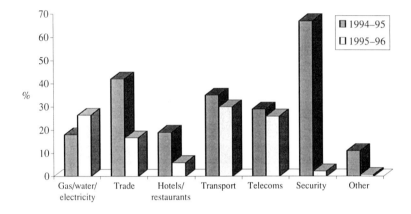

Figure 3.10 *Percentage of Sales Change, by Service, 1994–96*

Source: ALFS2.

The most rapid growth took place in trade (42 per cent in 1994–95 and 17 per cent in 1995–96), transport (35 per cent and 30 per cent), and security (67 per cent and 2 per cent). The highest turnover was in the larger, generally state-owned enterprises in telecommunications and the public utilities—the average value of sales was also high in transport. Of course, we should approach these positive results with caution: most of these establishments were quite new—less than two years old—so that their rapid sales growth must be viewed from the perspective of a relatively low point of departure; moreover, services are generally prone to sales decline after an initial expansion.

The expansion of the small privatisation programme to all small and medium-sized units (enterprises with fewer than 300 employees or a book value of less than USD 500,000) in trade and services seems to have led to a rapid expansion of service sector activity. At the same time, these good performances were observed in all property forms: state-owned enterprises which had been in existence for a good deal longer were also found to be performing fairly well. In the final analysis, we have every reason to believe that these figures are a promising sign of the dynamism of services in Albania.

Service performance growth was highest in 1995–96 in the region of Durres, followed by Tirana, Fier, and Dibra.

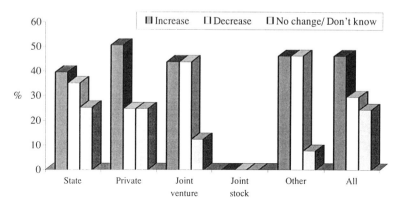

Figure 3.11 *Percentage of Establishments Registering an Increase or a Loss in Profits, by Property Form, 1994–96, Service Sector*

Source: ALFS2.

Nearly 50 per cent of enterprises in services reported an increase in profits in 1996 compared to 1995, while 29 per cent reported a fall in profits. The profitability increase was highest in telecommunications and lowest in hotels, and gas, water, and electricity. Private enterprises constituted a greater proportion of profitable enterprises (51 per cent) in contrast to state-owned enterprises, only 39 per cent of which were profitable as against 35 per cent which were less profitable. The high percentage of joint ventures in services which experienced profit losses should be noted, however. The regions of Dibra, Gjirokastra, Tirana, and Lezha showed particularly good results in 1996. Moreover, as in industry, there seems to be a direct relationship between employment changes and profitability: enterprises that cut employment were most likely to have suffered a fall in profits, and vice versa (*Figure 3.12*).

Again in sharp contrast to industry, services were operating much closer to full capacity in 1996—at an average of 83 per cent, compared to 80 per cent in 1995 and only 70 per cent in 1994. No great differences were observed in this regard between types of service, property forms, and regions, which shows that good performance in services was quite evenly distributed.

The above results are confirmed by official reports and statistics, which emphasise the significant increase in activity in these sectors in 1995–96. Growth in the construction sector was estimated at 12.5 per cent in 1995, much of it being attributable to increases in private construction, estimated to have doubled in 1995, though again from a low base. This growth, which was

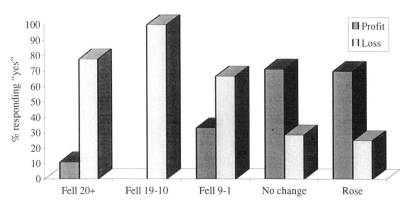

Figure 3.12 *Percentage of Establishments Registering an Increase or a Loss in Profits, by Employment Change, 1994–96, Service Sector*

Source: ALFS2.

helped by private control of real estate, strong earnings growth in agriculture, and rising private transfers from abroad, continued in 1996. Some other services, such as tourism, saw even more rapid growth. For example, the number of nights spent by tourists increased by 46 per cent in 1995, as new hotels opened, especially in southern Albania. There has been a surge in tourism receipts, which rose at an annual rate of 10 per cent to reach USD 56 million in the first three quarters of 1996.

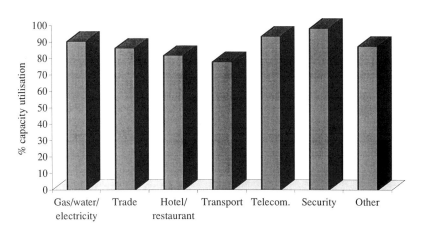

Figure 3.13 *Capacity Utilisation, by Service, Sept. 1996*

Source: ALFS2.

8 DIFFICULTIES AND SOCIAL UNREST REMAIN

Against this generally positive situation in services, however, a number of enterprises have encountered significant difficulties: appropriate policy action should have been taken to promote their survival. When asked to identify their main problem over the previous six months, 26 per cent of managers reported a fall in profits and 21 per cent the financial problems of their customers; nearly 10 per cent complained about high taxes. Eight per cent reported a risk of bankruptcy over the next 12 months, this percentage being particularly high in the public utilities of gas, water, and electricity (26 per cent of them). The main causes of bankruptcy were reported to be delivery claims (in 39 per cent of firms), lack of clients (37 per cent), customer claims (20 per cent), but also high taxes (7 per cent) and risk of strikes (5 per cent). Surveys conducted in Albania at the end of 1995 revealed the worst indicators concerning bankruptcies of new businesses in Central and Eastern Europe: out of 41,460 companies—half of which were operating in trade, followed by hotels and restaurants and transport—some 22 per cent had gone bankrupt.[2]

The problem of too localised networks was confirmed, with a number of enterprises in transport and trade complaining about inadequate supply. On the demand side, enterprises in trade (20 per cent of them) and hotel and restaurants (14 per cent) reported difficulties in selling their services. Poor working conditions were also found to be a major problem, reported by more than 15 per cent of enterprises, especially in state public utilities (24 per cent) and telecommunications (16 per cent) enterprises.

Moreover, although the income generated by services had increased over the last few years, in 1995 it was not much higher than in 1989 or 1990. Service incomes fell by nearly 20 per cent in the course of 1991–92. Construction saw a dramatic fall in 1990–92; and after a period of significant increases in 1993, it again fell back in 1994–95. But this official figure conceals the impressive development of construction in the informal economy. Transport in 1995 (476 million leks at 1990 constant prices) was also below its 1990 level (566 million leks). The share in GDP of services increased but this was mainly due to the collapse of industry. Many small entrepreneurs attempted to improve their often meagre profits by employing illegal workers on a full- or part-time basis.

2. See "Business Brightening and Falling", in the *Albanian Observer*, Vol. 2, No. 11 (1996), p. 10.

Albania in Crisis

Table 3.1 *Contribution of Services to GDP, 1990–95*
(million leks at 1990 constant prices)

	1990	1991	1992	1993	1994	1995
Construction	1 144	801	857	1 114	1 281	1 441
Transport	566	396	337	381	449	476
Other services	2 192	1 885	2 055	2 383	2 646	2 857
% change over previous period						
Construction	−12	−30	7	30	15	12.5
Transport	−10	−30	−15	13	18	6.0
Other services	−8	−14	9	16	11	8.0
Share of GDP at 1990 constant prices						
Construction	6.8	6.6	7.6	9.1	9.5	9.8
Transport	3.4	3.3	3.0	3.1	3.3	3.2
Other services	13.0	15.6	18.3	19.4	19.6	19.5

Source: IMF (1997b).

Moreover, 1996 was the year of social unrest in public services. The introduction of VAT at the rate of 12.5 per cent and the liberalisation of bread, flour, kerosene, and urban transport prices against a backdrop of rising inflation sparked a wave of serious industrial action. State enterprises in both industry and services were worst affected, mainly due to the strict wage controls to which they were still subject. In addition, our survey revealed that 12 per cent of enterprises in services (21 per cent of state enterprises) at the end of 1996 had had problems paying wages in the last 12 months, delays regularly reaching 3–4 weeks. One major strike was organised in October after the unions rejected the Government's offer of compensation based on a calculated 12.3 per cent rise in the value of a basket of 24 staple foods. The public sector unions demanded instead a price freeze and threatened to take the Government to the Constitutional Court for what they described as a breach of contract. This social unrest affected mainly large state enterprises, while working conditions became deplorable in new private service companies.

9 A LACK OF CAPITAL AND INTERNAL INVESTMENT

Most service enterprises were found not to be carrying out significant investment. This finding was also confirmed for very small units by INSTAT (1996). Most small companies reported a very low level of capital. According to financial experts, about 90 per cent of the capital circulating legally in

Albania is owned by less than one-fifth of the registered companies: 78 per cent of companies reported difficulties in obtaining access to capital and credit.

Moreover, service activities were particularly fragile because of their dependence on external remittances. Activities in private construction and other services were largely funded in this manner, either directly or through the borrowing of such funds in the informal financial sector.

Of 16,972 active enterprises in trade, only 17 per cent carried out investment in 1995; about 74 per cent of the latter were in the retail trade. Moreover, investment was dedicated mainly to the reconstruction and enlargement of buildings, and the purchase of machinery and equipment. There was little investment in new marketing or diversification of services: 44 per cent of respondents admitted a lack of knowledge about marketing and reported difficulties in finding a market for their goods and services.[3] As a result, only 6 per cent of service enterprises reported that they were planning to open a new establishment in the coming year. Our survey results confirmed that investment was non-existent in a majority of service companies.

Investment was more frequent in partnerships with foreigners (44 per cent). Among very small entities, investment was more widespread in cafés and restaurants (INSTAT, 1997)—32 per cent of them—but exclusively dedicated to the enlargement of buildings, rather than strategic investment (for the purpose of expanding into external markets, and so on).

Training activities were also rather limited, as shown in *Table 3.2*: on average, only 11 per cent of service employees benefited from training. Moreover, this training was generally limited to the period immediately following recruitment (in 79 per cent of enterprises), and was rarely extended to retraining to improve job performance or for upgrading. Joint ventures were found to be less inclined to promote training courses (only 9 per cent of the labour force), but more frequently introduced new technologies or diversified their services. The performance of other property forms in this regard were rather disappointing (*Table 3.2*).

---

3. See "Young, Alone, and with Initiative", in the *Albanian Observer*, Vol. 2, No. 1 (1996), p. 34.

Table 3.2 *Training, Work Organisation, and Technology, by Property Form, 1996*

	State	Private	Joint venture	Joint-stock	Other	All
Percentage of enterprises with:						
Initial training	72.8	84.5	56.3	0	84.6	*79.1*
Retraining to improve						
job performance	20.5	16.7	40.0	0	15.4	*18.7*
Training to upgrade employees	15.0	11.5	40.0	0	0	*13.3*
Total number of employees						
involved in training (%):	*7.0*	*13.5*	*9.5*	*0*	*16.1*	*11.0*
Percentage of enterprises that:						
Increased their product/service						
range	28.8	35.9	62.5	0	30.8	*33.8*
Introduced new technologies	26.7	19.1	56.3	0	15.4	*22.9*
Introduced changes in work						
organisation	23.9	20.1	40.0	–	30.8	*22.4*

Source: ALFS2.

10 POOR GENERAL INFRASTRUCTURE

During the 1990–92 crisis following the fall of communism, infrastructure in Albania was damaged with the destruction of state property; investment during that period fell from 26 per cent of output in 1989 to only 4 per cent in 1992. As a consequence, the country's infrastructure became seriously deficient and rapidly worsened. The lack of reliable services in transport, telecommunications, energy, and water have, from the start of the reforms, constituted a major impediment to investment and growth, and sometimes generated rather primitive services. The lack of water remains one of the most acute daily problems of Albanians.

Small shops and open markets for farm produce and handicrafts account for much of the retail sector. The availability of imported consumer goods has increased and they are also sold through such channels. Better-supplied shops are found only in the larger towns and cities of Tirana, Durres, and Vlora. Trade is often segmented and therefore very dependent on local suppliers, the poor transport system being far below the standards of other European countries. The road network is at best inadequate and in the remoter regions positively hazardous. The 18,000 kilometres of roads are constructed in accordance with the standards of the 1930s or earlier, and there is only one stretch of dual carriageway between Tirana and Durres, now being upgraded with loans from international organisations. There are approximately 742 kilometres of railway lines, linking Durres with the Montenegrin border and with the mining regions of the east, and Tirana with Vlora, but only four out of every five kilometres are operational.[4] There are two ports for maritime shipping: Durres, which also has ferry facilities, and Vlora—both need modernising. Tirana's airport has also been improved by reconstruction work and an increase in the number of European connections, but faces financial problems. The national airline Albanian Airways, which is 95 per cent owned by the Kuwaiti Al Kharafi Group, has incurred serious losses and was on the verge of bankruptcy at the end of 1996, according to press reports.

It is clear that increases in the level and amount of services are directly dependent on improvements in infrastructure and the utilities. Many essential services will not improve significantly until major investment programmes that have been scheduled for years are completed.[5] It is of course difficult to finance such programmes against a background of overall budgetary restrictions, so that the support of foreign donors will be a key component in this process. In the past, however, there seems to have been overreliance on foreign funding, without sufficient allocation of domestic finance from the budget.

This lack of infrastructure also represents a major obstacle to the development of tourism in a country with much tourist potential. The majority of the attractive tourist areas (for instance the southern cities of Saranda and Vlora) are in parts of the country where roads, telecommunications, and electricity are inadequate. The lack of infrastructure is also an obstacle to the internationalisation of Albanian services.

11 SHUT OFF FROM THE OUTSIDE WORLD

One way of overcoming the crisis afflicting many service companies would be to increase their range of foreign customers. In 1996, Albanian services still seemed hermetically sealed off from the external world. There was little growth in service exports, reflecting inadequate performance by transport, travel, communications, and tourism. As much as 97 per cent of all services were being provided for the domestic market: the highest proportion of services directed abroad—in telecommunications—was only 8 per cent, followed by transport (7 per cent), and trade (6 per cent). Hotels and restaurants, public utilities, and security services were operating exclusively

4. See EIU (1998a).

5. In particular, in 1993 the Government drew up a first comprehensive Public Investment Programme covering the period 1994–96, to identify and provide the investment necessary to support economic and social development. This programme was updated in 1995 for a new programme for 1995–97. See Monck (1995).

for the domestic market. Nearly 20 per cent of service enterprises mentioned difficulties exporting their services as the main cause of low efficiency.

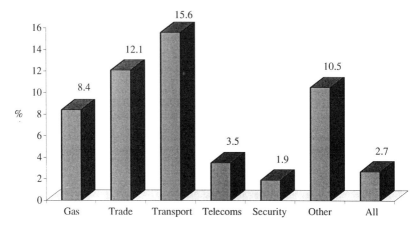

Figure 3.14 *Percentage of Services Exported, by Service, Sept. 1996*

Source: ALFS2.

12 FOREIGN INVESTORS MAINLY IN TOURISM

Joint ventures made up only 3 per cent of our survey covering service enterprises with more than 5 employees. This provides clear evidence of the difficulties faced by Albanian service enterprises above a certain size in attracting foreign investment.

This low percentage was also confirmed for very small units by INSTAT on the basis of a survey of 2,572 different trade enterprises and 591 café–restaurants, that were considered representative (in 1995 there were 16,972 trade enterprises and 4,198 café–restaurants): only 5 per cent of these enterprises in 1995 were joint ventures and only 1 per cent were foreign enterprises (INSTAT, 1997, p. 7). Enterprises with foreign funds were found to be concentrated in urban areas as well as in wholesale trade, where Greek and Italian funds dominate.

This number would seem to be much higher in very small trade companies. According to some estimates, at the end of 1995, there were 1,532 joint enterprises, around 1,000 of which were involved in trade and services.[6]

Moreover, for both sizes of enterprise—and despite the Government's attempts to entice foreign investors to participate in the financing of public

6. Data provided by EIU (1996), p. 43.

projects[7]—foreign investment in services seems to have been concentrated in a very limited number of sectors, mainly tourism and trade, where there are great opportunities for quick profits.[8] Total investment in tourism reached USD 70 million in 1995, mostly for hotel projects in and around Tirana, but also in other tourist areas.[9] In particular, foreign investors do not seem to have contributed much to the development of local suppliers of raw materials, goods, and services. In services, they also often registered more losses than profits (Chapter 9).

13 CONCLUSION

Despite clear and promising signs of rapid growth in the emerging service sector and its very good results, a more detailed analysis reveals its many weaknesses. First, the spectacular growth of micro private businesses was found to be based on a rather small number of simple traditional activities, such as basic trade and small restaurants and cafés. Their concentration in large towns led to a differentiated and unbalanced development of services by region. Their relative lack of capital and investment has become an obstacle to further diversification, with a clear risk of moving towards a "kiosk economy" already visible in the centre of Tirana: there has been an explosion in the number of very small and basic retail shops and cafés, generally financed by remittances from Albanian emigrants, that does not seem to have left much space—or capital—for other activities to emerge. When new services were developed—for instance, security services—they seemed to operate in a very narrow niche which was expected to disappear as the country developed—this sector seemed to have reached its limit, with slower growth, by the end of 1996. At the same time, larger state enterprises in public utilities were confronted by a serious economic and financial crisis, most of them experiencing a fall in sales and profits in 1995–96; poor infrastructure and overemployment were also major obstacles, undermining the return to profitability and their ability to carry out necessary restructuring. Poor

7. Projects included concessions for the financing and operation of a GSM mobile phone system; the financing, building, and operation of electricity generation plants, and water and sewage schemes; the stimulation of private sector housing developments; and investments in ports and airports.

8. Significant incentives have also been offered to foreign investors in this sector, including a tax holiday during the investment period, no profit tax for the first five years of operation, and a 50 per cent tax reduction for three more years.

9. During 1995–96, the Ministry of Tourism granted permission for around 40 new tourist developments, including hotel projects at Golem on the Adriatic, Llogara on the Ionian coast, and Drilon on Lake Ohrid.

working conditions and very low wages multiplied the risks of social conflict in these sectors. The privatisation of public utilities that might have brought with it the necessary innovation and investment was still in limbo at the end of 1996. A lack of access to external markets locked enterprises into a domestic vicious circle in which the simplicity and low quality of services was combined with poor working conditions and low wages, low levels of capital and investment, and little diversification. Foreign investors, who represented the most likely source of assets, fresh capital, new technologies, and access to foreign markets, continued to focus their attention and investment on a small number of sectors, such as trade and tourism, without bringing the expected higher returns.

In this context, what has been presented as another spectacular sign of Albanian recovery—and expected to compensate for the collapse of industry—could well turn out to be another Albanian "miracle" or "balloon of hope" that will dissipate rapidly rather than provide the basis for sustainable long-term growth.

4. The Missing Pillar: The Inadequacy of the Banking System

1 INTRODUCTION

Before the transition, Albania's banking system was typical of a centrally planned economy. The financial sector, like all the other sectors of the economy, was subject to extreme centralisation. There were only four financial institutions—all state-owned—with responsibilities divided along functional lines: (i) central and commercial, (ii) rural credit, (iii) collection of savings, and (iv) management of trade finance. For a long time, the State Bank of Albania was in charge of both central banking and commercial banking tasks.

The Government's comprehensive reform programme at the beginning of the transition set a number of financial objectives: decreasing the budget deficit, monitoring inflation, solving the foreign debt crisis, ensuring domestic convertibility of the lek, creating a two-tier banking system and a system of non-bank institutions, and initiating a modern legal framework for the financial system.

As an important first step, bank reforms in 1991–92 created a two-tier banking system with the Central Bank of Albania governing three state-owned second-tier banks: the National Commercial Bank (NCB), the Rural Credit Bank (RCB), and the Savings Bank (SB). Each of these second-tier banks was created with a view to it becoming a universal bank and engaging in both deposit taking and lending to households and enterprises. The volume of credit of these commercial banks, however, was to be monitored by the Central Bank through credit ceilings, the setting of interest rates for both loans and deposits, and a degree of control over exchange rates. Further steps were taken early in 1996, with the approval of a new Banking Law and a new Bank of Albania Law (in February), which confirmed the Central Bank's objective of influencing macroeconomic developments, such as inflation, by means of a tight monetary policy, a hard budget constraint, and other restrictive measures. Although such measures seemed likely to constitute a good basis for a strong new financial market, the banking system very soon revealed obvious weaknesses, some inherited from the previous regime—such as

55

outdated banking procedures and inexperienced staff—others generated by the new restrictive credit and banking system itself. In this chapter we will attempt to document the causes of these problems and to identify how they prevented the new banking system from performing its expected functions. Furthermore, the new system proved to be completely inappropriate in terms of the new developments in the economy, particularly the emergence of numerous private businesses and corresponding growth in investment and demand for credit.

2 BANKING AND OWNERSHIP STRUCTURES OF THE PAST

Outdated Banking System

Despite the progress made in one direction, the Albanians' lack of experience of modern banking techniques turned out to be a serious handicap. Most transactions were still carried out in cash,[1] even by Ministries, large enterprises, and—sometimes—foreign donors.

The banks provided few services to their customers, and at a standard far below the international norm. The range of credit and savings instruments was extremely limited. Transactions were effected and processed incredibly slowly. Currency transfer procedures were often archaic. As far as foreign exchange was concerned, the banks were seriously challenged by the more efficient and competitive free market operated by individuals in the street or from small private cash desks. The low quality of banking services was often due to the outdated infrastructure and an obsolete ledger system that made it impossible to implement modern payment techniques. Expertise and qualified staff to carry out proper credit analysis were also missing. In particular, we shall see how the banks were unable to structure financial arrangements with business borrowers in such a way as to address both the banks' needs related to risk and the credit needs of the business community. Insurance services, for instance, had not been systematically developed within the banking system. There was also a general lack of transparency.

No Changes in the Property Structure

The property structure did not change rapidly. The extension of our 1996 survey to include Albanian banks was an important departure. We interviewed the managers of the Central Bank and its 37 affiliates in the regions, and of

---

1. For instance, a new Law on Cheques had been drafted in 1995, but had not been approved and implemented by 1996.

the three secondary banks and their dozen or so regional affiliates, providing data on a total of 78 banks.

According to the survey results, at the end of 1996 there were still no private banks, and only two foreign banks had come on the scene to form joint ventures, the Arab Islamic bank and the Italian Albanian Bank, with an average foreign capital participation of 60 per cent. Only 2 per cent of bank managers reported having distributed or sold shares to employees.

Forty-three per cent of state-owned enterprises reported plans to change their property form, thus confirming that privatisation in the banking sector in 1996—that is, five years after the beginning of the reforms!—was still in the future. Although the Government approved a new privatisation strategy for state-owned banks in September 1996, it did not provide much detail about the timing and method of privatisation. At the same time, although private banks looked likely to emerge, legal restrictions limited their activities.

In the course of 1996, licences to engage in private banking activities were given to three private enterprises, all subsidiaries of established foreign banks.[2] However, state banks had part ownership in most of the new firms and their activities remained limited. It is important to note that at the end of 1996, the three state-owned banks between them held over 95 per cent of deposits in the formal banking system (IMF, 1997b). The two joint-venture banks at the end of 1996 served more as a facility for the transfer of currency than for deposits and credits.

Some progress was expected with the establishment of the new Tirana Stock Exchange as the first institution of the Albanian capital market in mid-1996, but this institution has yet to assume its intended role.

The prevalence of state-owned enterprises was even stronger in terms of employment, concentrating more than 99 per cent bank employees (*Figure 4.2*).

Large banks were also dominant. The average number of employees in each bank was relatively small, at 44 employees, the two joint ventures being smaller. Although most banks (86 per cent) had fewer than 50 employees (*Figure 4.3*)—except in Tirana, where the average was 177—nearly 50 per cent of employees were concentrated in banks of more than 200 employees (*Figure 4.4*).

---

2. But also of other, less well-established foreign banks—for instance from Greece and Malaysia—as described by Muço (1997), p. 3.

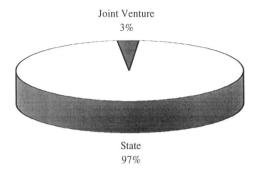

Figure 4.1 *Distribution of Establishments, by Property Form, Sept. 1996, Banking Sector*

Source: ALFS2.

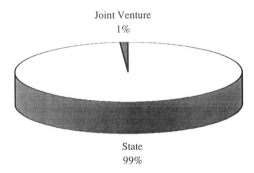

Figure 4.2 *Distribution of Employment, by Property Form, Sept. 1996, Banking Sector*

Source: ALFS2.

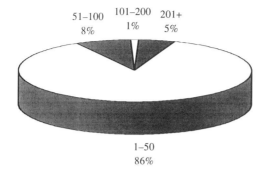

Figure 4.3 *Distribution of Banks, by Number of Employees, Sept. 1996*

Source: ALFS2.

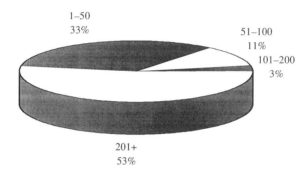

Figure 4.4 *Distribution of Employees, by Number of Employees, Sept. 1996, Banking Sector*

Source: ALFS2.

Regional Imbalances: The Gap between Tirana and the Other Regions

Finally, although the banks were fairly well distributed among the different regions (*Figure 4.5*), the bulk of the employees worked in the large national banks in Tirana (57 per cent). This concentration of large banks in the capital (*Figure 4.6*) is reflected in the difficult access to capital experienced by companies in remote areas, which often had to deal with banks located in Tirana, another reason behind their preference for alternative credit facilities at the local level.

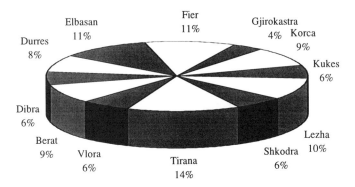

Figure 4.5 *Distribution of Establishments, by Region, Sept. 1996, Banking Sector*
Source: ALFS2.

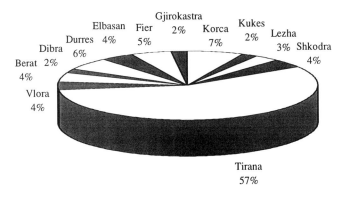

Figure 4.6 *Distribution of Employees, by Region, Sept. 1996, Banking Sector*
Source: ALFS2.

This regional imbalance was reflected in banks' profit levels by region. We asked managers of the 78 banks distributed in all parts of the country to report whether they had experienced an increase, a decrease, or no change in profits in the past year (*Table 4.1*). Huge differences were found between regions, with a majority of the banks in the capital (87.5 per cent) and in a few other large towns, such as Elbasan (62.5 per cent) and Korca (57.1 per cent), registering profit growth in 1995–96, while most other banks had to endure a fall in profits, particularly in Fier (62.5 per cent reporting a loss), Dibra (60 per cent), Berat, Durres, and Lezha (50 per cent).

Table 4.1 *Percentage of Banks Reporting an Increase in Profits, by Region, 1995–96*

	Increase	Decrease	No change	Don't know	Total
Berat	50.0	50.0	0	0	100%
Dibra	20.0	60.0	20.0	0	100%
Durres	0	50.0	25.0	25.0	100%
Elbasan	62.5	25.0	12.5	0	100%
Fier	12.5	62.5	0	25.0	100%
Gjirokastra	25.0	25.0	25.0	25.0	100%
Korca	57.1	14.3	28.6	0	100%
Kukes	25.0	25.0	50.0	0	100%
Lezha	12.5	50.0	25.0	12.5	100%
Shkodra	40.0	40.0	20.0	0	100%
Tirana	87.5	12.5	0	0	100%
Vlora	25.0	0	25.0	50.0	100%

Source: ALFS2.

This concentration of banking activities in Tirana also delayed the necessary modernisation and training of personnel in the rural areas. As shown in *Table 4.2*, only in Tirana were a majority of banks found to implement training courses for a significant proportion of their employees (33 per cent of employees involved against less than 10 per cent on average in all other regions). Banks in regions such as Gjirokastra, Vlora (both in the south), and Kukes (in the north) were not carrying out any training activities or only very rarely, generally on the job rather than "in the classroom", and for a very small percentage of their employees.

Table 4.2 *Percentage of Banks Implementing Training, by Region, 1995–96*

Region		Forms of training		
	% of employees involved in training	Initial training	Retraining to improve job performance	Training to upgrade
Berat	6.7	28.6	42.9	28.6
Dibra	9.0	0	60.0	60.0
Durres	16.7	50.0	83.3	83.3
Elbasan	17.1	37.5	57.1	57.1
Fier	21.8	50.0	75.0	66.7
Gjirokastra	0.8	0	0	0
Korca	35.0	50.0	66.7	66.7
Kukes	5.4	0	25.0	0
Lezha	11.8	12.5	25.0	28.6
Shkodra	6.2	20.0	60.0	60.0
Tirana	32.9	70.0	70.0	70.0
Vlora	0.6	20.0	20.0	20.0
All	**15.5**	**32.9**	**50.7**	**46.5**

Source: ALFS2.

The small percentage of banking employees who were involved in training at the national level at the end of 1996 (15 per cent) should also be noted. Moreover, less than half of the banks reported carrying out training activities, whether for new recruits, improving job performance, or upgrading. This weakness in terms of training accentuated the staffing problem and the low quality of services already identified.

3 THE LIQUIDITY CRISIS

Albanian banks were clearly confronted by a liquidity problem, for a number of reasons.

Non-Performing Loans

The commercial banks had to solve the problem of non-performing loans, having inherited a mass of loans to state enterprises, farms, and co-operatives which could never be collected. A complex web of interbank liabilities, dating from before the transition, also remained. This left the balance sheets of all the banks compromised and impeded the development of an interbank market.

The non-performing loans had multiplied mainly because of the inappropriate evaluation and selection of credit customers, and a lack of professionalism on the part of commercial bank specialists, who had no experience of risk-based lending. In too many cases preferential credit access had been given to state managers, with a considerable amount of corruption and bribery thrown in for good measure. The significant number of unsuccessful new businesses was another factor.

We tried to find out more about the reasons for this difficult situation by asking the managers of the 78 banks to report on their main labour efficiency problems (*Table 4.3*). It appears that working conditions were the most frequently mentioned difficulty (36 per cent). Difficulties in selling services were also a major problem, one that may have induced the banks to become less strict when issuing loans. This was particularly prevalent in Tirana (in 33 per cent of banks), and even more so in Korca (40 per cent), Dibra (50 per cent), and Vlora (67 per cent). The skills and qualifications of banking employees were judged by managers to be insufficient, a state of affairs often related to another significant problem, low wages. The absence of adequate supervision was also blamed, especially in banks in Tirana (by 33 per cent of them) and Durres (50 per cent).

Nearly 20 per cent of bank managers mentioned quality of work as the main employment problem expected in the next 12 months.

Table 4.3 *Main and Secondary Cause of Low Labour Efficiency, Banking Sector, Sept. 1996*

	Main problem	Secondary problem
Low skills	16.7	2.7
Poor working conditions	35.7	5.4
Low wages	11.9	29.7
Inadequate supervision	7.1	10.8
Absenteeism	2.4	0
Difficulties in selling services	20.9	24.3
Other	4.7	21.6
Don't know	0	5.4
	100%	100%

Source: ALFS2.

As a result, by the end of 1994, 27 per cent of loans made since June 1992, when the banks had started operating, were non-performing. By the end of 1995, in two of the three new banks, overdue loans accounted for almost half of total outstanding loans.[3] According to other sources, by April 1995 only 30 per cent of the loans issued by the three commercial banks had been repaid in due time.[4] Our 1996 enterprise survey also reveals (*Table 4.4*) that problems with debtors were the main difficulty reported by bank managers (nearly 37 per cent).

The mentality of customers also played a role: the belief was widespread that the state would not ask for the loans to be repaid.

Finally, the accumulation of bad loans can also be attributed to the lack of collateral, the virtual non-existence of the mortgage, and court delays in confiscating mortgaged assets in cases of default. Difficulties in properly defining collateral and its market value are the direct result of the frequent impossibility of registering intangible assets, and delays in establishing the legal framework necessary for buying and selling land.[5] Another reason is the lack of legal instruments available to banks to enforce overdue loan payments and to cancel loans entirely.

3. See IMF (1997b), p. 28. The report also mentions as a significant example poor credit evaluation in the Rural Commercial Bank in respect of its short-term loans to farmers to buy tractors and trucks, accounting for one-third of the bank's total lending and 80 per cent of its bad debts.

4. See *Monthly Statistical Bulletin* of the Bank of Albania (October 1995), also mentioned in Muço (1997), p. 5.

5. Many banks offered loans on the basis of the value of the customer's home. In most cases, however, particularly in the countryside, these dwellings had no market value following the large-scale migration of the rural population to the large towns. Disputes about land ownership made the situation even more complicated.

The failure to repay large sums in due time has given rise to a number of serious problems, many banks deciding as a consequence to limit their loans, so adversely affecting manufacturing. Loan default is also an obstacle to the privatisation of Albanian commercial banks, since potential buyers would have to take over non-performing loans. On the other hand, there can be no doubt that privatisation would do something to solve the problem of bad selection of applicants for credit and increase competition on the credit market.

A Lack of Deposits

The difficulties of the banks have also been generated by the unwillingness of the public to deposit its savings: our survey in 1996 confirmed this as one of the banks' major problems. This phenomenon is often explained in terms of the very low standards of living prevalent in Albania at the beginning of the transition—Albania was the poorest country in Europe—standards that in some cases have since that time declined even further (see Chapter 6). But this is clearly not the only problem, by any means: the evidence collected so far shows that there were sufficient funds—for instance, remittances from abroad—to accumulate high levels of savings and deposits. Estimates of the funds placed in the informal market at the end of 1996 and early 1997 confirm this view.

There are a number of other reasons for this peculiar state of affairs, which commenced after 1992–93, a period of high inflation. Depositors responded to the failure of the banks to counter the high inflation with high interest rates by reducing or even closing their accounts; to make matters worse, many banks did not agree to repay particularly large deposits, provoking a generalised crisis of confidence in the banking system. This crisis was compounded by the inability of the banks to implement an efficient giro system, which motivated people to hang on to their savings or to seek more liquid investments and places of deposit. This lack of confidence in the banking sector among depositors led them to refrain from tying up their funds for a long period. Money was henceforth deposited only on a short-term basis. Moreover, many people began to look for alternative placements. The fundamental fact that the Albanian economy is predominantly based on cash transactions, necessitating rapid access to capital, further enhanced the attractiveness of alternative investments offering high interest rates over a very short period of time and with rapid rotation.

Our survey results confirm the banks' liquidity problems: when asked to identify the main problem they had had to face over the last six months, most bank managers reported insufficient deposits or difficulties with their debtors. Nearly 20 per cent emphasised financial problems or falling profits, while others complained about the slowness of money turnover (*Table 4.4*).

Table 4.4 *Main Problem in the Last 6 Months, Sept. 1996, Banking Sector*
(percentage of establishments specifying problem)

Debtor problems	36.8
Insufficient deposits	28.9
Fall in profits	13.2
Financial problems of customers	6.6
Problems with speed of money turnover	5.3
Lack of new technology	5.3
Departure of experienced staff	1.3
Low motivation of employees	1.3
High taxes	1.3

Source: ALFS2.

Table 4.5 confirms the lack of deposits: in the first half of 1996, time deposits were reported in only 42 per cent of banks (at an average per bank of 760 million leks), demand deposits in 52 per cent (at an average per bank of 3,545 million leks), and foreign currency deposits in 36 per cent (2,640 million leks). Personal savings were registered in 78 per cent of banks, but amounted to an average per bank of 35 billion leks, representing a decrease on 1994.

Table 4.5 *Deposits, 1994–96, Banking Sector (million leks)*

	1994		1995		Jan.–Sept. 1996	
	% of banks	Amount	% of banks	Amount	% of banks	Amount
Deposits:						
Demand	41	2 615.3	45	4 005.9	52	3 545.7
Time	33	599.2	35	883.0	42	759.5
Foreign currency	24	2 603.5	26	3 319.1	36	2 639.6
Individual	67	45 116.0	70	35 075.0	78	35 010.0

Source: ALFS2.

The banks' liquidity problems were confirmed by changes in profits over the last year: 37 per cent of banks reported a fall in profits, while 38 per cent reported an increase. We have seen that the situation was more dramatic in particular regions (*Table 4.1*): profit falls were most frequent in Fier (in 63 per cent of banks), Dibra (60 per cent), and Lezha (50 per cent); while in Tirana, Elbasan, Berat, and Korca the banks reported profit increases. Tirana reported the highest profit increases in both 1994–95 and 1995–96.

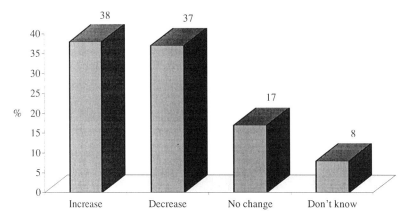

Figure 4.7 *Percentage of Banks Reporting Profit Increase, 1995–96*

Source: ALFS2.

According to the IMF (1997b, p. 30), "all banks have failed to meet required capital adequacy ratios". They also indicate that none of the three state-owned banks has a licence, having failed to meet the provisions of the Banking Law.

The majority of banks tried to improve matters by extending their range of services: 83 per cent of bank managers reported attempts to diversify, although 22 per cent noted extreme difficulties in selling new services. It is significant that of the 78 banks in our sample less than 5 per cent were planning to open new branches.

Once again, there was a direct positive correlation between profits and employment changes. Banks with increasing profits also increased their labour force, while banks that registered losses were also those that had to cut employment the most. This confirms that the profitability crisis in the banking sector had a direct impact on employment in several banks. This generalised relation between profitability and employment, observable in all sectors, is developed further in Chapter 5.

4 HARD BUDGET CONSTRAINT LIMITING CREDIT

Growing Credit Demand . . .

Rapid development of the private sector resulted in higher demand for credit. The creation of new small private enterprises required start-up capital and additional funds for necessary investment. At the same time, the privatisation of state-owned enterprises needed substantial investment in order to increase efficiency and renew their generally obsolete equipment and technology.

Many people willing to start a new business were often blocked by the very tough conditions imposed by the banks, most of which required a downpayment on loans that most new businesses could not supply.

. . . Not Met because of a Voluntarily Restrictive Monetary Policy

Direct instruments of monetary policy were first used by the Bank of Albania, in particular a tight credit policy through hard constraints, such as bank-by-bank credit ceilings imposed on commercial banks. Interest rates on loans and deposits were also indirectly set by the Central Bank. Quarterly distribution of the volume of credit has often led commercial banks to refuse customer requests for loans because they did not fit into their credit plan (Muço, 1997, p. 4).

The bank-to-bank credit ceilings were imposed from mid-1992 on the direct advice of international monetary institutions in response to the banks' poor credit evaluation and stock of bad loans. According to the IMF (1997b, p. 30), "[t]hese ceilings have been set at levels well below what the banks would like and probably at levels insufficient to meet the demand for credit in the private sector at prevailing interest rates. The limitations of the banking system made these measures sensible, indeed necessary, but their combination led to the emergence of an informal market, which provided alternative channels for the intermediation of savings." This clear economic policy choice, however, had much greater and unexpected implications, as the 1997 crisis showed (Chapter 10).

As predicted, this strict monetary policy clearly reduced the ability of commercial banks to satisfy increasing demand for credit in 1992–96. Only a very small percentage of credit requests could be satisfied, directing the private sector to the informal credit market.

In 1994, the Albanian Government, in co-operation with the IMF and the World Bank, restricted all new lending from public sector banks to the amount repaid on existing loans. In response, Albanian bankers restricted all new lending, using only 64 per cent of the authorised credit (Wortman, 1995). In the second half of 1995, only 42 per cent of the 1.4 billion lek credit limit fixed by the Bank of Albania for the whole banking system was used.[6]

This policy was guided by the need to keep inflation and other monetary indicators under control, and probably also reflected the difficulties of the banking sector in terms of liquidity and non-performing loans. However, we may question the effectiveness of such a restrictive policy, especially in a context of unsatisfied—and rapidly growing—credit demand from the private sector and the financial problems of most industries in the manufacturing

6. See "Revisit Bankare", Bank of Albania, October 1995, quoted in Muço (1997), p. 5.

sector. The rapid development of the informal credit market should also have served as an important warning signal to the Government and international monetary institutions to relax this policy.

Our survey results confirmed that the credits provided by the banks were very limited. In 1996, only 17 per cent of the banks reported having provided credits for industry (at an average of 111 million leks) and 23 per cent for services (217 million leks), so further deepening the crisis in these sectors. Access to credit was particularly difficult for state enterprises: less than 10 per cent of banks financed them in 1996, 70 per cent of banks concentrating on the private sector. A minority of bank managers reported having provided loans to other banks (4 per cent) or directly to the Government (only 3 per cent, but of very large sums). Individuals were able to obtain loans in 65 per cent of banks, the average amount per bank being 1,215 million leks. Most credits were provided by large banks, especially in Tirana, indicating a regional imbalance in credit access.

Table 4.6 *Credits, 1994–96, Banking Sector (million leks)*

	1994		1995		Jan.–Sept. 1996	
	% of banks	Amount	% of banks	Amount	% of banks	Amount
Short-term credits for:						
Public	14	110.4	11	159.6	10	128.0
Private	63	457.2	64	615.6	64	306.7
Whole economy	–	250.7	–	392.1	–	235.7
Long-term credits for:						
Public	5	342.1	2	527.7	2	454.7
Private	57	279.8	60	683.1	69	402.9
Whole economy	46	161.7	49	347.0	52	338.8
Total credits for:						
Industry	18	677.1	15	940.3	17	110.8
Services	17	87.5	19	113.3	23	216.8
Bank	3	89.8	3	97.5	4	60.0
Government	3	3 795.0	3	10 273.0	3	11 934.0
Individuals	58	3 113.2	60	1 966.5	65	1 215.5

Source: ALFS2.

5 THE GROWTH OF THE INFORMAL CREDIT SECTOR

All the above listed weaknesses of the banking sector and the difficulties in obtaining credit in the formal credit market led to the emergence of a flourishing informal market.

A Credit System by Default

The liquidity problems of banks have clearly limited their ability to respond to the demand for credit emanating from enterprises. The increasing range of loan conditions—such as downpayments and collateral—compelled most enterprises to seek more flexible arrangements. The lack of infrastructure and modern payment techniques, but particularly bureaucratic delays in obtaining credits after long discussion, also pushed customers into the informal market. In a survey carried out in 1996 (Muço and Salko, 1996), 53 per cent of entrepreneurs reported that their main reason for going into the informal market was a need for immediate funds.

To summarise, the formal banking sector did not function properly as a domestic financial intermediary, either as a collector of savings or as a credit provider for economic activity. As far as savings are concerned, the Bank of Albania tried to ensure that depositors were offered interest rates which were at least positive in real terms by setting minimum interest rates on time deposits (for the period 1993–95 these were in the range of 15–20 per cent). These were very low compared to the interest rates found in the informal market. Interest rates on deposits and credits, though fluctuating wildly during the period 1991–96, have always been around 5 to 6 times lower than those on offer in the informal market (Muço, 1997). As a result, as we see in *Table 4.5*, only 42 per cent of banks received any time deposits between January and September 1996.

A Phenomenon Fuelled by both Credit Demand and Supply

The informal credit market developed because there was both great demand for capital and a large supply. All new businesses that were unable to obtain bank loans directed their requests to the informal market. Outstanding formal sector bank loans to the private sector represented around 4 per cent of GDP at the end of 1996. These figures, when compared to the overwhelming share of private sector production in the whole economy, indicate that much of that production was financed through own resources or the informal market. On the supply side, there was a substantial volume of savings—chiefly remittances from emigrants—estimated at around USD 400 million a year. Emigrants began to lend their savings informally at high and competitive rates, taking advantage of the inability of the banking sector to respond adequately and in good time. The existence of capital is important because it contradicts the view often put forward that the collapse of the banking sector was a direct consequence of the economic crisis in Albania. The financial difficulties of the banks could probably have been overcome if the population's savings had been properly channelled into the banking sector and a better credit policy put in place aimed at financing manufacturing and the emerging new businesses.

Economic Policy Out of Control

The growth of the informal market led to a number of negative effects. First, it involved a higher degree of risk. Recourse to such credits in the informal market for long periods, often at very high interest rates, landed some businesses in serious financial difficulties. The result was either a higher probability of bankruptcy or diversification into illegal activities and money laundering. The suppliers of capital also faced greater risks, particularly in respect of non-existent or illegal collateral. The existence of this market resulted in more and more abuses and social problems. Another major adverse effect was the loss of state revenues, since unlicensed activities entail systematic tax and social contribution evasion. Furthermore, the informal market has swallowed individual savings that were thus not always used for productive investment. Finally, the growth of the informal market obviously limited the macroeconomic efficiency of the Central Bank. For example, it is possible that a market in which enormous amounts of money were changing hands influenced the inflation rate. Informal foreign currency exchange also undermined official exchange policy. Similarly, real consumption levels no longer reflected official income levels, while the general GDP growth was clearly not being generated by declining production.

6 CONCLUSION

We may conclude that the banking system was of little help to Albanian manufacturing in the crisis it faced from 1991. In fact, the failure of the banking system to act as a proper financial intermediary has depressed industrial activity even further. On the one hand, the banks were unable to attract savings from the population, especially remittances from emigrants; on the other, they provided only marginal credit to the productive sector, so failing to sustain the growth of a multitude of small businesses that had as a consequence to turn to the emerging informal credit sector. If this failure can be explained partly by the economic crisis and the accumulation of a series of non-performing loans which encouraged the banks to be more cautious, it was also clearly the result of a policy choice, on the advice of international monetary institutions, to implement a very restrictive monetary policy, including the limitation of credits.

According to the IMF (1997b, p. 14), "monetary policy has relied mainly on indirect instruments to control credit expansion to the non-government sector". This policy, however, has had catastrophic implications for the whole economy that have so far not been well documented, and on which we shall attempt to shed more light in the following chapters. The fact that large amounts were distributed to the Government rather than to productive enterprises means that the absence of productive credit was due not only to the absence of deposits but to the internal deficiencies—or the overt policy—of the banking sector. The presence of potentially very high savings in the economy confirms this view, as a number of observers have pointed out: "the irony of the situation is that while credit demand was very high and credit supply continued to grow . . . the amount of credit being dispersed was minimal" (Wortman, 1995, p. 11).

The progressive growth of the informal credit market as a "market by default" will further exacerbate tensions in the credit market and in the whole economy. The expansion of the informal market will clearly lead to a multiplication of abuses, with everyone attempting to maximise profits before the system collapses. The expansion of this informal market, combined with the Government's *laissez-faire* policy, progressively gathered all the elements that came together to provoke a generalised financial crisis in early 1997 (Chapter 10).

5. The Unemployment Shock

1 INTRODUCTION

Since the beginning of the transition in 1992 Albania has been beset by a deep economic and social crisis, with shrinking output and sales, numerous bankruptcies, and growing unemployment. The economic crisis, which was examined from all sides by our first enterprise survey in 1994, had not been overcome by 1996. In Chapter 2 we confirmed the depth of the crisis in industry.

As a result of the collapse of production, the lack of demand, and difficulties in finding external markets, the number of bankruptcies in Albania has been multiplying rapidly. In the two years which separated our two surveys, more than 20 per cent of all industrial enterprises declared themselves bankrupt and ceased operating. In November 1996, 30 per cent of the managers questioned reported that their enterprise was threatened with bankruptcy over the next 12 months.

One of the main aims of our analysis has been to quantify the direct effects on employment of the general demand crisis. We tried to estimate the extent of overemployment in the different sectors of the economy at the end of 1996 with the help of a range of measures, and then to analyse restructuring and lay-off policies in individual enterprises and industries. We also tried to assess how far the expansion in services could help to compensate employment cuts in industry. Employment trends in the banking sector were another central concern.

2 GENERALISED OVEREMPLOYMENT . . .

As a first indication we asked whether the enterprise had had enough work for its employees over the last two years: 38 per cent of managers in industry reported that they had not, particularly hard hit being chemicals (64 per cent), joint-stock companies (56 per cent), and large enterprises of more than 200 employees (40 per cent). In services, on the other hand, only 7 per cent of establishments reported having had too little work for their employees.

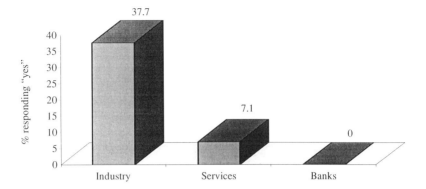

Figure 5.1 *Too Little Work for Workforce, by Sector, Sept. 1996, All Sectors*
Source: ALFS2.

Secondly, we asked managers if they thought they could produce the same output with fewer workers. Their answers confirmed that, despite restructuring, overemployment was still present in industrial enterprises, and to a lesser extent also in services and banks (*Figure 5.2*).

In industry, however, the situation at the end of 1996 appeared to be less dramatic than in 1994: 30 per cent of enterprises said that they could produce the same output with fewer workers, as against 45 per cent in 1994.

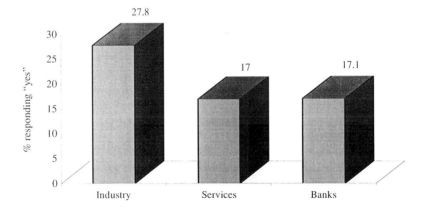

Figure 5.2 *Could Produce Same Level of Output with Fewer Workers, by Sector, Sept. 1996, All Sectors*
Source: ALFS2.

Restructuring and lay-offs occurred on a particularly large scale in the food industry—in which 22 per cent of employers reported in 1996 that they could produce the same output with fewer workers, compared to 45 per cent in 1994—and in leather and shoes (27 per cent as against 34 per cent). It is important to note that restructuring also occurred in minerals (where 26 per cent of employers reported overemployment, compared to 51 per cent in 1994), confirming the progress made in this sector. At the same time, as shown in *Figure 5.3*, the employment situation was found to be particularly bad in chemicals (where 47 per cent reported overemployment), mining (41

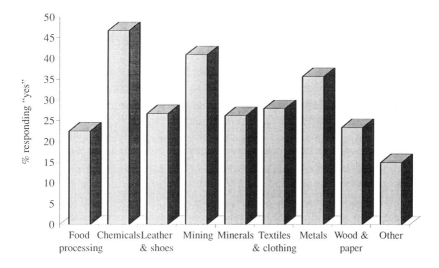

Figure 5.3 *Could Produce Same Level of Output with Fewer Workers, by Industry, Sept. 1996*

Source: ALFS2.

per cent), and metals (36 per cent). In services, the visible signs of overemployment were found in transport and trade (*Figure 5.4*).

An analysis of the situation in terms of property form confirms that restructuring has been implemented by enterprises of all forms of association, including state-owned enterprises, in which the percentage of employers reporting overemployment fell from 47 per cent in 1994 to 33 per cent in 1996 (*Figure 5.5*). Better employment prospects were registered in the private sector, with only 24 per cent reporting overemployment.

Restructuring between 1994 and 1996 was found to be distributed equally by size of enterprise, although more employers in large enterprises reported

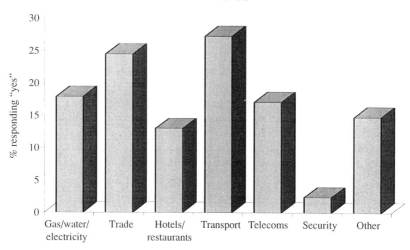

Figure 5.4 *Could Produce Same Level of Service with Fewer Workers, by Service, Sept. 1996*

Source: ALFS2.

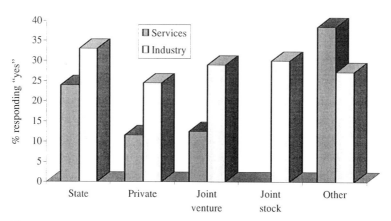

Figure 5.5 *Could Produce Same Level of Output with Fewer Workers, by Property Form, Sept. 1996, Industrial and Service Sectors*

Source: ALFS2.

that they could produce the same output with fewer workers (47 per cent as against 20 per cent in smaller firms). Employers in the regions of Lezha, Durres, Elbasan, and Kukes were also more likely to report this problem.

Despite the better economic performance of services, 17 per cent of establishments in this sector reported that they could maintain the same level of activity with fewer employees. This was most pronounced in the large state-owned enterprises in transport and the public utilities. Although trade, which is dominated by small private firms, was also significantly affected *(Figure 5.4)*, on average only 11 per cent of private service enterprises mentioned this indicator of overemployment, compared to 24 per cent of state-owned enterprises *(Figure 5.5)*. A direct relationship may also be observed between overemployment and enterprise size.

We also asked managers to indicate the percentage of workers required to produce the same output. Industrial enterprises reported that they could produce the same output with 80 per cent of their current workforce, thereby providing an initial overemployment estimate of 20 per cent. This figure is lower than the 30 per cent we arrived at in our enterprise survey in 1994, another confirmation of intensive restructuring among all Albanian industrial enterprises since that time. It was a high figure nevertheless, showing that restructuring was far from finished.

Moreover, the chemical (34 per cent) and mining sectors (28 per cent) reported percentages higher than the national average in 1996. Also noteworthy is the progress made in minerals, in which overemployment was reduced from 44 per cent in 1994 to 21 per cent in 1996. The situation had also improved significantly in food (from 30 to 17 per cent), and wood and paper (from 28 to 19 per cent), providing an additional indication of a modest recovery in these sectors.

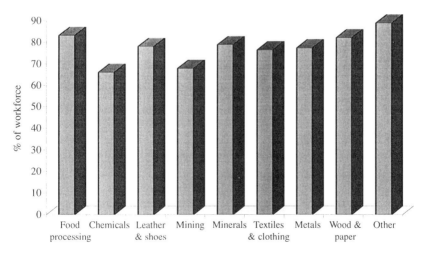

Figure 5.6 *Percentage of Workers Needed to Produce the Same Output, by Industry, Sept. 1996*

Source: ALFS2.

Albania in Crisis

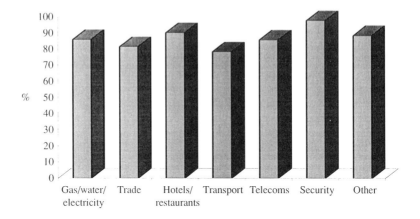

Figure 5.7 *Percentage of Employees Needed to Produce the Same Service, by Service, Sept. 1996*

Source: ALFS2.

In services, overemployment was estimated to be 13 per cent, with higher figures in transport (21 per cent). Nearly full employment was observed in security services despite the large number of firms (77) and the significant level of employment (7 per cent) in this activity.

In industry, there were no large differences by property form, enterprises across the board reporting average overemployment of between 19 and 25 per cent. Restructuring in state-owned enterprises has been particularly vigorous, overemployment falling from 35 per cent in 1994 to 25 per cent in 1996. Overemployment was lowest—19 per cent—in private enterprises. Joint ventures averaged 23 per cent overemployment, although the disaggregated figures reveal a marked disparity between those in minority foreign ownership, which reported only 10 per cent overemployment, and those in majority foreign ownership, which reported overemployment of 24 per cent. Surprisingly, property form differentials were much greater in services, overemployment estimates varying from 8 per cent in private enterprises to 19 per cent in public enterprises (*Figure 5.8*).

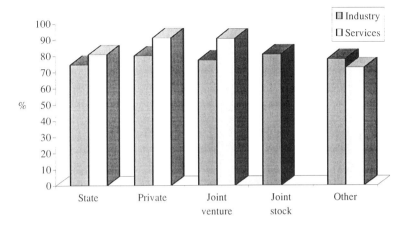

Figure 5.8 *Percentage of Workers Needed to Produce the Same Output, by Property Form, Sept. 1996, Industrial Sector*

Source: ALFS2.

A strong direct correlation was found both in industry and services between size of enterprise and overemployment, which was found to vary in industry between 15 per cent in small enterprises and 37 per cent in large enterprises, and in services between 9 and 27 per cent respectively (*Figure 5.9*).

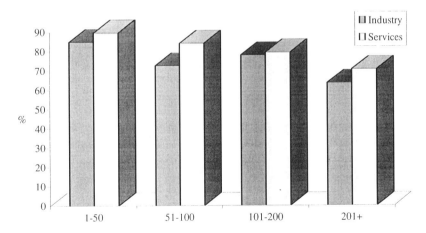

Figure 5.9 *Percentage of Workers Needed to Produce the Same Output, by Number of Employees, Sept. 1996, Industrial and Service Sectors*

Source: ALFS2.

There were also important regional differences in overemployment between
industry and services: overemployment in industry was highest in Kukes,
Lezha, Korca, and Durres, while in services it was highest in Vlora and
Tirana.

Although banks were found to be operating at nearly 100 per cent of full
capacity and managers did not report having too little work for their
employees, overemployment was found at the establishment level: 17 per cent
of bank managers reported that they could provide the same services with
fewer employees, adding that 86 per cent of the current workforce would be
sufficient. Overemployment was estimated to be higher in Shkodra (28 per
cent), Korca (25 per cent), and Berat (23 per cent), and lower in Tirana, Vlora,
Elbasan, Gjirokastra, and Kukes (below 5 per cent). In banks which had
already reduced their labour force over the previous two years, managers
continued to report average overemployment of nearly 50 per cent, directly
reflecting the serious financial problems of many banks (*Figure 5.10*).

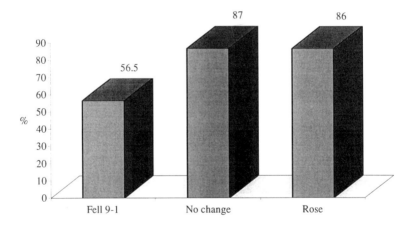

Figure 5.10 *Percentage of Employees Needed to Produce the Same Output, by
Employment Change, Sept. 1996, Banking Sector*

Source: ALFS2.

When asked to indicate what the main employment problem was likely to be
over the next six months, nearly 20 per cent of banks reported quality of work
(33 per cent in Tirana), and 15 per cent, lay-offs.

3 ... DESPITE ACTIVE RESTRUCTURING AND MASSIVE LAY-OFFS

These figures were even more alarming when we consider that most enterprises had already implemented restructuring programmes involving a substantial number of lay-offs. In our first survey we found that industrial enterprises had dismissed more than 50 per cent of their labour force in 1993–94: on average, 34 per cent in 1993 and 32 per cent in 1994. The results of our second survey show that this downward trend continued in 1995–96, with some sectors and regions being particularly hard hit. We found that on average industrial enterprises had dismissed 11 per cent of their labour force in 1995 and nearly 12 per cent in 1996.

Our first survey in 1994 revealed an extremely high proportion of workers dismissed in 1993–94. In food, leather and shoes, and textiles and clothing more than 70 per cent of the labour force were dismissed in 1993–94. The mining industry was also at the forefront of this process, releasing 25 per cent of the labour force in 1993, 29 per cent in 1994, 17 per cent in 1995, and 13 per cent in 1996 (*Figure 5.11*).

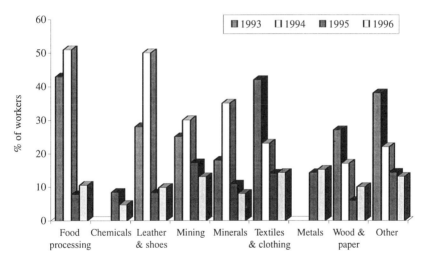

Figure 5.11 *Percentage of Workers Dismissed, by Industry, 1993–96*

Note: Chemicals and metals were included under "Other" in 1993–94.
Sources: ALFS1, ALFS2.

Although these figures indicate the existence of a a positive trend, showing that Albanian employers had already started restructuring, concern should have been expressed regarding the employment situation, particularly the unemployment rate. Industrial employment has continued to grow only in the textile industry, mainly due to the emergence of dynamic new small private enterprises. A proportion of employees dismissed from the food industry have also been integrated into the growing service sector, however, especially in trade. Private sector growth far from compensated for the enormous employment cuts in industry registered since the beginning of the reforms, however.

The signs of overemployment identified in section 2 show that dismissal programmes in sectors such as mining and chemicals will continue. Not surprisingly, low dismissal rates in sectors such as chemicals and minerals directly resulted in high overemployment, enabling us to predict significant employment cuts in these sectors in the future. By contrast, other sectors— such as food—reduced their labour force substantially in order to be able to continue operating in more favourable conditions. Enterprises in leather and shoes and wood and paper, having carried out significant restructuring in 1993–94, experienced less severe employment reductions in 1995–96. In other industries, employment reductions were more equally distributed between 1993 and 1996.

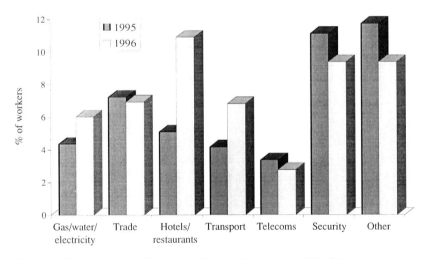

Figure 5.12 *Percentage of Employees Dismissed, by Service, 1995–96*
Source: ALFS2.

In services, dismissals (7 and 8 per cent on average in 1995 and 1996 respectively) seem to have been less dramatic and more equally spread between sectors,[1] although paradoxically the sectors with the largest

---

1. Although our first enterprise survey did not cover services, information collected by INSTAT tends to show that dismissals were also limited in services in 1993–94.

enterprises—such as transport, gas, water, electricity, and tele-communications—have been less inclined to implement mass lay-offs. Mass redundancies have only been postponed, however.

In the banking sector, managers reported the dismissal of 5 per cent of their labour force in 1995 and of a further 5 per cent in 1996. The smaller banks implemented larger labour force reductions than their big brothers. From our survey results it is clear that restructuring in the banking sector will continue and even increase in the near future. At the end of 1996, bank managers estimated that 7 per cent of the labour force would have to be cut over the next 12 months: the percentage was higher (10 per cent) in the large banks of more than 200 employees. According to high-ranking officials at the Ministry of Finance at the end of 1996, the three national banks at the secondary level, the Savings Bank (SB), the National Commercial Bank (NCB), and the Rural Commercial Bank (RCB), would have to undergo at least a 30 per cent staff reduction over the next few months in the course of privatisation: should privatisation fail, however, liquidation of these banks had not been excluded.

Analysis by property form shows that dismissals in industry were most extensive in state-owned but also joint-stock enterprises, confirming their commitment to restructuring, which will have to be continued in the future. Private firms and joint ventures were also found to cut employment when necessary. Interestingly, small enterprises of fewer than 50 employees were not found to have implemented many fewer lay-offs as a percentage of the total workforce than very large enterprises. Our survey also confirmed that among state-owned enterprises the restructuring process was much less advanced in services than in industry (*Figures 5.13* and *5.14*).

The regional distribution of restructuring was uneven. In industry, it was highest in the regions of Korca (13 per cent of the labour force dismissed in 1995, followed by a further 18 per cent in 1996), Vlora (11 per cent in 1995 and 17 per cent in 1996), and Gjirokastra (17 per cent and 11 per cent). The regional figures show restructuring being implemented at different times: enterprises in Elbasan and Berat, for instance, with large state enterprises, started in 1994, as a consequence of which employment reductions were lower in 1995–96; in Gjirokastra, Dibra, and Korca the process began in 1995; and in Kukes and Vlora it developed as late as 1996 (*Figure 5.15*). Employment reductions in services were highest in Berat, Dibra, Shkodra, Kukes, and Tirana (*Figure 5.16*).

Relatively lower dismissal rates in the banking sector (5 per cent on average in 1995 and again in 1996) hide important differences by region: there were more dismissals in Kukes (12 per cent in 1995 and 6 per cent in 1996), Elbasan (11 per cent and 4 per cent), and Dibra (5 per cent and 10 per cent).

Albania in Crisis

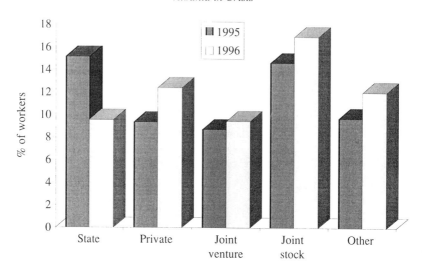

Figure 5.13 *Percentage of Workers Dismissed, by Property Form, 1995–96, Industrial Sector*

Source: ALFS2.

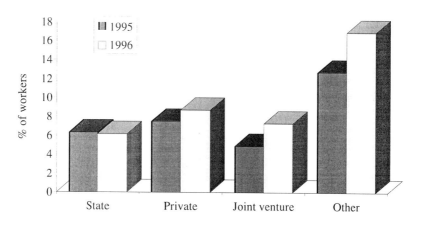

Figure 5.14 *Percentage of Employees Dismissed, by Property Form, 1995–96, Service Sector*

Source: ALFS2.

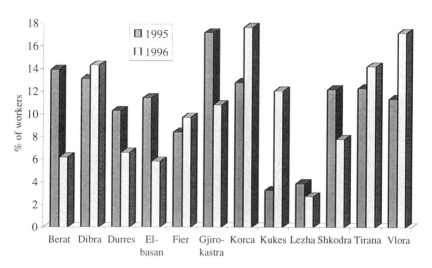

Figure 5.15 *Percentage of Workers Dismissed, by Region, 1995–96, Industrial Sector*

Source: ALFS2.

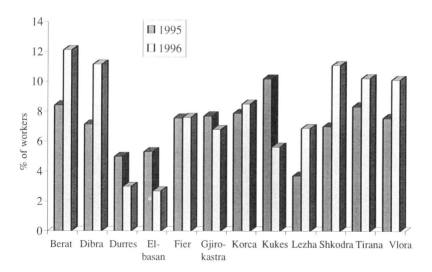

Figure 5.16 *Percentage of Employees Dismissed, by Region, 1995–96, Service Sector*

Source: ALFS2.

Albania in Crisis

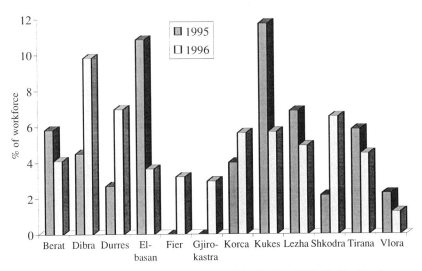

Figure 5.17 *Percentage of Employees Dismissed, by Region, 1995–96, Banking Sector*
Source: ALFS2.

4 REAL UNEMPLOYMENT: WELL ABOVE THE OFFICIAL FIGURE

Registered Unemployment and the Official Rate

The conventional view that unemployment started to decrease in Albania after a few years of reforms stems from a literal and uncritical reading of the registered unemployment figures. Briefly, after having reached its peak in the first half of 1993—at more than 30 per cent—the unemployment rate started to decrease in the second half of the year, establishing an annual average of 22 per cent. It fell to 18 per cent in 1994, 13 per cent in 1995, and 12 per cent in 1996. The basic statistics on official unemployment are presented in *Table 5.1*. Of the 1,282,000 persons economically active in Albania in 1996, some 1,116,000 were employed, while 172,000 were registered as job-seekers.

Table 5.1 *Official Unemployment Rates, 1991–96*

1991	9%
1992	27%
1993	22%
1994	18%
1995	12.9%
1996	12.3%

Source: INSTAT.

These figures led government officials and external experts alike to the conclusion that one of the major problems of the Albanian economy had been solved, in many cases finding expression in triumphalist statements: "Economic recovery was a major factor in absorbing registered unemployment, which declined from a peak of 37 per cent of the labour force in March 1993 to 13 per cent in 1995" (World Bank, 1996a, p. 1); and "Official unemployment is declining . . . this is generally attributed to the success of the government's economic reforms" (Economist Intelligence Unit, 1996, p. 41).

Clearly, many experts persuaded themselves that, despite restructuring and massive lay-offs and closures in large old state enterprises, the emerging private economy had managed to absorb both labour-force entrants and those leaving obsolete firms. This interpretation does not stand up to close scrutiny, however. The change in the percentage of registered unemployed was clearly due to changes in eligibility criteria. Furthermore, there are many reasons— listed below—that force us to conclude that registered unemployment was not (nor is it now) an appropriate measure of real unemployment and did not reflect the real tensions in the labour market.

Dismissal Rates

In the first place, our survey results have shown the horrendous decline in industrial production and the imposing dismissal rates in 1993–96. We also found that emerging services, rather than continuing to generate new jobs, were facing employment cuts. This assessment at the enterprise level clearly does not square with the official unemployment figures. This high rate of dismissals was mentioned in other documents, too: for instance, the IMF (1997b, p. 6) reported that "total public sector employment fell to about one-third of its pre-transition level . . . [I]n the 36 large enterprises taken over by the Enterprise Restructuring Agency, employment fell from 49,000 to about 10,500 by mid-1995".

Hidden Unemployment

Secondly, there is much evidence of overemployment at the enterprise level, with many enterprises putting part of their workers on administrative leave, either unpaid or on only partial pay. Such categories of worker—neither employed nor unemployed—are obviously not taken into account by the official figures, although they clearly reflect the inefficiency of the current labour market. There is also considerable hidden unemployment in agriculture, those receiving agricultural land being ineligible to register as unemployed, despite the fact that the small amount of land received by each family generally made it possible for only one member to be considered fully employed. This situation was particularly bad in the north and in the hillside or mountainous regions, where the parcels of land distributed to each family were especially small and families large. Part of the decline in official unemployment was due to the decrease in the size of the state agricultural sector after privatisation: the unemployed in this sector were re-classified as employed, even though their situation remained unchanged.[2]

We shall see that another factor in the high rate of hidden unemployment is the significant number of jobless people who failed to register.

Street Economy

A third important factor is the substantial informal economy and the underrecorded street economy. Although one might argue that many of those involved in the informal economy also have registered jobs, most of those participating in activities of this kind see them largely as a means of survival, and are still essentially unemployed. The pitiful sight of middle-aged men and women standing at the side of the road holding out bunches of bananas or offering to weigh you on their scales for a small charge is sufficient antidote to the claim that these people are employed in any meaningful sense of the term.

Informal Employment

Informal employment in both urban and rural areas is substantial. According to a December 1996 survey conducted in several regions by the Ministry of Labour, 65–70 per cent of all persons working (full- or part-time) in the private non-agricultural sector were not officially recorded as employees or as self-employed. On the one hand, this phenomenon could lead to an under-estimation of the number of employed, so overestimating the proportion of registered unemployed: for instance, the Ministry of Labour's decision in 1996 to grant legal status to a tranche of new private enterprises (whose 13,000 employees had hitherto been regarded as illegal) also helped to bring down the unemployment figures.[3] On the other hand, most activities in the informal sector are performed on an irregular and precarious basis, without any job security or income guarantee, so that when workers lose their job they cannot request unemployment benefits or any other form of compensation. Although no statistics exist on this phenomenon, the high bankruptcy rate of

2. See Mancellari, Papapanagos, and Sanfey (1996, p. 475).
3. As mentioned in Economist Intelligence Unit (1996, p. 41).

small businesses in the informal sector would seem to suggest that it represents a substantial source of poverty, workers suddenly falling from employment into inactivity and destitution without a social safety net to catch them. Official statistics on employment and unemployment do not reflect this particularly unhappy side of the Albanian labour market.

Emigration Moderating Tensions in the Labour Market

The fall in unemployment may partly be attributed to labour migration, 400,000 Albanians—15 per cent of the labour force—having gone to work abroad.[4]

While this labour migration may have moderated tensions in the labour market, it has also deprived Albania of many of its most flexible and skilled workers, who have succeeded in the more demanding labour markets of the advanced industrial countries. These workers might have helped to accelerate economic development if they had remained at home. In any case, such a release from the labour market should have not been interpreted as a consequence of economic recovery: on the contrary, this migration process was clearly the sign of a defective domestic labour market, and should have encouraged commentators to tone down their more optimistic assertions.

National Figures Conceal Sharp Geographical Distortions

It is important to analyse the unemployment rate by region, in order to obtain a more precise picture of the particular "balance of tensions" in different labour markets. In fact, very significant regional differences may be observed, unemployment rates at the local level in 1992 varying from 14 to 43 per cent. The highest unemployment rates were registered in the most rural areas of the north, such as Kukes (43 per cent), Dibra (31 per cent), and Shkodra (27 per cent), and in the central industrial districts of Elbasan (32 per cent) and Berat (26 per cent). The lowest rates were in Lezha and Fier. Unemployment was also relatively lower in the southern half of the country. In absolute terms, most of the unemployed were found in the cities and larger towns (Tirana, Berat, Durres, Elbasan, Fier, and Shkodra).

4. For some analysts, however, due to the short-term nature of most of the emigration, and the fact that much of it is clandestine, many of these emigrants have been included in the labour force figures, thus inflating the number of employees and further reducing the rate of the unemployed compared to the employed. See Mancellari, Papapanagos, and Sanfey (1996, p. 478).

Table 5.2 *Unemployment Rates, by Region, 1992–96 (%)*

	1992	1993	1994	1995	1996
Berat	26	24	18.6	19	20.8
Dibra	31	11	4.9	3.2	3.8
Durres	26	18	13.5	14.1	12.9
Elbasan	32	31	22.9	21.9	20.3
Fier	18	15	8.9	8.2	9.6
Gjirokastra	16	8	6.3	6.7	8.7
Korca	23	11	5.7	5.6	4.6
Kukes	43	22	15.6	14.2	21.1
Lezha	14	14	10.6	11	14.8
Shkodra	27	28	16	13.7	23.1
Tirana	25	21	19.7	14.6	18.2
Vlora	24	15	12.2	14.2	21.7

Source: INSTAT.

Tighter Eligibility Criteria

As already mentioned, the downward trend in the official unemployment rate can mainly be attributed to the introduction of new eligibility criteria for unemployment benefits.[5] Unemployed status is accorded to registrants who can demonstrate that they are not working, that they are capable of work, and that they are actively seeking and available for work. Under this new legislation, the unemployed were entitled to receive a flat-rate benefit for up to one year only, after which some became eligible for income support. Introduced in May 1993, the new law had an immediate effect on the figures for 1994: the unemployment rate, after having reached its peak at over 30 per cent in the first half of 1993, started to fall immediately on the application of the new eligibility criteria: as we have mentioned, the annual national average for 1993 was 22 per cent, falling further, to 18 per cent, in 1994. The number of unemployment benefit recipients fell even more sharply—according to INSTAT, from 35 per cent in 1993 to 19 per cent in 1994. The IMF gives even more striking figures, the percentage of unemployed receiving benefits falling from 18 per cent in 1993 to only 5 per cent in 1994, and to as low as 3.7 per

5. Unemployment benefits and conditions of eligibility are defined in Law No. 7703 of 15 May 1993, "On Social Security in the Republic of Albania", article 53. All persons meeting the following conditions are eligible: (i) they have made social security contributions for a period of at least 12 months; (ii) they are at present unemployed; (iii) they are willing and available for training or retraining; (iv) they do not receive any other benefit under this law, invalidity payments excepted.

cent in 1995.[6] In any case, both figures show a drastic fall in the number of recipients after the introduction of tight eligibility criteria in May 1993.

Table 5.3 *Unemployed Receiving Benefits (percentage of total unemployed), 1993–96*

	IMF	INSTAT
1993	18.1	35.4
1994	5.1	19.4
1995	3.7	26.9
1996	–	23.8

Sources: INSTAT, IMF (1997b, p. 57).

The fact that the unemployment rate had been officially reduced mainly because of the introduction of new criteria was admitted by the IMF in 1997: "the number of unemployment recipients has fallen due to the imposition of tighter eligibility criteria" (IMF, 1997b), in stark contrast to the explanation they had given in 1994: "The unemployment rate declined to 18 per cent by the end of 1993, reflecting a decrease in the number of unemployed state-farm workers following the distribution of land to them in July and a substantial increase in private non-agricultural employment" (IMF, 1994, p. 12): the tighter eligibility criteria were not even mentioned. According to the World Bank, moreover, "at one year entitlement duration and with average benefits being slightly higher than the minimum wage, the scheme could be considered quite generous" (World Bank, 1996b, p. 43).

Anyone who has worked in Albania or who has merely visited the country would readily agree that unemployment as defined by the new eligibility criteria poorly reflects Albanian reality. We will now look in more detail at the reasons for this, particularly the many obstacles that stand in the way of a higher rate of registration.

Long-Term Unemployed Excluded after One Year

Tight criteria were also applied to the duration of unemployment benefits—a maximum of one year—posing particular problems in a society with a high proportion of long-term unemployed (those without a job for one year or more) in total registered unemployment—more than 80 per cent in 1994 and

6. The difference between the two figures may be due to IMF recalculations, which include only the domestic labour force. There is no optimal methodology since it is very difficult, for instance, to estimate the number of those who are registered as either employed or unemployed in Albania but are living and working abroad.

73 per cent in 1995—men and women being affected equally. In 1996, for instance, probably as few as 24 per cent of registered job-seekers received unemployment benefits, since their one-year entitlement had expired, the remaining 76 per cent receiving nothing. For some, the situation was even more dramatic; for instance, according to the World Bank, "nearly every unemployed member has been out of a job continuously for more than one year" (World Bank, 1996b, p. 43).

This also means that official estimates fell short of the true level of unemployment: registration ceases to matter once the period of unemployment benefit has expired. As a result, most long-term unemployed were not even counted as officially unemployed.

We should emphasise that unemployment was found to be the main determinant of urban poverty.

Table 5.4 *Long-Term Unemployment (percentage of registered unemployed), 1993–96*

1993	64.5
1994	80.6
1995	72.7
1996	76.0

Source: INSTAT.

Other Labour Categories Not Counted

At the same time, new labour market entrants are ineligible for benefits; in any case, because the extent and quality of employment services and employment promotion programmes are still poor, school-leavers and others seeking to start their working lives are generally not interested in registration (they constitute only 0.2 per cent of the registered unemployed). It is also worth noting that smallholders are not eligible to register as unemployed, so that official unemployment rates do not take into account the growing unemployment in agriculture. This is why more than 80 per cent of the registered unemployed were found in urban areas, and why the unemployment figures fell so quickly in 1993–94—by around 160,000—as former state-farm workers, hitherto registered as unemployed, were allocated land and so removed from the statistics.

High Staff Turnover in the Emerging Private Sector

While the emerging private sector has been providing a significant number of new jobs, the life expectancy of the majority of new businesses is very low, at less than one year. The requirement that one has paid social security contributions for at least one year before one becomes eligible for unemployment benefit is almost impossible to fulfil for most of those who leave the private sector to register as unemployed.

Low Level of Unemployment Benefits—When Paid at All

The low level of unemployment benefits was a further discouragement to many to register as unemployed. For those entitled to claim it, average flat-rate unemployment benefit in 1995 was only 3,417 leks per month, well below any acknowledged measure of the subsistence minimum.[7] Moreover, since many of the unemployed come from low-paid jobs, they qualify for only the minimum amount, which is insufficient to cover minimum needs. Finally, not even all those who were entitled to the benefit in fact received it, because of the deficiencies of the unemployment insurance scheme (run by the Social Insurance Institute, and funded by a high payroll tax of 6 per cent).

Low Status of the Unemployed

For more than 50 years, unemployment was designated as "parasitic", if not criminal, and mainly restricted to former prisoners and the "unemployable". This discouraged many from registering. The unattractiveness of unemployment benefits and poor job prospects did little to change attitudes.

Financial and Time Costs of Registration

We should add that another barrier to registration was the financial and time costs involved. For some, the distance they would have had to travel was simply too great. Even if one did take the time and trouble, however, the low state of development of local employment offices meant that a great deal of time was spent queuing, only adding to the frustrations of being without work. The fact that jobless people had to register each and every month also discouraged many.

Delays in Payment

The fact that workers were not entitled to receive unemployment benefit immediately was another major deterrent to registration, since most workers confronted by unemployment for the first time—or for the first time in a radically transformed labour market—tended to believe they would find a job within a few months.

---

7. It has since fallen even further: according to information provided by INSTAT in 1997 it was only 2,500 leks.

Poor Quality of Employment Services

The low level of employment services is a result of high staff turnover, a lack of financial resources, and overly centralised control of labour offices, suppressing personal initiative. Labour offices are largely seen as institutions which dole out unemployment benefits to laid-off workers: their job mediation and other services are severely neglected. Active employment promotion programmes (labour market training, on-the-job training, business incubators, business clubs, and public works) were funded primarily by the World Bank, but tight central control and strict eligibility conditions for participation in these programmes have hindered their wider implementation.

Low Probability of Finding a Job

Job-seekers and employers alike have little confidence that they will obtain appropriate assistance from labour offices. In fact, most of the employers we interviewed reported that they had not recruited workers through local employment offices. The number of vacancies reported to local labour offices is very low, due to both depressed demand for (official) labour and the employers' lack of confidence. The number of unemployed persons who find work with the assistance of labour offices is extremely small—only 0.4 per cent.[8] Many persons ceased to register as unemployed because they did not expect to receive assistance in finding work from labour offices and so turned to the informal sector to work. In 1994–95, more than 125,000 failed to register as unemployed, probably because they had simply given up hope (UNDP, 1996, p. 2).

As a result, a significant proportion of those excluded from the labour market are simply not accounted for in the official statistics, a situation similar in some respects to what was observed in Russia, where the official unemployment rate of 1 per cent notwithstanding, more and more people have found themselves without a job.[9]

All the currently available statistics on employment and unemployment in Albania are inaccurate. As the EBRD says, "Unemployment figures in

8. Of those placed, 61 per cent are women, and 51 per cent are from the ranks of the long-term unemployed. Persons aged between 21 and 34 account for 54 per cent of those placed, while 13 per cent are young people below the age of 21. Persons above the age of 34 are already less attractive for employers, and their 33 per cent share in total placements is below their proportion in total unemployment.

9. See Standing (1996), especially Chapter 2, "The Mystery of Unemployment: Triumph or Wishful Thinking?", pp. 14–29.

Albania are very unreliable; the true unemployment rate is probably much higher (30-40 per cent) than the official one" (OECD–CCET, 1995, p. 21).

Employment data come mainly from the reports of state and large private enterprises, while in the small private urban and agricultural sectors only very rough estimates are available. Unemployment data refer to the registered unemployed: anecdotal information is all that is available on the extent of non-registered unemployment. Only a comprehensive labour force survey could provide the requisite labour market information and so provide an important tool for decision-makers: we develop this proposal in Chapter 16.

5 CONCLUSION

To summarise, we saw that the production crisis in industry has clearly resulted in dramatic employment cuts. More than 50 per cent of the industrial labour force was dismissed in 1993–94, a downward trend that continued in 1995–96. Surprisingly, significant employment reductions have also accompanied the growth of services.

Estimates of overemployment indicate that restructuring was far from complete at the end of 1996, especially in large state-owned enterprises in industry and services, and with privatisation and further restructuring in the banking sector on the horizon. The official figures on registered unemployment—17 per cent in 1995 and 12 per cent in 1996—were difficult to square with the results of our survey. The official statistics on unemployment have clearly been deflated after the adoption of much stricter conditions for eligibility. Moreover, they do not account for a great number of people excluded from the labour market, in both the formal and the informal sectors. They do not apply to rural areas, where all people of employable age are assumed to be engaged in agriculture in some way, although undoubtedly often on a less than full-time basis, if at all.

The poor incentives to register as unemployed, the low probability of benefit entitlement on registration, and the paltry and short-term benefits, which are often not even paid, have served to obstruct the provision of all but the most rudimentary assistance to those outside the labour market. This situation has also helped to render official unemployment figures totally misleading and therefore to give a false estimate of unemployment in Albania. Early in 1997, Minister of Labour Mr Elmaz Sheriffi, conscious of this problem, courageously estimated the true unemployment rate at over 50 per cent. The attempt to minimise the unemployment crisis—the Government's official line before 1997—made it difficult to determine the full gravity of the situation, so obscuring the considerable potential for a social explosion.

The unemployment shock described in this chapter, although not reflected in the official statistics, undoubtedly continued between 1993 and 1996, being fed not only by the economic crisis and the related large employment cuts, but by government policy, which consisted in limiting unemployment benefits to only a narrow band of those without work, leaving the informal market as the only possibility for many, and further degrading the official labour market. There can be no doubt that the unemployment shock was a significant cause of growing discontent in Albania, one which the widespread presentation of an improved economic situation and a fall in unemployment can only have exacerbated, culminating early in 1997 in a generalised rebellion.

6. Impoverishment Wages and Incomes

1 INTRODUCTION

The depth of the crisis in industry and the dramatic trend in unemployment inevitably had a direct effect on enterprise wage policies. While before the transition, in 1991, wage levels in Albania were the lowest in Europe, the economic crisis experienced in 1991–92, with the collapse of production and trade, further aggravated this initial situation. The stabilisation policy implemented in the first years of transition, which clearly identified wages as one of the main macroeconomic variables to be kept under control, does not seem to have done much to improve wage levels and living standards. The new coalition Government, led by the Democratic Party, which won the election in April 1992, sought to implement a radical market reform programme with the support of the IMF and other international institutions in the hope of stimulating economic growth. In this macroeconomic programme, a restrictive incomes policy figured prominently, with the aim of limiting inflationary pressures, while prices were partly liberalised. A range of instruments was used to control wage growth: direct limits on average wages, wage tariffs, control of the minimum wage, and fixed compensation for inflation instead of an indexation system.

Wage regulations consisted in fixing limits for the average wage for each ministry (Ministry of Industry, Ministry of Health, Ministry of Education, and so on), each ministry then having to apply it at the enterprise or institution level. The Ministry of Industry, for instance, had the task of fixing the average wage by industry, which was then applied at the enterprise level, according to the number of employees. Employers had to pay a punitive tax for every wage increase above the stipulated norms. In theory, managers had the freedom to redistribute the resulting wage fund (average wage multiplied by number of employees) among the different categories of employee, but in reality this freedom was limited by a very rigid tariff scale which fixed wage rates for each category of worker. Irregular adjustments of the minimum wage also constituted a way of controlling wage growth in the whole economy, since most wages, particularly in the public sector, as well as all social benefits, were directly linked to the minimum wage. Finally, instead of indexing the minimum wage and the average wage, the Government decided to provide fixed compensation for price increases, which were, however, only irregularly distributed and rapidly lost touch with real price increases.

The result of this policy has been a fall in real wages which plunged most Albanian workers well below the subsistence minimum. According to data collected by the Institute of Statistics (INSTAT), real wages fell by nearly 50 per cent between 1991 and 1994. Although an agreement was signed in November 1996 on wage indexation to take account of price increases, this agreement was never implemented. As a result, real wages continued to fall in 1995–96, leading to further poverty. The economic crisis also contributed greatly to limiting wage increases, but it was not the only factor: it is significant that more profitable enterprises have been prevented from paying higher wages by the strict wage controls in place since 1992.

We argue in the present chapter that this restrictive policy not only led to a further fall in living standards but also proved to be inadequate to deal with the deep crisis confronting the Albanian economy, characterised by a series of industrial stoppages and bankruptcies, in a context of low productivity, social conflict, and growing unemployment. To this end, we examine the pattern of wages, incomes, and social benefits in Albania since the beginning of the reforms through the analysis of our enterprise survey data. The richness of the data allows us to present in detail wage levels, structure, and differentials by branch, property form, size of enterprise, and region. This work has been carried out within the framework of a technical co-operation project that the ILO has been implementing in Albania for more than five years (1993–98) with the aim of helping the government to reform its wage and incomes policy. We also present figures on living standards and poverty which help to identify more accurately the social trends of the first five years of transition and make possible a better understanding of how these problems contributed to the 1997 crisis.

2 UNPAID LEAVE AND NON-PAYMENT OF WAGES

Unpaid Administrative Leave

In some industries, enterprises have responded to the crisis by putting part of their workforce on administrative leave, usually without pay: according to our survey, at the end of 1996 5 per cent of the industrial labour force (much higher in textiles and clothing) was on unpaid leave—the same as in 1994. Services and banks (less than 1 per cent of employees) were not similarly affected.

Difficulties in Paying Wages

In our survey, nearly 15 per cent of managers in industry and 12 per cent in services—but less than 2 per cent in banks—reported serious difficulties in paying wages over the last 12 months. In industry, the problem was particularly severe in mining (45 per cent of enterprises), leather and shoes (19 per cent), and minerals (17 per cent). In services, wage payment delays were found mainly in gas, water, and electricity (35 per cent).

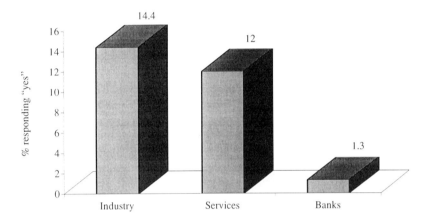

Figure 6.1 *Difficulty in Paying Wages, by Sector, Sept. 1996*
Source: ALFS2.

Workers in state-owned enterprises were hit hardest, with payment difficulties being reported in more than one-third of public establishments in industry and in more than one-fifth in services; 15 per cent of joint ventures were also affected, along with a smaller number of private enterprises (*Figure 6.4*). Large companies of more than 200 employees also had difficulties (more than 21 per cent of them). The non-payment of wages clearly affects a significant proportion of the industrial labour force. Some regions suffered more than others, probably reflecting local industrial restructuring and economic problems: in Kukes and in Dibra both industry and services were hit. The average period of non-payment was 6 weeks in services and 3 weeks in industry, although in wood and paper it reached 7 weeks, and in leather and shoes, 4 weeks. One industrial enterprise in Elbasan, for example, did not pay its workers for more than 12 weeks.

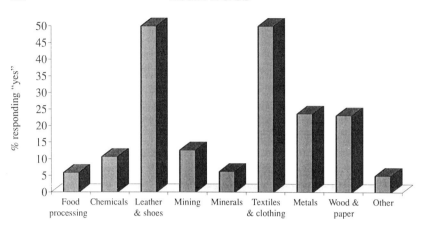

Figure 6.2 *Difficulty in Paying Wages, by Industry, Sept. 1996*

Source: ALFS2.

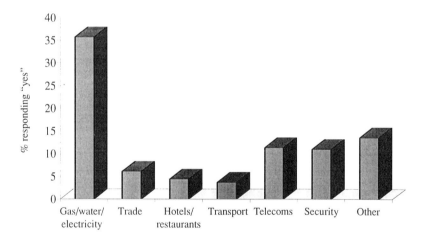

Figure 6.3 *Difficulty in Paying Wages, by Service, Sept. 1996*

Source: ALFS2.

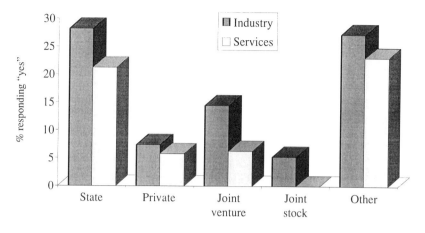

Figure 6.4 *Difficulty in Paying Wages, by Property Form, Sept. 1996, Industrial and Service Sectors*

Source: ALFS2.

3 VERY LOW WAGE LEVELS

Average Wages in Industry and Services below Subsistence Needs

In October 1996 the mean monthly average wage in industry was 7,880 leks per month (less than 50 USD); wage levels in services were slightly higher, at 8,600 leks.

Although there is no official calculation of the subsistence minimum or poverty line in Albania—despite the fact that it is prescribed in the new labour code—both the trade unions and independent researchers have put the individual subsistence minimum at more than 10,000 leks,[1] significantly above the average wage in both services and industry. This comparison leads to a first important result, namely that the average wage in Albania at the end of 1996 was still well below the poverty line. In other words, most Albanian workers were paid well below any subsistence minimum. The same situation had been observed during our first enterprise survey in 1994, with the average wage standing below 80 per cent of the subsistence minimum, showing that no significant progress had been made between 1994 and 1996 (see Vaughan-Whitehead, 1995).

---

1. See the estimate presented by Llubani (1997) and Ceni (1997).

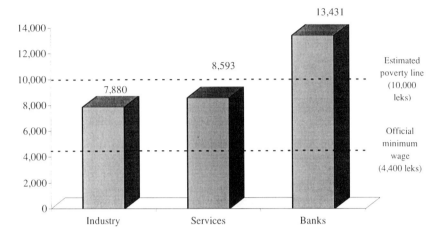

Figure 6.5 *Average Wages, by Sector, Sept. 1996 (leks)*
Source: ALFS2.

In addition to social unrest, this state of affairs also resulted in serious problems at the enterprise level. The majority of managers cited low wages as one of the main causes of poor labour efficiency. More than 35 per cent of enterprises in industry (and 40 per cent in services) also mentioned low wages as the main reason for the loss of newly recruited workers (most with aspirations to join the highly paid banking sector): more than 50 per cent of enterprises had decided to raise wages in order to halt this phenomenon, which was now widespread among skilled workers. We should emphasise that these low wages resulted from a combination of the economic crisis and a very restrictive incomes policy. In many sectors, they were a direct reflection of economic and financial difficulties. In more profitable sectors and enterprises, which were still limited by wage controls, they were the direct result of the Government's centralised incomes policy.

Higher Wages in the Banking Sector

The average wage in the banking sector was much higher: at nearly 14,000 leks it was almost twice the average wage in industry. To some extent, high wages managed to isolate the banking sector from the major social conflicts. The disaggregated figures, however, reveal significant differentials between individual banks. State banks were found to pay less (13,200 leks on average) than the two joint ventures (19,000 leks). As shown in *Figure 6.6*, large banks also paid higher wages (18,000 leks) than small banks (13,000 leks). In some regions, banks were paying much less than the national average, particularly in Kukes (an average of 11,400 leks), Lezha (11,600 leks), and Vlora (12,300 leks); while in Tirana and Durres the banks were paying much more (17,000 and 15,000 leks respectively). A direct relationship between average wages and employment changes was also identified. Average wages were found to be lower (11,000 leks) in banks where employment had been severely cut, while the highest wages (nearly 15,000 leks) were paid in banks that had increased employment. This relationship between employment and wage levels in some banks reflects the generalised problem of debt and profitability described earlier. As we shall see, categories of employees were also highly differentiated.

Banks were also found to have low labour efficiency: the main cause was reported by 35 per cent of bank managers to be poor working conditions; low wages were mentioned by 30 per cent. The problem of efficiency was reported on a large scale in the regions of Berat (by 67 per cent of banks) and Korca (40 per cent). The majority of bank managers reported that their principal weapon against low labour efficiency was an increase in basic wages (51 per cent) and improvements in work organisation (40 per cent).

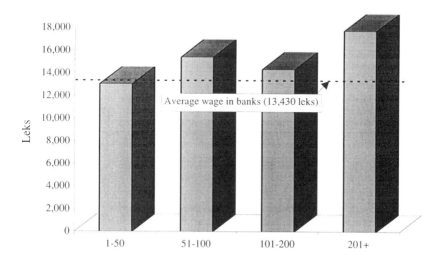

Figure 6.6 *Average Wages, by Number of Employees, Sept. 1996, Banking Sector (leks)*
Source: ALFS2.

4 WAGE DIFFERENTIALS PARTIALLY DISTORTED

Sectoral Differences Reflecting Monopolistic Positions

Some wage differentials were observed between industries. The most poorly paid industrial workers at the end of 1996 were those in textiles and clothing (6,800 leks), chemicals, and leather and shoes (6,900 leks). The highest wages in industry at the end of 1996 were being paid in minerals (10,100 leks). This probably reflects both productivity and demand factors: the low wages in chemicals, for instance, are mainly due to the difficulties encountered by enterprises because of low demand for their products, while the high wages in minerals are the product of, among other things, the abundance in Albania of natural resources such as chrome and copper; the presence of large monopolistic enterprises, for instance, large chrome companies; difficult working conditions which induce employers to complement the basic wage with a series of additional premiums for working conditions; and finally, the apparent strength of the trade union bargaining position in this industry. It is interesting that wages were lowest in the most export-oriented sectors, where foreign investors predominated—that is, textiles and clothing, and leather and shoes—confirming low wage costs as the main comparative advantage of these sectors.

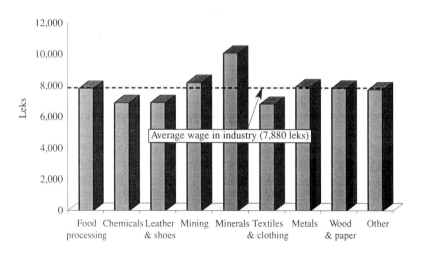

Figure 6.7 *Average Wages, by Industry, Sept. 1996*

Source: ALFS2.

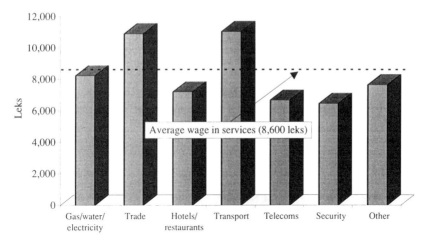

Figure 6.8 *Average Wages, by Service, Sept. 1996*
Source: ALFS2.

It should also be noted that a large gap—more than 3,000 leks—separated average wages in the most generous industry, minerals, and those in the least generous, chemicals (*Figure 6.7*). This difference had been much narrower— 1,000 leks—in 1994. The highest wages in services were being paid in transport and trade, and the lowest in security services (*Figure 6.8*).

Increasing Gap between Property Forms

One might hypothesise that privatisation would lead to higher wages: first, because the Government's attempts to restrict wage increases in order to limit expenditure could have led state enterprises to hold down wages more than other enterprises; and second, because new private enterprises could be expected to be more responsive to market pressures, and to take advantage of their greater autonomy in setting wages. In fact, *Figure 6.9* shows a huge difference—amounting to nearly 3,000 leks—between the average wage in state enterprises (7,300 leks for industry) and the average wage in joint-stock companies (10,200 leks) and joint ventures (9,800 leks). Joint ventures in majority foreign ownership paid 10,400 leks in contrast to the 8,000 leks paid by those in minority foreign ownership. Private enterprises were also among the lowest payers, although they tended to supplement low basic wages with other payments, as we shall see. A similar phenomenon was observed in services, where the highest wages were paid in joint ventures and the lowest again in state-owned enterprises. This increasing gap between public enterprise wages and those of other property forms was found to be a major source of worker discontent and social conflict, resulting in industrial action in a number of public enterprises. In industry, more than 15 per cent of state-owned enterprises reported between 1 and 3 strikes over the last 2 years, mainly because of low wages, in contrast to 4 per cent of private enterprises. A similar difference was observed in services.

On the one hand, these figures show that wage levels in industry—and to a lesser extent in services—were starting to respond to market forces, wage levels being lower in state-owned enterprises than in new enterprises with a different property form. On the other hand, these differences were also the direct consequence of strict wage controls in state enterprises compared to free wage bargaining in private firms. This policy led to economic distortions between the two sectors and to growing social discontent in the state sector.

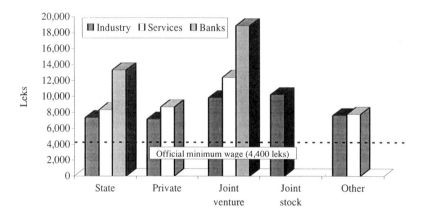

Figure 6.9 *Average Wages, by Property Form, Sept. 1996, Industrial and Service Sectors*
Source: ALFS2.

Regional Differences

This combination of wage differentials by industry and form of ownership also led to important wage differentials by region, often reflecting the industrial configuration of the region concerned. Traditional industrial regions, for instance Korca, Kukes, and Shkodra, dominated by large state-owned enterprises, were paying the lowest industrial wages in 1996 (6,500 leks), something already observed in 1994. Some regions changed over the course of time, however: for instance, the emergence of new dynamic private industrial enterprises in the district of Lezha, where the lowest wages had been paid in 1994, so boosted wages that by 1996 it had become the highest paying region (12,500 leks). Enterprises in cities such as Durres and Tirana paid wages close to the national average. Regional differentials were very variable in services, higher wages being found not only in Lezha, but in Shkodra, Tirana, and Durres.

Banking was not found always to follow industrial and service development or to reflect the dynamism of enterprises at the local level: for example, Lezha was found to pay the highest wages in industry and services—due largely to the emergence of successful new private enterprises—but among the lowest in the banking sector. It is important to note that most banking is concentrated in Tirana and Durres, where the highest wages in this sector are paid.

5 WAGE DETERMINANTS AT THE ENTERPRISE LEVEL

In order better to understand wage determination at the enterprise level, we asked management to indicate the main factor influencing the last wage increase at their enterprise. The majority in both industry and services responded that no single consideration had been predominantly responsible for determining wage increases. Twenty-six per cent of managers in industry mentioned an increase in production as one factor (only 12 per cent in state-owned enterprises compared to 37 per cent in joint ventures), while 18 per cent—particularly in very large enterprises—reported the implementation of wage increases mainly in response to price rises. Surprisingly, wages appeared to be much more closely linked to profitability in services: one-third of enterprises (including 40 per cent of joint ventures) reported that their wage increases were mainly determined on the basis of increases in production and profits, factors such as price increases playing a very marginal role (the main determinant in only 2 per cent of enterprises).

We complemented these statistical averages by an econometric analysis, which allowed us to identify more precisely the main factors influencing wage developments. The following equation was estimated:

$$\text{Lg(wages)} = a + b1\sum(\text{IND}) + b2\sum(\text{PROP}) + b3\sum(\text{REG}) + b4\text{EMPSIZE} + b5\text{EMPCH} + b6\text{SALECH} + b7\text{PTY} + b8\text{PROF} + b9\text{PEXP} + b10\text{PBC} + b11\text{PFEM} + b12\text{PPTIME} + b13\text{PUNION} + b14\text{PROSH} + e$$

where

       IND = a set of dummies for the industry of the enterprise;
       PROP = a set of dummies for the property form of the enterprise;
       REG = a set of dummies for the regional location of the enterprise;
       EMPSIZE = size of enterprise in number of employees;
       EMPCH = percentage employment change in the enterprise over the past two years;
       SALECH = percentage change in sales in real terms over the past year;
       PTY = productivity measured as the value added generated by the enterprise divided by the number of employees;
       PROF = profitability of the enterprise (cashflow/capital);
       PEXP = percentage of exported production;
       PBC = percentage of workforce in the enterprise classified as manual workers;
       PFEM = percentage of workforce consisting of women;
       PPTIME = percentage of part-time workers in the enterprise;
       PUNION = percentage of workers in a trade union;
       PROSH = dummy, 1 if the enterprise was operating a profit-sharing scheme, 0 otherwise;
       e = error term.

The wage function was estimated by means of ordinary least squares regressions, with the logarithm of average wages as the dependent variable. The results for the three sectors confirm the previously described variations between property forms, with levels in joint ventures and joint-stock companies being significantly higher (with a positive and highly significant coefficient in the equation) than in state-owned companies (used in the equation as the omitted property form). Interestingly, no statistically significant differences were observed between industrial sectors (probably already captured by the property form variables). Wages were found to be strongly inversely related to the number of employees, however, large enterprises paying the lowest wages. The regional dimension was found to be the most important determinant in the wage equation for the banking sector, all regional variables appearing with a negative, often significant, coefficient in comparison with the region of Tirana (taken as the omitted variable), where banks are clearly paying the highest wages. Wages also appeared to be significantly lower in the region of Korca for industry, and in Kukes, Berat, and Fier for services.

Table 6.1 *Log. Average Wages, 1996, All Regions, All Sectors (OLS regression coefficients)*

Variable	Industry		Services		Banks	
(Constant)	3.829	91.946	3.918	91.666	4.157	49.819
Sector[1]						
Industry						
Chemicals	−0.025	−0.055	–	–	–	–
Mining	0.033	0.852	–	–	–	–
Leather & shoes	−0.024	−0.465	–	–	–	–
Minerals	0.0025	0.079	–	–	–	–
Textiles & clothing	−0.0099	−0.275	–	–	–	–
Metals	0.015	0.323	–	–	–	–
Wood & paper	−0.0015	−0.048	–	–	–	–
Services						
Gas, water, and electricity	–	–	0.029	0.898	–	–
Hotels & restaurants	–	–	−0.035	−1.421	–	–
Transport	–	–	0.073	2.272**	–	–
Telecommunications	–	–	−0.029	−0.740	–	–
Security	–	–	−0.037	−1.264	–	–
Other services	–	–	0.012	0.436	–	–
Property Form[2]						
Private	0.031	1.106	−0.027	−0.967	–	–
Joint venture	0.101	3.255**	0.156	3.038***	0.254	1.058
Joint-stock	0.077	1.964*	–	–	–	–
Other	0.052	0.985	0.0082	0.156	–	–
Region[3]						
Berat	−0.022	−0.511	−0.068	−2.024**	0.159	−2.379**
Dibra	−0.033	−0.674	0.013	0.336	−0.081	−1.141
Durres	0.024	0.829	−0.007	−0.256	−0.071	−1.051
Elbasan	0.013	0.324	−0.046	−1.364	−0.091	−1.362
Fier	−0.029	−1.013	−0.093	−3.459***	−0.071	−1.033
Gjirokastra	−0.063	−1.023	−0.023	−0.579	−0.112	−1.367
Korca	−0.069	−2.303**	−0.043	−1.323	−0.131	−1.958*
Kukes	−0.087	−1.374	−0.136	−3.191**	−0.132	−1.731*
Lezha	−0.063	−1.393	−0.023	−0.637	−0.153	−2.392**
Shkodra	−0.032	−0.806	0.024	0.691	−0.084	−1.198
Vlora	−0.020	−0.524	−0.0051	−0.128	−0.146	−1.954*
Employment Size	−0.0003	−3.079***	−0.0005	−2.997**	0.0002	0.112
% Manual Workers/95	0.0005	6.062***	−0.0002	−0.620	–	–
% Women/95	−0.0011	−2.357**	−0.0003	−0.987	0.001	0.959
Part Timers	−0.0004	−0.690	−0.00004	−0.095	−0.0032	−2.403**
Profit-Sharing	0.011	0.376	0.054	2.644**	0.034	0.886
% Sales Change/95–96	0.0002	1.579	0.0006	0.858	–	–
% Emp. Change/94–96	−0.0001	−1.736*	0.0006	1.635	−0.0009	−1.259
% Unionisation	0.0001	0.714	−0.0002	−0.771	−0.0001	−0.279
% of Production Exported	0.00003	0.083	–	–	–	–
Productivity/95	−0.0002	−0.856	0.0001	1.078	–	–
Profitability/95	−0.000001	−3.443***	−0.000001	−3.075***	0.000001	0.096
R2		0.3032		0.1749		0.3464
F		3.7122		3.5845		1.3123

Notes: 1. Omitted: food.   ***   statistically significant at 1% level.
            2. Omitted: state.   **   statistically significant at 5% level.
            3. Omitted: Tirana.   *   statistically significant at 10% level.

Source: ALFS2.

If industrial establishments were beginning to respond to market pressures, one might have expected that wages would have risen less in enterprises that had cut employment by more than their competitors. In that respect, it did seem that the labour market was not really functioning to any appreciable extent, in that average monthly wages in industry were found to be negatively related to employment changes, showing that enterprises experiencing employment cuts were continuing to pay the highest wages. This result in industry was partly caused by the situation in the monopolistic mining, minerals, and metal sectors, where enterprises, although among the least profitable, often paid the highest wages. This also explains the strong negative relationship in the wage equation between wages and profitability. It is interesting to note, however, that this phenomenon was less prevalent in services, where wages seem to have responded better to market forces, being positively (in contrast to industry) influenced by the employment trend.

It is also worth noting the failure of productivity increases to bring about wage rises (in fact the productivity variable appears with a negative sign), a problem that we will analyse in detail in section 8. Good export and sales performances did not seem to result in higher wages either, although the variables for property form may already capture this phenomenon in part (joint ventures, for instance, export more and pay higher wages). The existence of a profit-sharing scheme was found to be positively correlated to wage levels in services, confirming that profit-sharing is being implemented in service enterprises that are already profitable and paying higher wages, for example, in trade (as we will see later). We will also explain in section 8 why the same variable was not significant for industry (it even appeared with a significant and negative coefficient in the same equation applied to 1994 data; see Vaughan-Whitehead, 1995, pp. 60–61).

Average wages also seemed to reflect the nature of the labour force, although there were differences between the three sectors: for example, wages were the lowest in workforces with a high proportion of women in industry, while in services, and even more so in banks, this was not the case. In industry, wages were higher in enterprises with a high proportion of manual workers. It is also important to note that trade unions did not appear to play an effective negotiating role in raising wage levels: although this may be the result of the centralised wage-fixing system at least in part, it is also due to the lack of a real tradition of wage negotiations at the enterprise level, and their total absence in the emerging private sector (see Chapter 7). In our view, trade union influence would have increased, and wages have reflected economic performance much more, if wage negotiations had taken place at the national level on a tripartite basis, complemented by local negotiations at the branch, regional, and enterprise levels between trade unions and employers.

6 SYMBOLIC OFFICIAL MINIMUM WAGE

Low Percentage of Workers Paid the Official Minimum Wage

The survey also gathered data on the statutory minimum wage. Since the beginning of the transition in 1992, there have been no regular negotiations between government, trade union, and employer representatives on the minimum wage, and its level has been only irregularly adjusted by government decision or decree. As a result, the minimum wage fell dramatically in real terms: in the year of high inflation, 1993, alone, it has been estimated that it fell by more than 65 per cent in real terms (see Kodra 1998, p. 94). As a result, it also lost ground with regard to the average wage, falling from 93 per cent of the average wage in 1991 to 52 per cent in 1996. It should further be emphasised that this took place in a period which was also characterised by a fall in average wages of over 50 per cent.

Table 6.2 *Minimum Wage and Average Wage, 1991–96*

	Minimum Wage	Average Wage	Minimum Wage/ Average Wage
1991	675	727	93%
1992	840	1 784	47%
1993	1 200	3 084	39%
1994	2 400	4 778	50%
1995	3 700	6 300	58%
1996	4 400	8 400	52%

Source: Kodra (1998).

At the time of our second enterprise survey (September 1996), the minimum wage was 4,400 leks—still well below the subsistence minimum or poverty line. It had fallen in fact to less than 45 per cent of the subsistence minimum—estimated at 10,000 leks—at the end of 1996. The minimum wage was still only 4,400 leks at the end of 1997. It is obvious that this official minimum was only a symbolic sum, not only for workers who needed much more to attain the subsistence minimum for themselves and their families, but also for employers who had to pay well above it in order to avoid industrial conflict and to motivate the workforce. This phenomenon was confirmed by our survey, which revealed that, at the end of 1996, only 4 per cent of all workers in industry were being paid the official minimum wage. This percentage in industry was the same at the end of 1994, showing that the few adjustments of the minimum wage had not had much effect on enterprise wage policy.

Albania in Crisis

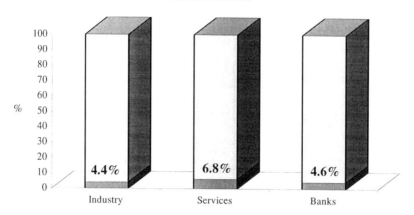

Figure 6.10 *Percentage of Workers Receiving the Official Minimum Wage, by Sector, Sept. 1996*

Source: ALFS2.

The percentage of workers paid at this level was slightly higher in particularly labour-intensive sectors, such as minerals (more than 6 per cent), but elsewhere no more than 5 per cent of the labour force received it. The proportion of workers paid the official minimum wage was found to be highest in state-owned enterprises (5.5 per cent) and joint ventures (5 per cent), and lowest in private enterprises (less than 4 per cent).

The percentage of employees paid the official minimum wage was also low in services and banks (6 per cent). As in industry, the percentage in services was higher in state-owned enterprises, especially in large enterprises in such monopolistic sectors as gas, water, and electricity (9 per cent), and telecommunications (7 per cent), but also in the small private companies providing security services (11 per cent) and in trade (7 per cent). In all other services, only a marginal percentage of employees were being paid at that level.

Clearly, the minimum wage did not offer any compensation to workers for the rapid growth of inflation, and it is no exaggeration to say that the minimum wage completely lost touch with reality. This situation, in which the minimum wage no longer performed either its social function of protecting the lowest-paid categories of worker, or its economic role as the basis of the wage structure, demanded urgent action and should have been given top priority by the Government in 1996–97.

Starting Wage Well above the Official Minimum Wage

In an effort to identify the lowest-paid workers more precisely, we asked managers to report on the minimum wage paid by their enterprise. The average minimum wage paid at the enterprise level in 1996 was 5,700 leks in industry (5,850 leks in services and 7,900 leks in banks): that is, 1,300 leks (1,450 leks and 3,500 leks) higher than the official minimum wage (*Figure 6.11*). This means that most employers, although they could have paid less, decided to pay higher minimum wages in order to avoid generalised worker demotivation and a further decline in output quality and all-round enterprise competitiveness. We can therefore postulate the existence of a kind of "efficiency wage" in Albanian enterprises, particularly in the banking sector, where managers reported that they had had to increase both starting and average wages in order to retain newly recruited employees and to avoid labour force demotivation. A starting minimum wage of 10,000 leks was offered in large banks (of more than 200 employees), most of which are based in Tirana where there is competition for banking specialists.

Some differences were observed between industries: the mineral industry paid the highest minimum wage, followed by wood and paper. The lowest minimum wage (5,000 leks) was reported in chemical enterprises. As far as property form is concerned, the starting wage was highest in joint ventures (6,200 leks) and private enterprises (6,000 leks), and lowest in state-owned enterprises (5,000 leks). A similar difference between joint ventures and state enterprises was observed in services. Sectors paying the highest minimum payment were trade and transport, with the lowest starting wages being paid in telecommunications.

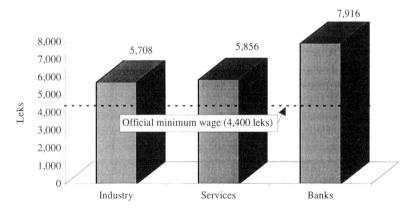

Figure 6.11 *Enterprise Minimum Payment, by Sector, Sept. 1996*

Source: ALFS2.

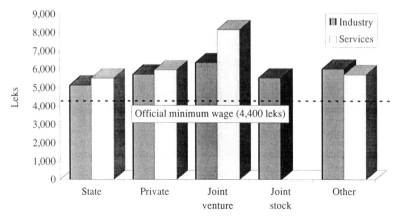

Figure 6.12 *Enterprise Minimum Payment, by Property Form, Sept. 1996, Industrial and Service Sectors*

Source: ALFS2.

7 AN EXTREMELY COMPRESSED AND DEMOTIVATING WAGE SCALE

Starting Minimum Wage Applied to Most Workers

The percentage of the labour force being paid the "enterprise" minimum wage was extremely high: 35 per cent in industry and nearly 50 per cent in services, showing that most employees were being paid at this starting level. In 1994, by contrast, only 20 per cent of employees in industry had been paid the starting wage. In 1996, the figure had risen to 50 per cent in food, and to 40 per cent in both metals and minerals; in security services it was close to 90 per cent and in trade to 60 per cent. By property form, the proportion of employees paid at this starting level was greater in private enterprises in both industry and services (45 per cent and 65 per cent respectively). These results mean that the starting minimum wage—clearly well above the official minimum wage—plays an important role in the wage scale at the enterprise level: nearly half of all employees, on average, are paid at this level. This is the first indication of the extreme compression characteristic of wage scales in Albania.

The situation was again somewhat different in the banking sector, where not only was the starting wage much higher, but only a small percentage (7 per cent nationally; 10 per cent in Tirana) of the labour force—general service employees—actually received it.

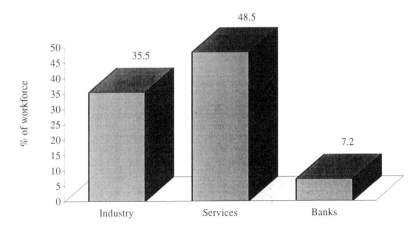

Figure 6.13 *Percentage of Workers Receiving Enterprise Minimum Payment, by Sector, Sept. 1996*

Source: ALFS2.

Starting Wage Very Close to the Average Wage

When we compared this starting wage with the average wage at enterprises we found that it represented nearly 80 per cent of the average wage paid by enterprises in both industry and services, and 60 per cent of that paid in banks. It was even higher—nearly 90 per cent—in industries such as leather and shoes, and in service sectors such as security (92 per cent). Surprisingly, in both services and industry, the wage scale was found to be most compressed in private enterprises, where the starting minimum wage was as much as 85 per cent of the average wage. The fact that this percentage was lower in state-owned enterprises may reflect a lower starting wage, however.

This suggests that the wage scale at the enterprise level is extremely limited and that no large wage differentials exist between different categories of worker. It indicates also that the basic payment system in the private sector—regardless of the supplementary payments which we shall turn to in a moment—was no better than that in the public sector and should have been reformed.

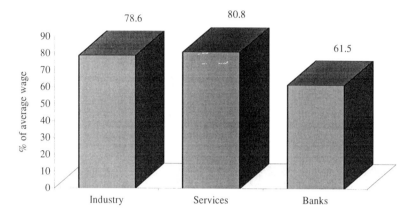

Figure 6.14 *Minimum Payment as Percentage of Average Wage, by Sector, Sept. 1996,*
Source: ALFS2.

Very Low Wage Differentials by Category of Employee

In an effort to obtain a clearer picture of wage differentials, we collected data
by type of employee in seven occupational categories in industry and
services: (i) managers, (ii) specialists, (iii) general service employees, (iv)
supervisors, (v) technicians, (vi) skilled workers, and (vii) unskilled workers;
and in three in the banking sector: (i) managers, (ii) specialists, and (iii)
general service employees.

The results—with the possible exception of the banks—confirmed the
existence of insufficient wage differentiation between categories of employee

Table 6.3 *Wage Ratio of Occupational Groups Compared to Unskilled Workers, by
Sector, Sept. 1996*

	Manager	Special-ist	General service	Super-visor	Techni-cian	Skilled worker	Other
Industry	2.49	1.77	1.39	1.78	1.56	1.25	–
Services	1.96	1.97	1.29	1.73	1.52	1.31	–
Banks	2.61	1.61	–	–	–	–	1.31

Note: For the bank sector wage ratio is calculated in comparison with general service employees,
i.e. the lowest paid.
Source: ALFS2.

within the same enterprise. In October 1996 managers in both industry and services were paid on average only slightly more than twice the wage of unskilled workers (*Table 6.3*); at the same time, the wages of skilled workers were on average a mere 25 per cent higher than those of unskilled workers. The fact that exactly the same percentages were found in 1994 shows that there had been no change at the enterprise level concerning wage grading and payment systems. The only variation on 1994 concerned wage differentials between different property forms in industry: a manager in an industrial joint-stock company or joint venture was paid at the end of 1996 more than three times what his unskilled employees received, compared to managers of state-owned enterprises in industry (which incidentally seemed to be trying to valorise the work of specialists and technicians) who received only twice that sum (*Table 6.4*). This appears to indicate that different payment systems were emerging in new joint-stock companies and joint ventures, which link wage levels much more closely to individual skills and training, and perhaps also to individual and collective performance (a matter to which we will return in the next section). Similar property form variations in wage differentials were not found in services—where wage differentials were found to be even lower in joint ventures and private enterprises than in the state sector. It is noteworthy that the low wage differentials prevailing between different categories of worker in private enterprises—in both services and industry—confirm our previous results on compressed basic wage scales in this property form (but also higher premia and profit-sharing; see section 8). Wage differentials were higher in the banking sector, where the wages of managers and specialists were, respectively, nearly three times and twice those of the lowest paid category, general service employees.

Table 6.4 *Wage Ratio of Occupational Groups Compared to Unskilled Workers, by Property Form, Sept. 1996, Industrial and Service Sectors*

	Manager		Specialist		General service		Supervisor		Technician		Skilled worker	
	Ind.	Serv.	Ind.	Serv.	Ind.	Serv.	Ind.	Serv.	Ind.	Serv.	Ind.	Serv.
State	2.38	2.13	1.84	1.98	1.39	1.30	1.89	1.73	1.68	1.52	1.24	1.25
Private	2.11	1.83	1.65	1.78	1.35	1.11	1.48	–	1.38	–	1.24	1.35
Joint venture	3.19	1.65	1.75	–	1.39	–	1.84	–	1.49	–	1.28	1.41
Joint stock	3.54	–	2.07	–	1.55	–	2.20	–	1.78	–	1.33	–
Other	2.47	1.90	1.82	–	1.33	–	1.93	–	1.69	–	1.29	1.36

Source: ALFS2.

One positive finding concerned wage differentials between men and women in the same job. Women's wages in industry were found to be almost 97 per cent of those of men in white-collar jobs and 96 per cent in blue-collar jobs; in services and banks, their wages were 95 per cent of men's. These percentages—very high compared to survey results elsewhere in Central and Eastern Europe—tend to show a relative absence of sex discrimination. Nevertheless, differences were identified by property form and industry, with higher wage differentials in small private enterprises in food and in textiles and clothing, although large state enterprises—for instance, in chemicals and metals—were paying women almost the same as men, reflecting the wage equalisation policy systematically followed under the previous regime. We also saw from our wage equation that wages tended to be lower in industries with a higher proportion of female workers (such as private textiles firms). These results by property form may indicate that wage differentials will grow in the future, as the private sector develops. Male/female wage differentials were also more marked in particular occupations, especially at management level. In the banking sector, for instance, a wage differential of 10 per cent was found between men and women in managerial positions. In addition, nearly 49 per cent of top managers reported a preference for men when appointing new bank managers—49 per cent indicated no preference and only 2 per cent reported a preference for appointing women.

8 WAGES DISCONNECTED FROM PRODUCTIVITY

One of the main characteristics of wages in a market economy is their responsiveness to market signals and to microeconomic performance. A traditional complaint against the wage-fixing system under the previous regime was that it was too rigid and so unable to adjust to changing demand or to provide incentives to increase labour productivity. We thus tried to test whether some wage flexibility had been introduced in the Albanian wage determination system, and whether wages were progressively reacting to market signals and were more closely related to productivity and other economic performance indicators.

Wage Levels Not Following Economic Results

We first compared wage trends with sales growth and observed significant differences between industries (*Figure 6.15*) that confirmed the total disconnection between wages and economic performance (represented by sales growth), identified earlier in our wage equation.

In the more profitable industries, such as textiles and clothing and leather and shoes, sales growth had not been converted into higher wages. Far from it: it was in these industries that the lowest wages were being paid. In contrast, in mining, wages were higher than the national average, despite the continuing sharp fall in sales in 1995–96. An even more extreme case was minerals, where wages 40 per cent higher than the average had nothing to do with performance and everything to do with the sector's monopolistic position. Only in chemicals have bad results and lay-offs combined to push wage levels 20 per cent below the national average. It is important to note that wages in 1996 seemed to be even more disconnected from performance than in 1994, when the more profitable sectors mentioned above reported wages higher than the national average. This trend is likely to continue if payment systems are not comprehensively reformed. These figures also confirm the disconnection (observed from our wage equation) between wages and employment changes: wages were found to be above the national average in industries that had the greatest number of dismissals, such as mining and metals (*Figure 6.15*).

This disconnection between wages and performance could also be observed by property form. While wages naturally remained depressed in the unprofitable state sector, good performance in private firms was not translated into higher wages: on the contrary, higher wages were found in poorly performing joint-stock companies. Only in joint ventures did sales growth seem to have been translated into higher wages.

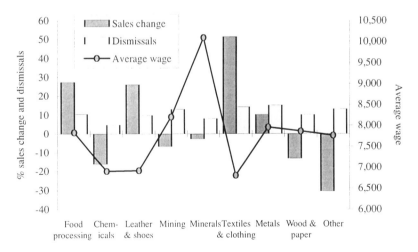

Figure 6.15 *Wages, Sales, and Employment Trends, by Industry, 1995–96*

Note: Zero level for average wage corresponds to average wage for industry (7,880 leks).
Source: ALFS2.

In services, wages seemed to be responding better to market forces, with higher wages in, for instance, private enterprises in trade, although good performances in some other sectors, such as telecommunications, did not seem to be translated into higher wages.

The Law on Profit-Sharing in Public Enterprises

From the above we can conclude that although some enterprises (for instance, joint ventures) have started to respond to market signals and microeconomic performance, the wage-fixing system remained too rigid and so unable to adjust to changing demand or to provide incentives to increase labour productivity. Some efforts had been made by the Government in this regard, however. Above all, in 1992 the Government decided to link wage increases to productivity by encouraging enterprises to implement profit-sharing schemes. In order to promote a measure of decentralisation in public sector wage determination, the Law on Complementary Remuneration in Addition to the Basic Wage was adopted in August 1992 for state-owned enterprises. These enterprises were henceforth permitted to make additional payments— linked to enterprise profits—up to a maximum of 15 per cent and with an annual limit per employee fixed at two monthly wages. (Apart from distributing 15 per cent to employees through profit-sharing, state enterprises could use their annual profits—after deductions—to create capital reserves up to a 5 per cent limit, to invest in research and work organisation without limitation, and to finance social assistance, again without limitation.) Such bonuses may not be distributed in enterprises where no profits are generated, although enterprises that have put aside special capital reserves from profits generated in the previous year may exceptionally pay their workers additional sums; such reserves are limited to a maximum of 5 per cent of annual profits after deduction of the previous year's losses.

The Decreasing Extent of Profit-Sharing

Our first enterprise survey in 1994 revealed that this law had been very effective in developing profit-sharing schemes: 53 per cent of state enterprises (98 per cent of them in accordance with the law) had introduced such a scheme, along with 23 per cent of private enterprises (surprisingly, 95 per cent of them also based on the law governing state-owned enterprises). Enterprises were also found to distribute substantial amounts in this way. This was particularly the case in public enterprises where basic wage increases were limited by central controls and where new legislation on profit-sharing brought them some flexibility to increase total earnings. In fact, it is significant that in those enterprises, an average of nearly 15 per cent of the basic wage was distributed in the form of profit-sharing, not far from the maximum limit of two monthly basic wages on annual profit-sharing amounts as stipulated by the legislation.

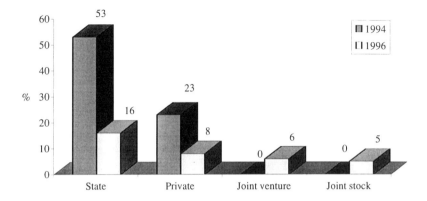

Figure 6.16 *Percentage of Enterprises Operating a Profit-Sharing Scheme, by Property Form, Sept. 1994 and 1996, Industrial Sector*

Note: There were no joint ventures or joint stock companies in 1994.
Sources: ALFS1, ALFS2.

In 1996, however, only 9 per cent of industrial enterprises reported that they were applying a profit-sharing scheme, and only another 8 per cent said that they were planning to introduce such a scheme in the next 12 months. Only 16 per cent of state-owned enterprises (as against 53 per cent in 1994) were still operating such a scheme, only 8 per cent of private enterprises, and only 6 per cent of joint ventures.

In services, 8 per cent of enterprises promoted a profit-sharing scheme, mostly in trade and hotels. In the banking sector, 20 per cent of banks—all of them state-owned—had introduced a profit-sharing scheme (the two joint ventures in our sample had not introduced such a scheme). Of the remaining banks, 9 per cent were planning to introduce a profit-sharing scheme. As in industry and services, most (90 per cent) profit-sharing agreements in this sector have been based on the Law on Profit-sharing in State-owned Companies, confirming its success among employers in all sectors of the economy: it clearly met a need for more decentralised wage fixing at the enterprise level. Many schemes were related to profits (45 per cent in industry), but also to quality of production (18 per cent in industry and nearly 30 per cent in banks), or to combined measures of performance (30 per cent in banks).

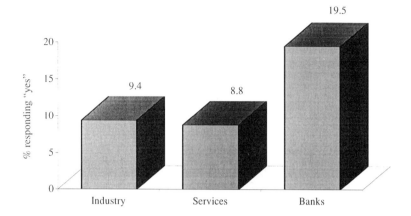

Figure 6.17 *Percentage of Enterprises Operating a Profit-Sharing Scheme, by Sector, Sept. 1996*

Source: ALFS2.

The survey results also show that, although profit-sharing bonuses remained substantial in 1996, enterprises that were still operating profit-sharing schemes were also distributing lower amounts than in 1994: on average 9 per cent of the basic wage (corresponding to 4,060 leks in industry and 4,640 leks in services), which was lower than in 1994—when enterprises distributed 15

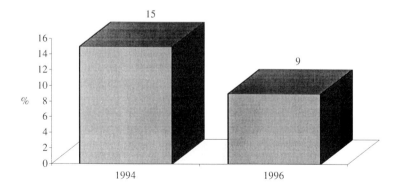

Figure 6.18 *Percentage of Wage Paid in the Form of Profit-Sharing, Sept. 1994 and 1996, Industrial Sector*

Sources: ALFS1, ALFS2.

per cent of the basic wage in the form of profit-sharing bonuses—and also less than 50 per cent of one monthly wage (that is, below the maximum allowed by the legislation). The percentage was higher for managers in both industry and services, however. Important differences were also observed by property form, private enterprises both in industry and services distributing higher profit-sharing bonuses than state enterprises.

Profit-sharing bonuses in 1996 were also extremely high in banking, an annual average of 31,000 leks being distributed to each employee, representing twice the average monthly wage in this sector, not far above the maximum amount of two monthly wages stipulated by the legislation. Profit-sharing in the banking sector was therefore used as an important supplementary payment system and source of income.

Profit-Sharing Used to Circumvent Central Wage Regulations

Figure 6.19 presents profit-sharing practices by sectors in industry in 1994, showing some surprising results. Although we might have expected more profitable industries to have a greater tendency to introduce and develop profit-sharing schemes, these schemes were found to be more widespread, and profit-sharing bonuses much higher, in less profitable industries, such as food (unprofitable in 1994), wood and paper, and mining. By contrast, these schemes were less prevalent (*Figure 6.19*) and profit-sharing bonuses lower (*Figure 6.20*) in the more profitable textiles, and leather and shoes. A similar process, although to a lesser extent, was observed in 1996.

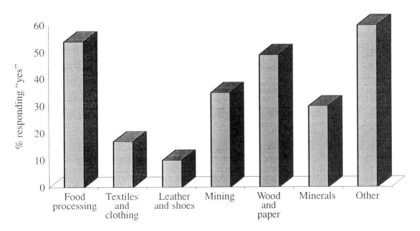

Figure 6.19 *Percentage of Enterprises Operating a Profit-Sharing Scheme, by Industry, Sept. 1994*
Source: ALFS1.

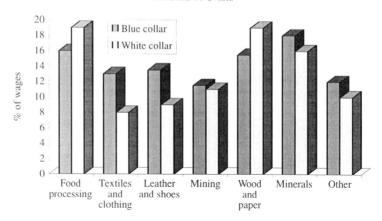

Figure 6.20 *Percentage of Wage Paid in the Form of Profit-Sharing for White- and Blue-Collar Workers, by Industry, Sept. 1994*

Source: ALFS1.

This result might be due to the combination of wage regulations with profit-sharing: as soon as they were introduced by the law, profit-sharing provisions seem to have been used by public enterprises to complement the basic wage that was limited by central wage regulations and rigid wage tariffs. These enterprises therefore redistributed their low profits, if any, in the form of profit-sharing bonuses instead of investing them in new technologies or changes in work organisation which could have improved the quality of production and progressively increased their productivity and profitability. These results show the limits of profit-sharing schemes in the centralised incomes policy that was imposed as part of the macroeconomic stabilisation programme. In such a context, profit-sharing bonuses have been used as a source of additional income, a sort of "efficiency wage" aimed at motivating the labour force.

Positive Performance Results

We should emphasise at this point that substantial evidence was found to indicate that profit-sharing schemes had helped Albanian enterprises to improve their economic performance. A number of statistical and econometric findings from the surveys pointed to a positive association between profit-sharing and productivity or other measures of economic performance.[2] Moreover, more than 42 per cent of enterprises with profit-sharing stated that these schemes had had a beneficial effect on productivity,

2. For a detailed presentation of these results, see Vaughan-Whitehead (1998b).

this percentage of satisfied answers being much higher in textiles and clothing (86 per cent stating it contributed to increasing productivity) and in paper and wood (50 per cent); 23 per cent of enterprises also found that these schemes improved the social climate in the enterprise. Interestingly, these schemes also contributed to the avoidance of lay-offs, according to 20 per cent of enterprises, particularly in those sectors confronted by the most difficult employment situation: 31 per cent of profit-sharing enterprises in the mining industry, for instance, stated that profit-sharing had helped management and workers find alternative solutions to lay-offs.

More than 75 per cent also reported that profit-sharing had led to increased worker participation in decision-making. In services, managers reported the beneficial effect of profit-sharing in facilitating the labour force's adaptation to new technologies.

These results seem to confirm the potential of profit-sharing schemes as a useful supplement to rigid low basic wages and as agents of greater flexibility in the wage determination system. They also point to the ability of profit-sharing to improve workers' motivation and productivity, while at the same time limiting lay-offs under crisis conditions.

The decrease in the coverage of profit-sharing schemes observed at the end of 1996 was therefore very much a negative development: while it may have been a sign of progressive decentralisation in wage policy—in the form of a progressive relaxation of wage controls—motivating state-owned enterprises to replace profit-sharing bonuses with normal wage increases, the abandonment of profit-sharing in the majority of enterprises was another worrying trend, given the positive benefits detailed above.

9 THE NEED FOR SUPPLEMENTARY SOURCES OF INCOME

Low basic wages and central wage regulations have motivated employers to diversify forms of payment.

Other Monetary Incentives

Apart from profit-sharing schemes, 21 per cent of industrial enterprises were found to be utilising other forms of monetary incentive, 25 per cent of banks, but only 11 per cent of enterprises in services. This form of payment was most widespread in industry—generally in the form of discretionary premiums for good individual performance—chiefly in the metal industry, followed by mining, and was least prevalent in leather and shoes. In services, enterprises in telecommunications (30 per cent of them) made most use of this type of payment system.

The two main monetary forms of incentive were (i) the distribution of a lump-sum payment for all or for a few categories of employee (generally on the basis of discretionary management decisions), found in 40 per cent of enterprises distributing such bonuses; and (ii) the payment of an additional monthly wage (found in 60 per cent of these enterprises).

Substantial amounts were paid in this way for the purpose of compensating insufficient basic wages. In industry in 1996 an average of 27 per cent of the total wage was paid in the form of additional monetary incentives in enterprises using this means of payment. Bonuses were highest in minerals and lowest in chemicals. Banks were found not only to be paying higher basic wages and larger profit-sharing bonuses, but to be distributing substantial additional monetary bonuses, in the amount of 24 per cent of total wages in 1996. In contrast, in services, if introduced at all, only 15 per cent of the wage was made up of monetary incentives, the highest bonuses being paid in telecommunications and security services.

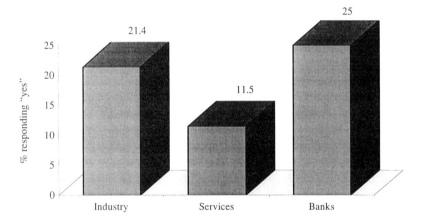

Figure 6.21 *Percentage of Enterprises Operating Monetary Incentive Scheme, by Sector, Sept. 1996*

Source: ALFS2.

A Wide Array of Social Benefits

Enterprises were also found still to be providing a great variety of benefits, which clearly constituted an important complementary source of income (*Table 6.5*). In industry, there were no great changes in this respect in relation to 1994, apart from a slight decrease in the proportion of enterprises providing such benefits and slight changes in benefit structure. Subsidies for consumer goods, for instance, were gradually being phased out (provided by only 47 per cent of enterprises in 1996 as against 81 per cent in 1994). All regular workers were equally entitled to all types of benefit. Other workers were in a much more precarious position, one which had deteriorated further since 1994.

Benefits were again highest in the banks, confirming the relative privileges of employees in this sector. The benefits provided by industry and services were very similar to one another, though some differences by property form were discernible (*Table 6.6*). In general, workers were much less likely to receive benefits in joint ventures and private enterprises, while state-owned and joint-stock companies continued to provide the same benefits as in 1994. New private owners in particular no longer provided funds for rent or supplementary pensions, nor did they subsidise transport, food, and other consumer goods to a significant extent. Differences were also found at the industrial and sectoral levels: industrial workers were less likely to receive benefits for instance in leather and shoes, wood and paper, and textiles and clothing, while service workers in trade and hotels were in a similar position. Small enterprises were also found to provide fewer benefits than large companies.

Table 6.5 *Type of Benefits Provided for Workers, by Sector, Sept. 1996 (percentage of establishments providing specified benefit)*

Benefits	Industry		Services		Banks
	Regular workers	Non-reg. workers	Regular workers	Non-reg. workers	All workers
Paid vacation	94.8	16.1	92.9	25.2	100.0
Rest houses	91.6	29.9	89.7	41.5	97.4
Sickness benefit	90.1	24.7	90.1	34.8	98.6
Subsidised rent	6.1	2.7	2.3	0.3	28.2
Subsidies for kindergartens	63.1	19.3	53.0	21.2	83.0
Incentive bonuses	34.2	9.8	38.8	14.9	63.8
Loans	8.5	1.8	5.4	2.0	30.3
Retiring assistance	25.7	7.5	29.9	11.4	52.4
Supplementary pension	3.8	1.5	5.5	1.0	0.0
Possibility for training	16.7	4.8	15.3	4.0	56.8
Subsidised food	28.6	12.2	28.6	12.3	25.0
Subsidised consumer goods	47.1	15.9	47.4	18.1	94.1
Transport subsidies	20.8	10.7	13.0	4.3	14.3
Other	1.2	0.3	3.1	1.7	9.1

Note: All employees in banks seem to be regular employees.
Source: ALFS2.

Table 6.6 *Type of Benefits Provided for All Workers (Regular and Non-Regular), by Property Form, Sept. 1996, Industrial and Service Sectors (percentage of establishments providing specified benefit)*

Benefits	Industry					Services			
	State	Private	Joint venture	Joint-stock	Other	State	Private	Joint venture	Other
Paid vacation	100.0	92.6	91.9	100.0	90.9	100.0	87.9	87.5	100.0
Rest houses	95.5	89.6	90.3	100.0	81.8	91.1	83.3	86.7	100.0
Sickness benefit	96.6	87.1	88.7	90.0	90.9	97.2	81.2	87.5	92.3
Subsidised rent	14.9	1.9	6.5	5.0	0.0	3.0	0.9	30.0	0.0
Subsidies for kindergartens	75.9	56.4	62.9	60.0	72.7	78.0	26.7	66.7	91.7
Incentive bonuses	37.5	33.7	30.6	35.0	36.4	37.0	31.9	58.3	30.0
Loans	3.4	12.4	6.5	10.0	0.0	1.2	3.1	20.0	0.0
Retiring assistance	31.0	21.6	29.0	25.0	27.3	35.3	18.2	45.5	20.0
Supplementary pension	11.4	0.6	1.6	0.0	9.1	9.1	0.0	0.0	0.0
Possibility for training	23.0	11.9	19.4	20.0	18.2	23.2	6.7	30.0	20.0
Subsidised food	50.0	14.3	19.4	70.0	45.5	36.4	17.7	18.2	33.3
Subsidised consumer goods	85.2	28.8	40.3	50.0	45.5	80.5	17.7	20.0	58.3
Transport subsidies	42.5	13.8	12.9	5.0	27.3	21.7	2.2	22.2	11.1
Other	1.1	1.9	0.0	0.0	0.0	4.3	0.6	28.6	0.0

Source: ALFS2.

To summarise, in the current crisis the enterprise-based social welfare system remains very strong, although differences are growing rapidly between regular and other workers and between property forms.

10 NO ACCESS TO HEALTH AND EDUCATION FOR MOST

While enterprises tried to limit the fall in real wages and living standards by providing extra sources of income and social benefits and services, the state was disengaging itself from providing free health services and education. The lack of funds to finance the health care system caused severe disruption in the health care delivery system that was previously fully financed from the state budget. Access to health services was more and more limited to people's ability to pay. Under-the-table payments and health insurance contributions became the only means of obtaining access to basic health treatment and medication. Similar developments occurred in education. This trend aggravated the depth of poverty, good health and education playing a key role in raising individual living standards and being an essential element in any poverty reduction strategy.

We should emphasise that these processes were the result primarily of the transition rather than of the previous regime. Albania, despite its low income per capita, formerly had relatively good education and health indicators, reflecting the priority typically given to these sectors by communist regimes. In 1990, more than 40 per cent of the adult population had completed secondary or higher education.[3]

The destruction of schools and many health facilities in 1992 brought all this to an abrupt halt, a development considerably aggravated by the Government's decision to reduce expenditure in these key public services, from 56 per cent of GDP in 1991 to 29 per cent in 1995. Social security expenditure decreased from 12.1 per cent of GDP in 1991 to 6.7 per cent in 1995. Subsidies to enterprises were almost completely stopped, falling from 20.4 per cent to a mere 0.6 per cent. Health expenditure fell from 4.3 per cent of GDP in 1992 to 2.4 per cent in 1995, while over the same period education expenditure fell from 4.4 per cent to 3.5 per cent. These developments were clearly reflected by the terrible state of schools and hospitals. School attendance also declined significantly. In the case of health services, many people from the poorest social groups did not seek medical treatment because of the expense.

As a result, a number of health indicators have deteriorated during the transition, especially infant mortality (now the highest in Central and Eastern Europe) and adult morbidity due to infectious diseases. In 1995–96 these indicators were particularly worrying in the North, with much higher rates of infant mortality (45 deaths per 1,000 live births compared to 18 in the South and a national average of 33 in 1995), a higher incidence of respiratory diseases for children, and nutritional problems (with nearly 30 per cent of children severely malnourished—see World Bank, 1996b). In addition, the bulk of the urban population received largely inadequate urban services and were afflicted by extremely unhealthy environmental conditions.

11 GROWING POVERTY AND INAPPROPRIATE SOCIAL INCOMES

No Reliable Data But Clear Evidence of Destitution

Few data are available on poverty in Albania, because of the absence of a nation-wide household survey. A first attempt was made to rectify this in 1993–94, although only the region of Tirana was covered. It is also difficult to measure poverty in the absence of a recognised poverty threshold, although its calculation is embodied in the labour code.

3. However, more than 5,000 schools were destroyed or damaged because they were associated with the communist regime. Many health facilities were also totally destroyed in 1992.

Poverty has grown in both rural and urban areas. In the countryside, one-quarter of the population lived on farms that were too small—less than one hectare—to sustain a family, condemning them to a hand-to-mouth existence. The poorest decile lived on agricultural incomes of less than USD 70 per year, and were unable to meet even their basic food requirements for the whole year. Extreme poverty was most widespread in the rural and mountainous areas of the North and Northeast, where the average farm size is only 0.5 hectare, and farm incomes are negligible because production is almost exclusively aimed at self-consumption (and not even attaining that), and there are no opportunities for off-farm employment. In these regions, more than half of the population was living in poverty.

Farmers were compelled to seek other sources of income: between 70 and 90 per cent of rural households had a source of income other than farming.[4] Particularly important were social transfers such as pensions (received by 35 per cent of farm families), social assistance (20 per cent), and unemployment benefits (in the rare instances of entitlement), although they were far from sufficient. The main means of survival for farming households was reported to be remittances from absentee family members.

The World Bank has attempted to measure the incidence of poverty in both rural and urban areas, estimating the relative subsistence minimum or poverty line as half the gross expenditure per adult (in rural areas, the gross expenditure of farm adults), before measuring what proportion of the population was below this minimum. In rural areas, a poverty incidence of 29 per cent was observed, while in urban areas, it was estimated at approximately 15 per cent. However, although this type of research is very helpful, the results very much depend on the selected poverty line. The World Bank chose one of only 2,200 leks per month (half the mean expenditure of around 4,400 leks for Tirana). When the poverty line was slightly increased at 2,850 leks, urban poverty doubled to 30 per cent. Finally, these figures are only relative figures based on average expenditure. The level of expenditure is misleading, however, especially in a poor country that has experienced a fall in living standards and so a decline in both the level and structure of consumption: the fact that 80 per cent of the household budget must be spent on food, generally of lower quality and with less protein, clearly means that average expenditure does not conform to what would normally be considered as an acceptable consumption pattern. This is the reason why most countries in the West and elsewhere in Central and Eastern Europe prefer to calculate an absolute rather than a relative poverty line, based on a basket of goods and minimum quantities needed for subsistence. This was the method selected by

4. For poverty in rural areas, see World Bank (1996b, pp. 23–35).

a number of Albanian experts who estimated the subsistence minimum at around 6,000 leks at the end of 1994, and 10,000 leks at the end of 1996. This approach transforms the picture of deprivation in Albania dramatically, plunging more than 70 per cent of the population into poverty. There is clearly a need to develop a robust methodology for calculating the subsistence minimum. It would also be important to involve both employers' and trade union representatives and their experts in the discussion of these questions, so promoting the establishment of an objective and widely recognised poverty line in Albania. A nation-wide household survey would also provide useful information on the level and structure of expenditure and also income, so making it possible to identify more accurately the poorest categories in the country (Chapter 16).

Social Assistance Programme: Only Directed to Targeted Groups

The situation in Albania is particularly unhappy because, although the elderly, the sick, and the long-term unemployed are the worst-affected groups, most of the population lives in poverty, so making nonsense of the kind of social protection system—or social safety net—that the Government, on the advice of international monetary institutions, has tried to implement, based on tighter eligibility criteria and narrower targeting. As the World Bank has also recognised (1996b, p. 21), it is very difficult indeed to "differentiate the poor from the very poor".

The social assistance programme (known as "Ndhime Ekonomike") introduced in July 1993 was intended to help families with no or insufficient income to meet their minimal subsistence needs. Although this assistance did play a role, it was found to have excluded many of the poorest. Payment levels were also very low,[5] declining even further—by more than 20 per cent in real terms—between 1993 and 1995. For families dependent on social assistance this has resulted in major hardship.

Pensions—a crucial source of income for rural families—also fell in real terms: among households with less than half a hectare of land, almost 40 per cent relied on pensions as their main source of income. Given the extremely low value of the agricultural pension (900 leks a month, or less than USD 10), these households tried to survive in a situation of extreme deprivation. Social assistance payments for farmers were not much higher (15,000 leks per year).

One may well wonder what further evidence would have been needed to induce the authorities to increase agricultural pensions—and pensions generally—when they had become little more than symbolic payments.

---

5. The average full assistance payment in 1995 was 2,533 leks per month.

Household Budgets Mainly Dedicated to Food

Another measure of falling living standards is offered by the structure of consumption, something which has completely changed over the years of transition. We have already seen that an important part of families had to limit their expenditure on health care and education. They also reduced their expenditure on cultural entertainment. By contrast, the share of total household consumption dedicated to food increased to 72 per cent.[6] The poorest quintile of persons spent 1,650 leks a month (USD 13), of which 85 per cent was spent on food. Expenditure on electricity and heating after their prices were liberalised also increased, to make up 12 per cent of the monthly household budget. It is important to note that the share of food expenditure in Western countries rarely constitutes more than 30 per cent of total household consumption. In many cases, within this global figure for food expenditure, the poorest households modified their dietary patterns by consuming inexpensive and less nutritious food, for example by spending a large part of their monthly food expenditure on bread alone and much less on meat, milk, and vegetables. According to a survey in 1995, 33 per cent of households reported consuming a narrower range of food items apart from bread, with meat and fish, and fruit and vegetable consumption falling the most (World Bank, 1996b, p. 50). INSTAT reports that bread dominated the consumption basket of all households, accounting for 10 per cent of total expenditure.

This process had serious effects on the quality and productivity of the labour force, but also on the nutrition of all family members. More than one-third of families had to deplete their savings in order to meet expenses, with 30 per cent falling behind in the repayment of debts. In the big cities, more than 50 per cent had to borrow from relatives or friends to make ends meet.

A majority also increased their consumption on the black market: unbilled services, undeclared activities or rents, shopping second-hand and at cheap street dealers, hiring illegal ("black") labour to carry out repairs and so on. On the supply side, permanently low wages in the formal economy have pushed a growing proportion of the labour force towards the informal economy.

12 CONCLUSION

The positive results registered in apparent GDP growth led to encouraging statements with regard to living standards. For instance, according to the IMF,

6. According to the first household survey that INSTAT conducted in Tirana of 3,179 households in 1993. A second survey was carried out in May–July 1994.

"[e]stimation of average urban per capita consumption indicates that the real income decline was less marked than suggested by income data, if it occurred at all" (IMF, 1994, p. 88), and, "[w]hile there was undoubtedly a very substantial output collapse at the beginning of the transition process, living standards now appear to be higher than in 1990" (IMF, 1997b, p. 6).

Our survey results, however, showed a different picture. We have seen that real wages fell by more than 50 per cent in the first years of transition because of the very rapid price liberalisation and the absence of wage indexation; as a result, average wages both in 1994 and 1996 were still well below any measure of subsistence minimum or poverty line. We also saw that the minimum wage had been adjusted only irregularly so that it had fallen in real terms even more, losing any connection with the average wage and—even more dramatically—with the poverty line. This situation not only concerned wages but also all other sources of income, most social allocations being calculated on the basis of the minimum wage. As a result, they also fell in real terms during the same period, plunging a growing number of workers and recipients of social benefits into total destitution. This was combined with the tightening of eligibility criteria for unemployment benefits described in the previous chapter that also contributed to leaving many unprotected.

Although this downward trend reflected the economic crisis, it was also the direct consequence of the adjustment strategy pursued by the Government. In particular, wages were deliberately controlled as a key anti-inflationary variable. This was an important policy decision for households and individual welfare since wages were typically the most important source of income. A majority of the population in 1995–96 was described as having fallen well below any measure of subsistence minimum or poverty line.

We have seen that this restrictive incomes policy led not only to increasing social unrest and growing poverty, but also to economic distortions. Wages were found to be totally disconnected from productivity. Wages in state enterprises were also kept at artificially very low levels by state control while they were entirely free in the emerging private sector, leading to a growing wage gap between the two sectors. These different movements led to distorted wage differentials, while very rigid tariff scales and the absence of occupational wage differentials impeded the closer harmonisation of wage patterns with qualifications, responsibilities, and performance. This reduced worker motivation even further, a problem so often mentioned by managers in our enterprise surveys. This is also the reason why employers themselves were systematically paying wages well above the official minimum wage, and supplementing basic wages controlled by the state with profit-sharing bonuses, other monetary incentives, and a significant range of social benefits.

At the same time, insufficient wages in the formal sector compelled workers to accept second and even third jobs in the informal economy, so further reducing the taxable sector and diminishing state revenues. Finally, the effects of this centralised policy on inflation are highly debatable since inflation in Albania, where labour costs as a proportion of total production costs are below 15 per cent, was clearly not fuelled by wage increases.

Similarly, we may wonder whether the implementation of a more balanced economic policy in Albania, allowing wages to adjust more closely to economic trends (not only prices but productivity and employment) and to play both their social and economic roles, would not have been more appropriate, especially considering the growth of social tensions within enterprises and in society as a whole. We may also question whether such a radical strategy of wage controls was the best option in the poorest country in Europe.[7] The social explosion of early 1997, partly fed by these radical adjustment policies and their adverse effects, will comprehensively cancel whatever short- and medium-term economic progress may have been made.

7. According to the IMF, such rapid adjustment was the only desirable approach: "One may ask whether adjustment could have been made less painful. The rapid pace of price liberalisation and price increases was chosen both because food security required a supply response in agriculture and because there was strong political support for improving the rural–urban terms of trade. Options to smooth the transition under these circumstances, without increasing the fiscal deficit, would have included better targeting of social assistance, which was not administratively feasible, or increased taxation of agriculture" (IMF, 1994, p. 88).

7. The Avoidance of Social Dialogue and Participation

1 INTRODUCTION

Social dialogue in Albania at the end of 1996 was still—as a post-communist country—in its early stages, with a history of no more than three years. Before this, all employer–employee relations had to be conducted within the totalitarian system.

A law on collective bargaining was put in place at the end of 1991 with the aim of progressively promoting a new industrial relations system.[1] However, the ingrained tendency of the state to overcentralise and the lack of preparation and weakly developed independence of the social partners rendered this a very difficult and lengthy process. Only after pluralism was made possible in Albania from December 1990 could trade unions emerge. In the first years of reform, however, these trade unions were characterised by constant internal conflicts, quite apart from the difficulties inherent in the transformation to a new system from what had been perhaps the most oppressive Stalinist regime in the region.

Trade unions first had to deal with the painful consequences of economic stabilisation reforms and restructuring, with massive lay-off programmes and falling real wages. They also had to develop a stance in relation to the new employment possibilities created by very small enterprises in the private sector, not only in industry but also in the relatively new service sector. The unions were also suddenly confronted with the recomposition of their own movement. A new national organisation was created, a large number of employees in some enterprises and sectors which felt unprotected by the confederations began to organise small trade unions of their own, with a strictly occupational character. By the end of 1996, 24 different trade unions had been registered by the Ministry of Justice, with two trade unions dominating: the Free Trade Union (KS) and the Independent Trade Union (BSPSH).

---

1. More exactly, in December 1991 the Law on Labour Relations and Guidelines of the Council of Ministers on the Fundamental Conditions of Labour Contracts were adopted.

Employers, on their side, also tried several times to establish their own associations. Their initial lack of success could be attributed mainly to the lack of tradition in Albania and attitudes reflective of the burden of the past. The predominant role of the state as employer is another obstacle to the emergence of independent employers' organisations in the public sector. In the private sector, the sheer variety of managers and businessmen has made collective action in pursuit of their own interests difficult. Employers' representatives have also had to define their negotiating role, which is very different from the responsibilities and tasks previously vested in the Chamber of Trade and Industry. Great interest has been shown in the establishment of corporate employers' associations, for instance in chromium, copper, and energy, which employ a significant portion of the national work-force. Private employers have attempted to establish occupational associations, for instance in the construction industry in the regions of Vlora, Fier, and Elbasan. However, sectoral or regional agreements have remained the exception rather than the rule.

Although national employers' organisations were also created, including the Union of Albanian Employers and the Confederation of Albanian Businessmen or KONBIS, they found it difficult to assume their new role, mainly because of their lack of representativeness. This also posed problems for the trade unions and the Government, particularly when trade union representatives trying to negotiate national agreements discovered that the national employers' organisations either lacked a mandate from their members to negotiate such an agreement, or, more importantly, they were unable to ensure that a national collective agreement would be followed by employers at more decentralised levels. The binding nature in principle of a national collective agreement was not always recognised by employers, especially those who were not members of the national employers' associations.

In spite of all these difficulties, the first forms of tripartism did eventually emerge at the national level. Legislation was passed in accordance with which representatives of trade unions and employers' organisations would be invited to sit on the boards of important national bodies, such as the Pensions' Board, the Board of Employment Foundation and Self-Employment, and a board set up at the Institute of Management and Public Administration. The Labour Code approved in July 1995 created the legal background for the institutionalisation of tripartite relations through the establishment of the National Labour Council, although the latter did not commence operations until the end of 1996. The permanent members of the Council comprise 10 representatives each from the trade unions and the employers' organisations, who sit together with representatives of the Government. Important steps were taken in this direction over the course of 1996: in September 1996, a tripartite agreement was concluded for the first time between the Government and the social partners concerning the creation of a tripartite committee on wage issues, which commenced operations in 1997. The envisaged role of this wage committee, which operates within the framework of the National Labour Council, was to discuss and prepare minimum wage increases, although other wage-related reforms were expected to come within its remit.[2]

However, while the tripartite process was launched at the national level at the end of 1996, our survey data revealed that social dialogue at the enterprise level was marked by worrying trends between 1994 and 1996.

The present chapter presents the evolving role of labour–management relations and the functioning of collective bargaining at the enterprise level over this period. We try to identify systematically the problems that were encountered in this process, and to take into account as far as possible different sectors of the economy, different property forms, size of enterprise, different regions, and a number of other specific enterprise or local characteristics. For this purpose, we adduce concrete data on trade unionisation, collective agreements, and direct forms of workers' participation, and attempt further to identify how all these variables changed over the period.

2 THE DECLINE IN TRADE UNION INFLUENCE

Lower Unionisation in Industry

According to our survey results, there has been a sharp fall in the proportion of workers unionised in industry—from 93 per cent in 1994 to 50 per cent in 1996. This fall was general across all sectors: although most pronounced in leather and shoes, food, and wood and paper, it was also observed in such traditional sectors as metallurgy and minerals. The trend can be explained by a combination of three major factors. First, the development of the private sector in which collective bargaining is less developed and the trade union presence more patchy. Secondly, the tough restructuring process involving

2. The creation of this tripartite agreement was the achievement of a tripartite working group set up by the Ministry of Labour—with the assistance of the ILO—in 1993. Composed of wage experts from the Government, but also from trade unions and employers' organisations, it prepared a first assessment of the wage situation in Albania (ILO–UNDP–Ministry of Labour of Albania, 1995 and 1997) and proposed very concrete policy recommendations. On the basis of this important preparatory and training work, the tripartite wage committee will not only have to negotiate increases in the minimum wage, but also prepare reforms in such different areas as the wage-fixing system in the budgetary sector, central wage regulations, collective wage bargaining, payment systems linked to productivity, and wage statistics.

massive lay-offs against which the unions have not been able to do much, so weakening their position at the enterprise level. The decline in trade union representation, for instance, was most marked in metallurgy and minerals, though paradoxically trade unionisation was strongest in mining, despite the fact that this sector had experienced the severest employment cuts. Thirdly,

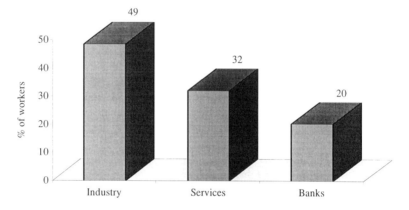

Figure 7.1 *Percentage of Workers Unionised, by Sector, 1996*

Source: ALFS2.

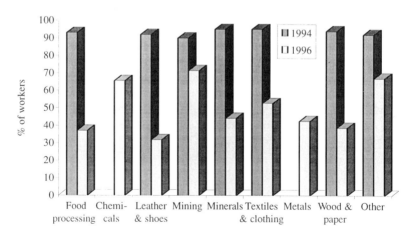

Figure 7.2 *Percentage of Workers Unionised, by Industry, 1994–96*

Note: Chemicals and metals were classified under "Other" in 1994.
Sources: ALFS1, ALFS2.

the sharp fall in real wages—and in some cases delays in the payment of wages—further contributed to reducing the trade unions' credibility.

The Marginal Position of Trade Unions in Services

Trade unionisation was found to be very low in services, covering only 32 per cent of the labour force. This low percentage was the direct result of the development of small private enterprises in trade, hotels and restaurants, and security, in which the proportion of unionised employees rarely exceeds 10 per cent (*Figure 7.3*). At the same time, trade union influence remained strong in the larger state-owned enterprises in telecommunications and the public utilities, accounting for more than 80 per cent of the labour force.

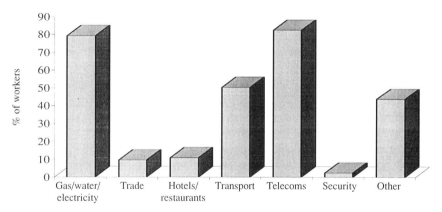

Figure 7.3 *Percentage of Employees Unionised, by Service, 1996*

Source: ALFS2.

The Absence of Trade Unions in the Private Sector

This big difference in services between the state sector and private property forms is made clear in *Figure 7.4*, which shows a 5 per cent unionisation rate in private enterprises compared to a 72 per cent rate in state-owned enterprises. Similar differences—although not to the same extent—were observed in industry, with trade unions managing to hold their position in state-owned enterprises and joint-stock companies (80 per cent unionisation), while losing ground in joint ventures (47 per cent) and, above all, in private enterprises (28 per cent).

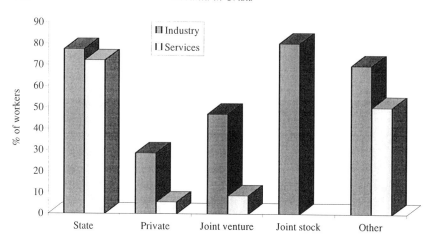

Figure 7.4 *Percentage of Workers Unionised, by Property Form, 1996, Industrial and Service Sectors*

Source: ALFS2.

It was significant that only 35 per cent of the industrial managers questioned reported the presence of a recognised trade union in their enterprise. In contrast, there was a recognised trade union in more than 84 per cent of state-owned enterprises. The situation by property form was even more contrasted in services, where only 6 per cent of private enterprises reported a recognised trade union, compared to 78 per cent in the state sector. Thirty-five per cent

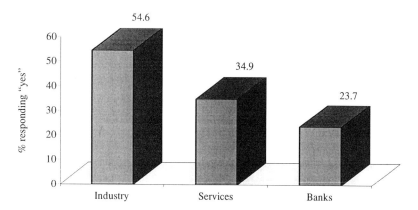

Figure 7.5 *Recognised Trade Unions in the Enterprise, by Sector, 1996*

Source: ALFS2.

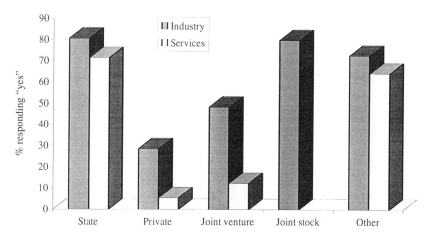

Figure 7.6 *Recognised Trade Unions in the Enterprise, by Property Form, 1996, Industrial and Service Sectors*

Source: ALFS2.

of employers in services as a whole had a recognised trade union in their enterprise.

The position of trade unions at the enterprise level (and therefore their bargaining strength) was therefore progressively being weakened. We saw from our wage equation that trade unionisation has not had a significant effect on wage levels, although the centralised wage-fixing system that continued to prevail was another important factor in this.

While the emergence of tripartite wage negotiations, complemented by progressive decentralised wage bargaining, could have left much more room for the social partners to reach agreement, the trade unions had to redouble their efforts at the enterprise level, especially in the new private companies. At the same time, the employers, especially new private owners, were still to be persuaded of the potential of enhanced social dialogue, not only to improve industrial relations in the enterprise, and to reduce workers' demotivation and high staff turnover, but progressively to increase productivity and product quality.

3 FEWER ENTERPRISE COLLECTIVE AGREEMENTS

Worrying Trends in All Sectors of the Economy

Between our two enterprise surveys, in 1994 and 1996, the percentage of enterprises signing collective agreements also seemed to have registered a significant decline. While most industrial enterprises signed a collective agreement in 1994, in 1996 only 50 per cent reported that they had done so and were able to indicate precisely what it contained. Enterprises in services were found to have a lower propensity to sign collective agreements: only 32 per cent of the 581 surveyed enterprises in services reported having a collective agreement and were able to indicate what issues it covered.

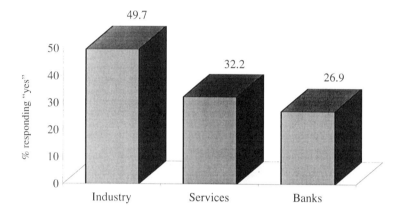

Figure 7.7 *Percentage of Establishments with a Collective Agreement, by Sector, 1996*

Source: ALFS2.

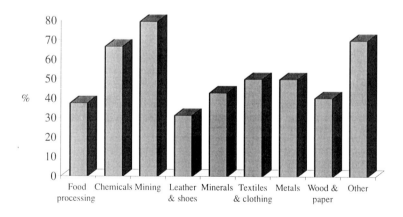

Figure 7.8 *Percentage of Establishments with a Collective Agreement, by Industry, 1996*

Source: ALFS2.

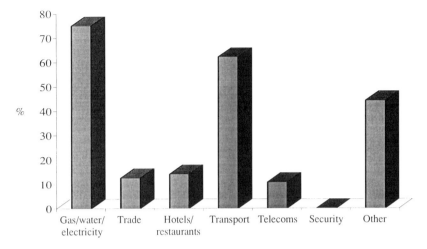

Figure 7.9 *Percentage of Establishments with a Collective Agreement, by Service, 1996*

Source: ALFS2.

Great differences were observed between sectors, however, most enterprises in transport and public utilities reporting such an agreement compared to less than 15 per cent in trade, hotels, and security. Banks registered the lowest proportion of collective agreements, at less than one-third.

The Absence of Collective Agreements in Private Firms

The percentage of collective agreements was much lower in private enterprises and joint ventures than in state enterprises. This trend was observed not only in industry but also in services (*Figure 7.10*). The smaller number of collective agreements in services might be explained by the predominance of small private enterprises in this sector: private employers have shown a marked reluctance to sign collective agreements. This lack of collective agreements was often combined with the absence of a recognised trade union. Although these enterprises were found to pay higher average wages and to distribute additional payments, pressure should be put on them to sign collective agreements and to get involved in traditional collective bargaining with workers' representatives.

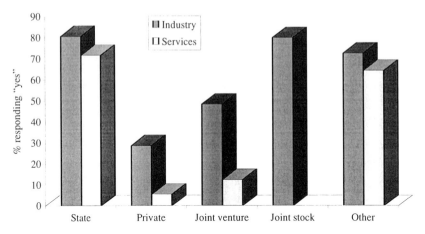

Figure 7.10 *Percentage of Establishments with a Collective Agreement, by Property Form, 1996, Industrial and Service Sectors*

Source: ALFS2.

A Greater Risk of Strikes

The number of strikes in Albania has been growing: 8 per cent of all industrial enterprises (and 6 per cent of those in services) reported between 1 and 3 strikes over the past two years. The number of strikes was particularly high, not only in large restructuring sectors such as chemicals, but in sectors with small private enterprises, such as leather and shoes (19 per cent reporting strikes) and textiles and clothing (15 per cent). It is clear that the trade unions will increasingly resort to this form of industrial action in order to obtain wage concessions if more traditional paths, such as collective bargaining and the signing of collective agreements at the enterprise level, remain closed to them.

The Contents of Collective Agreements

Most enterprise collective agreements (more than 80 per cent) were signed for a period of one year. Consequently, at the end of 1996, 77 per cent of the current collective agreements had been concluded that same year, as against 23 per cent that had been signed in 1995. Sixteen per cent of enterprises had concluded a collective agreement for two years, mostly state-owned enterprises and large companies.

The agreements continued to cover a wide range of issues, including working time, minimum wages, wage rates, job mobility, and promotion. However, significant differences had started to appear by property form: not only were private enterprises and joint ventures found to be signing fewer collective agreements, but these agreements were less likely to cover particular issues, such as task assignment, job mobility, and work organisation. Fewer issues were covered also in the collective agreements concluded in the banks.

Table 7.1 *Issues Covered by Collective Agreements, by Property Form, Sept. 1996, (percentage of establishments covering specified issue)*

	Industry					Services				Banks
Issue	State	Private	Joint venture	Joint stock	Other	State	Private	Joint venture	Other	State
Wage rates	77.8	77.6	80.0	58.8	85.7	83.1	24.1	66.7	66.7	46.9
Training	22.2	20.8	26.7	6.3	50.0	18.5	5.7	0.0	25.0	13.8
New technologies	18.1	16.7	16.7	18.8	25.0	16.0	3.8	0.0	12.5	23.3
Redundancy	9.7	8.3	10.0	6.3	12.5	11.0	5.8	0.0	0.0	13.8
Job mobility	59.7	41.7	56.7	37.5	62.5	66.9	22.6	66.7	55.6	23.3
Promotion	59.7	43.8	53.3	50.0	50.0	43.5	11.5	33.3	12.5	26.7
Task assignment	43.1	8.3	23.3	25.0	50.0	36.8	9.6	0.0	25.0	17.2
Work organisation	59.7	39.6	40.0	31.3	62.5	66.5	28.8	33.3	22.2	33.3
Minimum wages	65.3	75.0	73.3	43.8	75.0	58.1	21.2	66.7	50.0	43.3
Wage rates	75.0	79.2	83.3	68.8	75.0	63.3	24.5	33.3	77.8	41.9
Other	18.1	2.1	13.3	25.0	25.0	14.3	3.9	0.0	25.0	7.4

Source: ALFS2.

4 THE LACK OF DIRECT FORMS OF WORKER PARTICIPATION

While the trade unions were becoming more and more ineffectual, direct forms of worker participation were being promoted at the enterprise level.

Participation in Enterprise Decisions: A Lack of Transparency

Alongside the negative trends afflicting trade unions and the lower propensity of enterprises to sign collective agreements, we identified promising signs of increasing social dialogue, the majority of managers reporting the regular involvement of workers in enterprise decision-making: 63 per cent of industrial enterprises (61 per cent in services) reported that they both kept the workers regularly informed about enterprise developments and discussed enterprise results and objectives with them, while more than 75 per cent reported involving workers not only in wage determination and work organisation changes, but in discussions about investment and employment.

However, we should approach these statements with some caution since they were reported by the management, not the workers. In particular, trade unions reported that workers' representatives were only very rarely informed about decisions concerning lay-off programmes or partnership with a foreign investor. Moreover, our previous finding on the absence of trade union recognition by employers, especially in the private sector, was generally not a very positive and promising sign of the willingness of management to implement strong social dialogue and to involve the workers in key enterprise decisions.

Moreover, our results on workers' participation in decision-making were again clearly differentiated by type of enterprise. Wide variations were observed by property form (*Figure 7.11*): for instance, in industry only 54 per cent of private enterprises and 53 per cent of joint ventures reported regularly informing their workers about enterprise results and objectives, as against 85 per cent of state-owned enterprises (the same differences were observed in services). This kind of participation was also more widespread in very large enterprises, being found among 84 per cent of those of more than 200 employees, as compared to 54 per cent in enterprises of fewer than 50 employees.

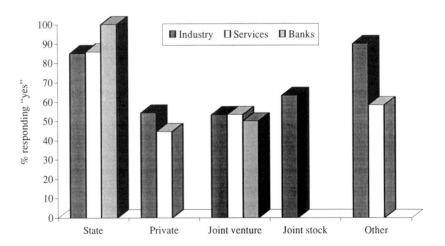

Figure 7.11 *Informing Employees Regularly About Results and Objectives, by Property Form, Sept. 1996*

Note: There were no joint-stock companies in services and banks, nor any private banks.
Source: ALFS2.

The level of worker participation was also found to vary substantially (*Figure 7.12*). In industry, state-owned and joint-stock enterprises were found to be developing worker representation on the board, while private enterprises and joint ventures gave preference to forms of worker participation in the workplace. Differences were also observed within joint ventures: those in majority foreign ownership (53 per cent) preferred workplace participation, while those in minority foreign ownership (56 per cent) developed worker participation at board level in a fairly systematic way.

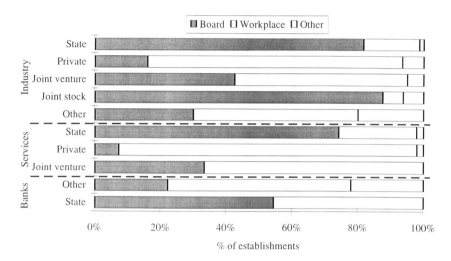

Figure 7.12 *Level of Worker Participation, by Property Form, Sept. 1996*
Source: ALFS2.

Participation in Enterprise Results: A Disappearing Phenomenon

The development of profit-sharing is another form of direct worker participation in the enterprise. We questioned managers on this subject in both 1994 and 1996. Three sets of results are particularly important.

1) We have seen in Chapter 6 that a decreasing number of enterprises were operating profit-sharing schemes. While the adoption of the 1992 law encouraging the development of such schemes had led to an explosion in the number of such schemes—involving 53 per cent of state enterprises—this number fell progressively in the following years, to only 16 per cent of state enterprises by the end of 1996. The proportion of enterprises practising profit-sharing schemes was lower in the private sector, at 23 per cent of enterprises in 1994, and also decreased substantially, to 8 per cent in 1996. Profit-sharing amounts per employee also decreased progressively.

2) Trade unions were found to be participating in this process less and less. While the majority of profit-sharing agreements (52 per cent in industry and 60 per cent in services) continued to be signed by workers' representatives in 1996, this represented a lower coverage compared to 1994, when the same representatives were involved in the signature of almost all (98 per cent) profit-sharing agreements. Moreover, as far as property form is concerned, 20 per cent of such agreements were signed by workers' representatives in private enterprises in 1996, as against 87 per cent in state enterprises (*Figure 7.13*). Only two years earlier, a majority of the few private enterprises (95 per cent of them) were involving workers' representatives in the introduction and signature of such schemes, almost on a par with state enterprises (99 per cent).

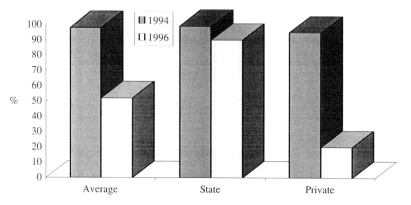

Figure 7.13 *Percentage of Profit-Sharing Agreements Signed by Workers' Representatives, Industrial Sector, 1994–96*

Sources: ALFS1, ALFS2.

3) We found that the introduction and development of profit-sharing schemes provided workers' representatives with a good opportunity to become involved in discussions with the management. Indeed, 75 per cent of managers in our survey reported that their profit-sharing scheme had resulted in increased participation of workers and their representatives in enterprise decisions (*Figure 7.14*). In fact, profit-sharing schemes were found to be quite democratic, in the sense that they were applied to the whole labour force, not only to white-collar workers. Indeed, the majority of industrial enterprises reported that they had introduced these schemes mainly in order to motivate blue-collar workers.

This outcome was not only a promising sign of the decentralisation of wage bargaining—a process which could be completed by the progressive abandonment of central wage regulation—but a positive encouragement to local employers and workers' representatives to engage in dialogue at the enterprise level even more intensively. Interestingly, 20 per cent of these enterprises in 1996 (and 15 per cent in 1994) reported that these schemes had helped them to avoid lay-offs, something which might have contributed to improving the social climate within the enterprise.

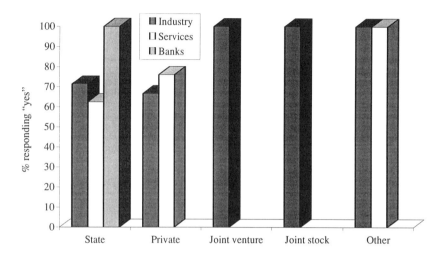

Figure 7.14 *Profit-Sharing Effect on Worker Participation, by Property Form, Sept. 1996*

Source: ALFS2.

In light of these results, the removal of profit-sharing schemes from enterprise payment policies was an unexpected and disappointing phenomenon. It also meant that an additional element of economic democracy was increasingly absent at the enterprise level.

5 CONCLUSION

Alongside privatisation, a general worrying trend at the end of 1996 was the decline in trade union membership and the propensity not to sign collective agreements in newly privatised enterprises. There was also little formal institutionalisation of labour relations in the form of trade union recognition and therefore limited signing of collective agreements in newly created private enterprises, especially in small industrial businesses; the rapid growth of small and medium-sized enterprises, for example in services, had also found trade unions incapable of responding. Significant differences had also started to appear between property forms with regard to the contents of collective agreements: not only were private enterprises found to be signing fewer collective agreements, but these agreements were less likely to cover particular issues, such as task assignment, job mobility, and work organisation. Many foreign investors have also been hostile to trade unions and the signature of collective agreements.

Trade unionisation decreased substantially, even in the state sector, while it reached marginal levels—less than 10 per cent of the labour force—in the private sector. This trend was primarily due to the economic crisis, reflected in falling living standards and growing unemployment: the trade unions' apparent inability to ameliorate these processes seriously harmed their credibility. Three additional factors contributed to declining trade union membership: privatisation, foreign direct investment, and the emergence of small firms.

Other forms of direct workers' participation were also not often developed. Workers and their representatives in the first years of transition were too rarely involved in decisions concerning employment reductions or change of ownership, despite their direct implications for their job and living conditions. Although workers' participation in profits and enterprise results was extensively promoted by employers in 1993–94, in many sectors this was more of an attempt to circumvent central wage regulations than to involve workers in enterprise management and results on a permanent basis. However, these schemes were found to improve the social climate within the enterprise and in some cases to contribute to solving conflicts concerning lay-offs. They also seemed to lead to higher worker motivation and productivity, and to provide greater wage flexibility. The progressive disappearance of profit-sharing schemes therefore represented another negative social development. We should also note that the absence of employee-ownership in the privatisation process was a distinctive feature of the Albanian transition compared to other Central and Eastern European countries (see Uvalic and Vaughan-Whitehead, 1997).

To summarise, precisely at a time when social dialogue could have helped to limit social tensions due to growing unemployment and falling living standards, and at least to some extent reduce the heavy burden of the transition on employees, reverse tendencies and practices could be observed at the enterprise level. Neglecting workers' involvement rapidly became a deliberate management policy in the implementation of necessary restructuring. Profitability margins were improved without any consideration of working conditions.

This absence of social dialogue and workers' participation at the establishment level could only reinforce the feelings of isolation and frustration among a growing majority of the population.

8. The Failure of the Mass Privatisation Programme

1 INTRODUCTION

Since the beginning of the reforms in Albania, privatisation has been considered a key element in the successful transition towards a free market economy. After a regime under which all assets were the property of the state, privatisation clearly involved a radical transformation of the economy and was expected to influence all other elements of economic reform. In common with other transition countries, Albania has put considerable emphasis on its privatisation programme, which has been designed largely on the basis of one determining factor: speed. As clearly stated by President Berisha, "Privatisation is the most important factor in economic reform in Albania . . . Its acceleration is the most important task at present."[1] In circumstances of serious budget crisis, a quick privatisation process was considered to be an important means of reducing the burden placed by subsidised state-owned companies on the state budget, and of generating state income through taxation. It was also considered essential for the development of corporate governance, given the inefficiency of state-owned enterprises and the need to bring in fresh capital and investment, and rapidly to renew obsolete technology, especially in industry. Quick privatisation was also seen as necessary for the purpose of changing attitudes, and reducing corruption, bureaucracy, abuse of services, and illegal activities (Muço, 1995). Sales of public capital were intended to be performed quickly and simply, without requiring prior large-scale restructuring or institutional capacity-building.

The first steps were taken in agriculture, and in small-scale privatisation, which was expected to lead quickly to more productive use and more efficient allocation of resources.[2] Although the Albanian medium-term programme of 1993 theoretically envisaged a range of possible privatisation methods, such as auction, tender, buy-out, direct sale, privatisation vouchers, and joint

---

1. As quoted in the *Albanian Observer*, Vol. 1, No. 1 (1995), p. 20.
2. Mainly by Decree of the Council of Ministers No. 248 of 25 March 1993, "Some Measures for Accelerating the Privatisation of Small and Medium-sized Enterprises".

ventures with foreign capital, the main method employed since 1995 has been mass privatisation through the distribution of vouchers. One of the main objectives of this approach was to involve Albanian citizens in the transition process; we analyse below why it is precisely in this respect that the privatisation programme has failed completely.

Box 8.1 *Legislation on Privatisation, 1991–96*

Law 7501 (19/07/91)	Land (amended by 7715 [02/06/93])
Law 7512 (10/08/91)	Privatisation (amended by 7653 [23/12/92])
Law 7631 (29/10/92)	Bankruptcy of state-owned enterprises
Law 7638 (19/12/92)	Commercial companies
Law 7652 (12/02/93)	Privatisation of housing
Law 7698 (15/04/93)	Restitution of property
DCM 190 (16/04/93)	Creation of the National Agency for Privatisation
DCM 19 (16/04/93)	Restarting the privatisation process
DCM 47 (07/05/93)	Valuation of state-owned property
DCM 248 (27/05/93)	Acceleration of privatisation of small and medium-sized enterprises (amended by 203 [May 1995])
July 1993	Creation of the Enterprise Restructuring Agency
DCM 386 (26/07/93)	Renting state-owned property
DCM 510 (26/10/93)	Privatisation of agricultural enterprises
Law 7764 (10/11/93)	Foreign investment (replaces Law 7496 of 8 April 1992)
DCM 93 (28/02/94)	Transformation of state-owned enterprises into commercial companies
DCM 51 (30/01/95)	Limits further privatisation by National Agency for Privatisation
DCM 1030 (23/02/95)	Issue and distribution of privatisation vouchers
DCM 203 (May 1995)	Privatisation of small and medium-sized enterprises (sale by auction)
DCM 244 (22/05/95)	Mass privatisation programme
July 1996	Creation of the Ministry of Privatisation replacing the previous National Agency for Privatisation and the Enterprise Restructuring Agency

Note: DCM: Decree of the Council of Ministers. For more, see Hashi and Xhillari (1998).

---

2 PRIVATISATION IN AGRICULTURE: DISMANTLING CO-OPERATIVES

Agriculture was the first sector to be privatised, mainly through the dismantling of agricultural co-operatives. Prior to 1991, the majority of agricultural production took place within the framework of state farms and co-operatives. Although, according to some, following the fall of the communist government, "farmers *spontaneously* dismantled agriculture co-operatives and distributed the land and livestock among themselves",[3] this process was

3. See IMF (1997b, p. 31).

clearly based on the Government's decision to ban co-operatives in agriculture, which was implemented through the programme of land privatisation approved by the Parliament in 1991 (Land Law No. 7501, 19 July 1991). Under this law, the land controlled by the co-operatives was allocated to families living in the villages of the co-operatives in accordance with a number of criteria: (i) land was to be distributed proportionately to every family according to the number of family members as of 1 August 1991; (ii) land was to be graded on the basis of irrigation, declination, and quality in order to make the distribution more equitable; and (iii) land planted to tree crops was assigned a different value in the distribution process. In 1992, the privatisation process was extended (under Decision 452 of 17 October 1992) to include land controlled by state farms.

By the end of 1993, 92 per cent of agricultural land had been privatised, including 93 per cent of former co-operative land and 91 per cent of former state farm land.[4]

Although this privatisation programme was implemented relatively quickly, it led to a series of problems, the distribution process being accompanied by discord and even violence. The Government encountered serious difficulties in distributing the remainder of the co-operative land, resolving boundary disputes, and establishing a land registry. In particular, it had great difficulty satisfying the claims of former owners who became eligible for financial compensation rather than restitution of property: a significant number of the claims of former owners are still outstanding; some have still not been registered, while others have been reluctant to accept the compensation offered.

Moreover, this privatisation led to the excessive parcelling out of agricultural land—certainly the most striking outcome of land privatisation— most of it coming into the ownership of individuals and their families, each parcel averaging no more than 1 hectare in size.[5] As a result, there are today some 400,000 smallholders working in agriculture and producing mainly for personal consumption. This is partly the outcome of the failure to develop an

---

4. State farms accounted for 24.1 per cent of the cultivated land and often possessed the best agricultural land.

5. As of mid-1995 365,000 families controlled 426,000 hectares of land formerly belonging to co-operatives, divided into 1.5 million parcels or plots. Furthermore, the average holding of around one hectare is divided into four parcels. In many cases, in order to ensure that all received comparable allotments, fields were divided so that every household in the village received one parcel of each particular type of land. This led to irrationally fragmented holdings reminiscent of pre-Revolutionary Russia (see Richard Pipes, *The Russian Revolution*, 1990, p. 103). Surveys also indicate that about 50 per cent of households received even less than one hectare of land (World Bank, 1996b, p. 25).

ambitious agricultural policy, instead of which a policy of "survival" has been adopted, with significant implications for the future of this sector. This trend has impeded the achievement of any economies of scale in agriculture, and has obstructed significant investment in new technology and marketing.

The rapid removal of the old agricultural system of co-operatives also disrupted the traditional distribution and marketing channels for agricultural inputs and created a vacuum which has not yet been filled. Moreover, significant damage was done during the political crisis of 1991–92. A lot of restoration work is needed, particularly in order to improve water network maintenance and irrigation systems. The level of mechanisation is also very low, and the traditional system of machine and tractor stations has been dismantled and needs to be replaced by a new system. The Government and the local authorities have not been able to improve the situation because of a general lack of financial resources. Finally, the small size of smallholdings is considered by experts to constitute a major obstacle to attracting foreign investment into agriculture.[6]

3 A LACK OF TRANSPARENCY IN SMALL-SCALE PRIVATISATION

Albania started its small-scale privatisation process in the middle of 1991, with the Privatisation Law of 10 August 1991. The National Agency for Privatisation (NAP) was established in order to organise and monitor the process. The rapid privatisation of small-scale entities was implemented in transport, trade, and services. Many problems arose in the course of implementation, however. More than 20,000 retail outlets were hurriedly distributed to workers and managers for a very low price. Because of the prevailing disorder, and the inadequacy of the legal framework, there were a lot of irregularities, and a generalised lack of transparency. Most privatisation was carried out quickly and without proper payment being made. All this intensified the demands of former owners for restitution, which has rendered the situation even more complicated.

In May 1993, privatisation was extended to small and medium-sized enterprises—defined by Decree No. 248 (completed by Decrees No. 47 and 244) as having fewer than 300 employees or a book value of less than USD 500,000. It gave responsibility for the system to the National Agency for Privatisation and established the auction as the preferred method of sale.

6. See "Looking Forward to the Market", in *Albanian Observer*, Vol. 2, No. 11 (1996), p. 32.

Systematically Avoiding Auctions

The auction method was used only in a very small number of cases, however. Preference was given to the former owners who had the pre-emptive right to purchase assets at their depreciated book value prior to their going to auction. The price paid by former owners has been considerably lower than the value at auction. Preference was also given to former political prisoners and those subject to political persecution, as well as—at least in theory—to present and former employees. In practice, many enterprises were sold directly because there was only one bidder. Foreign investors did not show much interest. The avoidance of auctions as the main method of privatisation did not promote competition: in 1993, only 3.8 per cent of privatised enterprises and 7 per cent in 1994 were subject to auction. Moreover, many of these enterprises have been sold at their initial price, without the value being increased as a result of the regular auction process, so resulting in a substantial loss of privatisation revenues for the state. To illustrate the difference, we might mention the privatisation of the hotels in Fier. The price of one hotel of 800 square metres which was auctioned in the regular fashion was increased from USD 150,000 to USD 520,000. By contrast, a similar hotel close by was sold at its initial estimate, without being auctioned: that is, at less than one-third of the potential price. A similar process occurred in respect of industrial enterprises.[7]

Local Privatisation Board Abuses

The privatisation process was decentralised to local privatisation boards which proceeded to use their powers to exclude bidders, to exempt units from auctions, and to request business plans. In practice, less than 5 per cent of small and medium-sized enterprises subject to privatisation went to competitive auction due to prior claims by former owners or political prisoners (36 per cent), or to the presence of only one bidder (59 per cent). In this process, many state-owned enterprises were split up during privatisation into more than ten enterprises.

Extensive small-scale privatisation continued from the middle of 1992 until 1994, when it was considered almost complete, especially in trade, handicrafts, transport, and housing. Although the government stated that the process had been implemented extremely quickly, it became obvious in early 1995 not only that there had been a great deal of corruption, but also that only a limited number of small enterprises had been privatised.[8]

7. See *Albanian Observer*, Vol. 1, No. 1 (1995), p. 20.
8. Analysts have called it "privatisation on paper", *Albanian Observer*, Vol. 1, No. 1 (1995), p. 20.

The Absence of Employee Share Ownership

According to the IMF, the buy-out method was given priority, with workers and former owners being preferred: half the purchases of small and medium-sized enterprises in 1993 and 40 per cent in 1994 "would have been operated" by employees.[9] However, although this has been observed in the case of very small ("micro") enterprises with fewer than five employees—especially in small enterprises producing wood, clothes, construction materials, bread, and oil—very few medium-sized or large enterprises seem to have followed the employee-ownership option, so contradicting the IMF assertion. According to our enterprise surveys, in almost all industrial enterprises with more than ten employees, there was no sign of employee ownership (with the exception of some services), and employers reported that there had been no distribution or sale of shares to employees. On the contrary, an average percentage of shares owned by employees of close to zero clearly makes Albania the only country in Central and Eastern Europe that has not developed any form of employee ownership. This is not surprising since the Government has brought forward no legislation, specific fiscal incentives, or other public provisions in order to favour this property form in the privatisation process. In fact, we would be justified in asserting that employee ownership has been totally absent from the privatisation process in Albania.

In many cases, indeed, employees have been discriminated against in the privatisation process, priority being given to the former victims of political persecution and/or—as already mentioned—to the former owners. In the case of the Rozafa Hotel in Shkodra and the Drini Hotel in Tirana, local privatisation committees gave them to former victims of political persecution, despite the buy-out plans proposed by former employees and their official complaints of discrimination and a series of petitions sent to the Prime Minister and the President.[10]

4 DIFFICULTIES IN THE PRIVATISATION OF LARGE ENTERPRISES

The privatisation of large-scale enterprises included state-owned enterprises with more than 300 employees and a value of more than USD 500,000. Around 300 enterprises came into this category, some of which could be split up and sold as small and medium-sized enterprises in accordance with Decree No. 248. Preliminary discussions commenced in 1994 concerning the selling-

---

9. IMF (1997b, p. 32).

10. See "Shareholders Still Far from the Share Market", *Albanian Observer,* Vol. 2, No. 7 (1996), p. 26.

off of state-owned utilities, such as water, hydroelectric power generation, power distribution, and telecommunications, with a view to increasing their efficiency and eliminating shortages, but no concrete steps were taken. The privatisation of the mining sector was also planned, but has met with strong opposition from the trade unions because of the adverse social effects and unemployment that would result.[11]

The Enterprise Restructuring Agency (ERA) was established in July 1993 as part of the privatisation strategy, to deal with 32 of the largest and most problematic industrial enterprises, which required managerial and financial assistance prior to either privatisation or closure. Partly financed through a World Bank IDA credit, this agency had funds to engage Western technical experts to undertake full-scale business audits and market reviews to determine how these large enterprises should best be reorganised. While this Agency played a role in assisting and downsizing enterprises (employment was reduced from a pre-1992 peak of 50,000 to less than 7,000 by early 1996), it succeeded in privatising only ten enterprises, and in liquidating only one. As a result, in July 1996 the government decided to abolish this agency and to transfer control of these enterprises to the Ministry of Privatisation.

5 THE COLLAPSE OF VOUCHER PRIVATISATION

Only in February 1995 did President Berisha announce a new programme of privatisation—issuing a new Presidential Decree—to be implemented through mass privatisation based on vouchers. The purpose of the programme was to transfer ownership of state enterprises into private hands and to spread this ownership amongst the population speedily and transparently. The fundamental objectives were to extend private ownership in order to facilitate the development of a market economy, and to increase the efficiency of these enterprises, so reducing the burden they place on the fiscal budget. At the same time, it was based on the belief that private citizens would have more respect for enterprise property if it were in private hands. Mass privatisation was also seen as a way of accelerating the privatisation process. The programme—supported by the World Bank and the IMF—was built on the experience of other mass privatisation schemes, notably in the Czech Republic, and had three main objectives (Monck, 1995, p. 82): "1) political: to involve and commit the population at large to the economic transformation process; 2) social: to achieve some form of distributive equity through the distribution of shares to the general public; 3) economic: to quickly privatise

11. See the two articles, "Mines Privatisation Begins", and "We Are against Privatisation of the Mines", in *Albanian Observer,* Vol. 2, No. 2 (1996), pp. 40–41.

a large number of firms to deepen market forces and competition within the economy."

In order to prepare the way, the Government intended to take a number of standard steps: (i) develop the legal framework; (ii) distribute vouchers to eligible participants; (iii) prepare state-owned enterprises for privatisation, including the corporatisation of the enterprises to be privatised, and the preparation of the prospectus on the assets to be included in the sale; (iv) prepare an integrated programme to inform voucher holders and company employees about the privatisation process; (v) organise auctions for the sale of the enterprises being privatised; (vi) develop investment funds in which private citizens would invest their vouchers—the funds would build up a portfolio of shares in a wide range of privatised companies; (vii) develop a securities market to enable individuals and funds to trade in the shares of privatised companies; (viii) restructure and refinance the privatised companies.

A presidential decree of May 1995 ordered the distribution of privatisation vouchers to all citizens above the age of 18, in three rounds. The average value of these vouchers after the three rounds, initially set at USD 200, was expected to be USD 750: the reality will be very different.

The President has on many occasions presented this process as a key point in the Democratic Party programme aimed at "transforming Albanians into owners"—for instance, during the discussions on the privatisation of large companies, including the oil company Albpetrol.[12] At a press conference given at the end of 1995, President Berisha announced the advent and success of the "first Albanian shareholders' society".[13]

As Democratic Party privatisation experts stated, "The Czech theoretical formulae, without being verified by the Czechs themselves, were materialised in Albania in less than a year".[14] Unfortunately, the final outcome did not turn out to be any more successful than the Czech privatisation programme, and began to show the same weaknesses.

In fact, this process was totally unsuccessful and experienced problems from the beginning, for a number of reasons: first, the government did not take all the necessary preparatory steps; secondly, mass privatisation took no account of Albanian reality; thirdly, the flawed nature of several of the most basic features of the voucher scheme, which have also given rise to problems in other countries where they have been implemented on a large scale.

---

12. See *Albanian Observer*, Vol. 1, No. 12 (1995), p. 17.
13. Ibid., p. 10.
14. See *Albanian Observer*, Vol. 2, No. 3 (1996), p. 28.

Voucher Devaluation to a Mere Fraction of their Nominal Value

From the start of the process, the supply of vouchers exceeded demand for shares in the enterprises to be sold, with the result that although only about one-fifth of the vouchers were issued initially, their price on the secondary market fell to about 16 per cent of their face value.

Pensioners began to exchange them at 10 per cent of their value. They exchanged the 20,000 lek (about USD 200) vouchers for 2,000 leks in cash, on the principle that it is better to have an egg today than a hen next year. This happened mainly because at the beginning of the voucher distribution process, no information was provided on the enterprises to be privatised. As a result, most of the capital has not been put to work. At that time, the vouchers could have only an abstract value, since the Government had not yet issued a list of enterprises that were to be auctioned and privatised. In total, there have been four rounds of auctions with 83 enterprises being put on offer. But the first list—of 20 enterprises—was made public five months after the distribution of vouchers, by which time half of all pensioners and many others had already exchanged them for cash: by selling their vouchers, a significant portion of citizens chose not to participate in mass privatisation.

The press has strongly criticised the Government for "allowing" these drastic falls in value. After the first list of enterprises to be privatised was made public in October 1995, vouchers rose to 40 per cent of their face value; then their value began to sink slowly. One year after the first distribution round, the vouchers' value again fell sharply. In April 1996, mass privatisation vouchers were being exchanged on Tirana's free market at 14 per cent of their nominal value. This was the second big drop in value since May 1995, when the Government first issued the vouchers (and after the law was passed). This is largely because only a small percentage of the Government's initial list had been privatised one year later. The main factor, however, was clearly the lack of publicity. In practice, it was impossible for voucher holders to invest in the companies being privatised.

A second group of 30 companies was offered in a second phase, but only 7,150 people had chosen to become shareholders by early 1996. The total value of the shares incorporated in these companies was 1.37 billion leks. According to Mr Niko Gliozheni, Chairman of the Privatisation Agency, however, in 1995 savings banks distributed 5.2 billion leks in vouchers for the mass privatisation process.[15]

The registration of 20 companies for the third phase started in February 1996, although it had been scheduled to take place much earlier. Later in the

15. See *Albanian Observer*, Vol. 2, No. 1 (1996), p. 30.

Box 8.2 *Time Schedule of the Mass Privatisation Programme, 1995–97*

May 1995	Presidential Decree and first distribution of vouchers (immediate fall in value of vouchers to 16 per cent of their face value)
October 1995	First list of privatised enterprises is made public (their face value increased by 40 per cent)
December 1995	Second list of enterprises (30 enterprises)
February 1996	Third list of enterprises (20 enterprises)
Mid-1996	Fourth list of enterprises (13 enterprises)
April 1996	Second big drop in value: vouchers are exchanged at 14 per cent of their nominal value
November 1996	Remaining vouchers are issued. Their price falls to 4 per cent—and then to less than 1 per cent—of their face value
End of 1996	The process is halted
1997	Not in operation

year, the Government made public the fourth list of 13 enterprises (and even a fifth list) to be privatised through vouchers, but this did not arouse much interest either.

The creation of the first investment fund in April 1996 was expected to increase public interest, but encountered a number of problems. In order to facilitate the participation of foreign investors, the Parliament decided in October 1996 that foreigners could use privatisation vouchers to invest in enterprises being sold.

When the remaining vouchers—400,000 at a value of 20,000 leks, and another 1.35 million at a value of 40,000 leks—were issued in November 1996, the price of vouchers on the secondary market fell immediately to 4 per cent of their face value. The failure to give them a stock exchange listing as initially planned also contributed to reduce their value. The total amount issued by the end of the second phase will be 62 billion leks (610 million USD).

The presence of pyramid schemes has also been presented as a factor that might have contributed to reduce people's interest in vouchers. The very high interest rates offered by some companies and funds might have enticed many people to convert their vouchers at a reduced value.[16]

Moreover, the voucher scheme concentrated on a very small number of profitable companies, sidelining the rest. In particular, people have mainly

16. See "Pyramid Schemes Hitting the Voucher [Programme]", *Albanian Observer*, Vol. 2, No. 11 (1996), p. 9.

invested in the privatisation of public services, especially the privatisation of a 30 per cent stake in three electric power distribution enterprises: one in Vlora (128 million leks), one in Elbasan (115 million leks), and the company Petrolimpeks (131 million leks). Other companies did not attract the same number of vouchers.[17]

At the same time, a few people made enormous profits from the decline in voucher values, buying a large number of them at a very low price and then investing them in privatised enterprises. This phenomenon was particularly striking in the case of the tourist sector: for example, the Kamberi company was able to acquire 72 per cent of the Llogara tourism project.[18]

According to the Minister of Privatisation himself, "there are therefore people who bought large quantities of privatisation vouchers at 2–3 per cent of their value". In total, however—the Minister added—according to 1998 figures from the Ministry of Public Economy and Privatisation, "of vouchers [issued so far] worth about 90 billion leks . . . only 16 per cent have been used . . . although [a lot more] should have been used in the course of the much publicised privatisation [process] . . ."[19]

Three years after the beginning of the process, the Minister of Public Economy and Privatisation admitted that "large-scale privatisation has failed".[20] He added that "A privatisation process that is based mainly on privatisation vouchers has not turned out to be very successful and effective in Albania, and in the other countries of Eastern Europe."

In the course of 1996, when vouchers had fallen below 1 per cent of their face value, the process was halted and had ceased to function by 1997.

Problems of Corporate Governance

A number of problems have been identified in the enterprises privatised with vouchers. First, a credit system was lacking in a situation in which many privatised enterprises have made almost no progress in bringing their technology up to date since they were privatised. A related problem is that of enterprise governance. Although some investors—and even one investment fund—have bought vouchers on the secondary market and have used them to buy substantial stakes in enterprises to be privatised, for the most part the ownership of privatised enterprises has been spread among many bidders, leaving the existing management in effective control of the company, and

17. See *Albanian Observer*, Vol. 2, No. 1 (1996), p. 30.

18. See *Albanian Observer*, Vol. 2, No. 5 (1996), p. 36.

19. See interview with the Minister of Public Economy and Privatisation Mr Ylli Bufi in *Albanian Observer*, Vol. 4, No. 4 (1998), p. 12.

20. Ibid.

giving shareholders little opportunity to challenge this control. Privatisation experts have also said that, because of this, these companies cannot be listed on the stock exchange: there are enterprises in which some 90 per cent of the shares have been distributed between 400 and 700 shareholders.

As an example, while a majority of shares have been accumulated in the power generation plant Petrolimpeks, management is difficult because the shareholders are scattered throughout Albania's 12 districts.

The creation of investment funds was expected to offer privatisation voucher holders the chance to invest in a portfolio, while creating opportunities for better corporate governance through the concentration of shares.[21] The Law on Investment Funds was passed by the Parliament in July 1995.[22] Foreigners were allowed to be founding members on condition that the Albanian partner(s) owned at least 50 per cent of the shares.

However, investment funds did not have much success. By the end of 1997, only 1.2 per cent of Albanians had deposited their vouchers with such funds. This lack of interest also reflects the population's preference for selling vouchers. According to analysts of the investment funds, it is also due to "the clear imbalance between the number of vouchers issued to the population, and the availability of objects to privatise using these vouchers".[23]

The high number of stolen vouchers was another obstacle impeding the development of investment funds.

Of the three funds licensed by the state to deal in vouchers, two, New Albania and Nobel, have failed to collect any vouchers. The other, Anglo-Adriatica, has managed to stay in business, but it has been criticised for accumulating vouchers above the number allowed by the law. This fund has attracted 41,182 shareholders, representing 10 per cent of the issued vouchers and 13.1 per cent of the privatisation money.

The Absence of a Stock Exchange

The development of a stock market was urgently required in order to attain more efficiency in capital allocation. But difficulties in resolving restitution issues and the absence of a computerised share register prevented this. The

21. For a description of the first investment fund to manage vouchers, see *Albanian Observer*, Vol. 2, No. 11 (1996), p. 33.

22. To receive the temporary licence, for two months only, fund founders have to deposit USD 20,000 as a guarantee against any problem they might have with their clients in the future. They may receive the final licence only after satisfying a number of other criteria, including the making of a deposit with a particular bank. See DCM 7979.

23. See the article "Investment Funds without Investors", in *Albanian Observer*, Vol. 3, No. 11 (1997), p. 31.

Albanian Stock Exchange did not open until May 1996.[24] Expectations at the time of its creation were high: for instance, the Minister of Finance Dylber Vrioni announced in December 1995 that "the first part of shares bought in the newly privatised enterprises will soon be registered in the stock exchange. This will be an institution which will be based on the experience of the countries of Central and Eastern Europe, due to the almost similar conditions during this transition period."

A law on the Stock Exchange was proposed by the Government in 1996. Transactions could be carried out in leks and privatisation vouchers. The law would also create a bond market, defining the government's terms and responsibility for the bonds. The proposed law also set down guidelines for a securities exchange commission, comprising three elected members. However, none of the initial expectations has been met. So far, the Albanian Stock Exchange has traded only Treasury bills and privatisation vouchers.

6 ENTERPRISE SURVEY: CONFIRMING SLOW PRIVATISATION

The enterprise survey provided a unique opportunity to examine the evolving distribution of establishments by property form.

An Entirely New Ownership Configuration . . .

Impressive changes took place in the ownership structure of the Albanian economy between 1994 and 1996: while in 1994 state-owned enterprises represented 63 per cent of all industrial enterprises, by the end of 1996 their share had fallen to only 27 per cent. Over the same period the share of private enterprises increased from 34 to 48 per cent. Leaseholding and co-operative forms progressively disappeared, while new property forms—such as joint ventures and joint-stock companies—emerged. At the end of 1996, 6 per cent of industrial enterprises were joint-stock companies and 18 per cent were joint ventures.

24. For more details about the creation of the first Albanian stock exchange, see *Albanian Observer,* Vol. 1, No. 12 (1995), p. 21; and also Vol. 2, No. 3 (1996), p. 25.

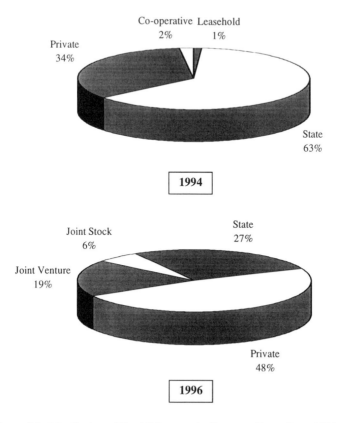

Figure 8.1 *Distribution of Establishments, by Property Form, Sept. 1994 Compared to Sept. 1996, Industrial Sector*

Sources: ALFS1, ALFS2.

. . . Due More to New Small Private Businesses than Privatisation of State Enterprises

This impressive change was due more to the emergence of private enterprises than to the privatisation process, which has been very slow. The distribution of employees by property form confirmed the predominance of large state-owned enterprises, which still accounted at the end of 1996 for 55 per cent of industrial employment, while the private sector, dominated by the new small businesses, employed only 17 per cent of the total labour force in industry. Particularly encouraging, however, was the growing employment in joint ventures, which accounted for 22 per cent of the industrial labour force.

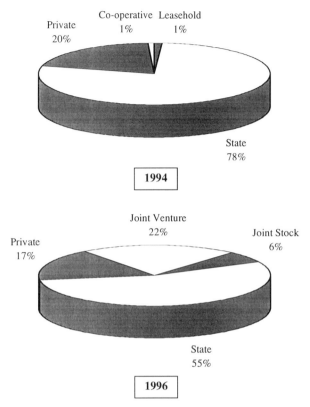

Figure 8.2 *Distribution of Employment, by Property Form, Sept. 1994 Compared to Sept. 1996, Industrial Sector*

Sources: ALFS1, ALFS2.

At the time of the second survey at the end of 1996, 20 per cent of enterprises were planning to change their form of ownership, including more than 50 per cent of state-owned enterprises. The fact that 60 per cent of these had expressed a similar wish in 1994 is further confirmation of the slowness of the privatisation process. The willingness of 22 per cent of joint ventures to change property form corresponded to their plans to increase the share of foreign capital, shifting from minority to majority foreign ownership. For joint-stock enterprises, it corresponded to the plans to increase the share of private capital so that it would acquire majority shares and control.

7 CONCLUSION

Despite several legislative changes and different government privatisation plans, by the end of 1996 it was clear that privatisation had moved only very slowly. While in the course of 1991–93 agriculture and small and medium-sized enterprises had been privatised very rapidly, the process had given rise to a number of deficiencies as regards ownership distribution and (as a consequence) corporate governance. In agriculture, it led to excessive parcelling out of the land and disruption of former distribution and marketing

Table 8.1 *Plans to Change Property Form, by Current Property Form, Sept. 1994 Compared to Sept. 1996, Industrial Sector*

	1994	1996
All	40	20
State	60	51
Private	24	2
Co-operative	15	–
Leasehold	0	–
Joint venture	–	22
Joint stock	–	11

Sources: ALFS1, ALFS2.

channels, so turning most production towards household self-consumption rather than the market. Privatisation of small and medium-sized enterprises had also led to a number of abuses, with the systematic avoidance of the auction method, despite the fact that this had been selected as the major privatisation method. Most privatisation of small and medium-sized entities was carried out quickly and without proper payment being made, so depriving the state of much-needed revenue. Employees have been discriminated against in the privatisation process, priority being given in practice to the former victims of political persecution or the former owners or only the managers. In fact, the Government brought forward neither specific legislation, nor fiscal incentives, nor any other suitable provisions in order to encourage employee ownership, in sharp contrast with other Central and Eastern European countries, which promoted this property form on a large scale in their privatisation processes.[25] Finally, and most significant, was the

25. See Uvalic and Vaughan-Whitehead (1997). See also ILO *Experts' Policy Report* (1998).

failure of mass privatisation through the distribution of vouchers. Although it was intended to make it possible for all citizens to participate in the distribution of public capital, this did not happen because of a number of mistakes made in the course of implementation. The enormous delays in publishing the lists of enterprises to be privatised despite the fact that vouchers had already been distributed in early 1995 did not give the holders of these vouchers any real investment opportunity. Their face value soon fell dramatically, and continued to fall in 1995 and 1996, eventually to below 1 per cent of their original value. This obliged the Government to halt the process of mass privatisation at the end of 1996. We saw that a number of problems also emerged with regard to corporate governance, because of the dispersion of ownership, the failure of investment funds, and the absence of a real stock market. Our survey results confirmed the slowness of the privatisation process, the change in the ownership configuration being explained largely by the spectacular growth of new small private enterprises rather than the successful privatisation of large state enterprises.

All these concerns led the Government to set up a new Ministry of Privatisation in July 1996, subsuming the old National Agency for Privatisation—which continues to function as part of the Ministry—and also the Enterprise Restructuring Agency. The first statements from the new Ministry emphasised the need to sell majority shares in large enterprises, where possible to strategic investors. In 1996, for example, preliminary agreements were reached with an Italian company to purchase most of the chromium mining industry. It was envisaged that strategic investors would also be sought for other mining companies and for the public utilities.

The new Ministry has also been subject to constant delay, however. By the turn of 1997, privatisation had still not touched the banking system or the large utility sector, including many large enterprises in mechanical industry, the electrical power sector, the mines, chromium and copper processing, and telecommunications.

The new Government intended to continue mass privatisation by improving the principal methods, although no new distribution of vouchers was foreseen. In early 1997, the new Minister of Privatisation announced that "1997 was going to be important for mass privatisation". The subsequent crisis, however, swept away every opportunity to proceed in this direction.

9. Limitations and Drawbacks of Foreign Capital

1 INTRODUCTION

After the extreme economic isolation of the decades under communist rule, the Albanian economy has opened itself up to the world. From the beginning of the transition, foreign investment has been considered as crucial for relaunching the Albanian economy; successive governments have given it top priority and over the last few years it has remained one of the main objectives of economic policy.

The constitution that prohibited investment was changed and in 1993 the Parliament passed one of the most liberal laws on foreign investment in Central and Eastern Europe.[1] The law was aimed at liberalising the procedures for attracting foreign investment. Foreign investors no longer had to obtain special permission from the Ministry of Foreign Affairs, and the law legitimised all forms of co-operation between Albanian and foreign investors, including participation in the privatisation process, joint ventures with Albanian partners, and green-field investment. The opening of the Tirana Stock Exchange at the end of 1996 was also expected to offer opportunities for portfolio investment.

The Law on Foreign Investment awarded the foreign investor equal treatment with local investors, and protected him against expropriation and nationalisation. It made possible the free transfer of profits and capital, and did not impose limits on equity participation. It even allowed losses for three consecutive years. The Government also offered a package of incentives to foreign investors operating in the country, particularly in manufacturing and tourism: a profit-tax exemption for a period of four years for those investing in production; other tax facilities for those reinvesting their profits;[2] and a five-year tax holiday for companies operating in tourist development zones.[3]

---

1. Law 7764 on Foreign Investment, dated 10 November 1993.
2. There is a 60 per cent reimbursement of profit tax for reinvested profits in production. Materials that are to be re-exported in the form of ready-made goods may be imported duty-free.
3. According to Law No. 7665 of 21 January 1993 on Priority Tourism Development Zones.

A new law on duty-free zones was passed by the Parliament in February 1996, allowing the establishment of special economic zones and industrial parks. The aim of this law was to develop, in particular areas, new investments and production for export, and to facilitate and accelerate the entry of goods and capital, promoting modern technology and creating new jobs.[4] For this purpose, many incentives have been offered to these zones, such as exemption from customs obligations, excise duties, and VAT, and exemption from profit tax in the first seven years. Finally, obstacles in the agricultural sector related to the acquisition of land by foreigners would be solved by the end of 1996.[5]

This orientation was clear in the Government's statements: "The Albanian government programme is a wide-ranging programme which is pro-business, pro-exports, and pro-direct investment. All the efforts we have made and are continuing to make to reconstruct legislation, institutions, and the economy serve this aim directly or indirectly: the creation of the most attractive and secure environment possible for foreign investment."[6] The Government also signed co-operation agreements and trade and investment treaties with different governments—for instance with the USA, Italy, Greece, Turkey, Germany, and France—to urge them to invest in Albania. At the same time, different associations, such as the Albanian Centre for Promoting Foreign Investment,[7] were created to facilitate the growth of such co-operation between Albanian and foreign investors.

In such a positive climate, it was important to obtain an assessment of foreign investment and to check in particular whether the very favourable conditions offered to foreign investors had in fact resulted in significant growth in foreign investment flows in Albania, and more importantly, if they had generated the economic growth and balanced economic development expected by the Albanian authorities.

---

4. Free zones must have a surface area of 30–50 hectares, and be close to ports, airports, or special zones of international transport. The procedures for these free zones will be enforced by the newly created Free Zones Administration (NIAFZ). The possibility of starting a free zone in Durres was already being studied at the end of 1996.

5. There was a clause in Article 2 of the 1993 Law on Foreign Investment concerning "land ownership", which was amended by the new law on "Buying and selling urban land" which allowed foreign investors to buy land for investment purposes, on the sole condition that the value of the investment should be three times the value of the land.

6. From the speech given by Mr Selim Belortaja, State Secretary for Economic Relations at the Foreign Ministry, at the Third Forum on Foreign Investment, held on 29–30 November 1996, in Tirana. See *Albanian Observer*, Vol. 2, No. 12 (1996), p. 18.

7. Created in February 1993, this association became a member of the World Association of Foreign Investment. See the interview with its president in *Albanian Observer*, Vol. 2, No. 11 (1996), p. 18.

Our final assessment is much more "nuanced" than the reports familiar from official economic reports and newspapers. In particular, we try to emphasise the limits that have been observed, not so much in the extent of foreign direct investment, but in its quality and in respect of sectoral and regional distribution. To this end, we try to analyse the dynamics of the influx of foreign direct investment in Albania between 1991 and 1996, relying on two different sources: (i) national statistics, which include all enterprises with foreign capital, including the smallest, and (ii) our enterprise survey, which covers larger enterprises. Our survey results also shed light on some of the effects of foreign investment in terms of economic and social developments.

2 LIMITED FLOWS OF FOREIGN CAPITAL

Despite attractive legal provisions and welcoming statements, foreign investment during the first years of reform was sustained but limited, well below what had been expected by the Albanian authorities. By May 1996 cumulative foreign investment had reached USD 270 million—or USD 85 per capita—well below the average in most Central and Eastern European countries.[8]

To give an idea of the comparatively small figure this represents, we might mention that remittances for 1995 from Albanians working outside the country were in the range of USD 350–400 million; total estimated foreign investment since 1991 did not equal this sum.[9] Revenues from emigrants in the period 1992–96 brought into Albania approximately USD 1.6 billion.

The ratio of accumulated foreign direct investment to GDP in 1994 was 8 per cent, which was still low compared to other Central European countries, such as Hungary (20 per cent) and the Czech Republic (12 per cent), or, in the EU, to Britain (20 per cent), France (11 per cent), Greece (23 per cent), or, in Asia, to Malaysia (47 per cent) and Singapore (97 per cent).

8. Hungary had reached USD 671 per capita in 1994.
9. As emphasised by Mr Don N. De Marino, Director of the Anglo-Adriatic Investment Fund. See *Albanian Observer*, Vol. 2, No. 12 (1996), p. 30.

Table 9.1 *Direct Foreign Investment, 1991–96 (million USD)*

	1991	1992	1993	1994	1995	1996
FDI per year	10	20	58	52	70	90
Cumulative FDI	10	30	88	140	210	300
Per capita FDI	3	10	28	44	65	85

Source: INSTAT.

We also tried to assess the extent of enterprises with foreign capital in our enterprise survey. From our sample of 1,005 enterprises in all regions of Albania, we found that only 80 enterprises—or 8 per cent—had foreign participation.

Among the factors that limited foreign investment, the lack of infrastructure was often reported by foreign investors. Political instability and overall country risk also remained important discouraging factors. Bureaucratic obstacles were often mentioned, particularly during business registration and at customs offices.

Low Level of Foreign Involvement

According to the Institute of Statistics, at the end of 1995 there were 1,532 joint ventures and 890 wholly foreign-owned companies in Albania. Most of them were very small companies with few employees: only 8.3 per cent involved more than ten people. The total number of employed was 19,000, and the average value of direct foreign investment for each project was about USD 87,000, well below the average in Central and Eastern Europe (approximately USD 260,000).[10] There was little direct foreign investment of more than USD 1 million in the productive sector.[11] While this small average size might have helped to revitalise the small-industry sector, it has had no impact on the strategic industries or the physical infrastructure of the country.

In our enterprise survey, we concentrated on larger enterprises with more than ten employees in industry and with more than five employees in services and banks. All enterprises with foreign capital were joint ventures; there were

10. This is even more remote from the average in developed countries, set by some experts at around USD 4 million. See I. Gedeshi in *Albanian Observer*, Vol. 3, No. 6 (1997), pp. 32–3.

11. Investments from well-known large Western multinational companies have so far been much rarer than in other Central and Eastern European countries, such as Hungary and the Czech Republic.

Table 9.2 *Number of Joint Ventures and Foreign Companies, by Level of Employment, End of 1995*

Number of employees	Joint ventures	Foreign companies
1 employee	553	463
2–4 employees	742	330
5–9 employees	97	35
10 employees and more	140	62
Total	1 532	890

Source: INSTAT.

no cases of wholly foreign-owned enterprises. A great difference was found between industry, where the average size of enterprises with foreign capital was 166 employees, and services and banks, where the average size was much smaller, at 27 employees. There were no great differences in size between enterprises with majority and with minority foreign capital, with the exception of services, where joint ventures with majority foreign capital were found to be much smaller. In general, joint ventures were found to be larger than the national average in industry and much smaller in services and banks.

Table 9.3 *Average Size of Enterprises with Foreign Capital, by Sector, Sept. 1996*

	Total joint ventures	*with majority foreign capital*	*with minority foreign capital*	National average
All	136	142	126	87
Industry	166	170	161	157
Services	27	13	30	54
Banks	27	27	–	44

Source: ALFS2.

Mainly Partnerships with Albanians

Wholly foreign-owned capital is to be found in much smaller enterprises. Their limited total number, however—fewer than 900 compared to more than 1,500 joint ventures—is also characteristic of foreign investment in Albania. This configuration was the direct result of the specific economic and political conditions prevailing in the country. In terms of ownership control, foreign investors could choose between three forms of foreign involvement: (i) direct acquisition of a state-owned company in the course of privatisation; (ii) creation of a joint venture in association with either private or state capital; and (iii) establishment of a totally new enterprise. These three forms of foreign involvement have co-existed in Albania. The first form ensures full or majority control of the assets and management of the enterprise; at the same time, it can entail high restructuring costs for the foreign investor, in terms of reducing excess labour, training workers, appointing new managers, setting up new production lines and objectives, improving distribution systems, and coming to terms with the enterprise's industrial relations and "social" inheritance, including working conditions and trade unions. This option was generally taken by large foreign companies with international experience in restructuring; they tended to choose enterprises that were already well established. In March 1997, for instance, the French company Ciment Français in the course of privatisation purchased a 70 per cent share in the cement factory and limestone quarry in Elbasan.

The establishment of new enterprises is privileged when the cost of restructuring in existing state-owned enterprises is too high—in terms of employment reductions and replacement of outdated equipment—or when the foreign investor prefers an immediate transfer of technology and the setting up of new buildings in a specific location. This was the case, for example, with Coca-Cola and with brand new hotels, such as EuropaPark in Tirana. It is also the option generally chosen by small operators: for instance, some 592 new foreign companies—66 per cent of the total—operated in trade (*Figure 9.2*).

The main preference of foreign investors, however, seems to have been the second form, association with a local partner. Initially, the strategy of foreign capital in Albania has been to establish commercial contracts with local partners, with simple forms of co-operation (production by order, co-production, and so on) that, when successful, have led to the creation of joint ventures. The prevalence of this involvement has also been determined by economic insecurity, which has discouraged the establishment of new enterprises, and the slow pace of privatisation, which has hindered many investment plans. Until the end of 1993, 70 per cent of foreign investment operations took the form of joint ventures with state-owned enterprises. By the end of 1995, this percentage had fallen to less than 63 per cent, after the Government decided to privatise state shares in joint ventures; these were then purchased by several of the foreign partners involved with a view to obtaining majority or full control.

In our enterprise survey at the end of 1996, we found that the great majority of foreign investors (75 per cent) had obtained majority capital, the all-enterprise average being 55.6 per cent, with higher participation in industry and banks, and lower in services. However, it is important to note that, with the exception of the two banks, most enterprises reported that they were not planning any increase in the share of foreign capital. This means that the foreign investor who has already obtained majority control with more than 50 per cent of the shares does not want to invest more capital, preferring to limit his participation. This is another indication of the rather limited involvement of foreign partners.

Table 9.4 *Share of Foreign Capital in Joint Ventures, by Sector, Sept. 1996*

	Enterprises with majority foreign capital (%)	Enterprises with minority foreign capital (%)	Average share of foreign capital	Percentage enterprises planning to increase this share
All sectors	75	25	55.6	2.3
Industry	77	23	58.0	3.2
Services	65	35	46.0	0
Banks	100	0	60.0	15.0

Source: ALFS2.

The main aim of foreign investors was to obtain majority control rather than full ownership. We will see later—on the basis of our enterprise survey— whether enterprises with majority foreign ownership reacted differently in terms of restructuring (lay-offs, training, changes in work organisation) compared to local enterprises or enterprises with minority foreign participation.

3 A LIMITED NUMBER OF PARTNERS

If we turn to the matter of country of origin, we find that 50 per cent of enterprises with foreign participation in early 1996 had been set up with capital from Italy, 20 per cent from Greece, and 17 per cent from Germany, the remaining 13 per cent being made up of a range of other countries, mainly Austria, Switzerland, Turkey, Croatia, Slovenia, and the USA.[12] The fact that more than 70 per cent of foreign firms or joint ventures are Italian or Greek indicates that foreign direct investment in Albania at present depends largely upon geographical proximity, a foreign investment situation quite different to that in the rest of Central and Eastern Europe.

12. Turkish investments include the operations of the Turkish construction company Gintas Alb Konstruksion in Tirana (see *Albanian Observer*, Vol. 2, No. 12, pp. 20-21); for Germany, (*cont.*)

The Italian capital that accounts for the lion's share of investment in Albania is mainly concentrated in the western areas of Albania, particularly in the cities of Tirana, Durres, Elbasan, Lushnia, Shkodra and Vlora. According to

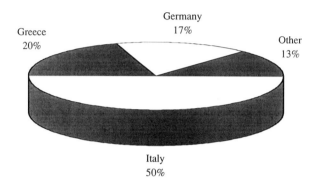

Figure 9.1 *Foreign Direct Investment, by Country of Origin, 1996 (%)*

Source: INSTAT.

the Centre for Foreign Investment Promotion, 21 per cent belongs to light industry, mainly textiles and shoe-making, 8 per cent to the agri-food industry, 35 per cent to construction, and more than 16 per cent to trade and services.

According to the Italian Economic Centre, at the end of 1996, Italian investors had invested more than USD 110 million. Most investors came from Southern Italy, from Puglia: according to the Centre, these businessmen were able to make greater profits and more quickly in Albania than at home. As explained by L. Fabbri, President of the Association of Italian Entrepreneurs in Albania, "they are motivated to invest in Albania because the average wage is equivalent to LIT 150,000 and they would have to pay for the same job in Italy up to LIT 1.5 to 2 million, that is ten times more".[13] They were attracted not only by low labour costs but by the relatively sizeable Albanian market:[14] in fact, most of the Southern Italian investors seemed to owe their survival mainly to their Albanian investments.

we may note the plans of Siemens and investments already made by Mercedes-Benz (*Albanian Observer*, Vol. 2, No. 12, pp. 21, 25–26) or by UMB-Agro Deutschland in agribusiness (*Albanian Observer*, Vol. 2, No. 10, p. 29). There was also US investment at the end of 1996, from the company Elba; see *Albanian Observer*, Vol. 3, No. 1 (1997), p. 27.

13. See *Albanian Observer*, Vol. 3, No. 2 (1997), p. 25.

14. According to the President of Bari's industrialists, interviewed by the BBC's Albanian Service. See *Albanian Observer*, Vol. 3, No. 1 (1997), p. 26.

However, the Centre also underlined that more than one-third of Italian businessmen were only attracted by quick profits and did not intend to establish stable economic activities.[15]

The Greek foreign direct investments are concentrated mainly in the southern and south-eastern part of the country, in the cities of Korca (26.4 per cent), Gjirokastra (16.1 per cent), and in the two cities in the region of Vlora, Delvina (4.6 per cent), and Saranda (22.9 per cent). These areas are close to the Greek border and are therefore used as an area of commercial trade between the two countries. These cities also concentrate the Greek minority and so have strong traditional economic and cultural links with their neighbour. It should be noted that the Greek foreign direct investment is directly subsidised by the Greek Government.[16] In 1994, 64 per cent of the 100 enterprises with Greek capital in Albania had benefited from grants from the Greek Government. Another characteristic of Greek investment is that 93 per cent involves new enterprises; only 3 to 7 per cent comprises privatised enterprises. It is mainly concentrated in trade, with annual profits of up to USD 48 million.[17] They are completely lacking in industry, however: only a few Greek companies (representing 1.3 per cent of Greek investors in Albania) operate in light industry (textiles, garments, leather), agri-food, and tobacco processing.

In total, Albania concentrates 25 per cent of all Greek investments abroad.[18] Early in 1996, the National Bank of Greece and a number of other Greek banks were licensed to open branches in Tirana. Nevertheless, by early 1997, there were still no large Greek companies in Albania.[19]

4 A NARROW RANGE OF SECTORS

Foreign investment has been concentrated in a very limited number of sectors. More than 65 per cent of enterprises with foreign investment up until 1996 were in trade, with less than 20 per cent in industry, and only 6 per cent in other services, particularly tourism (hotels and restaurants).

The very small percentage of foreign enterprises in agriculture is also worthy of note. Although many were created in 1992–94, most went

---

15. As reported in *Albanian Observer*, Vol. 3, No. 1 (1997), p. 26.

16. Subsidies of 35 per cent are provided by the Greek Government for amounts over 35 million drachma, according to the Law on Greek Development and Investments.

17. See "Greece 'attacking Albania'", *Albanian Observer*, Vol. 2, No. 10 (1996), p. 10.

18. Other privileged countries for Greeks to invest in are Bulgaria and Romania, with respectively 10 and 2.6 per cent of Greek investments.

19. See R. Goro, "Greek investment good but could be better . . .", *Albanian Observer*, Vol. 2, No. 12 (1996), p. 37.

bankrupt. Foreign partners in this sector were not appropriately selected: most did not bring the necessary new production technology and capital.[20] Only those who invested in processing agricultural products managed to survive, mainly in Durres, Kavaja, and Lezha. Moreover, the very small farms (one hectare on average) turned out to be a major obstacle to foreign investment, particularly in respect of land privatisation, so undermining the future of Albanian agriculture.

Table 9.5 *Distribution of Enterprises with Foreign Capital, by Sector, 1996*

	Joint ventures	Foreign companies	Total ent. with for. cap.	Domestic enterprises	Total	Enterprises with foreign capital/total
Agriculture	26	7	33	283	316	10 per cent
Industry	292	123	415	1 394	1 809	23 per cent
Construction	71	53	124	961	1 085	11 per cent
Trade	1 002	592	1 594	3 655	5 249	30 per cent
Transport	64	48	112	280	392	29 per cent
Services	77	67	144	505	649	22 per cent
Total	1 532	890	2 422	7 078	9 500	25 per cent

Source: INSTAT.

As far as foreign investment flows are concerned, the distribution was different, with tourism in first place with 34 per cent of foreign direct investment—in which large amounts are invested per project—then light industry (20 per cent), agri-food (18 per cent), construction (15 per cent), and transport (6 per cent). These four sectors concentrated more than 80 per cent of foreign capital flows in Albania. The relatively low amounts in trade render this sector marginal in terms of foreign investment flows, despite the large number of very small enterprises involved.

20. As reported by Mr Ismail Beka, Director of Programmes at the Ministry of Agriculture and Food, *Albanian Observer*, Vol. 2, No. 11 (1996), p. 30.

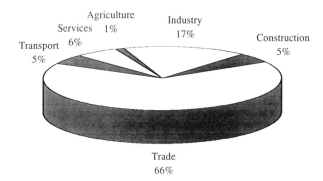

Figure 9.2 *Distribution of Enterprises with Foreign Investment, by Sector, 1996*

Source: INSTAT.

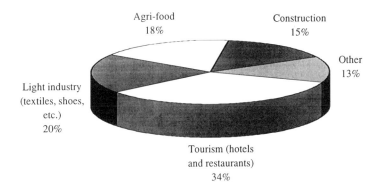

Figure 9.3 *Distribution of Foreign Direct Investment, by Sector, 1996*

Source: INSTAT.

Our enterprise survey confirmed the concentration of foreign capital in a limited number of sectors. From our sample of 1,005 enterprises, 80 had some foreign capital: 62 were in industry, 16 in services, and 2 in banking. Within industry, more than 31 per cent were operating in textiles and clothing, 18 per cent in food, 15 per cent in leather and shoes, 13 per cent in wood and paper, and 11 per cent in minerals (*Table 9.6*). In services, 79 per cent were in trade and 14 per cent in hotels and restaurants (*Table 9.7*).

Table 9.6 *Distribution of Enterprises with Foreign Capital, by Industry, Sept. 1996*

	All enterprises with foreign capital	with majority foreign capital	with minority foreign capital	With no foreign capital
Food	18.0	17.0	21.4	23.8
Chemicals	1.6	2.1	0.0	4.8
Leather & shoes	14.8	14.9	14.3	2.4
Mining	6.6	6.4	7.1	13.8
Minerals	11.5	8.5	21.4	12.1
Textiles & clothing	31.1	36.2	14.3	16.9
Metals	0.0	0.0	0.0	4.8
Wood & paper	13.1	10.6	21.4	13.4
Other	3.3	4.3	0.0	7.9
Total	100%	100%	100%	100%

Source: ALFS2.

Table 9.7 *Distribution of Enterprises with Foreign Capital, by Service, Sept. 1996*

	All enterprises with foreign capital	with majority foreign capital	with minority foreign capital	With no foreign capital
Gas/water/electricity	0.0	0.0	0.0	14.9
Trade	78.6	77.8	80.0	24.2
Hotels/restaurants	14.3	11.1	20.0	16.0
Transport	0.0	0.0	0.0	9.8
Telecoms	0.0	0.0	0.0	6.2
Security	0.0	0.0	0.0	14.6
Other	7.1	11.1	0.0	14.2
Total	100%	100%	100%	100%

Source: ALFS2.

5 CONCENTRATION IN A FEW REGIONS

Over 90 per cent of foreign enterprises and joint ventures are located in the western cities of Tirana, Durres, and Shkodra (more than 60 per cent of them in the Durres–Tirana corridor) and in the south-eastern part of the country, in the cities of Vlora, Gjirokastra, Korca, and Saranda. This coincides with the geographical proximity of Italy and Greece: Vlora, Saranda, and Durres, for instance, concentrate Italian investment, and Gjirokastra Greek. Tirana is in first place in terms of both number of enterprises with foreign capital (70 per cent) and foreign investment flows (60 per cent of invested capital).

This regional concentration has created a number of problems, mainly by enlarging the already existing regional differentials, in terms of wages, employment, economic development, and social indicators. There seems to have been a lack of regional policy aimed at attracting foreign investment to less developed areas.

Survey results at the end of 1996 confirmed this regional distribution. In industry Korca was found to have the greatest number of joint ventures, followed by Tirana and Durres (concentrating 30 per cent between them), and also Shkodra, Fier, Vlora, and Elbasan. Joint ventures in services were even less dispersed, with 57 per cent of them concentrated in Tirana, and 14 per cent in Durres. All joint ventures in banks were located in Tirana.

Table 9.8 *Percentage of Enterprises with Foreign Capital, by Region, Sept. 1996, All Sectors*

	Industry	Services	Banks	All
Berat	1.6	0.0	0.0	1.3
Dibra	0.0	0.0	0.0	0.0
Durres	14.8	14.3	0.0	14.3
Elbasan	8.2	0.0	0.0	6.5
Fier	11.5	7.1	0.0	10.4
Gjirokastra	4.9	7.1	0.0	5.2
Korca	18.0	7.1	0.0	15.6
Kukes	0.0	7.1	0.0	1.3
Lezha	3.3	0.0	0.0	2.6
Shkodra	13.1	0.0	0.0	10.4
Tirana	14.8	57.1	100.0	24.7
Vlora	9.8	0.0	0.0	7.8
Total	100.0	100.0	100.0	100.0

Source: ALFS2.

6 INVESTMENT MAINLY EXPORT-ORIENTED

On the basis of the list of enterprises and our enterprise surveys, foreign investors can be classified in terms of four main categories: (i) companies which import raw materials from the home country and then re-export products at different stages of processing; (ii) companies which use local raw materials and export the product; this happens in wood but mainly in the agri-alimentary sector; (iii) companies which produce for the Albanian market generally using local raw materials; (iv) individual and handicraft micro-companies operating in the commercial sector.

The majority of foreign investors were found in the first two categories. In enterprises in the first category, the production process is very labour-intensive, and is located in Albania mainly for the very low labour costs; all raw materials are generally imported, and then processed in Albania, before the totality of the production is sent back to the home country, where it is sold at local prices. We visited, for instance, an Italian clothing company in Vlora, where all the fabrics were imported from Italy, and very simple clothes were made by 50 Albanian women before being exported by boat to Italy. The technology was not sophisticated and the pace of work was relentless. There was no unionisation. Most enterprises in the second category process natural agricultural or sea food. A few Italian investors, for instance, specialise in lobsters for the Italian market. Several other joint ventures process agricultural products. Industrial enterprises with foreign capital producing for the local market are much rarer. This was confirmed by our enterprise survey results, which helped systematically to identify differences in economic performance between enterprises with foreign capital and those without.

As shown in *Table 9.9*, enterprises with foreign capital were found to perform better. In 1995–96, nearly 2 in 3 were found to be profitable and even to have registered an increase in profitability (compared to 1 firm in 2 in the case of enterprises without foreign capital). Even in industry they were functioning, on average, at 74 per cent of their production capacity, that is, above the national average for industry of 66 per cent. Productivity rates were also higher, a result which may, however, be due to the higher rate of dismissals in foreign companies. The widest gap was observed in respect of exports: in 1996 in industry, enterprises with foreign capital exported 52 per cent of their production as against a national average of 13 per cent. Several differences were also observed between enterprises with majority and minority foreign ownership: the first were much more export-oriented, with 60 per cent of their production sent to external markets; they were consequently working at higher production capacity and also registered better profitability and productivity. It should be noted, however, that the majority of enterprises with foreign capital working in services registered a fall in profits and productivity in 1996, a crisis that seems to have affected all types of foreign enterprise.

Table 9.9 *Economic Results, by Type of Enterprise with Foreign Capital, by Sector, 1995–96*

	All joint ventures				with majority capital				with minority capital				Firms with no foreign capital				Nat. Av.
	Ind.	Serv.	Banks	All	Ind.	Serv.	Banks	All	Ind.	Serv.	Banks	All	Ind.	Serv.	Banks	All	
Percentage of production capacity	74	78	100	74	78	80	100	77	57	78	–	62	66	82	94	78	78
Percentage of production exported	52	4	0	39	61	7	0	43	30	0	–	30	13	4	0	12	15
Profitable in 1996	59	–	–	58	60	–	–	60	54	–	–	50	63	46	–	60	60
Increased profits 1995–96	64	44	38	63	64	43	38	62	64	40	–	58	48	46	36	47	47
Change in productivity 1995–96	+0.93	–0.19	0	+0.68	+1.24	–0.63	0	+0.92	+0.03	–0.16	–	–0.02	–0.6	–1.8	–3.6	–1.6	–1.4
Productivity in 1996	5.8	2.5	0	5.0	7.6	2.1	0	6.5	0.2	1.3	–	0.5	1.5	–0.98	–8.2	–0.8	–0.4
Change in profits 1995–96	–2.26	+0.18	0	–1.72	–2.96	+0.05	0	–2.4	–0.14	+0.49	–	+0.02	+0.03	+0.11	+0.012	+0.08	–0.07
Profitability 1996	0.20	0.36	0	0.23	0.19	0.3	0	0.20	0.26	0.61	–	0.35	0.26	0.45	0.024	0.36	0.35

Source: ALFS2.

183

7 RESTRUCTURING POLICY

We tried to identify the restructuring policies of enterprises with foreign capital, in terms not only of employment, but also work organisation and global restructuring. Managers had first to reply to several questions related to employment—for instance if they had dismissed part of their labour force, or put workers on unpaid or paid leave, or implemented internal transfers. The employer had also to indicate if he had carried out training activities, in three major forms: (i) initial training, (ii) retraining to improve job performance, and (iii) training to upgrade skills. We also investigated diversification of product ranges or services. Finally, the manager had to report whether he had carried out changes in work organisation—for instance, job rotation and increased workers' autonomy—and introduced new technology. *Table 9.10* provides a synoptic view of restructuring measures that have been implemented, by type of enterprise.

It appears that enterprises with foreign capital—especially those with minority foreign capital—did not implement more dismissals than other property forms. Instead, they resorted to internal transfers between units or different establishments within the company. They also seem to have preferred to place part of the labour force either on unpaid or partially paid leave, probably in order to avoid the administrative procedures of dismissal and to keep a reserve of workers in case business should suddenly pick up. This put a growing proportion of the labour force in a precarious situation, however, since they were not being paid wages—or only in part—but neither were they entitled to unemployment benefits, a phenomenon that induced most of them to start working in the black market. In terms of training, enterprises with foreign capital did not implement many initial courses, preferring to promote retraining for improving performance or upgrading. Training remained limited to less than 20 per cent of the labour force (higher than in other enterprises). It is mainly with regard to changes in work organisation, job rotation, and the introduction of new technology that the participation of a foreign partner appears to have been determinant (*Table 9.10*). The main change in work organisation reported by joint ventures was the introduction of a "just in time" system (in 33 per cent of them compared to 9 per cent in other enterprises), alongside an expansion of international activities (mentioned by 16 per cent of them, compared to only 8 per cent of purely Albanian enterprises), which confirms the export-oriented character of their production.

Table 9.10 *Restructuring Measures, by Type of Enterprise with Foreign Capital, 1995–96*

	Enterprises with foreign capital	*with majority foreign capital*	*with minority foreign capital*	Enterprises with no foreign capital	National average
Percentage of dismissals	11.8	13.4	7.5	9.9	10.1
Increased unpaid leave	10.0	12.5	0	7.9	8.3
Increased paid leave	8.7	5.6	2.5	4.7	5.1
Percentage of labour force on unpaid leave	21.0	24.0	0	3.6	6.4
Transferred workers to other units or establishments	26.1	22.2	50.0	18.7	19.5
Diversified products/services	55.0	60.3	42.1	38.8	40.1
Initial training	35.0	34.5	36.8	57.4	55.7
Retraining to improve job performance	38.5	37.5	42.1	22.4	23.6
Training to upgrade	36.7	36.2	38.9	19.3	20.7
Percentage of labour force trained	18.7	19.6	18.7	11.3	12.0
Introduced job rotation	31.6	32.8	26.3	24.8	25.3
Increased workers' independence	16.1	12.0	20.0	18.5	17.9
Introduced change in work organisation	40.8	44.6	27.8	26.2	27.4
Introduced new technology	51.3	55.2	42.1	28.6	30.5

Source: ALFS2.

8 THE SOCIAL DEFICIT

The enterprise survey also came up with interesting results with regard to the social policy of enterprises with foreign capital. While they were found to pay higher wages than the national average, and also higher basic payments for the lowest categories of worker, joint ventures were found to perform extremely poorly in terms of social dialogue. Trade unions were not recognised in any of the service enterprises with majority foreign capital, nor in any of the foreign banks. Collective agreements were not signed in more than 80 per cent of service enterprises. Only industrial enterprises maintained dialogue with trade unions, probably because of strong unionisation in previously state-owned enterprises that had become joint ventures, and also because of fears of strikes interrupting production.

Workers' participation in decision-making was also less widespread among joint ventures, and when it was practised, it took the form of informal involvement in the workplace rather than the formal presence of workers' representatives on the board of directors. Participation in enterprise results through profit-sharing systems was also less developed in joint ventures.

Table 9.11 Social Indicators in Enterprises with Foreign Capital, by Sector, 1995–96

	All joint ventures				with majority capital				with minority capital				Firms with no foreign capital				Nat. ave.
	Ind.	Serv.	Banks	All	Ind.	Serv.	Banks	All	Ind.	Serv.	Banks	All	Ind.	Serv.	Banks	All	
Recognised unions	51	12	0	42	52	0	0	41	50	20	–	42	55	36	24	41	41
Unionisation	47	8	0	38	48	0	0	39	41	9	–	32	49	33	21	37	37
Signed collective agreement	41	18	0	38	40	20	0	33	43	11	–	42	52	55	36	53	51
Informed workers regularly about results	53	53	50	53	53	44	50	52	50	60	–	53	66	61	100	65	64
Level of participation																	
Board	42	33	50	41	40	25	50	39	56	50	–	54	46	44	54	45	45
Workplace	52	67	50	54	53	75	50	56	44	50	–	46	49	53	46	51	51
Introduced profit-sharing	1.7	6.3	0	2.6	2.2	11.1	0	3.5	0	0	–	0	11.0	8.7	20.0	10.4	9.8
Plans to introduce profit-sharing	3.5	7.1	0	4.2	0	14.3	0	1.9	16.7	0	–	11.8	9.1	8.6	8.8	8.8	8.4
Sold/distributed shares to employees	0	0	0	0	0	0	0	0	0	0	–	0	2.5	0.6	1.8	1.3	1.2
Plans to sell/distribute shares to employees	0	6.7	0	1.3	0	12.5	0	1.9	0	0	–	0	2.6	1.0	7.7	1.9	1.9
Ave. wage*	9 831	12 398	18 843	11 934	10 401	11 677	18 845	12 781	8 080	12 138	–	9 148	7 466	8 511	19 039	9 030	9 244
Min. wage*	6 367	8 167	13 000	6 893	6 499	8 253	13 000	6 995	5 775	7 840	–	6 311	5 570	5 786	7 746	5 880	5 950
Difficulty in paying wages	14.5	6.3	0	12.5	15.0	0	0	12.1	14.0	0	–	15.8	14.3	12.4	1.3	12.1	12.2
Strikes in last two years																	
none	88.7	100	100	91.0	87.7	100	100	89.5	92.9	100	–	94.7	93.0	94.0	100	94.1	94.0
1–3	11.3	0	0	9.0	12.8	0	0	10.5	7.1	0	–	5.3	7.0	6.0	0	5.9	6.0

* Leks.

Source: ALFS2.

186

We should add that foreign companies not only did not sign many collective agreements, but in many cases were found not to issue individual labour contracts. This is why many Italian companies came into conflict with their employees. Filanto, a joint venture with the former state-owned shoe-making company of Tirana, was closed down for nearly one year by a strike organised by workers' representatives because of work contracts and working conditions. The company Italduri in Elbasan was also blocked for several months for the same reasons: the problems between its leaders and the trade unions ended up in court. Paradoxically, this enterprise, employing 600 people and with an investment of USD 9 million, was found to have the most up-to-date equipment and technology.[21]

While not developing much social dialogue at the enterprise level, foreign investors tried to organise themselves in national associations in order to enhance their presence in the social dialogue taking place at the national level. In December 1995, for instance, Italian businessmen created an association aimed at improving dialogue with the Government. At the end of 1996, they asked (without success) to be represented on the newly created tripartite national council. A similar association of Greek investors was also established.

9 PROBLEMATIC JOINT VENTURES

Misbehaviour on the Part of Foreign Investors

A number of irregularities and instances of corruption were also observed on the part of foreign investors. The Government was partly responsible for this, because it failed to select foreign partners on the basis of technical criteria, preferring spontaneity and subjectivity. This happened mainly in strategic sectors such as copper. In many cases, errors were made, including overestimation of the foreign partner's contributions in kind and absence of control of the enterprise's economic and financial results. This was the case with the privatisation of the copper corporation Albbakri. The two Italian partners disappeared after having signed an agreement to form a joint venture

---

21. The Italian press has also reported cases of misbehaviour on the part of their small entrepreneurs in Albania. *La Stampa* (2 October 1996) depicted the working conditions in Italian-owned factories; it reports one entrepreneur from Albaco Shoes as saying: "It took some effort to get them used to sitting still for seven hours . . . But now their productivity has reached 80 per cent of that of Italian women workers, at £12 a week net." A few days after these interviews were published, these same workers organised a 48-hour strike. Production was brought to a standstill and the Italian bosses suddenly felt less secure. They could feel the hostility of the local population. As a result, some of the Italian staff employed at the factory asked to be moved elsewhere (Wood, 1997).

with the Albanian Government. False privatisation of this kind seriously impeded the copper industry in Albania for more than three years. The Government had to annul the privatisation after a lengthy procedure.[22]

Bankruptcies

Many joint ventures had to be declared bankrupt after only a few months. This happened on a large scale in joint enterprises in agriculture and food. Of the 27 joint ventures that were created up to early 1997, only 13 remained in business: 4 out of 15 enterprises in agriculture and fishing, and 9 out of 12 in food. The others did not close but registered heavy losses. Ministry of Agriculture experts reported that all fishing joint ventures had registered losses, estimated at USD 10 million. Similar losses were recorded in joint ventures in food, estimated at USD 6 million. The Coca-Cola Company was also mentioned as having accumulated losses.

This led the Ministry of Agriculture to sound the alarm early in 1997 and to propose the privatisation of the most problematic joint enterprises. The dissolution of some of these enterprises has been accompanied by court proceedings, however, sometimes even extending to the international courts. In most cases, the foreign partner was unwilling to acknowledge the decision of the Albanian court to declare the co-operation contract void, and took legal action through the international courts.[23] The Albanian state risks losing millions of dollars from these "divorces" involving foreign partners.

Similarly, the two joint venture banks—both involving Albania's National Commercial Bank, the two partners being the Italian Banca di Roma (established in 1993) and the Arab–Albanian Islamic bank (established one year later)—have registered very unsuccessful results for three successive years (1994–96). No profits have been generated yet. These two institutions were created with the intention of attracting foreign investment to Albania and to augment banking services. The reported figures clearly show that these attempted marriages of Albanian and foreign capital have failed so far.

22. See G. Pilika, "Privatisation only on paper", *Albanian Observer*, Vol. 3, No. 2 (1997), p. 36.

23. This seems to have happened, for instance, with the joint ventures Alb-Italia, Tale-Lezha, Hamallaj, Rrushkull, Spitalle, Fruit Enterprise Durres, Fruit Enterprise Kavaja, Sheep, Mussels Preservation Saranda, and many others. See "Joint companies in crisis and bankruptcy: $16 million losses", *Albanian Observer*, Vol. 3, No. 7–8 (1997), p. 25.

10 CONCLUSION

There is no doubt that, since the beginning of the transition, Albania has managed to attract foreign investment, so ending its long period of isolation. This was a major achievement for the Albanian economy: enterprises with foreign capital were found to out-perform their rivals in terms of profitability, productivity, and access to external markets. They were also found to introduce new technologies and new expertise into production and marketing.

At the same time, direct investment flows seem to have remained well below official expectations despite very favourable legislative provisions and a variety of attractive incentives. They also remained well below what the Albanian economy would have needed to revive its economy and to help it integrate in international markets. Foreign investment has also been much too concentrated in a limited number of sectors and regions. In particular, productive industries other than textiles and shoes—and services other than trade—have yet to benefit. Poorly developed regions have also been excluded from this process, which was supposed to benefit the whole economy but has instead enlarged the gap between the few privileged cities and the less developed parts of the country.

Foreign capital has remained too limited to investment on the basis of geographical proximity, and too often motivated by quick profits generated by labour-cost differentials: the benefits of long-term comparative advantage and development have so far not figured in the plans of foreign investors. This strategic policy was reflected in the basic orientation of foreign investors towards exports, and their poor contribution to the development of the local market.

At the end of 1996, a clear gap was visible between the strategy that Albanians would have liked foreign investors to pursue, and the one that most of them in fact followed. This gap was reflected in the growing number of joint ventures going bankrupt, mainly in the service sector, and of those against which the state was pursuing reprivatisation, risking long trials before international courts. The gap was further reflected in the uncongenial social climate prevailing in joint ventures, where trade unions were only rarely recognised, and the conclusion of collective agreements regularly avoided. The absence of individual labour contracts also led to a series of strikes and legal conflicts with the workers.

No doubt the Government was also partly responsible for this, with its poorly worked-out industrial policy, insufficient public funds dedicated to infrastructure, and lack of clear guidelines for the localisation of foreign companies and closer monitoring of their strategic motivations. The developments described in previous chapters may also have contributed to limit foreign investment and to concentrate it in a small number of sectors.

The total collapse of industry and the state's withdrawal from any form of industrial development must have discouraged many foreign investors from seeking to operate in that sector. The absence of a secure banking system also served to obstruct better circulation of capital flows. At the same time, the fall in real wages and erosion of purchasing power led to very low levels of domestic consumption, and reduced the potentialities of the domestic consumer market. This combination of low wages and poor market prospects seems to have attracted a particular type of foreign investor, eager to take advantage of a very low-paid labour force and to export at considerable profit. A different pattern of social development, with an increase in real wages and living standards, would probably have attracted a different type of investor, willing to produce for a stronger local consumer market, and looking for a more stable and long-term involvement in the country. Finally, the failure of voucher privatisation limited the involvement of foreign investors in privatised enterprises. The decision to involve foreign operators in this process at a later stage did not cause them to overcome their initial reluctance to be associated with this form of privatisation, although a few that did get involved were able to realise high profits.

To summarise, despite the Government's great expectations, foreign investment was not able to ameliorate the serious economic crisis in Albania. This led some experts to question the prioritisation of foreign investment by successive governments. The failure of a number of joint ventures seemed to justify this view, overshadowing others who were making a more positive contribution to Albania's development into a strong and open market economy. The 1997 crisis drew an even more marked line of demarcation between these two types of foreign investment.

10. The Collapse of the Albanian Pyramid

"The pyramid is the pillar that holds power aloft. If it wavers, everything collapses."

Ismail Kadare, *The Pyramid* (1992; English translation 1996: p. 8)

1 INTRODUCTION

The failure of the banking system to act as a proper financial intermediary and severe restrictions on credit policy led to the growth of the informal financial market (Chapter 4). While there was urgent demand for credit from new businesses in the private sector, emigrants had considerable financial resources at their disposal. The informal sector started up in order to establish the financial market which the banking sector had singularly failed to provide.

A number of companies decided to meet their financial needs by drawing on personal savings, offering interest rates higher than those in the banking system. As the Government continued to delay banking reform, pyramid schemes flourished throughout Albania.

The explosion of these lending activities, however, led to greater competition between the different funds, which had to increase their interest rates to keep their depositors. At the same time, institutions not based on any form of real economic activity also had to offer very high interest rates, taking the form of pyramid funds *tout court*, the deposits of the next person being used to pay the interest (and principal) on the deposits of the first: these schemes were clearly doomed to perish in bankruptcy. Such schemes normally collapse when the number of creditors at the base of the pyramid becomes so large that they cannot be repaid. However, most of the Albanian funds managed to survive for a number of years—more than five—due to a combination of political, economic, and social factors, as we shall see. Partly legitimated by political actors, partly hidden behind respectable economic activities, publicised by the local press, fed by emigrants, and ideal for money-laundering purposes, these schemes were able to attract colossal amounts of money until the end of 1996, when the first schemes started to go bankrupt, compelling the international monetary institutions and the Government finally to tackle the problem, the public authorities freezing the accounts of most of these companies. The ultimate collapse of the funds revealed the extent of the phenomenon, with deposits of more than USD 2 billion, and the participation of more than 75 per cent of Albanians. The funds operated throughout the transition period, and when they fell they suddenly revealed the true face of Albanian capitalism: for years the main pillar of Albania's economic miracle had been dubious pyramid funds. The fall of most economic indicators throughout 1996 were clear signs of the fragility of the economy and the forthcoming crisis. The pyramid schemes thus collapsed, and with them the Albanian success economy, the "Albanian pyramid".

The population lost all their savings almost overnight, representing the final straw that they were unable to bear. This led to the worst crisis post-communist Albania had had to face so far, plunging the country into violent protests and popular eruptions, regional rebellions, and finally chaos and violence. This provoked the fall of the Government, which was replaced by a temporary administration of national reconciliation. The depth of the crisis also required the intervention of a multinational military force (6,000 Italian-led troops), which remained to secure general elections in June 1997.

In this chapter we describe the history of this crisis, trying in particular to explain how these pyramid funds sank—and were allowed to sink—such deep roots in the Albanian economy, with an analysis of the political, economic, and social factors that generated their astounding growth.

2 THE COLLAPSE OF THE PYRAMID SCHEMES

At the beginning of the transition, informal credit came to be used mainly by private individuals in the wholesale trading of goods and in the service sector. Progressively, large companies managed to attract the major part of the population's savings, so concentrating the informal market in a few hands. Some—such as Vefa, Gjallica, and Kamberi—bought parts of enterprises, former state-owned assets that needed reconstruction. Others began to operate only as funds with borrowing and distribution operations, such as Sude, Populli and Xhaferri. Some were operating at the national level, with their headquarters in Tirana, such as Vefa and Gjallica. Others were regionally based, such as Populli and Xhaferri in Lushnia and Fier, and Kamberi and Cenaj in Vlora. All companies opened significant branches in Vlora and other cities in the south of Albania, which had the highest number of emigrants sending money to their families.[1]

---

1. See F. Moravia, "Vlora, capital of lending", *Albanian Observer*, Vol. 2, No. 9 (1996), p. 8.

How the System Survived for Five Years

The pyramid companies in Albania were considered to be the first Albanian capitalists. They were regarded as normal businesses borrowing money to raise capital and, eventually, to invest. Their borrowing activities had their legal basis in the Albanian civil code that considered a mutual agreement entered into by a borrower and a lender as quite acceptable.[2]

The proof of deposit was the receipt (or bill) given to the lender by the registered company. These receipts displayed the principal sum, the date of agreement, the period, and the interest rate with the final signatures of the lender and the cashier. The companies—though not the funds—legalised the contract through a lawyer. The companies also stated that they had mortgaged their property in case of non-fulfilment of the contract, although this was done only orally, and without mentioning the value of the property (see Muço, 1997). The interest rates offered by these companies quickly drew in an increasing number of people. Thousands of small kiosks with a cashier were opened all over the country to collect people's savings, money inflow and outflow being regulated from headquarters. Since the credibility of the whole system was essential to its survival, these funds ensured payment on time and in full. The apparent reliability of these investments, combined with very good interest rates, led to exponential growth in the number of depositors and the amounts deposited. During 1995 and early 1996, these pyramid schemes consolidated and grew. While some of them—those which were not based on any official economic activity or unofficial business—started to find it difficult to reimburse their depositors, other companies that had launched legal activities, or had access to money generated by illegal activities, became very powerful economic groups. Most regional funds expanded at the national level. By 1995, nearly every major city in the country had at least two such organisations operating in it.

These funds were able to survive, apart from their self-sustaining mode of functioning (earlier depositors being paid with the deposits of later ones), thanks to the existence of a range of revenue sources: remittances from emigrants, personal savings, revenues from private legal activities, and also—probably accounting for the major part—money laundering generated by criminal activities such as prostitution, the trafficking of illegal emigrants—mainly from Asia—across the Adriatic, and of drugs, weapons, and goods to break the Yugoslav embargo.[3] Geographical position and proximity to the Italian Mafia favoured such activities. At the cross-roads between the Islamic

---

2. This was often repeated by the pyramid companies and others to legitimise their activities (see Muço, 1997).

3. According to the Albanian economist Zef Preci, the Albanians—probably alongside the *(cont.)*

and the Western world, and between Western Europe and Central, Eastern, and South-Eastern Europe, the easy passage through Albania made it possible to pursue illegal trafficking into the heart of Europe.[4] The war in Yugoslavia and the prolonged embargo also favoured different forms of illegal traffic, especially fuel, passing from Greece or Turkey to the former Yugoslavia.

Most of these illegal activities were pursued—and most of the money they generated ended up—in the southern part of the country, cities such as Vlora becoming centres of the Albanian Mafia.[5]

The political support given to these funds, especially during the electoral campaign, and their presentation as success stories in the media helped to convince people of their reliability.

Market Saturation at the End of 1996

In summer 1996, after the elections, when for political reasons action against these funds seemed impossible and undesirable, a bitter struggle commenced among the pyramid schemes to attract depositors and to capture market share. They started to offer very high interest rates, 20 to 30 per cent a month, and shortened the repayment period—for instance from six or seven months to three. They also sought to attract more medium-sized and large deposits. This increased demand for capital met with a huge supply response: emigrants began to send more money to their families with the express purpose of investing in the schemes, hoping for immediate returns.

The virus seems to have quickly contaminated all types of people, including the best-educated strata, most people seemingly unable to think rationally any more. Many even sold their homes to increase their deposits, while others, on the basis of assumed future income, invested in new and larger ones.

According to observers, the capital inflow to each of these schemes increased from USD 500,000–600,000 per day in July to USD 3.5–4 million at the end of August.[6] The mass saving hysteria increased further in the

Italian Mafia—managed to earn USD 600,000 a day—one-fifth of total national income— smuggling petrol and diesel into Montenegro. He believes that up to USD 1.3 billion from those revenues was placed in the pyramid schemes. See *Albanian Observer*, Vol. 3, No. 5 (1997), p. 32.

4. In particular, immigrants from the Middle East (Egyptians, Kurds, and others) were found to reach Tirana Airport by plane (generally via Istanbul) before reaching the south-western port of Vlora, from where they embarked for the Italian coast. The average price of the trip was approximately USD 4,000. It is estimated that 400 people from the Middle East arrived at Rinas Airport every month. The bribe required to pass through the airport was approximately USD 400. See "Smugglers make millions from human cargo", *Albanian Observer*, Vol. 3, No. 11 (1997), p. 18.

5. See G. Pilika, "Vlora, like Palermo?", *Albanian Observer*, Vol. 2, No. 8 (1996), p. 8.

6. See A. Hoxha, "Why did it happen?", *Albanian Observer*, Vol. 3, No. 3–4 (1997), pp. 30–31.

following months, culminating at the end of autumn 1996. In October, it became evident that collapse was unavoidable and was coming closer and closer.

In October, the IMF insisted that the Albanian Government intervene, causing the Minister of Finance to call the attention of the media to the uncertainty and danger of the pyramid companies and funds. Meanwhile, the Government delayed taking legal steps. In November and December, the majority of schemes increasingly registered a negative daily net cash flow. In the course of the last quarter of 1996, the two funds Xhaferri and Populli increased their interest rates to 100 per cent per month on three-month deposits, while the Sude fund offered an interest rate of 50 per cent per month. Panic set in among the population and crowds gathered in front of the kiosks of the different schemes. In December, Sude failed to pay its creditors and several times could not meet the deadline of its contracts. In early January, it announced bankruptcy and, as a result of large-scale popular unrest, its proprietor was arrested and put in jail on 18 January.[7] The funds Populli and Xhaferri then collapsed. The first investment company, Gjallica, which had shown signs of difficulty at the end of the previous year, also announced bankruptcy.

In January 1997, the Bank of Albania restricted the daily withdrawals of funds and companies to a maximum of USD 300,000, a decision which was more motivated by fears of inflationary pressure due to massive capital movements rather than a real attempt to limit the activities of these funds, which nevertheless complained about such a restriction.

As the situation rapidly got out of control, the Parliament approved a law establishing a special investigative commission, charged with determining the source of these companies' capital and whether they were operating as "genuine" pyramid schemes or not.

In the middle of January, the government froze the current accounts—totalling USD 250 million—at state-owned banks of the two funds Xhaferri and Populli, which had accumulated 360,000 creditors. All the other funds simply stopped paying their creditors.

This action led to a massive wave of protests and popular unrest, with widespread demands for the resignation of the Government. It is important to note that many people remain convinced that most of the funds or companies would have reimbursed all their creditors if they had not been closed "prematurely". This is also the reason why the popular anger was oriented mainly towards the Government rather than towards the presidents of the

---

7. This scheme was operated by Maksude Kademi, a young gypsy woman who seems to have been one of the few people to be jailed for the financial disaster; see *Albanian Observer*, Vol. 3, No. 5 (1997), p. 32.

pyramid schemes.[8] The population could not understand why the Government, seemingly overnight, closed down schemes that they had allowed to operate for years.

The Estimated Extent of the Crisis

A few months after the outbreak of the crisis, the number of depositors was estimated at 400,000, which meant that at least half the families in Albania— but probably many more—had become involved in the pyramid schemes. The authorities also estimated the total net debt of the schemes towards their creditors at around USD 2 billion, that is, a sum equivalent to the annual national GDP.

Most of this money rapidly "disappeared" (often with the founders of the schemes), having probably been transferred abroad. The largest company was Vefa: in April 1997, the investigative commission appointed by the Parliament published a perfunctory report on its activities. Later on, the Parliament approved a law demanding transparent investigation into the economic activities of all five major pyramid companies.

4 POLITICAL LEGITIMATION: "NEGLIGENCE" OR "*LAISSEZ-FAIRE*"?

Political legitimacy seems to have played an important role in the progress of this financial disaster.

The Government did nothing to dissuade investors, nor did it thoroughly investigate the schemes. A number of explanations of this have been put forward. On the economic side, the influx of such large amounts of money seemed to boost the economy, and in some way compensated for the collapse of the industrial sector. The presentation of Albania as a success story was also highly expedient in the context of the 1996 election campaign. Moreover, the suspension of the pyramid schemes would have immediately provoked a rise in inflation and devaluation of the lek *vis-à-vis* stronger currencies such as the US dollar and the Deutschmark, as did in fact happen in spring 1997. On the political side, the Government was accused not only of negligence in connection with the schemes, but also of profiting from them. There have been allegations that no government action was taken because the ruling

---

8. Out of 1,492 people interviewed at the end of 1997 concerning who was responsible for pyramid scheme losses, nearly 60 per cent mentioned the Government, while less than 15 per cent blamed the owners of the schemes themselves. See UNDP, *Albanian Human Development Report 1998*. Seventy-eight per cent also reported that they themselves or someone they knew had lost money in the pyramid schemes.

Democratic Party received substantial funding from these schemes for its 1996 electoral campaign, as election posters featuring a photograph of Democratic Party leaders together with the logos of some of the largest pyramid companies—such as Vefa—can easily testify.[9] At the same time, the pyramid schemes Populli and Xhaferri (the first to be closed down by the Government) were said to be close to the Socialist Party.

The Government, with the help of the international monetary institutions, could have probably put a lid on the pyramid schemes with the requisite political will. In the event, a sort of "*laissez-faire*" policy or generalised "negligence" prevailed—interpreted by some analysts to indicate straightforward corruption and the pursuit of personal and party interests. A number of important measures were not taken by the Government at crucial junctures. Let us look at the most significant examples.

First, the Governor of the Central Bank could easily have banned the pyramid firms from collecting deposits, since the banking law clearly states that deposit collection is the monopoly of licensed banks—the pyramid companies were certainly not licensed. Alternatively, the banking system could have strictly monitored the activities of these funds. In 1992, the Albanian Parliament passed a banking law which appointed the Central Bank as supervisor of the commercial banks. The term "banks" should normally have included all enterprises engaged in banking activities, regardless of what they called themselves—for example, "fund". Moreover, Article 28 of the law provided that the Central Bank could impose particular tasks on commercial banks in consideration of their "environment", for example, in respect of their rates of interest and other duties. When a bank was deemed to be paying dangerously high rates of interest, the Central Bank, as supervisor of the commercial banks, was supposed to require that it establish a reserve fund at the Central Bank to safeguard its depositors. Such provisions could easily have been extended to cover pyramid schemes.

At the end of 1994, the opportunity came when a draft law on bankruptcy was also discussed in Parliament. It included a special article on banks which provided that they would have to establish deposit insurance funds supervised by the Central Bank. However, this clause was scrapped because the Government believed that normal bankruptcy procedures should not be applied to banks in order to avoid multiple cases of creditors of an insolvent bank demanding that it cease operations. As a result, the deposit insurance

9. Early in 1997, charges of campaign fund misuse were made against the Democratic Party by the Democratic Alliance. As the crisis intensified, DP Interministerial Committee Chairman Blerim Celia admitted that by 25 February 1997 the DP had indeed received at least USD 50,000 from the Vlora-based pyramid fund Gjallica. Other evidence was gathered which suggests close ties between members of the Democratic Party and the failed pyramid schemes.

scheme and the full application of the insolvency law to banks were left out
of the new Banking Law passed by the Parliament in February 1996, under
which only Central Bank supervision remained to safeguard depositors
against dishonest banks.

Finally, according to Central Bank Governor Kristaq Lukiku, in early 1996
a money-laundering law had been proposed by the Central Bank: as already
mentioned, most of these pyramid firms were fronts for shady criminal
enterprises. Nothing was done by the Government, however, and a general
attitude of forbearance predominated.[10]

When, in early October 1996, the World Bank and the IMF representatives
in Albania began to warn the Government of the likely outcome should the
pyramid schemes falter, their warnings were largely ignored.

The question remains whether the Government was aware of the potential
risks.[11] It is in this connection that the international monetary institutions had
a role to play.

It is important to note that the intervention of the IMF in October 1996 was
a decisive factor in obliging the Government to address the problem of
pyramid funds, and government action may be dated from this time, first in
the form of public announcements of the danger, followed by the freezing of
assets and closure. This intervention was not well received by the public and
the media, since it forced Albanians to face the harsh reality. A few months
later, in May 1997, the Albanian Government approved a new Law on the
Transparency of Pyramid Schemes. Moreover, the IMF obliged the
Government to close down all pyramid companies as a condition of
proceeding with the second ESAF agreement (concluded in May 1998 in the
amount of USD 47 million) for a period of three years.

Nevertheless, given the major influence of international monetary
institutions such as the IMF and the World Bank, we may question why they
decided to intervene decisively so late in the day, when it had already become
obvious that Albania was heading for financial ruin.[12] Many Albanian
analysts have been highly critical of this prevarication:

10. To some observers, other provisions—such as legally obliging pyramid companies to make
public their balance sheets—would also have been useful steps towards greater transparency,
although they could easily have been manipulated by the pyramid companies.

11. Inside the Democratic Party itself, many members clearly stated that, although the situation
was known to all, nobody took action. At the meeting of the National Council of the Democratic
Party on 18 January, Tomor Malasi, for example, clearly stated that "the Democratic Party lacks
ethics and we cannot continue like this anymore" (*Albanian Observer*, Vol. 3, No. 1 (1997), p. 5).
In fact, this meeting led to a split in the party, with many high-ranking political leaders—such as
former Deputy Prime Minister and Minister of Labour Shehi—distancing themselves from
President Berisha.

12. As indicated by the IMF: "By the end of 1996, it became clear that a collapse in this market
was imminent" (IMF, 1997b, p. 31).

The International Monetary Fund and other international financial institutions supported the reforms in 1992, signing agreements for credits and assistance. Money came, delegations as well, and statements such as "Albania is successfully conducting capitalist reforms" fell from everyone's lips. Suddenly everything was distorted and all the blame was placed at the doorstep of the pyramid investment schemes, forgetting that the IMF, the World Bank, and the diplomatic corps had witnessed it all. They all praised Albania and murmured silently about the pyramid schemes. (A. Gjata, *Albanian Observer*, February 1998)

It was only in September last year, when the Albanian pyramids had gobbled up all the Albanians' savings, amounting to about USD 1.2 billion, that IMF Director General Michel Camdessus wrote to President Berisha to warn him of the catastrophic consequences which had by then become inevitable. The pyramids had absorbed almost three-fourths of the country's money, obliterating any opportunities for serious investment. The IMF hoped that the country to which it had given so much publicity would control the situation, but it perhaps did not predict that Berisha had linked his political future to the moneylenders . . . At any rate, the IMF preferred not to speak out in public, for the sake of the zeal that Berisha and Meksi, the IMF's model pupils, had shown. ("IMF an Accomplice in Moneylending", *Koha Jone* [major Albanian daily newspaper], 29 January 1997)

Others insisted that the IMF had done nothing to put the protection of depositors at the core of the Albanian banking system. In particular, the new Banking Law of 1996 was prepared by the Central Bank with the direct assistance of the IMF, which could have insisted on retention of the deposit insurance scheme and the full application of the insolvency law to banks. The IMF's failure to do this may have been motivated by fears that the few Albanian banks would go under. More generally, the IMF was severely criticised for "not having used its influence to make the Central Bank carry out its supervisory duties and stop the pyramids in time".[13]

When the IMF finally asked President Berisha and his Government to act—in October 1996—it was far too late for any kind of soft landing.

---

13. As the World Bank representative in Tirana rightly stressed, "[a]fter all, the pyramids developed to the point [they did] because the regulatory and enforcement mechanisms were weak". *Albanian Observer*, Vol. 3, No. 2 (1997), p. 5.

5 ECONOMIC LEGITIMATION: THE MIRAGE OF BURGEONING WEALTH

The pyramid investment companies, for the purpose of giving small investors the impression that their money had been well invested and to increase their profits, became involved in a whole series of economic activities. They were chiefly oriented towards the most immediately profitable sectors, such as food and tourism. They also tried to get involved in the sectors potentially attractive to foreign investors, such as the exploitation of mining companies. They took advantage of the low price of state-owned enterprises sold in the privatisation process. They were more reluctant to take an interest in production in key industrial sectors (which would have been a more positive way of regenerating the Albanian economy). In 1996, the largest of them asked permission to open a private bank, an action intended to further reinforce its economic legitimacy.

Vefa Holding tried to present itself as a giant of the Albanian economy. It supplemented the pyramid schemes with investments in food factories, and built restaurants in tourist areas and a network of supermarkets. Vefa Holding also obtained exclusive dealerships from Fiat, Kia, Heineken, Ballantines, Baccardi, and many other well-known European brands. This image of successful entrepreneurship was supported by a large-scale publicity campaign, with posters plastered everywhere and announcements in every newspaper and magazine.[14] Vefa also started a private television channel and a modern printing house in Tirana.[15]

The President of Vefa Holding, Vhebi Alimucaj, rapidly became one of the richest men in Albania and was listed repeatedly as one of the most successful Albanian businessmen. At the end of 1996, a few months before the collapse, he was insisting that "the future of Vefa Holding is in the creation of a solid company which operates in many spheres and which influences the economic life of the country".[16] Alimucaj was also one of the country's representatives to NATO in Brussels. His company directly helped to fund the Democratic Party's campaign in the 1996 general elections.

The company Kamberi also tried to invest in meat processing and in tourism. In the mass privatisation process, the company bought the Llogara tourist complex—one of the most beautiful tourist areas in the country, 800 metres above the Ionian Sea—for USD 600,000. Its president and sole owner

14. For an example, see the announcement "Vefa Holding: Albanian Miracle", in the *Albanian Observer*, Vol. 3, No. 1 (1997), p. 11.
15. See "Nothing but capitalism", *Albanian Observer*, Vol. 2, No. 4 (1996), p. 34.
16. Interview in the *Albanian Observer*, Vol. 2, No. 2 (1996), pp. 38–9.

stated at the end of 1996: "We know the danger of this form of activity [borrowing through pyramid funds] and we try to accompany an increase in the money deposits with an increase in the invested capital."[17]

This accumulation of businesses enriched the presidents of these companies enormously, giving them wealth which they immediately converted into luxurious villas and sport cars, visible signs of burgeoning wealth and "successful" Albanian capitalism. In September 1996 one of the schemes (Gjallica) sponsored a "Miss Europe Contest", with the aim of putting Albania on the glamour map. Another pyramid company bought Brazilian and Nigerian players for its local football team and installed a former Argentinean international as the coach.[18]

After the scandal exploded, a government investigation was launched in 1997, with the help of a group of independent consultants. They shed more light on the activities of five of the companies suspected of being pyramid schemes (Vefa, Silva, Cenaj, Kamberi, and Leka). According to Farudin Arapi, head of the government investigation, over 80 per cent of the five companies were not functioning. He added that the five companies together had spent over USD 60 million on preparing proposals for projects that never got off the ground.[19]

"It is more than clear that all the [five] loan-receiving firms operated on the basis of pure pyramid schemes."[20] In other words, they were financing due interest payments from new deposits rather than from returns on investments. "[This] is also proved by the fact that as soon as the loan-taking process stopped, they halted pay-outs."

Similarly, according to the IMF, "[a]lthough a few companies have acted as intermediaries that on-lend funds to the private sector, the bulk of the funding raised has been for their own account" (1997b, p. 31).

The huge debts and obvious liquidity crisis of the pyramid investment companies were also clear—and sad—evidence of the organised cheating which lay hidden behind their economic activities. They owed USD 376 million to their creditors. The designated accountants Deloitte and Touche, which administered the companies after November 1996, said that all of them

---

17. Interview with Ferdinand Kamberi in the *Albanian Observer*, Vol. 2, No. 10 (1996), p. 5.

18. The 1978 World Cup winner Mario Kempes was hired as coach for the soccer club Lushnia for USD 300,000, a monthly salary of USD 1,500 and a luxurious apartment in Tirana. He was recruited by the President of the club, Pellumb Xhaferri, son of Rrapush Xhaferri, President of the Xhaferri fund. See "Foreigners attack soccer", *Albanian Observer*, Vol. 3, No. 1 (1997), p. 44.

19. See *Albanian Observer*, Vol. 4, No. 2 (1998), p. 8.

20. See *Albanian Observer*, Vol. 4, No. 3 (1998), p. 29.

were bankrupt and that their assets—estimated at USD 50 million—were far from sufficient to cover their accumulated debts.[21]

Table 10.1 *Debts of the Five Principal Pyramid Companies, 1998*

	Debts in USD, excluding interest	Assets*
Vefa	253.0 million	33.0 million
Silva	22.2 million	5.8 million
Cenaj	46.8 million	5.1 million
Kamberi	42.2 million	3.5 million
Leka	11.7 million	2.5 million

* According to first estimates by Deloitte and Touche.
Source: *Albanian Observer*, Vol. 4, No. 3 (1998), p. 29.

Vefa alone owed USD 253 million to more than 80,000 creditors, while it had only USD 7 million in the bank and 33 million in assets.[22] The administrators Deloitte and Touche issued an order forbidding the owner of Vefa, Vehbi Alimucaj, to direct the company, effective as of 1 March 1998. Similar decisions were taken against the owners of the other companies. The Government's failure to take action against the pyramid schemes made it possible for these companies to pose as good examples of Albanian capitalism. As late as January 1997, Prime Minister Aleksander Meksi, in answer to a question concerning whether some of these companies could compensate their obligations to depositors by means of returns on investments, replied: "With good investments and production, that possibility surely still exists. As they have said themselves, they will turn into shareholders or investment funds."[23]

21 We should add that this figure is based on the list of creditors that the companies submitted, which may well understate the true situation. Moreover, there were many other pyramid companies, larger (such as Gjallica) or smaller (Grunjasi, Blini, Bendo, Arkond, and so on) for which exact estimates were still not available at the time of completion of this book. It is very difficult to evaluate what exactly their inflows and outflows were, not to mention their liquidity situation. Only after long and detailed examination of the accounts of these companies, and the provision of more precise information on the number of their creditors and the amounts they invested, could an accurate picture start to emerge. In any case, the true figures will never be available because of the funds that disappeared from Albania, generally into Western banks.

22. This company tried to overestimate its assets, notably by increasing its capital by USD 8 billion two days before the June 1997 elections. See *Albanian Observer*, Vol. 3, No. 9 (1997), p. 22.

23. Interview with the *Albanian Observer*, Vol. 3, No. 1 (1997), p. 9.

IMF and World Bank optimism about the Albanian recovery seems to have helped consolidate the economic legitimation of these pyramid companies. This is also the reason why the IMF intervention in late 1996 took the Albanians by surprise, a fact abundantly reflected in the local press: "The IMF, this mystical institution, shocked Albanian public opinion when in October 1996 it criticised the functioning of the pyramid schemes to the Albanian Finance Minister at the IMF annual meeting at the end of September."[24] Furthermore, "Albania, considered a year ago the IMF's best pupil, has today seen the first cracks appear in its relationship."[25]

The storm that this intervention provoked led to more cautious statements from international experts. In November 1997, the head of the IMF delegation from its Washington headquarters tried to explain that it was not the IMF's task to decide whether to close the pyramid schemes: "Pyramid schemes are a problem of the Albanian government, and not ours."[26] One month later, the World Bank executive for the whole region reiterated its support: "The World Bank esteems Albania on the basis of its high rates of economic development as a place of particular success. Many of our experts have . . . praised . . . the achievements here, that's why the World Bank supports and will strongly support Albania in the future."[27] In January 1997, the resident representative of the World Bank in Tirana tried to minimise the crisis, stating that: "At present, though two or three pyramid schemes have already gone bankrupt . . . I do not see any serious irregularity in the Albanian financial sector."[28]

6 SOCIAL LEGITIMATION: EASING THE PAIN OF TRANSITION

The regular payment of interest to a growing number of people made it possible for the pyramid schemes to acquire a certain social legitimacy. At the beginning, profits from this market supported consumption and the level of aggregate demand. Earnings from money-lending became an important, if not the main, source of income for thousands of Albanian families. Indeed for several it may well have represented the only means of surviving the period of transition, although we have no assessments of the average amounts that

24. See "Albania in dilemma: should it listen to the IMF or not?", *Albanian Observer*, Vol. 2, No. 12 (1996), pp. 1–2 (quotation on p. 2). The title on the cover of the review was, quite significantly: "Golden apple: IMF or usurers".

25. Ibid., p. 2.

26. Ibid.

27. Speech by the Regional Executive Director of the World Bank addressed to President Berisha. Reported in ibid., p. 5.

28. Interview with the *Albanian Observer*, Vol. 3, No. 1 (1997), p. 17.

the families involved would have received on a monthly or three-monthly basis. It may also be that only a few—generally the richest who had substantial amounts to invest at hand, and who entered the scheme first because they were better informed—really benefited from it, while the poorest, who invested smaller amounts and joined later (being more cautious about their savings) may not have gained so much.[29]

Whatever the true figures are, there is no doubt that these schemes may have contributed for some years to smooth the pain of transition. This is why they became so popular. As far as the Government is concerned, political capital was to be made by giving the pyramid schemes room to manoeuvre. The relief afforded by these schemes also helped to moderate—at least temporarily—the social discontent caused by growing unemployment, very low wages, and the restrictive incomes policy, thus reducing popular pressure on the Government's macroeconomic policy.

This social legitimation was a determining factor in the growth in the number of small depositors and the overall development of these schemes, which would have collapsed much earlier if they had not managed for a time to provide a regular source of income for the majority of families. Receipt of this income pushed many to ask their relatives working abroad to invest their savings, in increasing amounts, in the pyramid schemes.

This whole affair will have terrible social consequences. First, it progressively increased the dependence of Albanian families on such schemes. The value of work may also have been degraded in the same way. The duration and extent of the phenomenon created the illusion of an easy welfare society, and did not push people into work, especially not for the usual miserable wages which could not compete with the high interest rates provided by the pyramid schemes. While unemployment—both official and hidden—was rapidly increasing, and the eligibility conditions for unemployment benefits were tightened up drastically, the existence of these schemes may have persuaded some unemployed persons not to register and to concentrate instead on obtaining high returns on their investment, in other words, to prefer queuing at the investment kiosk rather than at the local labour office. A consumer society began to emerge, at least for the minority profiting from the system, with an increasing number of imported goods becoming available.

The awakening was brutal. The poorest Albanians, who put all their savings into these schemes, lost everything, especially agricultural peasants who had to sell their only horse or cow or their one hectare of land to invest in the schemes. We analyse the profundity of this social disarray in Chapter 14.

---

29. In the literature on pyramid schemes, this aspect seems to have been neglected. We urge researchers to investigate these issues.

7 INSTITUTIONAL CRISIS AND POPULAR UPRISING

The collapse of the first pyramid schemes suddenly generated generalised chaos, with a total absence of control, either from institutions or political parties, so throwing a harsh light on the weaknesses of the system and the Albanian people's disaffection for all political parties.

Institutional Weaknesses

The transition in Albania was not accompanied by deep institutional reforms. The institutions inherited from the previous regime were extremely weak, and the necessary changes—such as a new constitution, new political institutions, and new basic rules governing society—were constantly delayed. In the new market economy, a whole series of changes was required, including the definition and implementation of a new tax regime, the adoption of market regulations, and the reform of the banking sector with a greater role for the Central Bank (Muço, 1997). Important changes in this direction were made, with the adoption of a new taxation system (including the introduction of VAT) and a large number of laws regulating political and economic life, together with laws on the banking system and market regulations. However, a significant number of institutional reforms that should have been carried out right at the beginning of the reform process were still missing at the end of 1996. Despite long discussions, Albania was still without a new constitution. The crisis took place partly on the back of the fragility of public authority and institutions—for example, in terms of public order, tax collection, and so on —combined with the inherited lack of a culture of responsibility. This led, for instance, to the deterioration of the budget due to the Government's total inability to collect taxes and to obtain the necessary revenues for the state. The weak legal system also contributed to the increasing number of illegal activities, including trafficking of every conceivable kind. The public authorities have not responded to this institutional deficit by encouraging the appropriate organi- sation of civil society and developing a bridge between the state and the citizens. Civil society was basically non-existent. At the same time, we also saw that the Government did not leave much room for discussion of these serious economic and social developments with trade unions or employers' representatives, further increasing frustration among workers and the population as a whole. The political leaders, especially the President, turned Albania in 1996–97 into almost a dictatorial regime, with no power-sharing and systematic muzzling of opposition parties and popular aspirations.

Political Authoritarianism

The crisis was also generated by political reasons and we can trace its roots to the general lack of democracy in Albania past and present. This democratic deficit became obvious in 1996–97. The two general elections— parliamentary in May and local in October—that took place in 1996 were dubious. They led first to a number of political confrontations, with less and less political freedom. The various political parties started to accuse each other of abuses of funds and employment of the pyramid schemes for electoral gain. The economic policy debate was also dominated by the rosy picture of economic activity presented by the ruling Democratic Party. While Albania was presented as a success story, essential debates on key issues such as privatisation policy, financial system reform, and institutional reform did not take place (Muço, 1997).

Even more seriously, clear evidence of electoral fraud by the Democratic Party confirmed by external observers led to a major political crisis.[30] The boycott by the opposition parties after the May elections—they abandoned their seats in the Parliament in protest—practically blocked Albanian political life. For months, they continued to call for a re-run of the 1996 elections.

The significant attack on the democratic life of the country by President Berisha and his party is one of the factors that led the Albanian people to demand the Government's resignation and to fight against its dictatorship and total monopolisation of power. Popular unrest was also motivated by the Government's inability to stop corruption, smuggling, and the illegal activities behind the pyramid schemes, while the majority of people had to endure a fall in real wages, rising unemployment, and the consequent overall fall in living standards. The role of the Government in the collapse of the pyramid schemes, but also the difficulty they had accepting it publicly, was another important factor. In January 1997, when the funds began to go under, Prime Minister Aleksander Meksi clearly stated: "People have entered the game of usuries like entering bingo, gambling, lotto. It is well known that in such games the money is won by some and [lost] by others. The money of those who have entered this game [is] won and lost together . . . [for] four years they [have continued] in [this] manner and people [have taken a] risk. He who likes to speculate takes risks."[31]

---

30 Days after the May elections, the Organisation for Security and Co-operation in Europe (OSCE) criticised the elections as rigged. The electoral results—that gave 122 seats out of 140 to the Democratic Party—held despite protests by the European Union and the US State Department.

   31. Interview with the *Albanian Observer*, Vol. 3, No. 1 (1997), pp. 8–9.

The Popular Explosion

Following the collapse of several pyramid investment schemes throughout the latter part of 1996 and the first few months of 1997, the country was immersed in a generalised popular uprising. The movement, naturally enough, began in Tirana. But it acquired its most radical expression in the city of Vlora in the south, before spreading swiftly through other towns and villages in that part of the country. The southern rebels seized heavy weapons and took control of most of the major cities south of Tirana, while in the capital President Sali Berisha holed up in the Presidential Palace and, with a force of civilian militia, secret police, and remnants of the army, continued to hang on, refusing to relinquish power. The movement that expanded all over the country, however, provoked the fall of the Government, which was replaced by a temporary administration of national reconciliation. The depth of the crisis also required the intervention of a multinational force, which remained to secure early parliamentary elections on 29 June. Albanians delivered their votes to the Socialists, giving them an absolute majority in the Parliament. It also marked the progressive return to normal political life and the re-establishment of public order.

The chronology of the unrest (*Box 10.1*) testifies to the violence of the crisis—the number of victims was approximately five hundred, according to some estimates. It also shows how the pyramid schemes played a catalytic role, with the movement of discontent and protest being transformed into a general popular uprising or rebellion against the political power of the President and the Government—demanding their resignations—and suddenly giving expression to years of frustration. Although this chronology relates the main events taking place mainly in the south, where the movement emerged and developed, it also gives examples of cities in the north where the movement also expanded. In this regard, although the aim of this book is neither to reproduce nor to explain the different political features of this movement, we thought it was important to attract the reader's attention to two aspects of the crisis that were emphasised in almost all the international press and yet do not seem to correspond to reality:

1) The media presented the situation in Albania as total "chaos" and often portrayed the movement as totally disorganised and composed mainly of "criminal gangs", the only aim of which was looting and widespread anarchy. This was certainly President Berisha's opinion: "The committees are a Socialist Party creation . . . they are run by mafiosi and relatives of Socialist Party members . . . who have adopted a Leninist strategy . . . of votes and violence."[32] Far from it. Although the rebellion was clearly chaotic, with

---

32. As quoted in the *Albanian Observer*, Vol. 3, No. 3–4 (1997), p. 2.

uncontrolled groups emerging in different cities, including groups of armed criminals, there was a clear attempt to organise and monitor the movement at the local level. Local committees were created in the rebel areas, to co-ordinate and direct the struggle, to organise supplies and impose some kind of order.[33] In Vlora, the rebels organised themselves into a defence committee called the "Committee for the Salvation of Vlora". Similar salvation committees were created in other cities. In cities such as Gjirokastra and Saranda, residents decided to set up their own local government. A regrouping of local committees was also achieved, with all the insurgent forces in the south putting together a unified National Committee for Salvation and Democracy, composed of representatives from Vlora, Saranda, Tepelena, Delvina, Berat, and Kucova, that is, all the main towns in the rebel-held areas.[34] Although the exact composition of the salvation committees was never totally clear, all sorts of people seem to have joined these organised groups: representatives of political parties, including the Socialist Party,[35] but even some dissident members of the Democratic Party, as well as military officials and ordinary citizens.[36] Plenty of workers participated in this movement, as shown by the constitution of strike committees—with elected delegates from workplaces—that then joined the salvation committees. Students and young people in general also actively participated, as witnessed by the hungerstrike organised by students from the University of Vlora. Members of the armed forces and the police also took part in the movement.[37]

33. These defence or salvation committees in the south took measures, for instance, to introduce order, to take weapons from children, and so on.

34. The *Financial Times* (12 March 1997) reported: "Rebels in southern Albania meanwhile formed a committee for the first time grouping all rebel forces. They rejected the moves in Tirana to form a coalition government, demanding instead that the president resign and that rebel representatives be included in negotiations to set up a new government . . ."

35. Although the rebellion was mainly against the Berisha regime, with the participation of Socialist members in local committees, the real leadership of the movement has never been shown to have been in the hands of the political opposition. As an example, the attempts of the Socialist leaders to patch up a deal with the rebels never came to anything. Furthermore, the newly formed Government of National Unity had only been in existence for 24 hours when fighting broke out in the capital itself and the rebellion spread all over the country.

36. In the Italian newspaper *Il Sole–24 ore* (8 March 1997), the leader of the Salvation Committee of Vlora, "Berti", explained that the Committee was made up of 31 individuals representing 17 political formations, among which there were even "dissidents" from Berisha's Democratic Party. Berti said: "This is the committee of the honest people, which has been joined by the strike committee that co-ordinated the protests during the last few weeks."

37. This wide and spontaneous participation led many observers to call this popular uprising a true "revolution"; so, for instance, R. Qosja: "In reality, Albania experienced a delayed democratic revolution" (UNDP, *Albanian Human Development Report 1998*); see also Woods (1997).

2) Many Western media sources reported that the crisis was mainly a North–South conflict,[38] involving a major risk of civil war. Although President Berisha warned repeatedly of the break-up of Albania, in what has been analysed as a desperate and deliberate attempt to play on North–South divisions, the crisis was clearly not led by a regional conflict: the widespread rebellion and number of victims all over the country proves this,[39] not to mention the number of destroyed enterprises (see Chapter 11) and police stations in every region of Albania. The North, supposedly a stronghold of Berisha, also rose and armed itself. Northern cities such as Shkodra, but also Lezha and Kukes, were witness to violent demonstrations against the President and the Government and also to the destruction of state institutions, shops, and enterprises.

38. See, for instance, "North versus South", *Newsweek* (March 1997).

39. According to the Ministry of Interior (12 April), at least 206 Albanians had died and 600 injured since 1 March, all over the country. According to the same estimates, at least 34 people died in Vlora, and more than 20 in Saranda, Korca, and Berat respectively. In the northern part of the country, the city of Shkodra had at least 18 dead. More than 10 also died in Gjirokastra, Tepelena, Durres, Tirana, and in Fier. The greatest number of injured, averaging between 30 and 50, were in the regions of Vlora, Gjirokastra, Saranda, Shkodra, and Tirana. See the *Albanian Observer*, Vol. 3, No. 3–4 (1997), p. 20.

Box 10.1 *Chronology of the Unrest in Albania, January–June 1997*

January 16 The Government freezes USD 255 million deposited in the state-owned banks by the two pyramid schemes Populli and Xhaferri. Demonstration in Vlora, where people stone the city hall after a local firm postpones payments.

January 19 General protest in Tirana. Some 3,000 people, led by the opposition parties, break through police cordons to demonstrate in Tirana's main square, Skanderbeg.

January 21 The Government forms a commission to investigate the crumbling investment schemes.

January 23 The Albanian Parliament quickly passes a law banning pyramid schemes in Albania, punishable by 20 years' imprisonment and confiscation of assets for the main organisers and operators, and 10 years' imprisonment for employees and collaborators. Demonstrations of hundreds of investors in the northern city of Shkodra, and also in the port of Durres.

January 24 Around 5,000 people go on the rampage in the southern city of Lushnia.

January 25 Demonstrators attack Foreign Minister Tristan Shehu in Lushnia.

January 26 Protests spread, sparking the worst violence seen in Albania since 1991. Thousands of people converge in the centre of Tirana and clash with riot police. Government and Democratic Party buildings are attacked and set on fire in several cities. The Parliament calls the army in to guard government buildings.

January 30 Ten opposition parties form the Forum for Democracy to stage protests across the country. The Forum asks President Berisha to dismiss his Government and to set up a technocratic government to solve the crisis.

February 5 The President of the pyramid scheme Gjallica announces bankruptcy. A crowd of more than 1,000 angry investors march in the port of Vlora demanding their money back and clashing with 200 policemen.

February 6 An even greater number of people (estimated by some at more than 30,000) take to the streets, besieging the police station.

February 8 Police in Tirana use batons to prevent the opposition from holding a rally; 15 opposition leaders beaten or detained.

February 9–10 Protesters attack Vlora police station. Two people die and 40 are injured in the fighting.

February 10 The Prime Minister asks the Parliament to introduce a state of emergency in Vlora to quell disorders.

February 11 30,000 people attend the funeral of an anti-government demonstrator in Vlora, shouting their defiance and outrage at the police, who stay discreetly out of sight.

February 12 A policeman is shot dead in Vlora.

February 15 At a meeting in Tirana, President Berisha admits mistakes in his handling of the pyramid schemes, but also blames investors and insists the state will not compensate them. 5,000 protesters skirmish with police in the southern town of Fier, 100 km from Tirana, while protests continue in Vlora.

February 16 More protests in the three southern towns of Fier, Vlora, and Saranda.

February 18 President Berisha launches a campaign to win back support. He again admits mistakes in the town of Lushnia. Promises to suspend all taxes for two years for all residents to help them to recover their losses.

February 19 President of Vefa Holding, Vehbi Alimucaj, intervenes on television to say he will start to repay over the next two to three weeks all small investors (who invested up to USD 5,000), in order to calm and disperse hundreds of people waiting outside Vefa offices for the past month.

February 20 President Berisha travels to Elbasan, former central industrial town, to calm the people there. In Vlora, 3,000 marchers turn out for a candle-lit evening procession in commemoration of the people who have died in the clashes the previous week. A group of 46 students start a hunger strike in protest against the Government.

February 21 The European Parliament adopts a resolution expressing concern over the crisis in Albania and the violence used to quell demonstrations. It urges President Berisha to open talks with the opposition, and to find solutions to repay lost savings of the population.

February 23 In Vlora, 5,000 demonstrators march on the main boulevard to Vlora University where they express their support for the students who have gone on an anti-government hunger strike.

February 24 Italian police round up a total of 125 people illegally trying to enter the southern part of the country by boat.

February 25 Glyn Davies of the US State Department says that the United States is deeply concerned about recent developments in Albania, and urges local leaders of demonstrations not to use violence and the authorities to permit peaceful demonstrations. The US ambassador in Tirana urges the Government to draft a new constitution and call early elections.

February 26 The Council of Europe adopts resolutions calling for constructive dialogue and respect for the fundamental principles of democracy and international obligations.

February 28 Democratic Party and the opposition Socialist Party hold first talks since general elections last May. The Socialists repeat their demand for the formation of a technocratic government and early elections.

February 28–March 1 Explosion of violence in Vlora after the Albanian secret police, the Shik, fails to halt the students' hunger strike. They are prevented from doing so by thousands of demonstrators. Night-time gun-battle in the city.[40] At least three civilians and one secret policeman (five according to the secret police) die, and more than 20 people are injured. Protesters later burn down the headquarters of the secret police, assault prisons and police stations. They seize weapons from police armouries and distribute them amongst the population.

March 1 A general strike is declared in the city that then spreads to most of southern Albania. In Lushnia, people block the roads and railways in support of the Vlora protesters. Several other road blocks are set up in the south. In Tirana, 5,000

---

40. The bitter conflict between the secret police and the populace is reflected in a number of press reports: "Vlora was where the latest violence was triggered last Friday as Shik, the plainclothes security police, fought a gun battle with demonstrators after failing to halt a hunger strike organised by students at the university. At least nine people were killed, three apparently in cold blood by Shik officers and the rest caught in the crossfire or trapped in Shik headquarters as it was torched and ransacked" (*Daily Telegraph*, 5 March 1997).

protesters clashed with riot police, overturning police vehicles, forcing the police to withdraw. President Berisha says the Government will resign, and the ruling Democratic Party will form a successor cabinet after consultations with opposition parties.

March 2 Protesters in Vlora demand that Berisha dissolve the Parliament and hold immediate elections; moreover, he must not stand for re-election. In Saranda, demonstrators sack police headquarters, seizing weapons, looting shops and banks. Police flee, troops desert army barracks. Four people are killed, and 22 are wounded by gunfire in southern Albania. The Parliament declares a state of emergency: a ten-article law bans public gatherings of more than four people, gives security forces the power to open fire to disperse crowds, restricts political activity, imposes controls on the media.[41] The Government of Aleksander Meksi resigns.

March 3 The Parliament elects Berisha unopposed for a second five-year term. The Parliament orders armed insurgents in the south to surrender their weapons by 1300 GMT or face being shot without warning.

March 4 Army troops begin enforcing emergency rule. At Delvina, in the direction of Saranda, Albanian Air Force MiGs are apparently sent to bomb the rebels.[42] Two air force pilots defect to Italy with their MiG planes rather than obey orders to fire on civilians. Berisha rejects the opposition calls for coalition government.

March 5 Stung by the series of humiliating setbacks, Berisha summarily dismisses his Army Chief of Staff General Sheme Kosova, who is said to have failed to guarantee security against insurgents.[43] Tanks are sent to the south to crush the rebellion. However, faced with the people in arms, the Government's armoured columns come to a halt outside rebel territory. In Saranda, rebels seize an army tank and set up a line of defence at the entrance to the town.[44] Gun-battle in Saranda, many people are injured. In Vlora, three dead and two injured.

March 6 President Berisha, backed by the opposition parties, suspends military action against the rebels and offers them an amnesty. Anti-government forces take firm control of the southern town of Tepelena.

March 7 Rebels reject the amnesty and refuse to lay down arms. The West urges Berisha not to relaunch military campaign against them. All political parties call on people to hand in arms.

March 8 Failed attempt by the Government to reinforce the key garrison at Gjirokastra by sending in 60 élite troops by helicopter. Their arrival at the town's police station provokes the anger of the population. The rebels finally seize the last southern government of Gjirokastra and ransack the main army base after

41. Scenes of violence against the media were also observed, with a handful of journalists being beaten up, and some independent newspapers firebombed. As *The Independent* (4 March 1997) reported: "The offices of Albania's most popular newspaper, *Koha Jone*, were left smouldering after a group of men burst in overnight and set fire to the building and lobbed Molotov cocktails in all directions."

42. As reported by the Italian newspaper *Il Sole–24 Ore* (4 March 1997).

43. He will be replaced by Major General Adem Kopani, the President's personal military adviser and member of the secret police.

44. According to the *Corriere della Sera* (6 March 1997): "Saranda . . . is completely in the hands of the insurgents . . . They have 10–15,000 armed men . . . They have even taken control of 6 warships that control territorial waters."

government troops flee; they capture a helicopter as well. The OSCE envoy, Franz Vranitzky, comes to Tirana. Talks between political parties commence.

March 9 Berisha concludes an agreement with the leaders of all political parties calling for a government of national unity and elections by June. They settle on 29 June. Former Berisha aide General Agim Gozhita is elected leader of Gjirokastra's 150-member rebel council.

March 11 Arms depots in northern Albania looted.[45] Bashkim Fino is nominated Prime Minister of the new Government. The first foreigners are evacuated from Albania.

March 12 The European Parliament passes a resolution suggesting military intervention in Albania. In Tirana, many shootings and mass looting. The international airport Rinas is blocked. Looting and killing in Elbasan, at least two dead in Mjeka. Four dead in Shkodra. The new Government calls for foreign military intervention and asks for an urgent meeting of the UN Security Council.

March 13 The prisons of Tirana are opened. All state buildings are on fire in Lezha. A state bank is burnt in Shkodra. Many enterprises destroyed all around the country. Berisha's family leaves for Italy.

March 14 Culmination of the exodus of Albanians to the region of Puglia in Italy. The chief of the secret police, Bashkim Gazidede, resigns. The Fino Government wins a vote of confidence in Parliament.

March 19 State of emergency in Italy because of massive arrival of Albanian refugees.

March 21 Southern committees gather in Tepelena demanding Berisha's resignation.

March 22 Six dead in Fier.

March 23 Peace rally in Tirana's Skanderbeg square.

March 24 Fino meets his Italian counterpart Romano Prodi in Rome. The European Union reaches a decision: EU troops are to go to Albania.

March 25 An armed band kills three policemen in Vlora.

March 27 The OSCE agrees to send troops to Albania. Tragedy in Tirana when a bus is hit by bullets. Another tragedy in Levan in which 20 people die.

March 28 The UN Security Council approves a mandate of three months for the Multinational Protection Force. It will be led by the Italians with 2,755 troops, but also comprise 923 troops from France, 345 from Spain, 630 from Greece, 691 from Turkey, and 116 from Austria.[46] It will operate within the co-ordinating framework of the OSCE. Tragedy in the Otranto straits, 30 miles from the port of Brindisi, when

45. We must say that we heard different versions of the reports of looting of arms depots. According to some, arms depots were attacked by the rebels; others say that the arms depots were abandoned by the army in sympathy with the rebels; others report that the army had received instructions to leave the depots open to the rebels. Incidentally, on 23 August 1998 the former defence and interior ministers were arrested for "allegedly having incited the rebellion", for (allegedly) "having ordered the use of the army against civilians—including chemical weapons—", and for (allegedly) "having distributed weapons to provoke their use between civilian groups" (see *Albanian Daily News*, 25 August 1998, pp. 1–2).

46. Romania (10 April), but also Slovenia (25 April), Denmark (2 May), and Portugal (mid-May) also decided to join the multinational force, see the *Albanian Observer*, Vol. 3, No. 5 (1997), pp. 3–5.

a boat full of Albanians headed for Italy sinks after a collision with an Italian police boat. At least 80 people die.

March 30 The Albanian Parliament passes the law on foreign military intervention.

March 31 National day of mourning for the Otranto tragedy.

April 1 Prime Minister Fino makes his first visit to the south since insurgents seized control of the region the previous month.

April 4 The Defence Minister visits the rebel-held town of Vlora to calm the anger of the people against Rome over the Otranto tragedy, and to prepare for the deployment of the Multinational Protection Force.

April 8 The multinational security force led by Italy will be known as "Operation Alba".[47] Romano Prodi wins a first vote in the Italian Parliament on the multinational force for Albania. It is a mission of peace, motivated by humanitarian objectives, to protect aid and help to promote stability. It will withdraw one month after the elections.

April 9 Italy's lower house of parliament votes in favour of deploying the Italian-led security force in Albania. The main opposition party returns to the parliament nearly a year after it had abandoned its seats to protest against widespread election fraud. The Parliament approves a measure lifting press restrictions.

April 10 Parliaments of different countries—for instance, Turkey and Romania—approve the dispatch of troops to take part in the international peacekeeping force in Albania.

April 11 Several newspapers resume publication after a month. King Leka I returns home after 58 years in exile to try to restore the monarchy through a referendum.

April 13 The Italian Prime Minister Romano Prodi is welcomed as a hero in Vlora. This ensures the welcome of the Multinational Protection Force two days later.

April 12 According to Interior Ministry sources, a total of 206 people have been killed and approximately 600 wounded since 1 March. To these we should add the more than 80 people who died in the Otranto straits.

April 15 More than 1,000 Italian-led troops begin to arrive by air and sea to spearhead the international protection force. The Democratic Party rules out general elections until rebels controlling the south have been disarmed.

April 25 Teenagers injure 20 people by blowing up an arms and explosives depot in the village of Gryke Manat near Lezha.

April 27 A boat originally built to carry only 50 people reaches Italy with 571 Albanian refugees on board. A total of approximately 14,000 refugees is estimated to have crossed the Adriatic since the collapse of the pyramid schemes.

April 28 The rebel-held southern port of Vlora organises a rally to commemorate the victims of the Otranto tragedy and to call for international help to recover the bodies. 103 are now estimated to have drowned.

April 30 In-depth exchange of views at the UN Security Council on the implementation of the International Advisory Mission within the co-ordinating

---

47. "Alba" being the Italian word for "dawn".

framework of the OSCE, and the Multinational Protection Force in Albania. The Council expresses its satisfaction that the situation is gradually becoming more stable, but urges the political authorities in Albania to implement the agreement of 9 March to create the necessary conditions, including appropriate legislation, for early, free, and fair parliamentary elections and for a new constitution.

Early May Albanian Parliament approves the Law on Transparency for the Pyramid Schemes.

May 4 Three armed men attack an Italian military camp in southern Albania in the first direct assault on the Multinational Protection Force.

May 6 Italy repatriates a total of 2,712 Albanian "undesirables".

May 7 Italy threatens to pull out if the deal between the political parties to organise elections by the end of June is not implemented.

May 12 President Berisha affirms that the elections will take place and he supports a simultaneous vote on the return of the monarchy. The US Secretary of State says the United States will not tolerate attempts to impede parliamentary elections set for the end of June.

May 13 Parliament passes a controversial new election law, paving the way for the June elections, but the law is opposed by the Socialist Party, which threatens to walk out of the coalition government if it is passed.

May 14 European envoy Franz Vranitzky arrives in Tirana for talks to plan new elections and try to stop the violence. The Albanian President postpones the signing of the decree on elections that most opposition parties have threatened to boycott. Greek consulate in border town of Gjirokastra and the main crossing into Greece are closed after another wave of violence. A Greek citizen is killed after being caught up in shooting. Explosion in southern Albania rocks a munitions dump. One army officer killed.

May 15 Macedonia seals its western border with Albania to halt a wave of illegal immigration by Albanians fleeing unrest and food shortages.

May 16 Albanian President calls early elections aimed at stopping violence, although most political parties are still threatening to boycott it. Berisha sets the date for 29 June. European envoy Vranitzky in the course of another mission urges Albanian political parties to compromise on crucial elections.

May 17 The European Union threatens that failure to hold elections by the end of June could prompt it to reconsider its support. Opposition political parties issue an ultimatum to President Berisha demanding changes in what they call "flawed elections".

May 19 Fino tries to reach a compromise over planned elections.

May 20 The Prime Minister appeals to the West for help in the political crisis.

May 22 President Berisha in a meeting with the Albanian Premier informs him of his decision to delegate the procedural competence to appoint electoral commissions to the Prime Minister and the Council of Ministers.

May 22 Albanian political parties agree to go ahead with general elections on 29 June. Vranitzky ensures that the international community will now do everything possible to help prepare the poll and post-election reconstruction.

May 25 President Berisha refuses government request to lift curfew before next month's elections.

May 29 Memorandum of understanding signed between the Albanian Government and the OSCE, ensuring the necessary status for this organisation in Albania to prepare and monitor the elections all over the country.

June Electoral campaign and diplomatic efforts to ensure the holding of free and fair elections in June. The campaign of the Socialist Party is led by the opposition leader Fatos Nano, and Prime Minister Fino. President Berisha leads the campaign of the Democratic Party.

June 1 Italian Prime Minister Romano Prodi ensures that the troops of the Multinational Protection Force provide "broad protection" on polling day.

June 2 Bomb attack injures 27 people at a bus stop in the middle of Tirana. At least seven people are injured, three critically. Another bomb injures 20 people in a crowded café a few hundred metres away from the central Skanderbeg square.

June 4 A hand grenade is thrown at Albanian President Berisha during an electoral rally in Shkallnuer, near the port of Durres, but fails to explode. State television broadcasts pictures.

June 11 An Italian coastguard patrol boat exchanges fire off the northern Albanian coast with a boat carrying several hundred people. Gunmen open fire on the Multinational Protection Force on the road from Elbasan to Tirana.

June 12 Eight people are injured by shooting close to an election rally addressed by President Berisha in Elbasan.

June 16 Two leaders of the Socialist Party are shot on their way to an election rally.

June 17 Five men and a woman are killed and 14 people injured in a dispute and battle over land in the village of Kapinova in southern Albania.

June 18 International conference on Albania in Rome at ministerial level, also involving international organisations, to discuss political, economic, and financial matters. The dismantling of the pyramid schemes and changes in the law on the transparency of pyramid schemes are also discussed.

June 29 The early parliamentary elections take place without major incidents, returning the Socialist Party with a majority, marking the gradual return to normal political life and the re-establishment of public order. The return of the monarchy is rejected. Berisha resigns. A new government is formed, with Fatos Nano nominated as the new Prime Minister, and Bashkim Fino as Deputy Prime Minister. Rexhep Meidani is elected new President of Albania.

Note: This table is an attempt to depict the major events of the Albanian crisis on the basis of different sources of information. Because of the great confusion, however, the absence of a diversified local press, very contradictory reporting by official sources (particularly in respect of the number of victims in the regional conflicts), and not always reliable international press coverage, there may be omissions or discrepancies. Future researchers seeking to reconstitute the chronology of this sad period in more detail would be performing a service to historical accuracy. Needless to say, we have not been able to take account of all the official—and behind-the-scenes—diplomatic contacts aimed at solving the conflict, mainly from the OSCE but also other international organisations, and Albanian and Western diplomats.

8 CONCLUSION

We have seen that the disruption of the pyramid schemes in early 1997, in a context of weak institutions and political turbulence, was the main catalyst in the overall crisis.

On the economic side, the fact that these schemes were able to expand for years is evidence of the extraordinary amount of cash Albanians had been able to amass in the four or five years after the fall of communism. This money could have been put to the service of the country's economic development if the banking system had been working efficiently and if an appropriate credit policy had been put in place. The amounts of money involved were considerable, comparable to national GDP, and more than six times the total foreign direct investment since 1991.

Pyramid funds have appeared in other countries,[48] but the Albanian version had two distinctive features: the longest duration (more than five years) and the greatest extent, with nearly two-thirds of the population becoming involved. It was the combination of conditions specific to Albania that generated the schemes and promoted their development. In particular, they benefited from political, economic, and social legitimacy, aspects of their success which seem to have been mutually sustaining. Political legitimacy—so important for obtaining the general trust of the population—clearly helped the pyramid companies to build up their economic legitimacy; in turn, the apparent economic success of the pyramid companies, echoed in the media, was an asset to the Government. They became the basis of what we have called "the Albanian pyramid".

The failure of the international monetary institutions to intervene until late 1996, and their systematic presentation of positive economic indicators—again largely echoed in the domestic and international press—also indirectly contributed to reinforcing the economic and political legitimacy of the schemes.

Finally, social legitimacy helped the pyramid schemes to convince the Albanian people that they were crucial for economic prosperity and for improving their individual and family living standards. Social legitimacy, and the huge popular support that went with it, pushed policy-makers into turning a blind eye to the internal workings of the schemes. The Government was eventually to be 'hoist with its own petard': the decision to close down the schemes became ever more difficult as more and more people invested more of their savings, and when closure could not be postponed any longer, the anger of the Albania people was exacerbated by their feeling that the

---

48. For instance in Romania in 1992–93 with the Caritas fund.

Government had supported the schemes—and even profited from them—until the last possible moment.

The collapse of the investment schemes suddenly revealed the real character of the Albanian economy, based on pyramid schemes and the laundering of money from illegal activities rather than on real production growth. The Albanian miracle vanished overnight.

Years of suffering and frustration of the Albanian population may explain the sudden intensity of the crisis. The sudden explosion, contrary to what has been said in most of the Western media, was due not only to the collapse of the pyramid schemes, however, and by no means suddenly interrupted positive economic growth. On the contrary, as we have tried to show, the collapse of the pyramid funds was the last straw, piled upon a whole series of political, economic, and social problems, causing the Albanian people finally to seek to radically change a regime that had been shown to fail in so many respects in its management of the country's transition to a market economy.

The extent of the protest and its implications—the subject of the second part of this book—confirm this interpretation of the crisis, with a general destruction of enterprises, public offices, and local activities and investments that simply cannot be satisfactorily explained in terms of the population's exasperation at the pyramid schemes' closure, but must be sought in more global and varied sources of dissatisfaction.

Part Two
Prospects: Albania after the Storm

11. The Extent of the Destruction

1 INTRODUCTION

It was important to provide a first assessment of the crisis. Our enterprise survey carried out at the end of 1997 gives us a first overall view, providing precise data on the number of enterprises that were totally destroyed in the spring events, and allowing us to identify the worst affected regions, as well as the hardest hit economic sectors, and types of enterprise ownership and management. The survey collected data on 1,014 enterprises in industry, services, and banks, which makes the results fully representative of the Albanian economy. The survey also gives us the opportunity to provide, for those enterprises that were attacked, a first "statement" of the value of their losses and, more generally at the national level, the distribution of damaged enterprises among sectors of activity, industries, regions, and size of enterprise.

On the basis of this first general (and depressing) picture of the destruction, we pursue an analysis of the data in order to try to understand what combination of factors led to such violent waves of devastation. A detailed econometric analysis allows us to identify the most important determinants of the Albanian people's sudden rage to destroy or damage their local enterprises and institutions. If the crisis as a whole seemed to be caused by a series of factors outside the enterprise, with the collapse of the pyramid schemes and other political and institutional developments playing a key role, it appears from the survey results that a number of factors inside the enterprise may also have contributed to the exponential increase in the anger of workers and others, making necessary for the investigator an examination of the recent economic and social experience of Albanian enterprises.

2 THE OVERALL DESOLATION

The enterprise survey reveals the widespread desolation in every region, area, and city in Albania. No part of the country was untouched by the events. Enterprises seem to have paid a particularly high price, with more than half of all enterprises suffering injury during the crisis. The valuation put on their losses by Albanian enterprises is astronomical: approximately 407 billion leks, that is, USD 2,713 million. The enterprise average is 496 million leks (USD 3 million).[1] This represents structural damage to buildings and factories, and losses in machinery and equipment. In terms of the number of companies destroyed or damaged, the spring rebellion is comparable in extent to a civil war.

The banking sector seems to be the most affected with 68 per cent of banks concerned, followed by industry (59 per cent) and services (57 per cent). The average value of damages is also much higher in the banks, which have been the first to be attacked by demonstrators who wanted back their savings accumulated by pyramid companies at state-owned banks. The greatest amount of damages, however, was registered by enterprises operating in services.

Table 11.1 *Percentage of Enterprises Reporting Damage and Value of Damage (million leks), Dec. 1997*

	Percentage of enterprises reporting damage	Average value of damage per enterprise	Total value of damage
Industry	59	487	118 469
Services	57	404	213 246
Banks	68	1 501	75 068
All	58	496	406 743

Source: ALFS3.

While a majority of enterprises were damaged during the events, many enterprises—162 enterprises to be precise, that is, 16 per cent of those surveyed—were totally destroyed, generally burnt out by the insurgents. More than 60 per cent of destroyed enterprises were operating in services, while only one bank was affected.

---

1. After the destruction, many enterprises tended to overestimate the value of their losses in order to obtain more reimbursement and aid. This was especially the case with Greek and Italian joint ventures that were eligible for special financial assistance from their home country. In other cases, managers themselves stole the equipment (computers, and so on) before declaring it had been stolen by the workers and other demonstrators. The confidential nature of our enterprise survey, a feature that we repeatedly emphasised to managers, makes the data it contains the most accurate available.

Table 11.2 *Percentage of Destroyed Enterprises, by Sector, 1997*
(% of total number of enterprises in each sector)

	Percentage	Number
Industry	19.6	59
Services	15.4	102
Banks	2.0	1
All	16.0	162

Source: ALFS3.

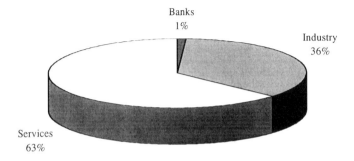

Figure 11.1 *Distribution of Destroyed Enterprises, by Sector, 1997*

Source: ALFS3.

3 STATE INSTITUTIONS A PRINCIPAL TARGET . . .

Survey results confirm that public institutions and enterprises were the main target, more than half of the enterprises that reported damage being state-owned. Numerous private enterprises were also attacked, amounting to 36 per cent of the total.

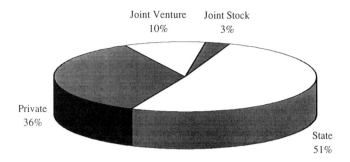

Joint Venture   Joint Stock
10%   3%

Private
36%

State
51%

Figure 11.2 *Distribution of Enterprises Reporting Damage, by Property Form, Dec. 1997*

Source: ALFS3.

Among state-owned enterprises, 74 per cent reported damage, against 42 per cent on average in private companies. Nearly 80 per cent of state banks were also attacked. The extremely high percentage of joint ventures (72 per cent of them) which reported damage is significant.

Table 11.3 *Percentage of Enterprises Reporting Damage, by Property Form, Dec. 1997*

	Industry	Services	Banks	All
State	71	74	79	74
Private	47	40	–	42
Joint venture	74	72	25	72
Joint stock	52	100*	–	56

* only 2 enterprises with this ownership form.
Source: ALFS3.

Average damage was much higher in state enterprises, something that certainly reflects the larger size of such companies: average damage is clearly strongly correlated with company size and number of employees. But although damage was limited in small enterprises in absolute terms, this does not mean that such businesses were spared closure, since by their very nature they are much more vulnerable than large enterprises. Private enterprises also registered significant injury.

Table 11.4 *Average Value of Damage per Enterprise, by Property Form, Dec. 1997 (million leks)*

	Industry	Services	Banks	All
State	2 030	983	1 787	1 278
Private	151	75	–	97
Joint venture	49	4	–	35
Joint stock	6	3	–	6

Source: ALFS3.

Table 11.5 *Total Value of Damage, by Property Form, Dec. 1997 (million leks)*

	Industry	Services	Banks	All
State	99 498	193 659	75 068	368 225
Private	16 536	18 967	–	35 503
Joint venture	2 124	70	–	2 194
Joint stock	128	7	–	135

Source: ALFS3.

Large enterprises had a greater probability of being attacked—78 per cent of enterprises with more than 200 employees, compared to 52 per cent of small enterprises with fewer than 50 employees. This might also reflect the concentration of attacks on large state enterprises. Public utilities were also systematically destroyed.

Table 11.6 *Percentage of Enterprises Reporting Damage, by Size, Dec. 1997*

	Industry	Services	Banks	All
1–50	56	49	65	52
51–100	53	70	83	64
101–200	66	71	100*	70
201 +	72	85	67	78

* only one bank in this category

Source: ALFS3.

Banks—almost all in the hands of the state—were clearly perceived as a symbol of the central authorities. The decision of the Government to freeze the accounts of a number of pyramid companies and foundations in state-owned banks also led many insurgents to concentrate their attacks on such banks in order to try to recover their lost savings. Nearly 80 per cent of all banks were attacked, although the results of the assaults are extremely differentiated according to type of bank. Large banks—concentrated in Tirana—were surrounded by substantial police cordons so that no serious damage was done (below 1 million leks on average), generally due to stone throwing or Kalashnikov bursts directed at the windows and facade. Attacks in other cities were much more serious, banks (generally small or medium-sized, with below 50 employees, and only a few larger ones) reporting very high average damage. One of them, in Vlora, was totally burnt out, since the local police were compelled to defend their own headquarters, which came under attack for several days, not to mention military barracks where weapons were kept, another of the first targets of the revolt.

With the exception of the banks, average damage was clearly related to establishment size (larger companies had much higher fixed assets), since enterprises operating in industry and services did not benefit from special police protection. Generally speaking, state enterprises were left totally without defence,[2] leading to scenes of looting, while the protection of private enterprises was left to the owners. The attempts of private owners and managers to protect their factories also explain the lower average value of damage reported by this property form. Foreign owners/managers in particular hired, at very high wages, a significant number of armed guards to protect their enterprises day and night, before leaving the country. In some cases, however, the foreign owner simply fled the country with the enterprise's financial assets, a retreat which enraged the workers, who destroyed their companies, as if to ensure they would never have to work for them again.

4 ... BUT DESTRUCTION OF JOINT VENTURES

The distribution of enterprises that were totally destroyed both compares and contrasts with that of enterprises that simply incurred damage. The attacks were directed against other types of owner, not only against public institutions. A particularly striking feature of the destruction process that emerges clearly from the survey results is the high percentage of joint ventures that were destroyed: while only 1 per cent of total state enterprises were destroyed, more than 13 per cent of joint ventures were totally burnt out. Private enterprises were also a target, with more than 5 per cent of them being totally swept away by the rebellion: given the large number of small private enterprises, this accounts for a lot of businesses.

---

2. Only banks, government offices, ministries, and important public institutions seem to have been protected by the police.

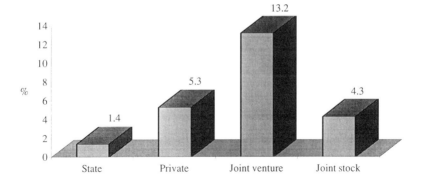

Figure 11.3 *Percentage of Destroyed Enterprises, by Property Form, 1997*
(% of total number of enterprises in each property form)

Source: ALFS3.

The distribution of destroyed enterprises also points to sectors dominated by joint ventures, such as textiles, wood and paper, and leather and shoes in industry and trade in services, where about one-quarter of enterprises were totally destroyed.

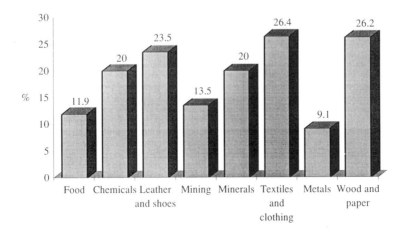

Figure 11.4 *Percentage of Destroyed Enterprises, by Industry, 1997*
(% of total enterprises in each industry)

Source: ALFS3.

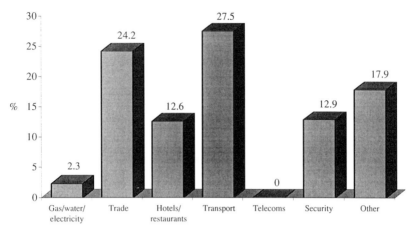

Figure 11.5 *Percentage of Destroyed Enterprises, by Service, 1997*
(% of total enterprises in each service)

Source: ALFS3.

Numerous examples have been reported in Shkodra of Italian textile enterprises that were totally burnt out by the workers. We interviewed the workers of an Italian–Albanian shoe factory in Shkodra that was totally destroyed; all of them were young women 18–25 years of age. They reported that they had had to work for very low pay while maintaining a punishing work rate, accumulating hours of overtime that were never remunerated. The fact that many workers would even collapse during the production process did not move the manager, who was obsessed by production volumes and profitability. The workers happily admitted having devastated the company during the crisis, breaking every single machine and piece of equipment.[3]

5 A CLEAR REGIONAL MAPPING OF DISCONTENT

Our enterprise results from different sectors (industry, services, banks) seem to converge on particular regions, chiefly the five regions of Berat (79 per cent of all enterprises, 100 per cent in industry), Gjirokastra (80 per cent), Korca (78 per cent), Vlora, and Shkodra (both 74 per cent). Damage was also frequent in industrial enterprises in Kukes and Dibra, services in Lezha, and banks in all regions except Tirana (for the reasons already given).

3. A series of interviews with the workers and managers of destroyed enterprises will be prepared by the author in co-operation with the National Statistical Institute of Albania.

Table 11.7 *Percentage of Enterprises Reporting Damage, by Region, Dec. 1997*

	Industry	Services	Banks	All
Berat	100	72	100	79
Dibra	71	61	67	64
Durres	34	36	75	37
Elbasan	47	44	60	47
Fier	53	48	100	51
Gjirokastra	71	80	100	80
Korca	77	79	80	78
Kukes	75	36	67	50
Lezha	55	62	50	59
Shkodra	85	66	100	74
Tirana	44	47	20	44
Vlora	70	76	75	74

Note: Banking establishments, with the exception of the concentration of large banks in Tirana, are spread over the whole of Albania, so that the numbers given above often represent only a few establishments per region.
Source: ALFS3.

The level of damage testifies to the intensity of the destruction process in some regions. Industrial and service enterprises in Fier, for instance, were often completely destroyed. Industrial enterprises, but also the few banks in Korca, were also devastated. Regional results confirm the extent of bank losses in Vlora and Lezha. Service companies in Durres and Tirana also reported great destruction.

Table 11.8 *Average Value of Damage per Enterprise, by Region, Dec. 1997 (million leks)*

	Industry	Services	Bank	All
Berat	26.1	9.7	5.2	11.8
Dibra	7.3	1.3	3.9	2.7
Durres	1.5	227.0	3.5	136.4
Elbasan	52.2	15.8	2.8	25.7
Fier	3 469.6	2 137.9	1.0	2 457.8
Gjirokastra	19.5	101.9	63.1	78.8
Korca	157.3	6.1	14 520.6	846.4
Kukes	13.3	141.5	13.3	91.6
Lezha	63.3	3.0	173.5	32.6
Shkodra	26.8	5.5	12.0	12.4
Tirana	12.4	322.8	0.0	216.0
Vlora	15.8	7.3	444.5	59.7

Source: ALFS3.

Table 11.9 *Total Value of Damage, by Region, Dec. 1997 (million leks)*

	Industry	Services	Bank	All
Berat	182	349	21	552
Dibra	51	33	12	96
Durres	52	13 167	14	13 233
Elbasan	940	585	14	13 233
Fier	107 557	160 343	3	267 903
Gjirokastra	136	2 037	189	2 363
Korca	7 548	254	72 603	80 405
Kukes	53	1 556	40	1 649
Lezha	696	64	347	1 107
Shkodra	536	224	48	808
Tirana	557	34 214	0	34 771
Vlora	158	152	1 778	2 088

Source: ALFS3.

The regional mapping of totally destroyed enterprises is also instructive. Surprisingly, high percentages of enterprises totally destroyed were not confined to the south of Albania—with Berat in first place—the central districts of Durres and Tirana also suffered heavily, one-quarter of enterprises being swept away by the popular revolt (*Figure 11.6*). In the north, more than 40 per cent of industrial enterprises were destroyed in the town of Shkodra, and 30 per cent of service enterprises in Kukes.

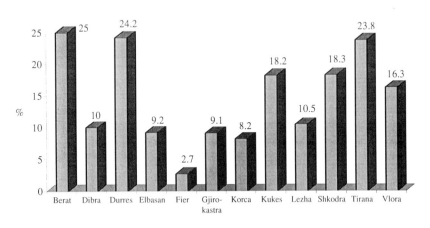

Figure 11.6 *Percentage of Destroyed Enterprises, by Region, 1997*
(% of enterprises in each region)

Source: ALFS3.

When we look then at the regional distribution of destroyed enterprises, we observe that 40 per cent of them were located in Tirana, 19 per cent in Durres, 9 per cent in Berat, and 8 per cent in Shkodra, confirming the mass destruction in these very different regions, which concentrate the largest number of enterprises. In the other regions a smaller number of enterprises were systematically ruined by local people.

Table 11.10 *Regional Distribution of Destroyed Enterprises, 1997 (% and number of enterprises)*

	%	Number
Berat	9.2	15
Dibra	2.5	4
Durres	19.1	31
Elbasan	3.7	6
Fier	1.9	3
Gjirokastra	1.9	3
Korca	4.9	8
Kukes	2.5	4
Lezha	2.5	4
Shkodra	8.0	13
Tirana	39.5	64
Vlora	4.3	7
Total	100	162

Source: ALFS3.

On the basis of these regional results, we can make a number of observations.

First, although there were regional differences in its extent, the wave of destruction spread all over the country: there does not seem to be any region or area of the country in which enterprises did not report damage. In fact, no less than 40 per cent of enterprises were affected in each of the 12 regions, and in all regions at least some enterprises were completely destroyed. This contradicts the statements repeatedly made during the crisis that the rebellion was concentrated in only a few areas of the country.

Second, there does not seem to be a particular gap between the north and the south of Albania. While the extent of the crisis was clearly very great in the southern cities of Vlora, Fier, and Gjirokastra, where the fighting between the police and the people was the most intense, it was also widespread in the northern regions of Kukes, Shkodra, and Lezha. The centre of the country was also damaged, with a high concentration of totally destroyed enterprises. This also contradicted the reports that presented a crisis limited to the south of the country, with the risk of civil war between north and south. Although the south was worst hit, becoming totally beyond the control of the central authorities, northern and central regions also expressed their opposition to the regime in no uncertain terms.

Third, there does not seem to be a particularly striking difference between urban and rural areas. The animosity was generalised, with the rural population becoming particularly militant in Lezha and Korca. Although having fewer factories, these regions reported a significant number of damaged companies, in many cases workers and peasants—coming down from the mountains—uniting to destroy enterprises. This also contradicts the statements that the rural population, although in a precarious economic situation, were reasonably happy about the transition, particularly in respect of privatisation and agricultural reform.

6 DESTRUCTION CONCENTRATED IN LABOUR-INTENSIVE ACTIVITIES

More detailed figures by sectors of activity show that the extent of the crisis was differently distributed according to type of economic activity. Within the industrial sector, almost all mining enterprises (97 per cent of them) incurred damage, with average losses of more than 3 billion leks. A significant proportion of enterprises in food, textiles and clothing, and leather and shoes were also affected.

Table 11.11 *Percentage of Enterprises Reporting Damage and Value of Damage (million leks), by Industry, Dec. 1997*

	% of damaged enterprises	Average damage per enterprise	Total damage
Food processing	56	287	16 387
Chemicals	47	194	2 924
Leather and shoes	57	16	222
Mining	97	3 114	96 550
Minerals	57	24	675
Textiles and clothing	59	9	480
Metals	54	10	106
Wood and paper	41	35	1 122

Source: ALFS3.

In services, the state utilities of gas, water, and electricity were the worst affected—85 per cent of enterprises—probably because they undoubtedly represented the public management and central authorities against which the rebellion took place; 77 per cent of telecommunication enterprises also reported damage. Security services were the least affected, probably because such enterprises were well equipped to defend themselves. As we shall see, these enterprises and the individuals working for them flourished during the spring events as other managers and individuals sought their services. Every enterprise hired armed guards to keep away the rebels from their factories and to prevent looting.

Table 11.12 *Percentage of Enterprises Reporting Damage and Value of Damage (million leks), by Service, Dec. 1997*

	% of damaged enterprises	Average damage per enterprise	Total damage
Gas/water/electricity	85	517	43 452
Trade	49	1 110	128 828
Hotel/restaurant	47	16	1 157
Transport	44	392	14 111
Telecoms	77	216	6 685
Security	31	8	472
Other	56	192	18 273

Source: ALFS3.

Almost one in two trade companies was attacked, registering a significant (highest in services) average amount of damage—more than 1 billion (1,110 million) leks.[4] Tourism also suffered huge losses: six hotels alone reported losses of 227 million leks. Nearly 30 per cent of the total value of tourist resorts seems to have been destroyed.[5]

It is notable that the percentage of affected enterprises was much higher in labour-intensive sectors, such as mining and textiles and clothing, where wage costs represent a very high share (48 and 44 per cent respectively) of total production costs. Total labour costs (wage costs + other labour-related costs such as social contributions) in these two sectors also represent 63 and 60 per cent respectively of production costs. Popular anger seems to have concentrated on these two sectors in particular. A similar phenomenon may

4. Probably because means of transport, but also other heavy equipment, were systematically stolen or destroyed.

5. See "Tourist Industry Devastated by Spring Crisis", in the *Albanian Observer*, Vol. 3, No. 11 (1997), p. 22.

be observed in services, in which the sector with the highest share of wage costs and labour costs (52 and 70 per cent) in total production costs, telecommunications, was the most severely affected by the demonstrators. *Table 11.13* gives a first indication of the direct correlation between the share of wage/labour costs in production costs and the percentage of enterprises which were damaged, particularly in industry. This correlation is also confirmed by our regressions and econometric analysis of the crisis.

Table 11.13 *Percentage of Enterprises Reporting Damage, by Labour Costs, Dec. 1997 (percentage of labour costs in total production costs)*

	Industry	Services	Banks	All
< 35%	51	50	62	52
35–44%	52	51	50	51
45–54%	52	56	50	54
> 54%	62	57	86	60

Note: 45 per cent was the national average for labour costs/production costs.
Source: ALFS3.

This labour dimension goes well beyond the aspect of property form: all types of ownership seem to have suffered. For instance, while the labour-intensive mining sector was dominated by large state-owned enterprises, the textiles and clothing industry was mainly composed of private enterprises and an important concentration of joint ventures with majority foreign capital. The comparative advantage of these sectors is undoubtedly their labour force, available in abundance at very low cost. Many employers have systematically left this labour force without even basic social protection. The working conditions prevailing in these enterprises, in terms of unpaid overtime and the absence of individual contracts and collective agreements, seem to have contributed to the general desire of their workers to sweep them away. The high number of dismissals in labour-intensive sectors also contributed greatly to the discontent.

Again, the rebellion was not solely the result of the collapse of the pyramid schemes, but was strongly motivated by the internal functioning of enterprises. This labour dimension could also partly explain the regional configuration of the crisis; for example, why the percentage of enterprises incurring damage was so high only in industry in the regions of Kukes and Dibra (reported in 75 and 71 per cent respectively of industrial establishments), which also happen to be the most labour-intensive regions (labour costs of 60 and 55 per cent of total production costs). The traditional industrial areas of Berat and Elbasan are also labour-intensive, and it would not be surprising if the massive lay-offs that occurred in these two regions during the transition, without sufficient other economic activities emerging to compensate, were enough to explain the dramatic intensity of the crisis which engulfed them.

7 THE ROLE OF WAGE AND EMPLOYMENT POLICIES

We found that the probability of suffering damage was also dependent on the employment and wage conditions prevailing at the establishment: *Table 11.14* provides a first overview.

Table 11.14 *Wages and Employment in Damaged Enterprises, Dec. 1997*

	Enterprises reporting damage	Enterprises not reporting damage
Employment		
Employment change in past two years	−19.1%	−3.6%
Dismissal rate in 1996	6.4%	4.3%
Wages		
Wage costs/production costs	33%	30%
Average wage (leks)	8 600	9 100
Minimum wage (leks)	6 100	6 900

Source: ALFS3.

A direct correlation between the crisis and previous employment cuts was observed, enterprises which reduced more jobs over the previous two years having a higher probability of suffering damage and to a greater extent. To be sure, employment cuts partly reflect the poor economic and financial conditions of these enterprises, which might have led to the workers' generalised demotivation taking more violent expression during the crisis. At the same time, people seem to have exercised their wrath particularly on establishments that had not hesitated to carry out massive lay-offs and to plunge a large number of workers and their families into poverty. This correlation was observed in all types of enterprise and in all sectors (industry, services, and banks), as shown in *Table 11.15*. We further investigate this aspect in the econometric analysis.

Table 11.15 *Percentage of Enterprises Reporting Damage, by Employment Change (in past two years), Dec. 1997*

	Industry	Services	Banks	All
Fell 20+	72	70	80	72
Fell 19–10	65	65	33	63
Fell 9–1	53	75	78	68
No change	33	45	33	43
Rose	60	48	64	54

Source: ALFS3.

This is confirmed by comparison of unemployment rates by region in 1996 and the regional map of damage. We may observe that enterprises in the regions with the highest unemployment—such as Berat, Kukes, and Elbasan—suffered the most damage. The regional localisation of damage also corresponds to the results we obtained concerning dismissals during our enterprise survey at the end of 1996: in Korca, Gjirokastra, and Dibra (see *Figure 5.15* in Chapter 5), which reduced their labour force by more than 30 per cent in 1995–96, more than 70 per cent of enterprises were damaged in 1997. Other regions where the labour force was adjusted earlier in the transition, with employment cuts of more than 50 per cent—for instance, Elbasan and Berat in 1993–94—were also badly affected by the popular uprising. At the same time, damage seems to have been more frequent and more extensive in the enterprises that paid the lowest wages in 1996. This difference is particularly marked in industry and banks.

Table 11.16 *Percentage of Enterprises Reporting Damage, by Wage Levels in 1996, Dec. 1997*

Wage levels	Industry	Services	Bank	All
Below average	60	53	73	57
Above average	45	54	44	53

Source: ALFS3.

Past very low wages might have constituted an additional cause of rebellion and destruction. This was the case in very labour-intensive sectors, such as textiles, leather and shoes, and chemicals, which also paid the lowest wages (see Chapter 6).

We will see in section 8 that this relationship between low wages and damage affected all property forms and types of sector and enterprise.

8 DESTRUCTION DETERMINANTS AT THE ENTERPRISE LEVEL

In order better to understand the factors that led to destruction at the enterprise level, we complemented the above statistical averages by an econometric analysis. We estimated the following equation by means of ordinary least squares regressions, taking the reporting of destruction as the dependent variable (the dummy variable taking the value 1 if the enterprise was destroyed, and 0 otherwise):

$$(DESTROYED) = a + b1\Sigma(SECTOR) + b2\Sigma(PROP) + b3\Sigma(REG) + b4(EMPSIZE) + b5(EMPCH) + b6(PROD96) + e$$

where

SECTOR = a set of dummies for the sector (different industries and services);
PROP = a set of dummies for the property form of the enterprise;
REG = a set of dummies for the regional location of the enterprise;
EMPSIZE = size of enterprise by number of employees;
EMPCH = percentage of labour force change in 1996;
PROD96 = percentage of full production capacity in 1996;
e = error term.

Among the explanatory factors, in addition to the dummy variables for sectors, regions, and ownership forms, we included the size of the enterprise and the previous year's employment changes. The economic situation of the enterprise before the crisis was captured by the percentage of full production capacity at which enterprises reported they were operating at the end of 1996. The econometric results confirmed our previous statistical results. *Table 11.17* presents regression results for all enterprises and for the production sector. They emphasise the same results. The most significant variable represented joint ventures, confirming that this ownership type was at the forefront of the destruction in Albania. By contrast, state ownership seems to have been much less important. The most significant sectors were wood and paper and leather and shoes, which concentrated a high number of joint ventures. The northern district of Shkodra emerged clearly as the most significant region in this respect. The regions of Berat and Vlora also appeared with a positive coefficient. The size of enterprises was not as significant but still positively correlated to the destruction process, with a tendency for large enterprises to be more affected by the destructive wave. Interestingly, employment changes over the previous year clearly appeared with a negative and significant coefficient, showing that they somehow influenced the destruction process: the more lay-offs before the crisis, the higher the tendency for the enterprise to be destroyed.

Table 11.17 *Determinants of Enterprise Destruction, 1997 (OLS Regression Coefficients)*

	All		Industry	
Variables	Coefficient	T-statistics	Coefficient	T-statistics
Property form[1]				
State	0.01098	0.445	0.05290	0.759
Private	0.02358	0.940	0.08385	1.293
Joint venture	0.09058	2.938 ***	0.17688	2.523 **
Joint stock	0.02077	0.511	0.09234	1.203
Region[2]				
Berat	0.05624	1.603	0.23014	2.024 **
Dibra	0.00727	0.196	0.02911	0.269
Durres	0.01225	0.378	0.05199	0.646
Elbasan	0.03438	1.014	0.10798	1.216
Fier	0.01380	0.438	0.01959	0.233
Korca	0.00855	0.265	0.02523	0.314
Kukes	0.01252	0.280	0.04634	0.371
Lezha	0.00352	0.095	0.01248	0.133
Shkodra	0.07624	2.199 **	0.21599	2.503 **
Tirana	−0.01590	−0.521	−0.02409	−0.296
Vlora	0.05427	1.444	0.09592	0.999
Sectors[3]				
Chemicals	−0.03596	−0.838	−0.03259	−0.499
Leather and shoes	0.07573	1.851 *	0.06289	0.997
Mining	−0.03196	−1.053	−0.01553	−0.265
Minerals	−0.00318	−0.105	−0.00725	−0.154
Textiles and clothing	−0.00506	−0.208	−0.01941	−0.467
Metals	−0.01354	−0.284	0.01039	0.146
Wood and paper	0.06795	2.331 **	0.07267	1.559
Gas/water/electr.	−0.01650	−0.837	−	−
Trade	0.00354	0.198	−	−
Hotels/restaurants	−0.00906	−0.432	−	−
Transport	−0.01841	−0.677	−	−
Telecoms	−0.00976	−0.346	−	−
Security	−0.02833	−1.202	−	−
EMPSIZE	0.00003	1.604	0.00006	1.266
EMPCHG	−0.00006	−1.873 *	−0.00003	−0.617
PROD96	−0.00024	−1.037	−0.00016	−0.312
Constant	0.00339	0.081	−0.10055	−1.044
R^2		0.099		0.217
F		2.470		2.14

Notes: 1 Omitted: Other property forms.   *** statistically significant at 1% level.
2 Omitted: Gjirokastra.   ** statistically significant at 5% level.
3 Omitted: Food.   * statistically significant at 10% level.

Source: ALFS3.

Other variables proper to the establishment level could not be collected on destroyed enterprises due to the difficulties we had reaching managers and obtaining the necessary information, all books and accounts having been destroyed along with the enterprise. We complemented these first results on destroyed enterprises by carrying out a similar exercise on enterprises reporting damage. We took the reporting of damage (as a dummy taking the value 1 if the enterprise reported damage and the value 0 if not) as the dependent variable, and tested a series of possible explanatory factors, as follows:

$(DAMAGED) = a + b1\sum(SECTOR) + b2\sum(PROP) + b3\sum(REG) + b4(EMPSIZE) + b5(EMPCH) + b6(PROD96) + b7(AWAGE) + b8(SOCIAL) + e$

where

SECTOR = a set of dummies for the sector (different industries and services);
PROP = a set of dummies for the property form of the enterprise;
REG = a set of dummies for the regional location of the enterprise;
EMPSIZE = size of enterprise by number of employees;
EMPCH = percentage of labour force change in 1996;
PROD96 = percentage of full production capacity in 1996;
AWAGE = average wage in 1996 in logarithmic form;
SOCIAL = a constructed index of social dialogue in 1996;
e = error term.

We also added to this equation some of the social factors identified in our statistics. We first included the monthly average wage paid by the enterprise before the crisis, to test whether very low wages could effectively be retained as an important factor to explain the damage. Similarly, we constructed a variable to measure the intensity of social dialogue within the enterprise; we built a dummy variable taking a value from 0 to 4, with the enterprise accumulating points according to its 1996 social policy: 1 if there was a recognised trade union in the enterprise; 1 if the trade union membership was above the national average; 1 if a collective agreement existed in the enterprise; 1 if the manager reported regularly informing the workers about enterprise results and objectives. An enterprise in which social dialogue was strong, recognised trade unions had a strong presence, and the workers were directly involved and covered by a collective agreement recorded the maximum value. At the opposite extreme, enterprises neglecting social dialogue in all its forms recorded a very poor score. This indicator shows whether social dialogue helped to prevent general destruction, or conversely, whether the absence of it contributed to the wave of discontent. *Table 11.18* presents the results for all enterprises. It confirms the importance of the regional dimension, with the five regions identified earlier emerging significantly from the regression: Berat, Korca, Shkodra, Vlora, and Gjirokastra were undoubtedly the victims of the most intense destruction. Not only state enterprises but also joint ventures turned out to be the ownership forms worst affected by the rebellion, confirming the problem posed by foreign investors. Public anger against the state seems to have been directed particularly against mines and the public utilities of gas, water, and electricity. The positive effect of enterprise size may also capture part of this anger against large state institutions. It is important to note that social variables also emerged significantly from our econometric analysis. First, the negative and significant coefficient on average wages (AWAGE) confirms that the existence of previously very low wages may have constituted an additional factor of discontent, especially when combined with a poor—or non-existent—social policy. Social dialogue, or the absence of it, had an impact on the extent of the crisis: the deliberate and systematic attempt by managers in many new enterprises to avoid trade union action, forms of workers' participation, and the signing of collective agreements was strongly sanctioned by the workers and local people.

In this regard, some differences could be identified between industry, services, and banks (*Table 11.19*). Low wages seem to have been particularly prevalent in industrial establishments, while the absence of social dialogue was more significantly identified in the service sector where, as we have already seen, new enterprises only rarely implemented even a single element of social policy. Past lay-offs also played a role in services. The role of joint ventures in generating hostility was also found to be more visible in services, confirming the many problems that the state had with foreign partners in this sector (see Chapter 9).

Table 11.18 *Determinants of Enterprise Damage, All Sectors, 1997*

Variables	Coefficient	T-statistics
Property form[1]		
State	0.20604	2.658 ***
Private	−0.08689	−1.087
Joint venture	0.20992	2.132 **
Joint stock	0.22262	1.825 *
Region[2]		
Berat	0.34386	4.332 ***
Dibra	0.15092	1.771 *
Durres	−0.03009	−0.465
Elbasan	0.02630	0.366
Fier	0.10387	1.703 *
Korca	0.36743	5.727 ***
Kukes	0.10441	0.887
Lezha	0.12917	1.454
Shkodra	0.29207	3.865 ***
Gjirokastra	0.30226	3.291 ***
Vlora	0.32903	3.627 ***
Sectors[3]		
Chemicals	−0.15100	−1.183
Leather and shoes	−0.06370	−0.458
Mining	0.21384	2.282 **
Minerals	0.01307	0.135
Textile and clothes	−0.10695	−1.251
Metals	−0.09886	−0.646
Food	−0.00125	−0.017
Gas/water/electricity	0.15492	2.421 **
Trade	−0.04618	−0.762
Hotels/Restaurants	−0.04592	−0.651
Transport	0.01807	0.203
Telecoms	0.08590	0.939
Security	−0.20224	−2.552 **
EMPSIZE	0.00015	1.890 *
EMPCHG	0.00008	0.516
AWAGE	−0.20297	−1.759 *
SOCIAL	−0.04158	−2.162 **
Constant	1.19900	2.516 **
R^2		0.248
F		7.225

Notes: 1 Omitted: Other property forms. *** statistically significant at 1% level.
2 Omitted: Tirana. ** statistically significant at 5% level.
3 Omitted: Wood and paper. * statistically significant at 10% level.

Source: ALFS3.

Table 11.19 *Determinants of Enterprise Damage, by Sector, 1997*

Variables	Industry		Services		Banks	
	Coefficient	T-statistics	Coefficient	T-statistics	Coefficient	T-statistics
Property form[1]						
State	0.11469	0.701	0.20279	1.993 **	0.56109	2.339 **
Private	−0.04912	−0.318	−0.07740	−0.723	–	–
Joint venture	0.20825	1.237	0.29143	1.989 **	0.25624	0.573
Joint stock	0.22127	1.259	0.58788	1.783 *	–	–
Region[2]						
Berat	0.52138	2.164 **	0.25241	2.726 ***	0.82733	2.905 ***
Dibra	0.00888	0.042	0.15445	1.527	0.50108	1.590
Durres	−0.09972	−0.830	−0.02317	−.275	0.69717	1.732 *
Elbasan	−0.04122	−0.286	0.00298	0.033	0.46896	1.718 *
Fier	0.01226	0.094	0.07059	0.952	0.73261	2.167 **
Korca	0.33773	2.779 ***	0.31166	3.636 ***	0.61098	2.309 **
Kukes	0.22022	0.851	−0.09411	−0.643	1.08310	2.899 ***
Lezha	0.12059	0.726	0.08641	0.760	0.31043	0.878
Shkodra	0.29298	1.788*	0.22531	2.441 **	0.73286	2.363 **
Gjirokastra	0.18640	0.951	0.25476	2.290 **	0.85001	2.528 **
Vlora	0.26386	1.462	0.28591	2.376 **	0.70067	2.495 **
Sector[3]						
Chemicals	0.00386	0.024	–	–	–	–
Leather and shoes	0.10841	0.646	–	–	–	–
Mining	0.44878	2.874 ***	–	–	–	–
Minerals	0.14912	1.130	–	–	–	–
Textiles and clothing	0.01183	0.095	–	–	–	–
Metals	0.07031	0.380	–	–	–	–
Food	0.12702	1.078	–	–	–	–
Gas/water/electr.	–	–	0.17591	2.341 **	–	–
Trade	–	–	−0.05731	−.830	–	–
Hotels/restaurants	–	–	−0.04476	−.573	–	–
Transport	–	–	−0.01532	−.156	–	–
Telecoms	–	–	0.11682	1.168	–	–
Security	–	–	−0.16468	−1.854 *	–	–
EMPSIZE	0.00013	1.047	0.00021	1.790 *	0.00145	2.293 **
EMPCHG	0.00029	0.626	−0.00162	−2.629 ***	0.00003	0.161
AWAGE	−0.51733	−2.054 **	−0.13960	−.878	0.49729	1.234
SOCIAL	−0.02837	−0.825	−0.04508	−1.687 *	0.05561	0.684
Constant	2.29997	2.262 **	0.96997	1.507	−2.55167	−1.426
R^2		0.294		0.259		0.645
F		3.029		6.249		2.635

Notes: 1 Omitted: Other property forms.   *** statistically significant at 1% level.
           2 Omitted: Tirana.   ** statistically significant at 5% level.
           3 Omitted: Wood and paper.   * statistically significant at 10% level.

Source: ALFS3.

9 CONCLUSION

The picture of the destruction that emerged from the results of our enterprise survey confirms the extreme complexity of the recent Albanian crisis.

On the one hand, the geographical distribution of destroyed and damaged enterprises confirms the concentration of violence and devastation in the regions that were the core of the rebellion, such as the southern districts of Vlora, Fier, and Gjirokastra, mainly due to the successive collapse of local pyramid schemes and the strong political opposition of the people to the Berisha regime. On the other hand, our regional mapping of the crisis points to other regions and cities, such as Shkodra and Dibra in the north and the industrial regions of Elbasan and Berat, which also witnessed repeated scenes of enterprise destruction. Undoubtedly, a particularly important feature of this crisis was its widespread extent, involving all regions, cities, and areas of Albania. Large-scale acts of destruction in rural areas also reflected the general uneasiness among those making a living from agriculture, so confirming the inadequacies of an agricultural policy exclusively based on marginal cultivation on an extremely small scale. It is quite clear that privatisation and reforms in this sector were not as successful as local and international economic reports had been claiming for a number of years.

The situation is similarly complex in respect of different types of ownership. On the one hand, our enterprise results confirmed that state-owned enterprises were the main target of attacks because they symbolised presidential and governmental power and their responsibility for the fall of the pyramid schemes. For instance, public utilities in services, chemical factories and mines in industry, and local state banks were systematically destroyed or seriously damaged. On the other hand, beyond this expected outcome, we found that a significant amount of damage was also perpetrated against enterprises in other forms of ownership. In particular, foreign ownership turned out to be a common feature of destroyed enterprises, and a large proportion of joint ventures working in textiles and in leather and shoes were systematically destroyed in different parts of the country, from the north—for instance, in Shkodra—to the south, especially in Vlora.

A sectoral overview revealed that a range of industrial and labour factors may have actively contributed to the intensity of the crisis. We found, for instance, that enterprises specialising in labour-intensive activities—such as mining and textiles in industry and telecommunications in services—had particularly attracted the demonstrators' wrath. The figures speak for themselves: 97 per cent of mines and 77 per cent of telecommunications companies were seriously damaged during the crisis. A series of characteristics of the internal functioning or management style of enterprises also played a role. Very low wages, for instance, were found to have contributed to the general discontent and collective destruction, especially in industry. Previous employment cuts also motivated greater damage in enterprises, especially in regions characterised by already high unemployment rates. Where an enterprise's restructuring policy was based exclusively on external adjustments, through laying off a significant part of the labour force, destruction was more frequent and of greater extent. Social policy at the enterprise—or rather the absence of it—was also important. The great damage suffered by joint ventures, for instance, confirmed the problems brought about by this type of property form in terms of working conditions and workers' participation. More globally, the deficit of social dialogue at the enterprise level—in terms of trade union recognition and membership, collective agreements, and workers' participation—seems to have played an important role in the crisis, damage and closures having been limited where social dialogue was strong and based on a number of different channels; on the other hand, it was particularly acute where there was a bad social climate. All these factors often co-existed for years until the workers finally rebelled. External restructuring through lay-offs was often selected by enterprises where social dialogue was poor—or where lay-offs were facilitated by the absence of individual labour contracts—and where the management did not want to discuss alternative options, preferring to obtain greater short-term profits by imposing tougher time schedules and working conditions on the remaining labour force. This is what happened in some new private enterprises that were totally destroyed.

To summarise, our study confirms that the crisis was not generated by the pyramid fund losses alone. Conversely, the wide range of determining factors probably explains the wide geographical extent of the crisis: the crisis was by no means confined to the south, whose political opposition to the old regime was explicit. Industrial factors played a greater role in some regions, especially those dominated by traditional industrial conglomerates, such as Elbasan and Berat; other sources of dissatisfaction may have prevailed elsewhere, such as impoverishment incomes and a lack of social protection in rural areas. At the same time, similar reasons for discontent at the enterprise and local levels contributed to give the destruction process much more than a regional character. Massive dismissals, low wages, and difficult working conditions expanded worker discontent beyond the domain of the enterprise. Poverty in Albania knows no regional borders. More globally, years of suffering and the frustrations accumulated during the transition led almost inevitably to widespread revolt.

12. A Halt to Economic Activity

1 INTRODUCTION

After obtaining a first picture of the destruction, it was essential to analyse the direct effects of the revolt on economic activity. The richness of the data provided by our surveys allows us to determine precisely which enterprises and activities have been obliged to close down or to interrupt operations, and so to provide a first estimate of the overall effect of the crisis on economic activity in Albania. Our most recent enterprise survey was particularly timely, having been carried out in December 1997, that is, more than nine months after the culmination of the spring events, and six months after the successful organisation of elections in June, which marked the beginning of the return to normal life and the recommencement of economic activity. This period of time allowed many employers to restore their enterprise and to resume their activities. In this chapter we give a first assessment of the type of enterprises which had to terminate and those which were able to recommence operations. We are therefore in a position to report on the capacity of local economic actors after such a major crisis, and provide some insights into the real strengths of the Albanian economy. Closer identification is carried out by type of sector, industry, property form, size, and region. A series of microeconomic indicators at the enterprise level allows us to compare enterprise production and performance figures at the end of 1997 with those of one year earlier. They also help us to define what characteristics seem to have been essential for enterprises to survive the crisis. We identify which activities have suffered the most and which require urgent policy support.

Needless to say, the terrible state of enterprises and of local labour and statistical offices, many of which were also totally burnt out, made it difficult to collect the necessary data. Moreover, most enterprises having been either destroyed or—at least partially—closed down, statistical information on enterprise activity was difficult to obtain. Many managers simply did not know, less than one year after the crisis, how they were going to proceed. Others had simply fled abroad with their enterprise's data and money. We therefore cannot pretend in this first assessment to provide a full picture of what happened, but we believe that the data that we have collected are

sufficiently reliable and representative to furnish a faithful overview of the
economic implications of the crisis.[1]

2 THE EFFECTS OF THE CRISIS ON ALBANIAN ENTERPRISES

Enterprise results confirm the direct effects of the crisis on enterprises. In
total, 43 per cent had to interrupt their activities, either partially or totally; if
one adds to this the 16 per cent of enterprises that were totally destroyed, one
reaches a total of 60 per cent of enterprises directly hurt by the crisis. Most
enterprises that interrupted totally were found to have almost no chance of
starting up again: in many cases, the manager has left the country and is
unlikely to return. We should also emphasise that many enterprises that
reported only partial closure were in fact not operating: they simply kept the
enterprise open, but halted production. Others managed to maintain only the
core of their activities.

   Those which halted their activities altogether reported an average period of
closure of six months, while enterprises that only partially interrupted their
activities started something resembling normal operations again after an
interruption of three months. The periods of interruption given here may serve
only as indicative figures, however, since less than 25 per cent of enterprises
responded to this question. We suspect therefore that the figures presented
here underestimate the true duration of interruption.[2] No great differences

Table 12.1 *Enterprises Interrupting their Activities, by Sector, 1997*
(% of establishments totally or partially interrupting activities due to the crisis and average duration of interruption in months)

	Interrupted totally	Months	Interrupted partially	Months	Total interrupted
Industry	15.6	6.3	36.5	3.0	52.1
Services	14.9	6.0	24.1	3.6	39.0
Banks	3.9	1.8	41.2	2.3	45.1
All	14.5	6.0	28.6	3.3	43.1

Source: ALFS3.

   1. This first assessment will be complemented by technical reports on specific topics carried
out together with the Albanian Statistical Institute.
   2. Managers who were hesitating or not reporting had generally had a longer period of
interruption than others. Most had not resumed activities yet.

were observed between industry, services, and banks (see *Table 12.1*). We will see, however, that these national averages conceal great differences by region, type of enterprise, and activity.

The greatest variations were observed mainly by region: the three regions of Vlora, Korca, and Shkodra saw the most enterprises interrupting their activities. In Vlora and Shkodra, one-quarter of enterprises had to close down. Enterprises in other regions, however, were not spared. In Tirana, 20 per cent of enterprises interrupted their production totally. Half of all enterprises had to interrupt operations in Dibra, and 15 per cent ceased altogether. A similar situation was observed in Berat, Durres, and Gjirokastra. A lower proportion of enterprises seems to have been affected in Kukes.

Table 12.2 *Enterprises Interrupting their Activities, by Region, 1997*
(% of establishments totally or partially interrupting activities due to the crisis and average duration of interruption in months)

	Interrupted totally	Months	Interrupted partially	Months	Total interrupted
Berat	13.3	5.0	18.3	3.2	31.6
Dibra	15.0	1.2	35.0	1.3	50.0
Durres	6.2	6.1	36.7	2.7	42.9
Elbasan	4.6	7.0	18.5	3.4	23.1
Fier	8.0	5.1	24.8	3.5	32.8
Gjirokastra	12.1	3.8	21.2	3.2	33.3
Korca	6.1	6.1	54.1	3.1	60.2
Kukes	0	0	18.2	2.5	18.2
Lezha	7.9	7.0	28.9	4.3	36.8
Shkodra	23.9	8.3	32.4	3.9	56.3
Tirana	20.8	3.6	19.3	2.6	40.1
Vlora	25.6	8.0	46.5	5.1	72.1

Source: ALFS3.

Differences were also observed by type of ownership. A high percentage of joint ventures, nearly one-third of them, closed completely, and with a longer period of interruption: more than 60 per cent of them interrupted operations either totally or partially. If we add this to the 13 per cent that were destroyed, this gives more than 70 per cent of joint ventures directly hurt by the crisis. Most foreign investors decided to suspend their activities immediately when they saw the extent of the crisis, and did not return to the country for several months. This rendered a return to normal activity difficult, especially since foreign investors had a majority control in almost all joint ventures (with an average of 60 per cent of the shares). This difference shows a higher risk aversion on the part of foreign operators compared to Albanian employers who in many cases decided to continue in the midst of the chaos. The crisis also harmed small domestic private enterprises, however: nearly 60 per cent of them had to interrupt their activities totally or partially. By contrast, state enterprises continued operating despite considerable damage; in many cases, they were working well below normal production volumes, however.

Table 12.3 *Enterprises Interrupting their Activities, by Property Form, 1997*
(% of establishments totally or partially interrupting activities due to the crisis and average duration of interruption in months)

	Interrupted totally	Months	Interrupted partially	Months	Total interrupted
State	6.2	4.7	25.6	3.4	31.8
Private	19.8	5.3	39.5	3.3	59.3
Joint venture	26.3	6.4	34.2	2.9	60.5
Joint stock	8.7	4.5	39.1	2.8	47.8
Other	10.0	4.7	17.5	3.0	27.5

Source: ALFS3.

Results by industry show that textiles and clothing and leather and shoes had the highest proportion of enterprises interrupting their activities, followed by metals, minerals, and food.

Table 12.4 *Enterprises Interrupting their Activities, by Industry, 1997*
(% of establishments totally or partially interrupting activities due to the crisis and average duration of interruption in months)

	Interrupted totally	Months	Interrupted partially	Months	Total interrupted
Food processing	14.9	5.1	38.8	3.3	53.7
Chemicals	15.0	4.5	25.0	3.2	40.0
Leather and shoes	17.7	5.4	41.2	4.0	58.9
Mining	16.2	6.8	32.4	2.6	48.6
Minerals	8.6	5.7	48.6	2.8	57.2
Textiles and clothing	19.4	6.8	43.1	2.7	62.5
Metals	18.2	9.0	36.4	2.8	54.6
Wood and paper	14.3	6.7	19.0	3.2	33.3

Source: ALFS3.

Among services, hotels and restaurants were the first to be closed, both for security reasons during the crisis and because of the lack of customers after the crisis. Martial law, along with the curfew imposed in Tirana, and the political instability preceding the June elections did little for the profitability of restaurants and bars. People's lack of money after the fall of the pyramid schemes was another factor. At the same time, the hotels were hardest hit by the suspension of tourism: only a few businessmen and officials entered Albania in 1997. Trade activities were also interrupted, with more than 20 per cent of trading companies, generally the smallest and least robust, interrupting their activities for an average of six months. We shall see that many had not resumed activities by the end of 1997. Many transport companies also had to close down from the beginning of the events, because of the obstruction of the main road axes between the north and the south. Until the end of 1997, although traffic had been re-established, transportation could not be ensured without risk of attack or looting. This sector was among those which suffered the most from the revolt and its economic consequences. Telecommunications companies also had to interrupt their operations, at least partially, given the difficulty of access to many regions and the great damage inflicted on this sector during the revolt. Survey results confirm that security companies went through the crisis without interrupting or even reducing their activities. Gas, water, and electricity services, because of their importance for the population and for the economy, continued to operate despite destroyed agencies and equipment.

Table 12.5 *Enterprises Interrupting their Activities, by Service, 1997*
(% of establishments totally or partially interrupting activities due to the crisis and average duration of interruption in months)

	Interrupted totally	Months	Interrupted partially	Months	Total interrupted
Gas/water/electricity	3.5	1.3	8.1	2.8	11.6
Trade	21.5	5.6	28.0	3.0	49.0
Hotels/restaurants	20.6	4.1	39.1	4.4	59.7
Transport	9.8	5.6	41.2	3.3	51.0
Telecommunications	0.0	0.0	38.7	6.0	38.7
Security	7.1	8.0	8.6	3.2	15.7
Other	9.4	5.1	16.2	2.1	25.6

Source: ALFS3.

The characteristics of enterprises, especially in terms of employment, also influenced their capacity to continue without interruption. Although we found that large establishments clearly registered much greater damage, small enterprises were revealed to be the most vulnerable to the crisis: nearly 50 per cent of enterprises with fewer than 50 employees had to suspend operations, often for the totality of their activities. Most of these small enterprises were operating in trade, textiles and clothing, and leather and shoes. This was an additional sign of the fragility of the new small private enterprises, especially in services, a feature that we tried to describe in Chapter 3.

Table 12.6 *Enterprises Interrupting their Activities, by Level of Employment, 1997 (% of establishments totally or partially interrupting activities due to the crisis and average duration of interruption in months)*

	Interrupted totally	Months	Interrupted partially	Months	Total interrupted
1–50	11.2	5.9	38.3	3.3	49.5
51–100	7.5	5.8	35.0	3.6	42.5
101–200	8.0	3.5	28.7	2.7	36.7
201+	11.3	7.6	25.0	2.9	36.3

Source: ALFS3.

Employment changes over the past two years also seem to be somehow related to the capacity of the enterprise to resist the crisis. The propensity to interrupt was clearly much more pronounced among enterprises that had resorted to massive lay-offs (more than 20 per cent in the last two years), and the ability to resist the crisis much stronger in enterprises where employment had been less reduced or even increased in the past two years (*Table 12.7*).

Table 12.7 *Enterprises Interrupting their Activities, by Employment Change, 1997 (% of establishments totally or partially interrupting activities due to the crisis and average duration of interruption in months)*

	Interrupted totally	Months	Interrupted partially	Months	Total interrupted
Fell 20+	17.6	8.0	42.6	3.5	60.2
Fell 19–10	8.3	2.4	43.3	3.7	51.6
Fell 9–1	5.0	3.3	24.0	3.3	29.0
No change	8.3	3.4	35.2	3.2	43.5
Rose	5.4	3.7	36.6	2.7	42.0

Source: ALFS3.

This result might be due to different phenomena. First, previous employment cuts reflect the economic and financial strength of the firm. Enterprises that increased employment in 1995–96 may have been more profitable than the others and therefore better able to withstand the crisis. Secondly, we saw in the previous chapter that popular wrath was more frequently directed towards enterprises that had carried out massive lay-offs without much consideration for the fate of the workers. In most cases, this relationship between employment changes and probability of suspending operations is probably a combination of the two factors mentioned above.

In order better to understand the factors that led enterprises to interrupt their activity, we complemented the above statistical averages with an econometric analysis. We estimated the following equation by means of ordinary least squares regressions, taking the reporting of interruption as the dependent variable (the dummy variable taking the value 1 if the enterprise interrupted, and 0 otherwise):

$$(\text{INTERRUPTED}) = a + b1\sum(\text{SECTOR}) + b2\sum(\text{PROP}) + b3\sum(\text{REG}) + b4(\text{EMPSIZE}) + b5(\text{EMPCH}) + b6(\text{DAMAGED}) + e$$

where

> SECTOR = a set of dummies for the sector (different industries and services);
> PROP = a set of dummies for the property form of the enterprise;
> REG = a set of dummies for the regional location of the enterprise;
> EMPSIZE = size of enterprise by number of employees;
> EMPCH = percentage of labour force change in 1996;
> DAMAGED = a dummy for the reporting of damage;
> e = error term.

Among the explanatory factors, in addition of dummy variables for sectors, regions, and ownership forms, and the variables previously used concerning the size of the enterprise and employment changes, we added a variable for taking into account the damage suffered by the enterprise. The results presented in *Table 12.8* confirm many of our previous results. Enterprises had a greater probability of interrupting their activity if located in the districts of Vlora, Shkodra, Korca, or Dibra. All property forms appeared with a positive and significant coefficient when taking state ownership as the omitted variable, showing a lower propensity to interrupt in state enterprises. By contrast, private owners were found to have interrupted activities on a massive scale. This process was also reflected in the strong negative coefficient on the size of enterprises, small enterprises having systematically closed down or interrupted part of their activity soon after the uprising began.

Table 12.8 *Determinants of Enterprises' Interruption of Activities, All Sectors, 1997*

Variables	Coefficient	T-statistics
Property form[1]		
Private	0.26324	5.540 ***
Joint venture	0.13399	1.835 *
Joint stock	0.17914	1.678 *
Region[2]		
Berat	0.04224	0.552
Dibra	0.18110	2.235 **
Durres	0.07829	1.306
Elbasan	−0.07575	−1.119
Fier	−0.04544	−0.807
Korca	0.12723	2.074 **
Kukes	−0.13780	−1.252
Lezha	0.06049	0.731
Shkodra	0.15934	2.206 **
Gjirokastra	−0.03209	−0.365
Vlora	0.32717	3.772 ***
Sector[3]		
Chemicals	0.12144	0.994
Leather and shoes	0.33921	2.578 **
Mining	0.20514	2.326 **
Minerals	0.22104	2.438 **
Textiles and clothing	0.28308	3.709 ***
Metals	0.16618	1.142
Wood and paper	0.00901	0.098
Gas/water/electr.	−0.24621	−4.131 ***
Trade	0.05402	1.007
Hotels/restaurants	0.14135	2.230 **
Transport	0.25848	3.120 ***
Telecoms	0.05893	0.687
Security	−0.34057	−4.778 ***
EMPSIZE	−0.00022	−2.793 ***
EMPCHG	0.00007	1.339
DAMAGED	0.25448	7.073 ***
Constant	0.13054	2.469 **
R^2		0.314
F		10.410

Notes: 1 Omitted: State.   *** statistically significant at 1% level.
                2 Omitted: Tirana.   ** statistically significant at 5% level.
                3 Omitted: Food.   * statistically significant at 10% level.

Source: ALFS3.

Joint ventures and joint-stock enterprises were also unable to maintain operations for long. Econometric results by sector also highlight sectors dominated by private or foreign ownership, such as textiles and clothing (which appeared with a very high and positive coefficient), leather and shoes, and transport. For state-owned enterprises, mining and minerals were the most hurt by the crisis, with no other alternative than to close or slow down their activity. In services, only public utilities but also private security sectors (both with a negative and significant coefficient) continued their activity despite the generalised crisis. As expected, the reporting of damage turned out to be highly significant and positive, violent attacks having obviously had an adverse effect on the enterprises' ability to continue their activities. The large-scale damage inflicted in the worst-affected sectors, such as mining, minerals, and textiles, directly led to many companies simply closing down the plant.

Employment changes were not significant, probably as a result of two contradictory effects: while in large state companies operating in traditional sectors such as mining, past employment cuts must have contributed to public hostility and enterprises' propensity to interrupt activity, small private enterprises that were found to have suspended operations most widely had generally increased employment over the previous year.

3 A DIFFERENTIATED PROPENSITY TO RESUME OPERATIONS

In our survey we also asked enterprises to report on whether they had resumed their activities. Their responses provide information essential to any assessment of the ability of Albanian enterprises to overcome the crisis. Disappointingly, it seems that only a relatively small percentage of enterprises—slightly more than one-third of those which had to interrupt their activities—had resumed economic activity by the end of 1997. This provides further confirmation, if needed, that the crisis dealt an almost mortal blow to Albanian enterprises and economic activity. It is important to notice, however, that the propensity to restart was much higher in industry than in services. This serves to emphasise once again the weaknesses of the service sector (see Chapter 3), while at the same time underlining the greater potential dynamism of the industrial sector, despite its miserable condition after the crisis. More detailed analysis revealed other notable differences, as well as, even more interestingly, a number of totally unexpected results.

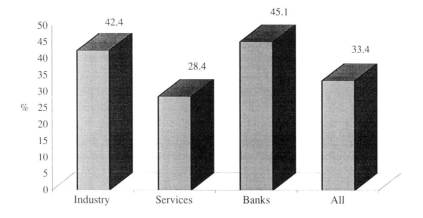

Figure 12.1 *Enterprises Resuming Activities, by Sector, Dec. 1997*
(% of establishments restarting activities after crisis)

Source: ALFS3.

The first unexpected outcome emerged from a look at the regions. While we might have expected that the regions most affected by destruction and interruption of economic activities would be less inclined to resume their activities, or at least to need more time to do so, the opposite seems to have been the case. The highest percentage of enterprises to have recommenced activities—more than 50 per cent—was found in the regions of Korca, Vlora, Dibra, and Shkodra, paradoxically the very regions most seriously harmed by the 1997 revolt. At the same time, enterprises encountering problems in restarting their activities were found in Kukes (especially in services, where only 7 per cent had restarted), but also Elbasan and Tirana. Industrial enterprises localised in Berat and Lezha also had problems restarting their operations. In the banking sector, none of the few banks (five) that had suspended their activities in Elbasan had resumed by the end of 1997, with two-thirds of banks remaining closed in Kukes and Fier.

Other unexpected results help us to identify the types of enterprise which were able to restart quickly: in industry, enterprises in minerals but also in textiles and clothing and leather and shoes; in services, hotels and restaurants and also transport. These were precisely the sectors in which more enterprises had to stop, either permanently or temporarily.

Table 12.9 *Enterprises Resuming Activities, by Region, Dec. 1997*
(% of establishments restarting activities after crisis)

	Industry	Services	Banks	All
Berat	30.0	23.9	50.0	26.7
Dibra	44.4	50.0	66.7	50.0
Durres	40.4	35.1	50.0	37.5
Elbasan	38.9	14.3	0.0	20.0
Fier	37.1	25.0	33.3	28.9
Gjirokastra	50.0	18.2	66.7	30.3
Korca	74.0	41.9	40.0	58.2
Kukes	50.0	6.7	33.3	18.2
Lezha	33.3	29.2	50.0	31.6
Shkodra	36.4	44.4	75.0	43.7
Tirana	25.0	19.8	40.0	21.9
Vlora	60.0	52.2	60.0	55.8

Source: ALFS3.

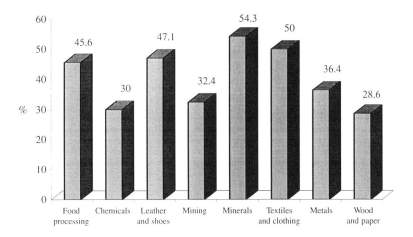

Figure 12.2 *Enterprises Resuming Activities, by Industry, Dec. 1997*
(% of establishments restarting activities after crisis)

Source: ALFS3.

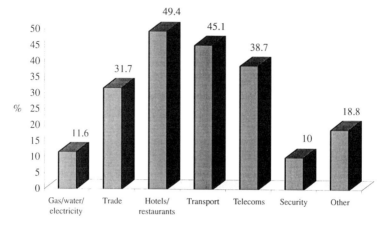

Figure 12.3 *Enterprises Resuming Activities, by Service, Dec. 1997 (% of establishments restarting activities after crisis)*

Source: ALFS3.

Among the various types of ownership, state enterprises were found to have the greatest difficulties resuming normal operations, although this group was less likely on the whole to have interrupted activities completely during the crisis. All other property forms reported a high propensity to restart, especially private enterprises, but also joint-stock companies and joint ventures. The relatively good result for joint ventures and private firms in industry may partly explain the high propensity to restart also observed in textiles and clothing and leather and shoes, the two branches in which they concentrate most of their activities. It might also explain the good results of Vlora and Shkodra, where joint ventures are mainly concentrated. The results of joint ventures in services seemed to be less promising, especially in trade.

Table 12.10 *Enterprises Resuming Activities, by Property Form, Dec. 1997 (% of establishments restarting activities after crisis)*

	Industry	Services	Banks	All
State	35.3	22.0	47.6	28.0
Private	58.4	41.3	–	46.6
Joint venture	42.2	36.7	66.7	39.5
Joint stock	47.6	50.0	–	47.8

Source: ALFS3.

Small establishments were also found to resume activities sooner than others: a direct and negative correlation between size and probability of restarting emerged from our enterprise survey results. Such establishments are generally private concerns but also joint ventures. Again, small enterprises were a group which had had to interrupt activities in massive numbers because of the crisis. Very large enterprises, on the other hand, also suffered a great deal of damage during the events, but, perhaps not surprisingly, have found it much harder to pick up the pieces again, especially in services.

Table 12.11 *Enterprises Resuming Activities, by Level of Employment, Dec. 1997 (% of establishments restarting activities after crisis)*

	Industry	Services	Banks	All
1–50	52.8	42.0	47.5	45.0
51–100	62.2	21.7	50.0	38.3
101–200	56.7	21.4	–	33.3
201+	39.5	14.7	33.3	28.8

Source: ALFS3.

We complemented the above results with an econometric analysis, this time taking the propensity to restart as the dependent variable. In addition to the variables we used in the preceding equations, we added factors that may have played a specific role in the ability of enterprises to restart operations. We included among the explanatory variables the variable for social dialogue, but also a series of dummy variables reflecting the main economic difficulty that the enterprise reported after the crisis: lack of demand, no investment capacity, and absence of raw materials. The variable of employment changes takes into account only the labour force adjustments made in 1997, that is, after the crisis.

We also included a dummy for complete interruption of activities: enterprises which were unable to avoid this were expected to face more problems resuming operations than those that suffered only a partial shutdown.

The equation was tested only on the sample of enterprises that reported having interrupted activities, either totally or partially. The results are presented in *Table 12.12*.

In a first equation, the variable for total interruption is the most significant, clearly showing that those who interrupted their operations completely generally have little capacity to restart: less than 10 per cent of those which interrupted their activities completely were able to resume their activity. In

Table 12.12 *Determinants of Enterprise Capacity to Resume Activities, All Sectors, 1997*

Variables	Equation 1		Equation 2	
	Coefficient	T-statistics	Coefficient	T-statistics
Property form[1]				
Private	0.06075	1.075	0.33347	3.754 ***
Joint venture	0.01025	0.154	0.19142	1.644 *
Joint stock	0.11123	1.135	0.17063	1.104
Region[2]				
Berat	0.08197	0.932	0.13207	0.823
Dibra	0.25843	2.997 ***	0.47769	2.955 ***
Durres	−0.00501	−0.083	0.00976	0.101
Elbasan	−0.03997	−0.526	−0.01291	−0.100
Fier	0.02276	0.388	−0.00150	−0.015
Korca	0.03338	0.537	0.15214	1.245
Kukes	−0.05705	−0.277	−0.35351	−1.738 *
Lezha	−0.05975	−0.731	−0.03064	−0.228
Shkodra	−0.01225	−0.177	−0.00321	−0.025
Gjirokastra	0.04509	0.511	−0.01325	−0.091
Vlora	0.00639	0.102	0.18488	1.446
Sector[3]				
Chemicals	0.10959	0.780	−0.05783	−0.344
Leather and shoes	−0.09669	−0.992	0.25124	1.206
Mining	−0.26091	−3.499 ***	−0.04001	−0.313
Minerals	−0.00639	−0.084	0.27806	1.833 *
Textiles and clothing	0.02031	0.283	0.24839	1.802 *
Metals	−0.27699	−2.063 **	−0.12104	−0.594
Wood and paper	0.07131	0.817	0.10007	0.680
Gas/water/electr.	0.10081	1.089	−0.06059	−0.484
Trade	0.03365	0.602	0.09946	1.032
Hotels and restaurants	−0.04279	−0.777	0.07721	0.782
Transport	−0.05866	−0.820	0.20795	1.664 *
Telecoms	0.03093	0.351	0.26172	1.778 *
Security	−0.05812	−0.541	−0.21749	−1.373
EMPSIZE	0.00006	0.589	−0.00009	−1.008
EMPCHG	−0.00008	−2.659 ***	−0.00007	−1.057
DAMAGED	−0.04606	−1.151	0.17156	2.548 **
NODEMAND	−0.07065	−1.880 *	0.03327	0.502
NOINVEST	−0.02331	−0.391	−0.04637	−0.514
NORAWMAT	−0.06474	−0.972	0.10909	0.923
TOTALINTRPT	−0.33580	−8.526 ***	NO	
SOCIAL	−0.00308	−0.154	−0.00585	−0.171
Constant	1.03207	12.969 ***	0.19844	1.632
R^2		0.551		0.257
F		5.145		2.758

Notes: 1 Omitted: State.   *** statistically significant at 1% level.
            2 Omitted: Tirana.   ** statistically significant at 5% level.
            3 Omitted: Food.   * statistically significant at 10% level.

Source: ALFS3.

this equation, enterprises in mining and metals were clearly found to have most difficulties restarting. Interestingly, the variable for employment changes in 1997 was highly significant, showing that the greater the employment cuts implemented in response to the crisis, the greater the possibility of restarting. Labour force reductions thus became one way of surviving for enterprises, a dimension we further investigate in Chapter 14. It was not surprising in this context that the social dialogue variable was not significant: while active dialogue with trade unions and workers may have helped the manager to resume activity—this happened in some state enterprises—small enterprises, in order to continue operating, were even less inclined than before the crisis to implement a social policy. Even in large state enterprises, the reduction of employment in order to operate without incurring unacceptably high losses was not the best way of enhancing social dialogue and forms of workers' participation. We will see in fact that almost all indicators of social dialogue at the enterprise level, especially trade unionisation, fell sharply after the crisis, even among state-owned enterprises. It is important to note that the lack of demand (with a negative and significant coefficient) turned out to be one determinant factor preventing enterprises from returning to normal activity, a problem confirmed by managers later in this chapter, and one which should be kept in mind with regard to policy recommendations.[3] We tested a second equation without the variable for complete interruption that we expected to capture the significance of other variables. Although the R^2 of the equation was significantly reduced, this allowed us to identify other important correlations. They generally confirm our previous main conclusion that it was precisely where the propensity to interrupt had been greatest that activity restarted, in sectors such as textiles and clothing, and minerals in industry, and transport and telecommunications in services.

Private enterprises were found to have the greater dynamism in restarting, along with, although to a lesser extent, joint ventures. The region of Dibra shows the most significant signs of economic recovery, in contrast with Kukes, where enterprises, especially those operating in services, had great difficulties recommencing operations. This may be due to the extremely high degree of damage registered in Kukes (Chapter 11): the suffering of damage represents in the equation another important factor preventing enterprises from getting back to normal business.

3. In the same equation for industrial enterprises only, which is not given here, the variable for the lack of raw materials also appeared with a negative and highly significant coefficient, indicating that the resolution of this problem may help enterprises to recover, a dimension which is also developed in our policy recommendations (Chapter 15).

As far as those managers who had not yet restarted are concerned, we asked about their future intentions: would they remain inactive or start up again in the course of the next six months, with an option for those who "did not know". Very few enterprises in fact responded with a definite answer with regard to their future operations, more than 95 per cent admitting that they were still unable to make a judgement. Only among those who had interrupted totally, 26 per cent clearly (33 per cent in services) stated that they would not start up again. In industry, nearly 15 per cent of enterprises in Berat, Dibra, and Gjirokastra reported that they would not recommence activities. Among the rest, uncertainty prevailed: 100 per cent of managers for instance in Kukes and Vlora, in all property forms and sectors, replied that they did not know. This answer illustrates faithfully the situation of generalised doubt and economic uncertainty that still prevailed at the end of 1997, more than six months after the supposed return to normal life.

Table 12.13 *Future Intentions among Enterprises that Had Not Resumed their Activities, by Sector, Dec. 1997 (%)*

	Industry	Services	Banks	All
Remain inactive	2.6	3.2	0	2.9
Restart in the next six months	2.6	2.0	0	2.1
Do not know	94.8	94.8	100	95.0
	100%	100%	100%	100%

Source: ALFS3.

4 BACK TO NORMAL?

While a certain number of enterprises resumed operations, at least in some sectors, it was important to check whether they had been able to recover previous performance levels. In this section we present a series of economic indicators in pursuit of such an assessment: production capacity, exports, profits, and sales change, complemented by information provided by the managers themselves on the main difficulties they encountered in 1997 and their prospects for the near future.

Production Capacity: Still below 1996 Levels despite Signs of Recovery

Employers reported that they were operating on average at slightly above 50 per cent of full capacity, a clear indication of the extent to which the crisis has affected the whole economy. Moreover, we should emphasise that this result reflects the capacity of the strongest businesses, those able to survive the crisis, and does not take into account all those which had to cease operating. Moreover, only 50 per cent of enterprises responded to this question, implying that the real average operating level is likely to be much lower than the one reported by enterprises, particularly given the fact that some enterprises reported having suspended part of their previous activities.

Amidst such darkness, however, it is important to seek potential sources of light, to identify the signs of hope. It is in this spirit that this 50 per cent average may be considered as encouraging—after all, Albanian enterprises were operating at an average of only 66 per cent of capacity in 1996. Whatever the true figures, these results show that some enterprises were at least well on the way towards resuming pre-crisis production levels. This slight recovery was particularly visible among private enterprises and joint ventures, while joint-stock companies were scarcely able to manage 40 per cent of full capacity.

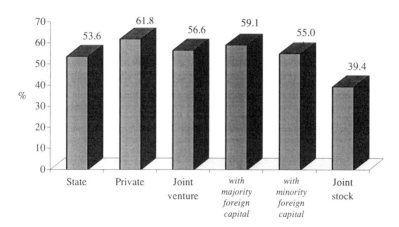

Figure 12.4 *Production Capacity, by Property Form, Dec. 1997*

Source: ALFS3.

In industry, enterprises in textiles and clothing and leather and shoes were again performing better, already operating at nearly 70 per cent of full production capacity. The mining companies had also recovered significantly, despite recent losses. Chemicals were left well behind. In services, security enterprises continued their good run, while transport companies and public utilities were rapidly recovering. The crisis did not seem to be over for hotels and restaurants and telecommunications, however. The few banks that responded (only 5) reported operating above 80 per cent of capacity: their high rate of failure to respond, however, confirms that most of them were still in limbo, especially state-owned establishments that were just marking time before their fate was determined by the privatisation process. Among the regions, Dibra and Lezha were found to have more enterprises back to high capacity levels, both in industry and services. Kukes also had a good record in services, by contrast with Berat, Elbasan, and Gjirokastra, where service companies were apparently finding it very difficult to emerge from the crisis. Industrial establishments in Elbasan and Vlora were showing signs of

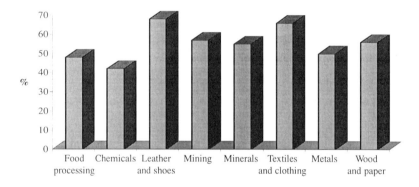

Figure 12.5 *Production Capacity, by Industry, Dec. 1997*

Source: ALFS3.

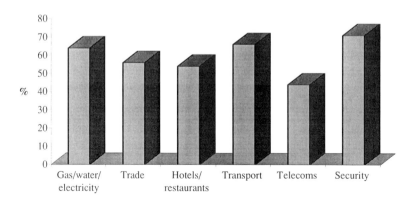

Figure 12.6 *Production Capacity, by Service, Dec. 1997*

Source: ALFS3.

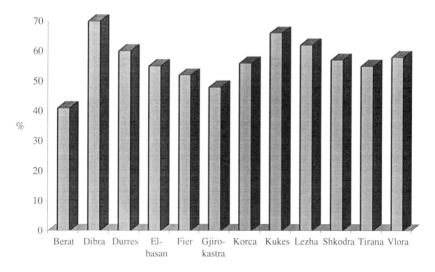

Figure 12.7 *Production Capacity, by Region, Dec. 1997*

Source: ALFS3.

production increase, while elsewhere, for example, in Shkodra, Gjirokastra, Fier, but also Tirana, much had still to be done.

Exports: A Return to Isolation during the Crisis

Enterprise export reports for 1997 reveal another dimension of the crisis: the almost total suspension of foreign trade. Exports suffered the most. The proportion of production exported fell from an average of 15 per cent in 1996 to less than 2 per cent in 1997. In highly exporting industries, such as textiles and clothing, accustomed between 1994 and 1996 to channel more than 80 per of their production into external markets, exports were drastically interrupted, and fell below 10 per cent of total production. They fell below 20 per cent in leather and shoes. The same process was also visible, although to a lesser extent, in wood and paper and in metals. Only chemicals seemed to continue exporting at levels comparable with one year earlier. An even more depressing picture was observed in services, with less than 1 per cent of services provided for foreign markets, the most notable export collapse being registered in the trade sector. Exports in the new private small service businesses, that only one year earlier had begun to contribute higher profits, were reduced to miserable levels in the space of a few months.

Albania in Crisis

Table 12.14 *Percentage of Production Exported, by Industry, 1996–97*

	1996	1997
Food processing	5.0	2.2
Chemicals	10.0	7.8
Leather and shoes	80.0	17.4
Mining	11.0	2.4
Minerals	3.0	3.8
Textiles and clothing	81.0	6.7
Metals	22.0	10.0
Wood and paper	21.0	11.0
All industries	11.0	3.3

Source: ALFS3.

This decline in Albania's external markets was occasioned mainly by the immediate retreat of joint ventures during the crisis: at the end of 1997, they were exporting only 13 per cent of their industrial production compared to more than 50 per cent in 1996 (even 60 per cent for those with majority foreign capital). In 1997, the collapse of exports was even more pronounced for many joint ventures in majority foreign ownership, which ceased trading when the foreign manager left Albania, while joint ventures in majority Albanian control continued. This is an instructive development for all those who claim that majority foreign ownership is the most profitable form of joint venture in Albania: while foreign investors dominated exports in 1996, their unwillingness to resume operations and low exports in 1997 will harm Albania's macro-economic development. As we explain in Chapter 13, this sudden fall in exports from joint ventures will contribute to a large trade deficit for 1997.

Table 12.15 *Percentage of Industrial Production Exported, by Property Form, 1996–97*

	1996	1997
State	12.0	4.5
Private	30.0	4.5
Joint venture	52.0	12.9
with minority foreign capital	30.0	24.0
with majority foreign capital	61.0	11.0
Joint stock	2.0	4.0

Source: ALFS3.

Regional figures show that traditionally exporting regions such as Vlora, Durres, and Tirana had substantially reduced sales abroad. Exports were mainly from regions close to the borders: textiles and leather from Gjirokastra directly to neighbouring Greece, or mining and metal products from Dibra and clothes from Korca, both situated close to the borders of Macedonia and Greece.

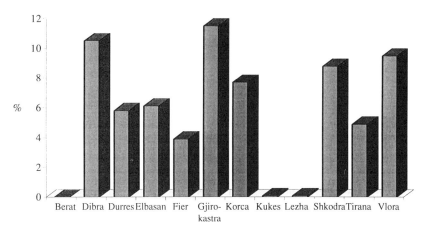

Figure 12.8 *Percentage of Industrial Production Exported, by Region, 1997*

Source: ALFS3.

Losses Endangering Survival

We have noted that the 50 per cent resumption of activities on the part of Albanian enterprises was a promising result, given that they had been operating at only 66 per cent of full capacity before the crisis. Nevertheless, these figures do not mean much unless the enterprises' financial results are factored in, particularly in respect of profits and sales. From this perspective, at the end of 1997 Albanian factories were in a parlous state: more than 30 per cent registered pure losses in 1997; 50 per cent of managements also reported a decrease in sales for the first nine months of the year. No major differences were observed between the main sectors of the economy, confirming that the crisis was widely generalised. The situation is even more alarming given that it comes after a long period of falling industrial output (see Chapter 2) and major difficulties in the service sector (Chapter 3). The fall in sales compared to 1996 levels is even more significant given the fact that less than 50 per cent of enterprises had reported increased sales that year. It is to be hoped, however, that Albanian enterprises touched bottom with the crisis of 1997 and that they can only generate progressively better results from now on.

The percentage of enterprises registering pure losses was highest in services, with nearly 50 per cent of enterprises. In industry, nearly 60 per cent of enterprises working in metals and mining were also in deficit, followed by 45 per cent of enterprises in minerals. Significant differences by size were observed between industry and services: while mainly large enterprises had a greater probability of registering losses in industry, a majority of small enterprises were in this situation in services.

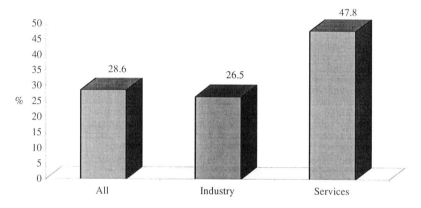

Figure 12.9 *Percentage of Enterprises Registering Pure Losses, by Sector, 1997*

Note: Not enough banks answered this question to make their inclusion meaningful.
Source: ALFS3.

Table 12.16 *Percentage of Enterprises Registering Pure Losses, by Sector, 1997*

	Industry	Services	All
1–50	23.3	60.0	26.5
51–100	25.5	50.0	26.5
101–200	28.0	40.0	30.0
201+	38.2	33.3	37.5

Source: ALFS3.

A majority of state-owned enterprises reported a total lack of profits. While private enterprises were found to be less seriously hurt by the crisis, joint ventures were found to be particularly vulnerable, nearly 40 per cent of them registering losses, especially among those with minority foreign capital (50 per cent).

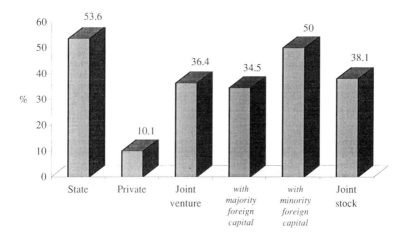

Figure 12.10 *Percentage of Enterprises Registering Pure Losses, by Property Form, 1997*

Source: ALFS3.

The proportion of enterprises in deficit was highest in the region of Berat, involving 62 per cent of all enterprises and 80 per cent of industrial enterprises. Gjirokastra, traditionally very dynamic as the closest city to the Greek border, was also found to be badly affected, with nearly 60 per cent of enterprises reporting pure losses in 1997. Service companies were also in deep deficit in their traditional fiefs, Durres and Tirana, with nearly 70 per cent of companies reporting a deficit.

The picture that emerges from sales changes compared to the previous year unfortunately does not show more positive developments: 50 per cent of enterprises reported decreased sales compared to 1996, with some sectors and regions registering even more depressing results.

Table 12.17 *Sales Change Compared to Previous Year, by Sector, 1997*
(% of enterprises in sector reporting sales change in real terms)

	Decreased	Increased	No change	Do not know
Industry	55	31	11	3
Services	49	26	19	6
Banks	40	28	4	28
All	50	28	16	6

Source: ALFS3.

Poor sales in 1997 were particularly common in the food industry, concerning nearly 80 per cent of enterprises, in mining (nearly 70 per cent), and in chemicals and metals (nearly 60 per cent). In services, hotels and restaurants continued to face a fall in sales (60 per cent), with generalised bad results in trade and public utilities. Our results confirmed the better prospects for textiles and clothing and leather and shoes.

Table 12.18 *Sales Change Compared to Previous Year, by Industry, 1997 (% of enterprises in sector reporting sales change in real terms)*

	Decreased	Increased	No change	Do not know
Food	76.4	14.5	5.5	3.6
Chemicals	57.1	35.7	7.2	0
Leather and shoes	25.0	66.7	8.3	0
Mining	67.7	19.4	9.7	3.2
Minerals	42.3	30.8	23.1	3.8
Textiles and clothing	34.8	50.0	13.0	2.2
Metals	55.6	44.4	0	0
Wood and paper	50.0	25.0	17.9	7.1

Source: ALFS3.

Table 12.19 *Sales Change Compared to Previous Year, by Service, 1997 (% of enterprises in sector reporting sales change in real terms)*

	Decreased	Increased	No change	Do not know
Gas/water/electricity	52.4	29.3	8.5	9.8
Trade	53.2	31.2	15.6	0
Hotels/restaurants	59.7	14.9	19.4	6.0
Transport	38.2	41.2	14.7	5.9
Telecommunications	45.2	45.2	6.5	3.2
Security	35.1	28.1	29.8	7.0
Other services	44.8	13.8	32.2	9.2

Source: ALFS3.

Large enterprises, with more than 200 employees, were found to have more difficulties overcoming the crisis than small enterprises: 61 per cent of them registered a fall in sales compared to 1996. Configuration by property form also shows that all types of ownership were affected by falling sales in 1997, with a higher probability of positive results for joint ventures. It is worth noting that a large gap was again observed between joint ventures with majority foreign control, most of which reported increased sales in 1997, and joint ventures with only minority foreign participation, a majority of which (67 per cent) suffered a fall in results. This should be viewed in the light of the fact that a much greater proportion of joint ventures with majority foreign ownership suspended operations completely during the crisis, while those with minority foreign capital continued their activities, although with poor results. More than 50 per cent of state enterprises also experienced falling sales in 1997.

Table 12.20 *Sales Change Compared to Previous Year, by Property Form, 1997 (% of enterprises in sector reporting sales change in real terms)*

	Decreased	Increased	No change	Do not know
State	51.5	24.5	12.8	11.2
Private	47.8	30.0	19.3	2.9
Joint venture	43.1	41.2	11.8	3.9
with majority foreign capital	40.5	45.2	9.5	4.8
with minority foreign capital	66.7	33.3	0	0
Joint stock	54.5	27.3	9.1	9.1

Source: ALFS3.

Other signs of the crisis emerged from the enterprise survey. It was significant, for instance, that less that 8 per cent of enterprises replied that they intended to open new establishments in the next 12 months. Clearly at the end of 1997, enterprises were fully engaged with trying to survive and to rescue as many of their previous activities as possible. Expansion would have to wait for better times.

The Main Reasons for the Decline

We asked managers to report the main reasons for decline in 1997, to obtain a better understanding of the direct results of the crisis, in terms of damage, equipment and establishments destroyed, and lost capital (some employers had also placed some of the circulating assets of their company in pyramid schemes), compared to other reasons more closely related to the globally depressed economic environment that prevailed after the events. These two dimensions are, of course, intimately related since the collapse of the pyramid schemes, apparently one of the pillars of Albanian capitalism, immediately led to a fall in consumption and, as we have described, multiple enterprise closures. The fall in macroeconomic indicators that we describe in Chapter 13 is further confirmation of the global economic slump in 1997.

A majority of enterprises clearly placed two main reasons for decline before all others: the physical damage incurred during the events (reported by

26 per cent of enterprises as the main cause of decline), and the lack of demand for their products and services (23 per cent). Direct and indirect effects thus combined to push most enterprises to the brink of insolvency.

All major sectors of the economy—including banking—were affected by physical damage. The industrial sector was also confronted in 1997—as it still is today—by the major problem of lack of investment, also partly due to the absence of credits made available to the production sector. Services were clearly hurt by the fall in demand that prevailed after the crisis.

Table 12.21 *Main Reasons for Decline in 1997, by Sector*

	Physical damage	Lost capital	Lack of invest-ment	Lack of raw materials	Absence of demand	Other
Industry	30.3	11.9	16.5	5.5	22.0	13.8
Services	23.9	12.4	9.4	7.3	24.8	22.2
Banks	25.0	5.0	10.0	–	15.0	45.0
All	25.9	11.8	11.6	6.3	23.4	20.9

Source: ALFS3.

As expected, the most direct effect of the crisis—physical damage—was most widespread in the sectors and enterprises that were the primary target of the wave of destruction. The sectors that suffered the most damage—mining in industry, and telecommunications and gas/water/electricity in services (see Chapter 11) also reported physical damage as the major cause of their 1997 economic decline. Enterprises belonging to leather and shoes, minerals, transport, and trade also lost considerable capital during the events, a fact that they reported as one important cause of their slump in 1997.

The indirect effects of the crisis have not been less harmful for enterprise activity. *Tables 12.22* and *12.23* help us to identify precisely the main problems afflicting the Albanian economy after the crisis of 1997, sector by sector: for example, food processing enterprises and hotels and restaurants have undoubtedly been the worst affected by the fall in demand. The main difficulty encountered in chemicals, leather and shoes, and also textiles, has been the lack of raw materials, mainly due to the destruction or closure of local suppliers and the temporary interruption of imports, particularly important in respect of joint ventures.[4]

---

4. As we saw in Chapter 9, many joint ventures with majority foreign capital, especially in textiles and clothing, often import all of their raw materials from the home country, before processing it in Albania and sending the output back to the home country in its totality.

Trade enterprises were directly harmed by the sudden lack of money and fall in purchasing power, one-third of them reporting lack of demand for their services. By contrast, security companies, because of the general climate of insecurity, did not suffer to the same extent from the generalised fall in demand.

Wood and paper enterprises suffered mainly from a lack of investment. Gas/water/electricity companies also reported a lack of investment as one of their major problems, along with the extent of the damage they had suffered, two factors that combined to afflict these public utilities which are so important for all (low demand is obviously less of a problem for this sector). Telecommunications, and to a lesser extent transport, will also probably require a number of years and significant financial assistance before they are able to reconstruct their devastated network.

Table 12.22 *Main Reasons for Decline in 1997, by Industry*

	Physical damage	Lost capital	Lack of invest-ment	Lack of raw materials	Absence of demand	Other
Food	22.2	5.6	13.9	2.8	36.1	19.4
Chemicals	0	0	0	40.0	20.0	40.0
Leather and shoes	14.3	28.6	0	42.9	14.3	0
Mining	33.3	8.3	16.7	4.2	25.0	12.5
Minerals	30.8	30.8	23.1	0	15.4	0
Textiles and clothing	22.2	18.5	7.4	22.2	11.1	18.5
Metals	0	12.5	12.5	25.0	25.0	25.0
Wood and paper	21.1	0	26.3	10.5	26.3	15.8

Source: ALFS3.

Table 12.23 *Main Reasons for Decline in 1997, by Service*

	Physical damage	Lost capital	Lack of invest-ment	Lack of raw materials	Absence of demand	Other
Gas/water/electricity	38.5	11.5	26.9	0	7.7	15.4
Trade	26.1	19.6	4.3	4.3	28.3	17.4
Hotels/restaurants	22.0	4.9	9.8	0	36.6	26.8
Transport	26.1	21.7	4.3	0	26.1	21.7
Telecommunications	75.0	6.3	6.3	0	0	12.5
Security	16.7	0	0	0	16.7	66.7

Source: ALFS3.

A look at the situation in terms of form of ownership confirms our previous results: state-owned enterprises were not alone in being targeted by popular discontent. In particular, a high percentage of joint ventures (33 per cent) reported physical damage as the main reason for their lower results in 1997. A good proportion of these enterprises—especially in leather and shoes, and in textiles—also mentioned lost capital as a factor. Physical damage was clearly the main source of poor results also among state-owned enterprises. By contrast, private enterprises and joint-stock enterprises seem to have suffered much more from the indirect effects of the crisis: private enterprises from the low demand and joint-stock enterprises from the lack of investment. In terms of size of enterprise, large enterprises placed physical damage as the main cause of decline, followed by the lack of raw materials, while small enterprises were mainly affected by the absence of demand.

Table 12.24 *Main Reasons for Decline in 1997, by Property Form*

	Physical damage	Lost capital	Lack of invest-ment	Lack of raw materials	Absence of demand	Other
State	23.6	9.4	8.5	9.4	18.9	30.2
Private	22.8	10.7	13.4	6.7	30.2	16.1
Joint venture	33.3	14.3	14.3	9.5	28.6	0
Joint stock	11.1	22.2	33.3	0	11.1	22.2

Source: ALFS3.

Results by region show that nowhere in Albania have enterprises been readily able to overcome their losses of equipment and plant. Physical damage prevailed as the main cause of economic decline in a majority of regions. In some areas, the destruction of public establishments, enterprises, and public utilities did not leave behind many signs of activity, resembling a war zone. The situation was the most dramatic in the regions of Berat, Korca, and Vlora, where nearly half of all enterprises reported physical damage as the main cause of falling profits.[5] Lost capital during the events was also reported in almost all regions, particularly in Durres, Lezha, and Shkodra. Enterprises localised in other regions seem to have been more affected by the economic implications of local demand, especially in Kukes (54 per cent reporting the problem), Tirana (34 per cent), and Gjirokastra (31 per cent). It is worth

5. These three regions were also those with the highest percentage of enterprises reporting damage (Chapter 11).

noting the lack of investment in Shkodra, where one-third of enterprises cited it as the main cause of their business difficulties. Traditional industrial areas, such as Elbasan, Fier, and Lezha, suffered in 1997 from the absence of raw materials, which explains why they operated at only a low percentage of their full production capacity.

Among other sources of difficulty in the last six months, managers also reported the periodic shortage of electrical energy (mentioned by 8 per cent of enterprises), obliging them to regularly cease production with high losses, and the high taxes (6 per cent) that they found particularly inappropriate in a phase of reconstruction.

Table 12.25 *Main Reasons for Decline in 1997, by Region*

	Physical damage	Lost capital	Lack of invest-ment	Lack of raw materials	Absence of demand	Other
Berat	53.3	6.7	0	0	13.3	26.7
Dibra	18.2	9.1	0	9.1	18.2	45.5
Durres	15.0	18.3	13.3	8.3	23.3	21.7
Elbasan	33.3	14.3	0	14.3	19.0	19.0
Fier	28.6	4.1	18.4	12.2	22.4	14.3
Gjirokastra	23.1	15.4	0	0	30.8	30.8
Korca	44.8	13.8	10.3	6.9	17.2	6.9
Kukes	33.3	0	16.7	0	50.0	0
Lezha	27.8	16.7	11.1	11.1	16.7	16.7
Shkodra	20.8	16.7	29.2	0	12.5	20.8
Tirana	15.2	7.6	15.2	2.5	34.2	25.3
Vlora	43.5	8.7	0	8.7	13.0	26.1

Source: ALFS3.

Risk of Bankruptcy

Considering the depressing picture of economic activity in Albania in 1997, it was important to determine whether enterprises were confident concerning their immediate prospects. Managers were asked whether they feared bankruptcy within the next 12 months: only 4.4 per cent considered there was a high probability of bankruptcy, while a further 22 per cent were uncertain. Despite the high degree of uncertainty, we can therefore say that bankruptcies seem to have taken place mainly in the few months following the crisis. Nevertheless, the risk of bankruptcy was perceived differently according to sector, property form, and region. No less than 22 per cent of firms in metals foresaw bankruptcy; other sectors in which pessimism was rife were mining (9.7 per cent), leather and shoes (8.3 per cent), minerals (7.7 per cent), and chemicals (7.1 per cent). By contrast, wood and paper plants (0 per cent) and service companies (less than 4 per cent) were relatively optimistic. Joint ventures appeared to be less confident about the future, with 8 per cent of them foreseeing bankruptcy, 17 per cent among joint ventures with minority foreign capital. By region, the risk of closure was perceived to be most acute in Vlora (among 10 per cent of managers), Korca (8 per cent), Kukes, Lezha, and Shkodra (6 per cent).

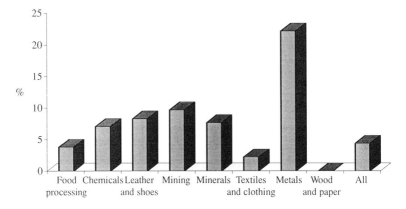

Figure 12.11 *Percentage of Enterprises Believing Bankruptcy Likely within a Year, by Industry, Dec. 1997*

Source: ALFS3.

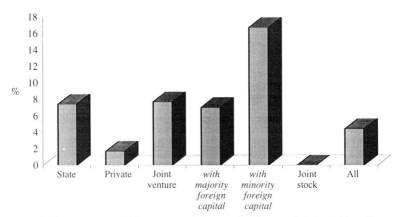

Figure 12.12 *Percentage of Enterprises Believing Bankruptcy Likely within a Year, by Property Form, Dec. 1997*

Source: ALFS3.

Overall, the main reason for expecting bankruptcy was the lack of customers, cited by one-third of all those anticipating bankruptcy (especially in food, chemicals, and hotels and restaurants), followed by 20 per cent who thought their firms would go bankrupt because of the raw materials price rises (especially in minerals and textiles, and in the regions of Gjirokastra, Durres, and Korca). Bank debts were also reported by 40 per cent of mining companies.

5 CONCLUSION

This first assessment on the effects of the 1997 crisis on enterprise activity in Albania does two things. First, it clearly confirms the picture of desolation already drawn in Chapter 11: a majority of enterprises have interrupted their activities, either partially or totally, because of the crisis. Among those that had to close down, nearly one-third reported that they would remain closed. If we combine the number of enterprises which were destroyed or closed down, we reach a figure of between 30 and 50 per cent of the total number of enterprises swept away by the events, without counting those which are trying to continue without much hope of avoiding bankruptcy, a prospect particularly strong in some traditional sectors, such as metals, mining, and chemicals.

For the survivors, the aftermath of the crisis has deeply affected their results. More than one-third of enterprises have registered pure losses, and half, a fall in sales compared to one year earlier. Most of them were operating well below capacity prior to the crisis, a reference period also characterised by a general economic slowdown. The decline in enterprise performance on external markets was also dramatic: in 1997, the percentage of production oriented towards export fell below 3 per cent. One of the most serious effects of the events of 1997 was to isolate Albania at the very moment it was trying to open itself up to the rest of the world. Sectors such as textiles and shoes, that in the first years of transition had managed to channel more than 80 per cent of their production towards external markets, almost stopped exporting altogether in 1997. The withdrawal of joint ventures was felt particularly strongly in these sectors, emphasising yet again the risk of industrial and trade policies which rely exclusively on foreign investors and their performance on external markets.

Analysis by sector and region also helped us to identify the reasons for the 1997 decline. The most immediate manifestation of the crisis, physical damage, had the most dramatic effect on economic results in those enterprises hardest hit by violence: mining, telecommunications, and public utilities. As far as ownership forms are concerned, state-owned enterprises and joint ventures were the worst affected, while among regions, Berat, Korca, and

Vlora suffered most. Other sectors and regions were not spared, having been hit by the deep economic depression that suddenly struck Albania: in particular, the fall in local consumption and overall demand has injured all types of enterprise and all regions, but especially Tirana and small private enterprises, which are now struggling for survival.

At the same time, amidst this generalised scene of devastation our enterprise survey has identified a few hopeful signs. Many enterprises that closed down during the events had already resumed their activities by the end of the year, not a few deciding to struggle on despite suffering terrible damage. Unexpectedly, it was precisely in those activities and regions whose propensity to close down had been highest during the crisis that more businesses started up again: small enterprises, either private or joint ventures—for instance, in textiles and clothing and leather and shoes—have shown greater dynamism in this respect: some had already registered positive results by the end of 1997; others were prevented from doing so mainly by the general fall in demand, implying that these enterprises might be able to return to normal as the Albanian economy picks up. By contrast, very large enterprises, that suffered enormous damage during the crisis, seem to have had more problems getting back to normal, especially in services. Moreover, these problems were not limited to the fall in demand, but included a series of more structural worries, such as the difficulty and cost of obtaining the necessary raw materials, and the lack of investment and new technology. Recovery in these sectors may take longer. At the same time, the good export performance of such traditional sectors as chemicals, which have offered some—though still insufficient—compensation for the fall in exports in other sectors, also represents a positive result, showing the importance of retaining more traditional—sometimes more reliable because better established— industries.

The regional dimension is crucial. Regions that were devastated by the crisis seem to be characterised by a dismal economic environment: even the most dynamic enterprises cannot survive or operate normally if they continue to be surrounded by multiple bankruptcies on the part of suppliers or customers, and no boost is given to local consumption and demand. We should remember that more dynamic small enterprises, especially in services, have shown considerable fragility. The few positive signs of recovery might turn to be only a mirage without a stronger and more generalised recovery (Chapter 13). In any case, economic recovery and growth could not be sustained without a rapid increase in the general level of demand, something that will never be achieved without rapid compensation for the recent, further dramatic fall in living standards (Chapter 14).

13. Macroeconomic Indicators Moving Backwards

1 INTRODUCTION

The widespread popular uprising of spring 1997 and the consequent interruption of economic activity in Albania sent all macroeconomic indicators into freefall. Indeed, the crisis managed to reverse macroeconomic gains, with negative GDP growth, a trade balance in the red, devaluation of the national currency, rising inflation, a dangerous widening of the budget deficit, a huge foreign debt, and a fall in foreign investment. For some economists, this fall in all economic indicators represented a real "economic earthquake", returning Albania to the situation of four years previously.[1]

The depth of the descent of the so-called "shining star", praised for its supposed strong economic foundations, even led some experts to revise their overoptimistic assessment of the pre-crisis situation, including a number of international monetary institutions: according to the World Bank, "[a] macroeconomic crisis was already in the making in 1996";[2] while for its representative in Tirana, "Albania was doing well until the crisis exploded, at least it appeared so on the surface . . .".[3] Such statements can be made to square only with difficulty with World Bank reports issued before the crisis which presented a range of indicators of Albanian economic success (see Chapter 1): we might have expected World Bank experts, who were diligent in presenting every possible sign of Albanian economic success, to have pursued their analysis "beneath the surface". For the Economist Intelligence Unit, "[e]arlier achievements were hollow" and "reforms appear to have been rather superficial".[4] Only a few months after the crisis, almost all the experts

---

1. See, for example, Zef Preci, "An Economic Earthquake Shattered Albania", in *Albanian Observer*, Vol. 4, No. 1 (1998), p. 27.

2. See World Bank (1997), p. 1.

3. See Carlos Elbirt, "Albania: Still under the Pyramids' Shadow", in *Transition* (the World Bank Newsletter on reforming economies), Vol. 8, No. 5 (October 1997).

4. See EIU (1998a), p. 13.

seem to have reached consensus concerning the past weaknesses of the erstwhile "Balkan tiger".

Although the second half of 1997 marked the beginning of reconstruction—and so generated better results—this was not enough to compensate adequately for the sharp fall in economic activity registered in the first six months. Moreover, the Albanian economy was still faced by a number of difficulties left over from 1996, before the crisis. In these circumstances, we must take care in our analysis of the declining macroeconomic indicators to distinguish between causes proper to the crisis and those due more to structural problems of the Albanian economy.

Table 13.1 *Main Macroeconomic Indicators, 1995–97*

	1995	1996	1997
GDP (million leks at current prices)	229 793	280 998	337 114
GDP (million leks at constant prices)	15 107	16 482	15 325
GDP growth (%)	13.3	9.1	−7.0
Industrial production (%)	1.0	13.5	−5.6
Agricultural production (%)	10.6	3.0	1.0
Inflation (end-of-year percentage)	6.0	17.4	42.1
Inflation (annual average)	7.8	12.7	33.2
Total exports (million USD)	205.0	243.7	158.6
Total imports (million USD)	679.0	920.5	693.5
Trade balance (exports minus imports)	−474.0	−676.8	−534.9
Exchange rate (leks for 1 USD)	92.7	104.5	148.9
Long-term foreign debt (million USD)	667.0	753.0	826.0
Budget deficit (billion leks)	23.4	36.4	49.0
Budget deficit (% of GDP)	10.4	11.4	14.0
Direct foreign investment (million USD)	70.0	90.0	47.5

Note: For the sake of coherence we present here the figures available for 1998 from the Ministry of Finance and the DEDAC (Department of Development and Aid Co-ordination). We should emphasise, however, that their estimates of GDP growth in 1995 and 1996 of 13.3 and 9.1 per cent respectively were far above those of the IMF (8.9 and 8.2), which we presented in Chapter 1. These differences show the problems—as well as the stakes—involved in the calculation of GDP in Albania. This table, however, helps us in our analysis by presenting the fall in GDP of 1997.
Sources: INSTAT; Ministry of Finance; DEDAC; IMF.

2 THE FALL IN GDP

The GDP figures unexpectedly reflected the halt imposed by the crisis on enterprise activity, at least in the first six months of the year. It also reflected the fall in demand that soon followed. In 1997, Albania's GDP was 337 billion leks, a fall of 7 per cent compared to 1996, interrupting the—according to official claims—period of high GDP growth from 1993 to 1996 (see Chapter 1).[5] According to Albanian statistics, the crisis has affected almost every sector of the economy. Transport was found to have been most badly affected by the crisis, with a 20 per cent decline in annual production, followed by a conspicuous fall in the service sector (which saw a 7 per cent decline), and construction (6.3 per cent). National statistics also confirm that all industrial sectors have experienced reduced production: total industrial production fell by 5.6 per cent on average. As a result, agriculture continued to account for more than 56 per cent of GDP in 1997, although it too was affected by the troubles, production virtually stagnating as in 1996 (1 per cent growth in 1996 and 3 per cent in 1997).

However, there is a significant gap between these official figures, published by the Government, and the results of our enterprise survey carried out in December 1997. Although the official figures confirm the overall drop in output in most sectors, they diverge considerably from the falls in profits and sales reported to us by industrial enterprises with over ten employees and by service enterprises and banks with over five employees, all over Albania. This also holds for aggregate GDP. Although the official figure is already significant, with GDP growth falling by 7 per cent, our enterprise survey would seem to indicate that the fall was much more dramatic, and that the official figure reflects only part of the picture. This is further justification for approaching GDP data in Albania with considerable caution:[6] it is important to remember that at the end of 1996 these data were still portraying Albania as a successful economy. The fall in industrial output of only 5.6 per cent also does not square with the results provided directly by the survey's microeconomic data, with between 30 and 50 per cent of enterprises having been swept away by the events and with almost all remaining enterprises reporting a fall in results (Chapter 12).

It is worth noting that the diminution of emigrants' remittances in 1997, earlier sums having been devoured by pyramid schemes a few months earlier, has probably also contributed to the slowdown of economic activity and the fall in GDP: in 1996, emigrants sent USD 558 million into Albania—in 1997, this fell by almost half, to USD 330 million. This would seem to indicate once more the extent to which economic growth had been supported by external transfers, as well as the fragility of an economy based on such transfers.

---

5. However, we must emphasise again our scepticism concerning GDP figures in Albania.

6. Surprisingly, this fall in GDP of 7 per cent had already been announced by the Government in July 1997, that is, five months before the end of the year; see *Albanian Observer*, Vol. 3, No. 7–8 (1997), p. 17.

3 TRADE IMBALANCES

As a direct result of the crisis, Albania experienced a significant trade deficit in 1997 of more than USD 500 million. Imports reached almost USD 700 million, although they remained below their 1996 level. According to INSTAT, import volumes have fallen substantially due to higher prices in EU countries —as a result of the devaluation of the lek—and lower purchasing power in Albania.

Analysts have attributed import growth in 1996 mainly to the increase in consumption consequent upon the returns from the pyramid schemes. Imports remained high in 1997, despite the fact that they had been suspended almost entirely during the three culminating months of the crisis (February–April). At the same time, exports decreased in 1997 to USD 158 million.

This unbalanced situation was clearly related to the terrible state of Albanian factories, leading to three distinct movements (described in the following subsections) that combined to worsen the trade balance: first, the poorer export performance of enterprises; secondly, increased imports of raw materials and equipment to supplement badly hit local supply; and thirdly, the need to import consumer goods to make up for the sudden domestic void.

Missing Exports

We have seen that exports in all sectors fell substantially in 1997. They reached zero level in March, and then increased progressively in the second half of the year. The low level of exports, as we saw in Chapter 12, is explained by the fact that domestic producers were operating well below full capacity, while some had simply been swept away altogether by the rebellion. It was also due to the greater difficulties enterprises now had in reaching external markets—for instance, because of transportation problems, roads being blocked or unsafe. Finally, in circumstances in which most enterprises were fighting for survival—many having been destroyed—with little or no funds with which to invest and raw materials hard to obtain, it was simply not feasible to produce high quality goods for external markets. The food industry exported little in 1997, and the processing of metals and raw materials ceased, so that products were exported mainly unprocessed, including minerals and metals, although fairly substantial volumes were attained (see Chapter 12). Textiles and clothing, and leather and shoes, normally primarily export-oriented industries, also drastically reduced their supply to external markets. The fall in exports was also due in large part (see Chapter 12) to the interruption of the activities of joint ventures, which had previously exported between 70 and 80 per cent of production: in 1997, this fell suddenly to below 10 per cent. The contribution of these enterprises to the balance of payments has traditionally been very important. This was not due to physical damage alone, however, but also to financial deficits accumulated over a number of years, especially in services (see Chapter 9). In addition to the interruption of existing joint ventures, 1997 also saw a fall-off in new foreign investment, a majority of projects remaining at the negotiation stage. A warning to this effect was sounded by the Centre for the Promotion of Foreign Investment in early 1998, which stated that in 1997 only USD 26 million of foreign capital had been invested in Albania, well below the level of previous years (Chapter 9).[7]

The Import of Raw Materials

We have seen that the lack of raw materials was one of the major causes of possible bankruptcy reported by enterprises (Chapter 12). They urgently had to replace local suppliers with international ones, with all the added transport costs and higher prices—due to currency devaluation—that this involved. Machinery and spare parts from abroad increased to form more than 15 per cent of total imports—electrical and mechanical equipment accounted for 59 per cent of this. As already mentioned, this was directly due to the destruction or bankruptcy of many local suppliers, hitherto particularly important in this sector (see Chapter 12). On the plus side, some affected enterprises were compelled to establish more modern production lines through the introduction of new technology.

Our survey results also show clearly that more than 80 per cent of enterprises in textiles and clothing and in leather and shoes, many of them joint ventures, complained about the absence of raw materials. This was confirmed by various reports that Greek and Italian enterprises producing textiles and shoes for export were having to import all their raw materials from home.[8] It is significant that in 1997, imports from Greece grew by 43 per cent compared to the previous year, Italian imports increasing more modestly, by more than 8 per cent. Indeed, 75 per cent of all Albanian imports in 1997 came from Greece. Finally, we should also mention the increase in imports of materials to be used in construction (over 70 per cent of such goods were imported in 1997), one of the most active sectors in Albania.

Escalating Imports of Consumer Goods

The total cessation of the production of domestic goods in the first half of 1997 also had to be compensated somehow by increasing imports: this

---

7. "Chaos and politics kill investment". Interview with President Selami Xhepa before he left office, in *Albanian Observer*, Vol. 4, No. 2 (1998), p. 40. The final figure will be USD 47 million.

8. See *Albanian Observer*, Vol. 4, No. 3 (1998), p. 39.

happened, for instance, with food items, normally exported, which accounted for over 30 per cent of total imports in 1997, 40 per cent of which comprised oil, butter, and other fats. The fact that in 1997 over 80 per cent of all foodstuffs were imported represents a significant paradox for an agricultural country trying to attract foreign investors into the food processing industry.

Lower Trade Deficit than in 1996

Although the three trends outlined above were peculiar to the period just after the crisis, we should note that the Albanian economy already had a large trade deficit: paradoxically, the trade deficit in 1997 was lower than the one accumulated in 1996, because the spring events blocked both imports and exports for a few months. This may indicate that the trade deficit was not a particularly distinctive feature of the period after the crisis, but instead may be rooted in structural problems characterising the production and industrial specialisation of the Albanian economy.

4 THE DEPRECIATION OF THE LEK

Albania did not represent an exception to the rule that the state of the domestic currency reflects that of the economy as a whole. The collapse of the pyramid schemes and the consequent political and economic crisis led to significant devaluation of the domestic currency. The collapse of the first schemes in early January led to immediate depreciation of the lek on the informal market conducted on the street, where the US dollar fell from 104 leks in late December to nearly 120 leks in mid-January.[9] This depreciation was confirmed by the official markets a few days later, furnishing a sudden contrast with the situation at the end of 1996, when the very high interest rates offered by the pyramid schemes strengthened the lek in relation to all Western currencies,[10] with the US dollar even falling below 100 leks in November. Confirmation of the fact that one billion leks in savings evaporated along with the fraudulent pyramid schemes doubtless led to a period of constant devaluation of the domestic currency. The devaluation of the lek was also a direct result of growing inflation earlier in the year, promoted by the Government's coverage of its huge budget deficit and internal debt with Treasury bills bought by the Bank of Albania. At the end of 1997, compared

---

9. See "Pyramid Schemes Deepen the Lek", in *Albanian Observer*, Vol. 3, No. 1 (1997), p. 14.

10. Particularly since two of the most popular pyramid funds, Xhaferri and Populli (but also others) accepted deposits only in leks; this compelled many Albanians who received money from relatives overseas to convert it into leks, so propping up the domestic currency.

to one year previously, the lek was 50 per cent weaker against the US dollar (exchanged at 150 leks).

The devaluation of the lek fostered among Albanians a general disaffection with their own currency, and a clear preference for transactions in US dollars. At the end of 1997 private operators were conducting a great part of their transactions in foreign currency. The purchase of an apartment or of any other real estate in Tirana was carried out in US dollars rather than in leks. In the south, on the other hand, the predominant currency became the Greek drachma. Even some state institutions began to request a switch to the US dollar, ignoring the lek.[11] As a result, the lek, after having resisted giving ground to the US dollar for several months, was devalued again in February 1998 (to 156 leks to the dollar), mainly due to the lack of hard currency in the market at a time when demand was increasing. Significant speculation by free market dealers was another factor in the oscillation of the exchange rate. The fact that more than 60 per cent of Albanian cash was still not deposited in banks also increased the scope for speculation, severely limiting the banking sector's room to manoeuvre.

5 GROWING INFLATION

Inflation had increased to 42.1 per cent by the end of 1997. This, however, was considered by the Government as something of an achievement after predictions that it would rise to 55 per cent in the course of the second half of the year. The collapse of the economy and the sudden withdrawal of foreign investors seriously affected confidence in the Albanian economy and its currency. The Consumer Price Index for March 1997 was 14 per cent higher than in February, a monthly inflation rate increase not registered since 1992. The price of some food items increased by as much as 30 per cent. A number of other factors contributed to the increase in inflation, from the liberalisation of bread prices at the end of 1996, to the devaluation of the lek in the first half of the year, but it is the Government's fiscal and monetary policies—which set new budget deficit records inevitably resulting in monetary expansion— that did the most to drive up inflation. At the end of 1997, money in circulation grew by 25 per cent, from 154 billion leks in December 1996 to 194 billion leks in December 1997. This increased money supply was not supported by an increase in production and consumption, only by the sudden need to cover the state deficit.

---

11. For example, the National Accommodation Organisation, a state-owned institution for citizens of the western town of Kavaje; see *Albanian Observer*, Vol. 4, No. 2 (1998), p. 30.

At the end of 1997, a number of other reasons contributed to push up inflation, such as the increase of VAT from 12.5 per cent to 20 per cent. This led, according to the Minister of Finance, to price increases of about 8 per cent—according to INSTAT, it led to an immediate price increase of more than 10 per cent for bread and milk, and of more than 18 per cent for vegetables, with 60 per cent increases for tomatoes, cucumbers, and a number of other vegetables in October. The price of petrol increased by more than 17 per cent.

Macroeconomic indicators often moved in tandem: for instance, in the first part of the year the devaluation of the lek and rising inflation fed one another. At the same time, the rise in imports increased the demand for hard currency, further undermining confidence in the domestic currency. After the elections, the new political situation and the return of many enterprises to economic activity stabilised both inflation and the exchange rate.

6 THE BUDGET DEFICIT

The crisis clearly had a profound direct effect on the state budget, the deficit reaching 49 billion leks or 14 per cent of GDP in 1997. (In more developed economies, the figure is usually around 1–5 per cent of GDP.)

The Absence of Tax Revenues

During the first three months of 1997, the state was able to collect less than 50 per cent of budget revenues, customs duties bringing in 7.3 billion leks, excise duties 5.2 billion. Government expenditure in 1997 was 93.2 billion leks. This gap was mainly due to the inability of the state to collect what was owed to it and to the high cost of maintaining a functioning administration. The insecurity and instability that reigned in the country and along its borders were aggravating factors. In April 1997, a particularly difficult month, customs revenues amounted to only 18 per cent of budget predictions. Control over customs checkpoints was resumed only later in the year.

In an effort to deal with this grave situation, the Government had to revise its budget plans, taking into account an increased budget deficit, a weakened tax collection system, and the need to cut public expenditure to the bone. The rate of increase of the budget deficit obliged the state to cut investment (financed through either internal funds or the reserve fund) and maintenance, which led to the rapid degradation of many state institutions and enterprises, at the very time they needed support to overcome the damage suffered during the crisis and to begin reconstruction.

Tax Reform

The Government decided on 1 October 1997 to increase VAT from 12.5 per cent to 20 per cent. Other taxes were also increased: the price ceilings were increased for oil products, excise duties on cigarettes and alcohol, and on domestic and imported goods were unified, while national and rental income tax rates were increased.

However, this did not improve the situation, the budget deficit increasing by 5 billion leks in the last two months of the year, compelling the Parliament to accept a 49 billion rather than a 44 billion lek deficit. This absence of revenues was due in great part to the dramatic fall in consumption. Moreover, the VAT increase immediately resulted in a general price increase, so adding to inflationary pressures.

Issuing Treasury Bills to Fund the Deficit

The monetary base expanded by 25.6 per cent during 1997, a result of increased government borrowing, Treasury bills being utilised to finance already high government expenditure. In 1997, the Treasury bills—worth 21 billion leks—issued by the Albanian Government were bought by the Bank of Albania;[12] they matured in 1998, and the Government must pay the maturity value in full.[13] Interest payments on this debt (accumulated over the last few years) have also grown considerably. During 1996, the Government paid 8 billion leks in interest, climbing to 18 billion leks in 1997. The crisis of 1997 shook Albanian finances to their foundations, leading to rising inflation which was translated into higher interest rates on government securities.

According to the Director of the Macroeconomic Department of the Albanian Ministry of Finance, "these high interest rate payments came as a result of the debt accumulation in previous years combined with high interest rates applied in the auctions where the bills are sold. These interest [rate]s are higher than what the banks pay for deposits of the same length."[14] The public debt accumulated by the end of 1997 reached 63 per cent of GDP, presenting a serious obstacle to economic development.

In 1996, the budget deficit had already reached a considerable sum—partly due to the amount spent on campaigning in the general election in May and in the local elections in October—equivalent to more than 10 per cent of GDP.

---

12. "Transferring money from one pocket to the other", according to Mitro Cela, *Albanian Observer*, Vol. 4, No. 2 (1998), p. 21.

13. See "Treasury Bonds Save the Day . . . But Could Backfire", in *Albanian Observer*, Vol. 3, No. 10 (1997), p. 29.

14. Statement by Artur Kasimati, as quoted in the *Albanian Observer*, Vol. 4, No. 2 (1998), p. 34.

As a number of international donors correctly observed, "prior to the current crisis, the fiscal situation had already deteriorated drastically".[15] Tax collection difficulties already existed, a situation about which the international financial institutions had already warned the Government. Many government debts had been contracted before the crisis, which aggravated the situation by increasing prices and so also interest rates on these debts. This is one more structural problem that Albania must solve.

7 FOREIGN DEBT

Albania's foreign debt at the end of 1997 totalled USD 826.3 million, nearly half of which was due to be repaid at that time (USD 384 million). Albania incurred this debt from states and international financial institutions on the basis of bilateral and multilateral agreements. A number of experts have stated that Albania's foreign debt situation is an accurate reflection of its overall economic condition: in 1997, only USD 13.2 million were repaid, a mere token. The debt—which is in US dollars, SDRs and German marks—represents 15 per cent of GDP; non-payment and the passing on of such a large burden of debt constitute great obstacles to economic development. In co-operation with the World Bank, the IMF, and other financial institutions, the Albanian Government has negotiated a debt restructuring programme. The Albanian authorities have multiplied their efforts to negotiate the debt with the countries concerned (for instance, an agreement was reached with Germany in 1994), covering the signing of existing obligations and a long-term rescheduling plan with concessionary interest rates. According to the Ministry of Economic Co-operation, the long-term foreign debt at the end of 1996 was USD 767.8 million, rising to USD 826.3 million in 1997. The annual interest payments on this debt amount to more than USD 20 million.[16]

Although many of these debts were contracted before the crisis, the inability of the Government to face its obligations in 1997—when it failed to repay part of the scheduled foreign debt—has only exacerbated the problem.

8 CONCLUSION

There is no doubt that the wave of destruction, which did untold damage to enterprises, leading many of them either to interrupt their activities or to the

15. World Bank et al. (1997), p. 9.
16. See Ministry of Finance, *Government Fiscal Statistics* (1998); see also the *Albanian Observer*, Vol. 4, No. 5 (1998), p. 24.

brink of bankruptcy, also affected Albania's macroeconomic performance. GDP fell for the first time since 1992, by 7 per cent. The dysfunctional state of Albanian enterprises and the withdrawal of joint ventures led to an absence of exports, and left the domestic market prey to increasing amounts of imported goods, resulting in a huge trade deficit. Foreign investment all but dried up in that year. Inflation, which had been relatively under control since 1993, jumped to nearly 50 per cent. At the same time, a confidence crisis depressed the domestic currency, which lost more than 50 per cent of its value against the US dollar. The generalised chaos and absence of state control also led to a major reduction in state revenues, causing the state to rely heavily on the printing of money and increasing internal debt through the issue of Treasury bills. This situation represented, in early 1998, a terrible potential risk with regard to inflation. Taken together with its external debt, this threatened Albania with bankruptcy.

For some, the crisis interrupted Albania's macroeconomic progress. However, while the crisis did indeed push the country backwards in terms of national growth, prices, and exchange rate stability, it is also true that all these signs of impending crisis were already present in 1996, with a constant trade deficit, imports outstripping exports, a huge budget deficit, and significant internal and foreign debt. Difficulties in collecting tax revenues were already known, and smuggling was rife. All these factors had led to a slowdown in GDP growth by the end of 1996, and had marked a return to two-digit inflation. Some experts had also warned in 1996 that the lek was overvalued and did not reflect deteriorating economic conditions.[17] We may assert in summary that the crisis rather aggravated the situation than created it, serving primarily to lay bare all the weaknesses of the Albanian economy: this distinction is particularly important for the chapter on policy recommendations, in which we try to respond to both its structural and its conjunctural deficiencies.

17. See for instance the *Albanian Observer*, Vol. 3, No. 5 (1997), p. 27.

14. The Social Abyss

1 INTRODUCTION

The collapse of the pyramid schemes and the consequent crisis will leave Albania in a miserable social state for a number of reasons: these events occurred after years of continuous impoverishment for many Albanians (see Chapter 6); a significant proportion of the population will be involved; and the most vulnerable categories of the population will be the hardest hit. In this chapter we shall attempt to describe the main elements of the crisis that have pushed (and will continue to push) most Albanians towards what one might call the "social abyss". We can group these elements within the framework of three main shocks: (i) the loss of life savings in the pyramid schemes, which will hurt most those who invested last and who put the whole of their savings and assets into the schemes—these are generally the poorest Albanians, mainly from remote agricultural areas; (ii) the destruction, bankruptcy, or diminished activities of enterprises, which will directly harm most workers and their families, plunging a growing proportion of them into unemployment; (iii) as if this were not enough, rising inflation will reduce virtually to nothing what was already only a token amount of social assistance and very low wages.

Moreover, the huge budget deficit and the authorities' decision to cut all expenditure—including that related to social protection—will make it difficult for the Government to provide an appropriate response to this emergency social situation, which will be particularly dramatic in some regions. Finally, as one calamity gives way to another, the massive influx of Albanian refugees escaping the conflict in Kosovo in 1998 will further exacerbate the economic and social problems, especially in the north.

Although no data are currently available on the full extent of the social effects of the crisis, we have tried to provide a first assessment from a wide range of publications and reports, complemented by the results of our enterprise survey which provide direct information on how Albanian enterprises dealt with the crisis in terms of employment, payment of wages, and its effects on workers and their families.

289

2 LIFE SAVINGS VAPORISED IN THE PYRAMID SCHEMES

The independent audit carried out on the pyramid companies after the disaster now enables us to see the full extent of the population's losses. The latest estimate of the total sum is USD 2 billion, more than 50 per cent—more realistically, at least two-thirds—of the population having invested in the pyramid funds or companies. Scenes of desperation—some committing suicide or discharging weapons wildly in the streets, others queuing day and night outside pyramid scheme kiosks—go some way towards capturing the full intensity of the drama that followed the abrupt announcement of the closure of the first two pyramid schemes. The sudden eruption of violence after the ensuing series of bankruptcies expressed the desperation of those who had lost everything. The statements rapidly issued by both government officials and the managers of the schemes to the effect that small depositors would be the first to be reimbursed also reflect their consciousness of the risk of social explosion. Most people will find it extremely difficult to recover: many even sold their homes in order to invest more in the funds, often after having acquired them at a low price in the course of privatisation, the only asset during the first years of transition which prevented most families from falling into utter penury. In the rural areas, thousands of farmers sold their cattle or their only piece of land in order to invest money in the schemes with the hope of suddenly increasing their desperately low income. Now they have lost even that.

As we explained in Chapter 10, the pyramidal structure of the schemes was based on new deposits that helped to meet the interest payments (and sometimes even the capital) due to those who joined first. Because the system worked for a few years, some people did benefit, but such persons were generally well informed about the functioning—and risks—of the game, being close to the company management; many were able to withdraw before the collapse. For the poorest people, the scenario will be very different: less informed about the risks of the schemes, particularly those living in remote agricultural areas, reassured by the political and economic legitimacy given to the schemes and by an impressive campaign in the media, they invested in the schemes at a later stage and, after receiving their first dividends, decided to invest whatever they had in the belief that this would finally end their daily struggle for subsistence. Peasant farmers, usually very conservative in character, were initially sceptical about the schemes, but in the end even they were unable to resist their allure. These farmers were the biggest losers in the pyramids' collapse,[1] which explains why their reaction was among the most violent.

1. See the *Albanian Observer*, Vol. 3, No. 5 (1997), p. 24.

In Chapter 10 we indicated that these schemes must have represented a source of income for some time, helping people to relieve the pain of transition: this gave the schemes a certain social legitimacy. However, we do not know exactly how long this went on, and the suspicion must be that the poorest Albanians gained little. The collapse of the schemes brought them back with a jolt to the hard realities of transition, with high unemployment, impoverishment wages, and miserable living conditions. Moreover, social peace in Albania had been possible in the first years of reform only because of the remittances sent home by friends and relatives working abroad. These transfers, however, having been swallowed up by the pyramid schemes in 1996, will fall by more than half in 1997. It is to be hoped that they will start to increase again in the not too distant future.

After the collapse of the pyramid companies, all political parties, especially during the election campaigns of June 1997, promised that something would be done to provide at least partial compensation for the thousands of creditors. President Berisha, for example, promised compensation for all victims of the pyramid schemes during a meeting of the national council of the ruling Democratic Party on 19 January 1997: "We shall return the creditors the money they have invested in the pyramid investment schemes to the last penny."[2] At several other meetings before the June elections (see *Box 10.1* in Chapter 10), he promised the money would be returned to the creditors together with the interest. Similarly, before the June elections—and before becoming Prime Minister—Fatos Nano had promised in a speech in Vlora in mid-1997 that Albanians would receive the maximum possible from the pyramid firms. Despite this promise, a year later most small creditors had still not been reimbursed, risking further social eruptions, the population having kept the weapons it obtained during the spring rebellion. Only two firms, Populli and Xhaferri, have returned any of the money; as far as the other firms are concerned, we await the results of the international auditors' investigation to see what can be recovered. Since these companies are completely bankrupt, in the best case only an insubstantial part of what was invested will ever be redistributed. As only one example of the depth of feeling which still exists, let us picture the angry man of 52 who waits every day, rain or shine, outside the barricaded gates of the company in which he invested more than USD 600, and who warns anyone hoping for a quick fix: "This is not over. Even if I have to stand here till 2010, it's not over."[3]

2. Quoted in the *Albanian Observer*, Vol. 4, No. 1 (1998), p. 39.
3. Quoted in the *Albanian Observer*, Vol. 3, No. 5 (1997), p. 35.

3 THE NEW UNEMPLOYMENT SHOCK

The Albanian people, after the injuries received from the collapse of the pyramid schemes itself, had to face the secondary effects: the interruption of the activities of most enterprises and the consequent renewal of massive unemployment. After having lost their life savings, many families also suddenly lost their main source of income, generally because their only working member lost his job during or after the crisis.

We have seen how deep the crisis was in terms of enterprise activity: taking together those enterprises that were totally destroyed and those which had to close down without any hope of starting again, between 30 and 50 per cent of enterprises were simply swept away by the crisis. Although there are no direct statistics on the effects of the crisis on employment, it is clear that a new unemployment shock will hit workers and their families, particularly because the generalised slowdown of economic activity cannot provide many employment alternatives. Finding a job seemed to be particularly difficult for unskilled workers and for women. According to the Employment Agency, the official number of unemployed was 190,000 in early 1998, 32,000 of them in Tirana alone.[4] The official unemployment rate was 15.9 per cent at the end of 1997. According to the Ministry of Labour, however, the number of unemployed in 1997 reached much higher levels: in the middle of the year the Minister of Labour estimated unemployment at around 450,000, one-third of the workforce; and this was before any assessment had been made concerning the extent of destroyed enterprises and interrupted activities. From our enterprise survey results (see Chapters 11 and 12), we can predict that unemployment is in fact much higher and that it will continue to grow: there can be no doubt that total unemployment, both official and hidden, at the end of 1997 must have been at least 50 per cent of the working population.

Those enterprises that were able to continue their activities have also found it difficult to start up again while retaining the whole of their previous labour force. We investigated this process through our enterprise survey, which revealed that in these enterprises on average nearly 9 per cent of the labour force had to be dismissed in 1997 (9.8 per cent in industry and 6.5 per cent in services). The banks, which had been less inclined to close down, despite considerable physical damage, were found to have dismissed a larger number of employees, approximately 22 per cent of their previous labour force.

The dismissal process seems to have been particularly significant in food (where enterprises reported an average of 27.4 per cent of the labour force dismissed in 1997), but also textiles and clothing (14 per cent) and, among

---

4. See "Few Chances for the Unemployed", in the *Albanian Observer*, Vol. 4, No. 5 (1998), p. 41.

services, in trade (18 per cent) and security (21 per cent). Perhaps not surprisingly, almost every enterprise in this last sector managed to stay open despite the crisis, but had to adjust its labour force accordingly. A greater percentage of dismissals was also observed among small private enterprises, confirming the weakness of this type of enterprise in crisis conditions. Regional mapping of dismissals placed Vlora first, with 16 per cent of the labour force dismissed, followed by Kukes (14 per cent), Korca (13 per cent), and Shkodra (11 per cent), all of which were among the regions hardest hit by destruction and the interruption of economic activity.

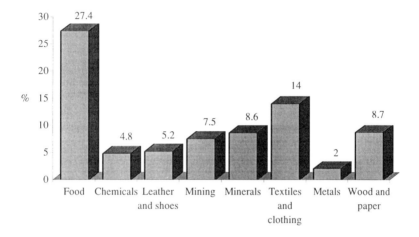

Figure 14.1 *Percentage of Labour Force Dismissed, by Industry, 1997*

Source: ALFS3.

These figures on dismissals must be added to the jobs lost in enterprises that were destroyed or had to close down. It is probable that such employment adjustments, as more enterprises start operating again and others close down, will continue. It is to be hoped that the progressive reactivation of the economy will partly compensate past and future dismissals, but the extent of the unemployment process, in a context of reduced economic activity, clearly calls for an ambitious employment policy from the Government. At the moment, most unemployed are left to their own fate. In 1997, the unemployment benefit of 2,500 leks (USD 17) was below the subsistence minimum. Moreover, less than 20 per cent of the unemployed were entitled to such assistance, leaving most of them in total destitution.

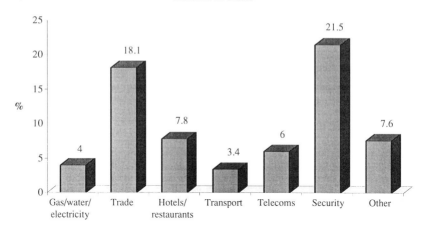

Figure 14.2 *Percentage of Labour Force Dismissed, by Service, 1997*

Source: ALFS3.

In addition, in 1993–96, the rise of unemployment had been somewhat limited by the massive emigration of approximately 15–20 per cent of the labour force. After the 1997 crisis, a steady stream of young people also tried to emigrate, both legally and illegally, but this time they were faced with very strict emigration controls imposed by neighbouring countries. This will prevent the process from happening again, at least on a large scale. Since then, a number of agreements on seasonal work have been made—for instance with the Italian authorities in early 1998—to relieve the tense political situation and in response to diplomatic pressure from the Albanian Government. But while they permit a certain number of Albanians to work in Italy for determinate periods these agreements are also a way of regulating the emigration flow.

4 RISING INFLATION ERODING PURCHASING POWER

The immediate increase in inflation in early 1997 increased the woes of the population. It was particularly visible in March 1997, when the Consumer Price Index rose by more than 14 per cent compared to February, a monthly inflation rate not registered since 1992. The rise was most significant in respect of the daily consumption products of the poorest categories: the prices of daily food and beverage products increased by nearly 19 per cent, while those of other no less essential sub-groups—such as fruit, sugar, coffee, and spices—increased by 30 per cent. The price of bread also increased by 30 per cent, adding to a large increase in 1996 that had already hurt the population. As if this were not enough, the measures taken by the Government—constrained by lower tax revenues—later in the year to increase budget revenues also hurt Albanian households: the increase of ceiling prices for oil and its products, and also the rise of VAT from 12.5 per cent to 20 per cent. Such measures limited consumption even further. In the first month after VAT was increased, the price of bread had already increased by 10 per cent, milk by 11 per cent, vegetables by 18 per cent, tomatoes by 60 per cent, and peppers by 51 per cent. The price of petrol increased by 18 per cent. Medical services, so important for the population, were not exempt either, dentists for example immediately incorporating the VAT increase in their prices.

Finally, we should mention that the increased number of imported goods, generally more expensive than local ones, to complement the collapse of domestic production and trade also hurt the population, while helping to drive up inflation.

5 THE NEW PLUNGE OF REAL WAGES AND INCOMES

The price curve continued its uninterrupted upward climb while real salaries and other income sources were devalued. Our enterprise survey carried out at the end of 1997 provides useful information on average wages in enterprises that continued their economic activity after the crisis.

As shown in *Table 14.1*, nominal average wages in 1997 stagnated approximately at the same level as in 1996, with a less than 2 per cent difference for the whole economy between the two years. If we compare this to inflation, it means that average wages in real terms lost almost 50 per cent of their purchasing power.

Nominal wages even decreased in services (–4 per cent), particularly in trade (–30 per cent in nominal terms) and in some industries, such as food, minerals, and metals. Although the average wage in industry increased by nearly 8 per cent in nominal terms, it remained well below inflation, thus leading to considerable erosion in real terms. This process was particularly dramatic for employees in services, especially trade, who saw their wages fall in real terms by more than 60 per cent in a single year.

It should be noted that enterprises continued to pay starting wages well above (by 50 per cent) the official minimum wage (4,400 leks); this was the only way of persuading workers to continue working.

Table 14.1 *Average and Minimum Monthly Wages, by Sector, 1996–97 (leks)*

		Leks		%
		1996	1997	1997/96
Average wage	All	8 660	8 332	+1.9
	Industry	7 880	8 492	+7.7
	Services	8 593	8 249	–4.2
	Banks	13 431	15 842	+17.9
Minimum wage	All	5 900	6 606	+11.9
	Industry	5 700	6 408	+12.4
	Services	5 850	6 466	+10.5
	Banks	7 900	8 771	+11.0
Annual inflation rate (%)			42.1	

Sources: ALFS2, ALFS3.

While real wages fell, their value in foreign currency terms also dropped with the depreciation of the currency (*Table 14.2*). In international comparison, Albania clearly had the lowest average wage in Europe, even behind Ukraine, Russia, and Moldova. It was even lower than those prevailing in Central Asian countries, such as Kyrghistan or Kazakhstan.[5]

Table 14.2 *Average and Minimum Monthly Wages, by Sector, 1996–97 (USD)*

		USD		%
		1996	1997	1997/96
Average wage	All	86.6	58.9	–47.0
	Industry	78.7	56.6	–39.0
	Services	85.9	54.9	–56.5
	Banks	134.3	105.6	–27.0
Minimum wage	All		44.0	
	Industry	57.0	42.7	–33.5
	Services	58.0	43.1	–34.5
	Banks	79.0	58.5	–35.0
Exchange rate (leks for 1 USD)		100	150	

Sources: ALFS2, ALFS3.

5. See IMF, *World Economic Outlook*, 1997a; and the *Albanian Observer*, Vol. 3, No. 7–8 (1997), p. 22.

The situation was particularly bad for employees working in state enterprises and budget institutions. While managers of private enterprises or joint ventures could increase wages to motivate their employees to start working again despite insecure or difficult conditions, managers of state enterprises continued to apply the restrictive incomes policy imposed by the Government. Employees in budgetary institutions also experienced a sharp fall in real terms of their monthly income, which had not been adjusted since before the election of May 1996. Employees in education and health, for example, continued to be paid less than 8,000 leks (USD 53) a month in 1997. Public employees, after pensioners and the unemployed, were among the poorest population groups.

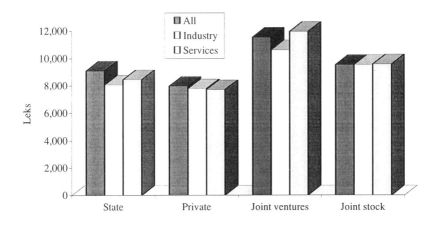

Figure 14.3 *Average Wage, by Property Form, 1996–97 (leks)*

Source: ALFS3.

The minimum wage (4,400 leks or USD 29) had not been increased since April 1996—all other social incomes directly related to the minimum wage necessarily remained constant throughout 1997. All social benefits fell in real terms. The minimum pension was also frozen at 4,000 leks (USD 26), well below the sum needed by pensioners to survive the price increases of basic commodities.

The minimum wage was finally increased, after nearly two years, in early 1998 (see Chapter 16), although the rise will not be sufficient to recover the purchasing power lost in 1997.

6 GENERALISED INTERRUPTION OF WAGE PAYMENTS

The statistics presented in the previous section show wage levels as they were reported by managers at the end of 1997. However, they conceal the massive interruption of wage payments that occurred during the first months of the crisis in early 1997.

Accordingly, the firms involved in the survey were asked if they had had severe difficulties in paying wages over the year. At the end of 1997, more than 20 per cent of enterprises reported they had had such difficulties: in fact, all those enterprises reported that they had had to interrupt wage payments. This process took place on a massive scale in some industrial sectors, such as mining, where 64 per cent of establishments interrupted wage payments, and minerals, where the figure was 33 per cent. Employees working in services were not spared, especially in public utilities (gas, water, and electricity) where half of enterprises reported this problem. Thirty per cent of enterprises in telecommunications were also affected. State enterprises had the most difficulties in paying wages (33 per cent of them), especially in industry (50 per cent), while more than 20 per cent of managers of joint ventures also had to interrupt wage payments. This might be due to the more significant damage that these two types of enterprise were found to have suffered during the crisis (see Chapter 11). As far as size is concerned, perhaps not surprisingly large enterprises had most problems in paying wages during the crisis. Employees working in the regions of Kukes (with 44 per cent of firms interrupting payments), but also Lezha, Vlora, Fier, and Berat (33 per cent) have been the most hurt by the sudden absence of wages.

Table 14.3 *Difficulty in Paying Wages, by Property Form, 1997 (%)*

	State	Private	Joint venture	Joint stock
All	33.6	9.8	21.2	18.2
Industry	53.1	9.5	27.3	15.0
Services	35.8	10.1	11.1	50.0
Banks	2.0	2.4	0	–

Source: ALFS3.

Table 14.4 *Difficulty in Paying Wages, by Size, 1997 (%)*

	1–50	51–100	101–200	200 +
All	15.6	23.3	26.4	39.4
Industry	17.9	19.6	23.1	41.2
Services	16.5	29.5	29.5	41.2
Banks	3.0	0	0	0

Source: ALFS3.

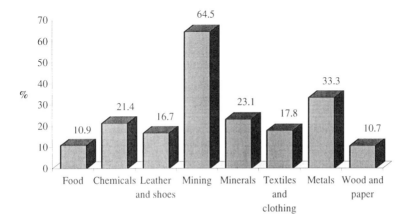

Figure 14.4 *Difficulty in Paying Wages, by Industry, 1997 (%)*

Source: ALFS3.

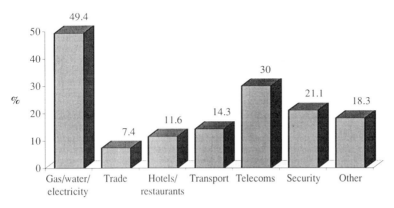

Figure 14.5 *Difficulty in Paying Wages, by Service, 1997 (%)*

Source: ALFS3.

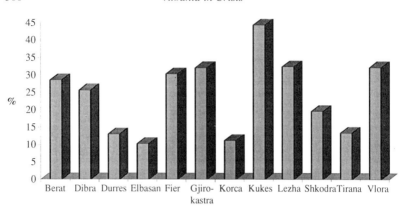

Figure 14.6 *Difficulty in Paying Wages, by Region, All Sectors, 1997 (%)*

Source: ALFS3.

It is important to note that those enterprises which did not interrupt their activity during the crisis were not found to have fewer problems in paying wages: on the contrary, most of them did interrupt wage payments for a long period. In effect, the burden of the crisis was simply shifted by many managers on to the workers' shoulders.

The average period of non-payment was 8 weeks, which corresponds to the major period of destruction of enterprises of February–March 1997. The length of the interruption of wage payments was found to be much longer for particular sectors and regions, however, including services, especially in the large enterprises in gas, water, and electricity (an average of 14 weeks), and in the small private firms operating in trade (16 weeks). Hotels and restaurants also reported not paying wages for a period of 12 weeks. The duration of this phenomenon confirms the difficulties with which these service industries were confronted during and after the crisis. The process also confirms the regions most seriously affected by the crisis: in Vlora, enterprises reported a period of non-payment of wages of more than 20 weeks, while employees in the regions of Berat and Fier had to wait more than 14 weeks before being paid. This absence of revenues over a period of months led very quickly, especially in a context of growing inflation, to an intolerable situation of extreme destitution.

7 WORKING WITHOUT EITHER REGULATION OR PROTECTION

Workers were also forced to endure deteriorating working conditions. Employees in many cases had to resume work in half-destroyed enterprises, without the most elementary safety and health provisions. Moreover, the availability of thousands of unemployed people motivated many managers to continue operating without any social and legal protection for employees. Many enterprises continued their activities in the black economy in order to avoid paying taxes and social security contributions. The Minister of Labour Elmaz Sherifi estimated that at the end of 1997 between 60 and 70 per cent of the total number of persons employed in Albania were without a labour contract.[6] This was observed mainly in small private enterprises, most of which were not registered at the Ministry of Labour.[7] Only very strict labour inspections could hope to change this situation: difficult at the best of times, particularly when resources are scarce, the lack of public order made this well-nigh impossible. According to the Director of the Labour Inspection Department at the Ministry of Labour, the level of employment control fell drastically in the first part of the year.[8] In Tirana, 60 private police officers had to help the Labour Inspection Department to enforce regulations.

We have seen in Chapter 6, however, that the absence of individual labour contracts was also observed among officially registered enterprises, for instance, in a number of enterprises operating with foreign ownership. A growing number of enterprises, motivated by public disorder and the absence of labour inspection, have pursued this option.

Our enterprise survey at the end of 1997 also reported the worsening of many of the adverse social trends observed one year earlier in a number of activities, and which seemed to have spread to other sectors.

We will first look at the total collapse of trade union influence at the enterprise level: although they continued to be recognised in nearly 40 per cent of establishments, trade unions lost most of their members, with an average of 12 per cent of the labour force unionised in 1997, compared to nearly 40 per cent in 1996 and as much as 93 per cent in 1994. This fall was particularly strong in industry, with only 14 per cent of trade union membership in 1997 compared to 50 per cent one year earlier. In services, the fall in trade unionisation already observed in 1996 was further pronounced in 1997, falling from 30 to 10 per cent: it even fell below 1 per cent in private

6. See "60 Per Cent of Labour Force without Contracts", in *Albanian Observer*, Vol. 3, No. 10 (1997), p. 36.

7. According to Ministry of Labour statistics, in 1997 there were 2,755 companies in Albania, employing 284,000 employees, most with formal labour contracts (ibid.).

8. Interview with Fatos Hodaj, Director of the Labour Inspection Department (ibid.).

enterprises in services. Although unions in state enterprises managed to retain a strong union membership—above 70 per cent of the labour force—trade union membership in all other property forms fell to historically low levels: 2 per cent in private enterprises, 9 per cent in joint ventures, and 19 per cent in joint-stock companies. While this might be only a temporary result of the crisis, workers having other priorities than trade union membership, it also means that the trade unions were not playing—or not being allowed to play— much of a role in the restructuring process after the crisis.

Table 14.5 *Social Dialogue Indicators, by Sector, 1997 (%)*

	Industry	Services	Banks	All
Recognised trade unions	51.8	35.4	24.5	39.5
Trade unionisation	13.7	10.5	32.9	12.1
Signature of a collective agreement	72.8	56.2	46.0	60.4

Source: ALFS3.

Table 14.6 *Social Dialogue Indicators, by Property Form, 1997 (%)*

	State	Private	Joint venture	Joint stock
Recognised trade unions	69.8	10.7	44.2	63.8
Trade unionisation	72.8	2.4	9.2	18.9
Signature of a collective agreement	60.4	46.3	59.6	95.0

Source: ALFS3.

At the same time, the absence of social dialogue in private enterprises was confirmed, only a small minority of them (10 per cent) recognising trade unions or signing collective agreements. In services, less than 40 per cent of enterprises reported having concluded a collective agreement. This percentage was the lowest in trade (30 per cent), security (35 per cent), and hotels and restaurants (37 per cent). In industry, it was the lowest in leather and shoes and in textiles and clothing. Less than half of the small enterprises with fewer than 50 employees had a collective agreement at the end of 1997 (*Table 14.7*). Nevertheless, we should emphasise that, overall, more enterprises signed a collective agreement in 1997 than in 1996, even among private enterprises. This represented a positive development in the middle of an otherwise dismal landscape, and may represent a sign of hope for improved social dialogue at the enterprise level in the future. It may be that enterprises—at least a good proportion of them—preferred to restart after the crisis on a better social basis than in 1996 in order to avoid future renewed production disruption. It is also possible that a good percentage of those enterprises that had been trying to avoid social dialogue of any kind in 1996 were swept away by the crisis. In any case, social dialogue at the enterprise level could not emerge without stronger trade unions, which, as we have seen, have been among the biggest losers of the crisis.

Table 14.7 *Social Dialogue Indicators, by Size, 1997 (%)*

	1–50	51–100	101–200	200 +
Recognised trade unions	20.7	60.3	77.8	90.3
Trade unionisation	4.1	29.9	35.1	38.6
Signature of a collective agreement	47.7	77.4	80.8	86.4

Source: ALFS3.

Finally, all forms of direct worker participation seem to have disappeared from enterprise management in 1997. Only 64 per cent of enterprises reported that they informed workers directly about company results, with less than 50 per cent of private enterprises and joint ventures doing so. Similarly, profit-sharing schemes were abandoned by most enterprises in 1997: 7 per cent reported applying such a scheme compared to more than 50 per cent in 1994. Less than 4 per cent of private enterprises and joint ventures had introduced payments related to performance or profit-sharing schemes. These direct forms of worker participation continued only in state-owned enterprises in mining, wood and paper, public service utilities, and telecommunications. Direct forms of democratic participation thus tended to disappear in the wake of the crisis.

Table 14.8 *Economic Democracy Indicators, by Property Form, 1997 (%)*

	State	Private	Joint ventures	Joint stock	All
Informing employees regularly about results	85.0	47.0	44.0	77.0	63.0
Worker participation in profits	11.0	4.0	3.0	10.0	7.7

Source: ALFS3.

These social tendencies—less social dialogue, less participation—clearly helped to put most employees in an even more precarious situation, despite an environment already dominated by poverty; they also added to the frustrations that the labour force and their families had to bear after the crisis.

8 MASS POVERTY: ABOVE ONE-THIRD OF THE POPULATION

The poverty situation described in Chapter 6 as critical will worsen even further, affecting a growing proportion of the population, constituting a form of mass poverty generally seen only in developing countries.[9]

According to different estimates, poverty increased by 30 per cent after the collapse of the pyramid funds, encompassing well over one million people.[10] Many of these—approximately 40 per cent or more than 500,000 people—are pensioners, living on an average monthly income of USD 22 in the cities, and USD 7 in the countryside. There are also the unemployed, people in rural areas, and all persons relying on social assistance or starvation wages. The number of families registered for social assistance in early 1998 was 165,000—representing 650,000 people—who lived on state assistance of no more than USD 21 a month. According to Minister of Labour Elmaz Sherifi, in mid-1997 about 600,000 Albanians eked out a meagre existence on welfare handouts of around USD 15 a month. Many social security and social assistance payments were interrupted in the early months of 1997.

A very close correlation was found between unemployment and extreme poverty. Among the urban poor, the poorest were those whose family's principal earner was unemployed. Next come multi-generational households in which the principal earner is a retired pensioner. Families with principal earners on low salaries constitute a third major group of urban poor.

In rural areas, the proportion of families below the poverty line is higher than the national average. Already at the end of 1996, one-third of the rural population was found to be living in poverty: needless to say, the collapse of the pyramid schemes which hit the countryside hardest will only make matters worse, estimated to have encompassed as much as two-thirds of the rural population. Living conditions in the countryside are shocking. This led in 1997 to growing internal migration, with villagers seeking to escape unemployment and poverty moving to the cities in search of a better life.[11] In Tirana and other large towns, however, although poverty is less widespread,

9. This has led a number of analysts to call Albania "Europe's Africa"; see Andrea Stefani, "Albania Marching towards Europe or towards Africa?", in *Albanian Observer*, Vol. 3, No. 7–8 (1997), p. 33.

10. According to the World Bank (1996b), already in 1996 more than 700,000 people were living below the poverty line.

11. See "Peasants Flood Cities in Search of Work", in *Albanian Observer*, Vol. 3, No. 10 (1997), p. 16.

it has begun to take hold: the number of homeless people has rapidly increased and hygienic provisions are at their lowest ebb—power cuts are a daily occurrence in Tirana and the water supply is regularly disrupted. This rural flux and concentration of the population in urban areas can only aggravate these already deteriorating conditions, especially in the suburbs.

The situation during the uprising was particularly dramatic: the country was facing a food shortage, government stocks having been exhausted and the trading system having ceased to function. At the beginning of the troubles, the International Committee of the Red Cross launched an emergency assistance programme for the most vulnerable people in Albania that lasted for eight months. This assistance was essential at a time when the country's social assistance network had ceased to function and many hospitals and social welfare institutions were in desperate need of food and medical supplies.[12] Other humanitarian aid and assistance were provided by the international community.[13] Beyond this emergency assistance, however, the Albanian authorities must bite the bullet and implement a more long-term programme to eradicate poverty (see Chapter 16).

9 CONFLICT IN KOSOVO: GENERATING NEW SOCIAL TENSIONS

The Undeclared War

The fighting in Koṣovo erupted in March 1997. The Serbians initiated security measures in response to "armed insurgency on the part of the Kosovo Liberation Army" (KLA),[14] carrying out heavy artillery and mortar attacks on villages from which they were alleged to be operating. Western Kosovo, a southern province of Serbia, has more than 2 million ethnic Albanians, accounting for 90 per cent of the population: it is one of the richest areas in the region. The operations of the Serb army rapidly took on the character of "ethnic cleansing": to some analysts, their actions represented an attempt to create a "sanitised corridor" free of ethnic Albanians, whom they consider a

12. In total, 50 tonnes of basic medical supplies and 187 tonnes of food have been distributed to 63 medical and social welfare organisations across the country. A total of 210,022 Albanian families received a parcel containing basic foodstuffs and items essential for maintaining hygiene. The ICRC also supplied chlorine and water purification equipment, and handed over 185 tonnes of food to the Albanian Red Cross as a winter reserve (Reuters, November 1997).

13. We might mention, for example, the humanitarian aid of ECU 4.7 million provided by the European Commission (EU Humanitarian Office) to provide food for vulnerable people and to rehabilitate emergency and public health facilities that had been pillaged and damaged all over the country.

14. Most of them have as their objective the unification of Albania with the Albanian ethnic minorities in Kosovo, Macedonia and Montenegro.

threat to minority Serb rule. Although no journalists were allowed to remain in the area, there were reports of systematic attacks with heavy artillery, grenades, and tanks, and the looting and burning of villages was systematically pursued close to the border, in order to force ethnic Albanians into a massive exodus. More than 300 Albanians had been killed in the crackdown at the time this book went to press.

The renewed fighting in the rump Yugoslavia revived concerns that the Kosovo tensions could spread to neighbouring countries, particularly if the fighting should divert the flow of refugees south to Macedonia. The Albanian Government, however, pledged that Albania would not be drawn into a Balkan war over Kosovo, as reiterated on several occasions by Prime Minister Fatos Nano[15]—"I commit myself to ensuring that Albania says no to any Balkan war waged by Albania and Albanians"—in favour of a diplomatic solution: "I have the impression that diplomatic shells are more powerful than artillery shells."

During the summer of 1998 the Western powers called upon Yugoslav President Slobodan Milosevic to end this offensive, but in vain, despite the huge Serb gains. From the time the fighting began, the Albanian Government called on NATO for protection from Serbian incursions, and indeed there was a massive display of air power in northern Albania in June 1998. However, threats of NATO military intervention were weakened by the insistence of leading EU states, such as Germany and France, that any action had to be sanctioned by the UN Security Council, at which Russia, which has close historical ties with Belgrade, seemed determined to continue to exercise its veto. The only significant step which the United Nations Security Council was able to make by late September was to call on the Serbs to halt the killing immediately, to assist the dazed and dispersed population with a view to helping them return home, and to start negotiations with the ethnic Albanians. At the end of October, after Kosovo had finally caught the world's attention and NATO had threatened the Serbs with air attacks, President Milosevic had nothing to lose in finally reaching an agreement just before the expiry of the NATO ultimatum. He agreed to withdraw his troops from Kosovo, but only after they had already driven out a large part of the ethnic Albanian population by means of mass killings and other atrocities.[16] As one Pentagon official said: "Milosevic has created a desert, and we are about to call it a peace; . . . We will present it as a victory, of course. The truth is, we are going in to pick up the pieces."[17]

---

15. See the *Albanian Observer*, Vol. 4, No. 6 (1998), pp. 13–16.

16. See *Newsweek*, 12 October 1998, whose cover headline was "War by Massacre", and the special report, "Time to Shoot or Shut Up", by J. Barry, R. Nordland, and R. Watson, pp. 10–17.

17. Ibid., p. 12.

Exodus

In the meantime, it was estimated that more than 15,000 refugees had fled from Kosovo into northern Albania, while about 7,000 had escaped to neighbouring Montenegro. According to humanitarian organisations, thousands more displaced persons were on their way.

The UN High Commissioner for Refugees had already registered 8,000 refugees by June 1997 and estimated another 4,000 had arrived without registering. A contingency plan was prepared for the arrival of about 10,000 more people.[18] Most refugees were concentrated in Bajram Curri, a border town 140 miles north of Tirana, while others stopped in Tropoja, the Albanian border town closest to the fighting, where thousands of Kosovo refugees had settled (see Map on p. xxiii).

UN officials estimate that a total of 265,000 people had been driven from their homes. About 65,000 of them fled to neighbouring Albania, Montenegro, or Macedonia. As many as 200,000 displaced persons were believed to be still inside Kosovo, many staying with friends and relatives, but 50,000 were sleeping in forests and on hillsides beyond the reach of Serbian guns.

Social Problems Exacerbated in the Poorest Region of Albania

The influx of thousands of refugees immediately created problems in the poorest region of Europe's most impoverished country. Many refugees were welcomed by local people, who shared what they could spare. Food shortages rapidly became the first problem,[19] followed by housing. Many were living in the open on the scant rations they had brought with them. According to one official responsible for humanitarian aid, "We already had a food shortage here before the refugees started coming . . . It is ridiculous to talk about humanitarian assistance in an area where there is already a food shortage."[20]

The relief effort was seriously hampered by the isolation and disastrous transport infrastructure of northern Albania. Rugged terrain posed severe supply problems for the UNHCR's aid efforts. In addition, the northern part of Albania is cut off from the south by a large lake, which can be crossed only

18. See "UN ready for 20,000 Kosovo Refugees", in the *Albanian Observer*, Vol. 4, No. 6 (1998), p. 10.
19. "A handful of rice. A tomato. A crust of bread. Asking Kosovo refugees what they have had to eat on any particular day is one way to measure their tragedy". *Albanian Daily News* (25 August 1998, p. 10).
20. See "Albania Urges 'Any Means' to Stop Kosovo Bloodshed", in the *Albanian Observer*, Vol. 4, No. 6 (1998), pp. 11–12.

by ferry, which was severely overworked. At the same time, donor nations were reluctant to send food and medicine to the region for fear that they would be stolen.

The coming winter (1998–99) is expected to be dramatic, a consideration which pushed Viktor Klima, Chancellor of Austria (which held the European Union presidency at the time) to call at the end of August 1998 for a UN Security Council debate on Kosovo, "to prepare humanitarian aid because thousands of refugees are in the forest today and the coming winter could cause dramatic problems".[21]

It was also estimated that Serbian shelling and arson had destroyed as many as 15,000 houses in Kosovo, making it impossible for a substantial number of those displaced by the fighting to return home. Many elderly people and children had already died on the road.

According to Eduardo Arboleda from the UNHCR, "diarrhoea, dehydration and disease were widespread among the displaced population", adding that in the winter "people will freeze to death, especially the most vulnerable groups . . . There is a lack of adequate food. It seems almost surreal to have people dying of starvation in Europe . . . but they could."[22] For Fernando del Mundo, also working for the UNHCR, there was no doubt: "What can we do if people stay in the hills and do not return to their homes before the winter? We are afraid that people are just going to die."[23] At the time of writing (December 1998) it is not possible to say whether this could be avoided, since no information seems to be available concerning either the extent of the Serbian military withdrawal from Kosovo or the return—and under what conditions—of the ethnic Albanians.

Economic Implications

The massive influx obviously had significant economic implications, particularly in respect of Albania's already stretched resources. In an interview, the Governor of the Central Bank Shkelqim Cani mentioned that the Kosovo crisis had put pressure on the Government to increase spending, while it would have a direct negative impact on foreign investment.[24]

There is no doubt that the risk of Albanian involvement in a war, the Government's statements notwithstanding, has discouraged foreign investors from coming—or returning—to Albania, especially after the events that shook Albania one year ago.

---

21. See *Albanian Daily News* (26 August 1998, p. 9).
22. Interview with Reuters, in *Albanian Daily News* (26 August 1998, p. 11).
23. See *Albanian Daily News* (25 August 1998, p. 10).
24. See *Albanian Daily News* (26 August 1998, p. 7).

The implications will be particularly severe for the northern regions of Tropoja and Kukes, the poorest in Albania. They subsist on low-productivity agriculture after the severe cut-backs in local chrome mining. About 40 per cent of Tropoja's 44,000 permanent inhabitants depend on welfare payments and handouts. In late June 1998, the Government ordered that those fleeing Kosovo should be given refugee status only if they were registered and remained in Tropoja district. This measure was intended both to facilitate the distribution of aid and to limit the conflict territorially, not to mention the criminality which the refugee influx seemed to have brought with it. At the same time, the Government has sought to promote co-operation among the population by creating a Youth Council, although tensions have been increasing. Every week looted guns kill two or three people in Tropoja's main town, Bajram Curri.[25] Tensions will not dissipate in the long term, considering the extent of the poverty and the poor prospects for jobs in this area of Albania. The burden will become heavier and heavier for both local and national budgets. We have already seen that the region of Kukes has the highest unemployment rate in Albania (Chapter 5).

10 CONCLUSION

The violence of the spring events, broadcast all over the world, clearly illustrated the sudden desperation of hundreds of thousands of Albanians. After reaching the conclusion—no doubt naively—that the transition would make things better for them, most Albanians lost all their life savings. Even the remittances from relatives or friends working abroad, that had served as vital means of surviving the first years of reform, were suddenly swallowed up by the pyramid schemes. The poorest people were the worst affected, especially in rural areas, where many were left entirely without means of subsistence, having sold their land and cattle to invest more. In the cities, many were left homeless for the same reason. But this was by no means the end of it. As the enterprise survey results show, the poorest people had to face a new assault, comprising the direct and indirect effects of the economic crisis. At the very moment workers wanted to return to work to start to recover their lost savings and to provide an income for their families, the destruction and closure of many enterprises left many of them without a job. The generalised slowdown of economic activity prevented them from finding alternative employment, leading to mass unemployment that the official statistics—frozen at the pre-crisis unemployment level—have yet to catch up

25. See EIU (1998c), p. 12.

with. Many had no other alternative but to enter the growing but insecure informal economy. For those "lucky" enough to find work, the situation was not much rosier. Enterprises that continued or resumed operations interrupted wage payments, and for months left workers without desperately needed earnings. Most enterprises also dismissed part of their labour force in a desperate attempt to continue, leading to large-scale lay-offs in some sectors and regions. The growing inflation that struck the most basic commodities was an additional factor that led many to abandon any hope of making ends meet. In the absence of indexation, average wages that were not increased for over a year lost nearly 50 per cent of their purchasing power. At the same time, the total collapse of trade union membership at the enterprise level, and the poor incentives of private enterprises to return to social dialogue in any form, combined with mass unemployment, has limited workers' ability to negotiate improvements in wages and working conditions. Social benefits, unemployment benefits, and pensions will also fall to merely symbolic levels, unable to ensure minimum subsistence needs. As if this were not enough, the sudden immigration of refugees fleeing the war in Kosovo will generate new social problems in northern Albania, already characterised by high unemployment. To summarise, all the recent economic, social, and political developments in Albania have combined to exacerbate the already precarious situation of Albanian families. The country fell suddenly into a huge social abyss, with one-third of the population plunging into an extreme poverty which cannot easily be imagined by Western readers.

15. Reviving Production Forces

1 INTRODUCTION

In early 1998, in the context of economic slowdown and social distress described earlier, it was far from obvious how economic recovery might be brought about, particularly because the improvement of the miserable social situation and the faith of millions of Albanians depended on its success. Faced on the macroeconomic side by a large budget deficit, trade imbalances, and growing inflation, and on the microeconomic side by the need to reconstruct a destroyed production sphere and to help enterprises restart their activities, the Government hesitated between different options. Assistance from the international community at this time was crucial. An important donors' conference in Brussels in October 1997, while testifying to a significant impulse of solidarity on the part of the international community, also came at the right time to motivate the Albanian Government to move ahead, despite the countless difficulties it faced. It also pointed the way towards economic recovery and, advised by international monetary institutions, a new budget was prepared for 1998, with a clear package of policy reforms. This led to a new wave of optimism concerning the chances of the Albanian economy to emerge from the crisis. In this chapter we analyse this package of reforms, and discuss its chances of bringing about the required economic recovery. We also try to go beyond the phase of reconstruction and to identify—taking into account past experiences, the mistakes described earlier, and the weaknesses of the Albanian economy and society highlighted by four years of enterprise surveys—what would seem to be the conditions that could best lead Albania towards long-term sustained economic growth.

2 INTERNATIONAL ASSISTANCE

The economic disaster in Albania required an appropriate response from the international community. The call was met by a wide range of diplomatic and technical missions aimed at assessing the situation after the crisis and the immediate needs of the country, as well as by the holding of a series of important international conferences to help Albania to ensure its longer-term economic recovery. In October 1997, a donors' conference was organised in Brussels under the aegis of a number of international organisations, which regrouped all international and bilateral donors. A comprehensive report—to which several international and national experts contributed—was also prepared for this purpose in order to make it possible for the most important technical co-operation projects and funds to be channelled towards the most needed reforms (see World Bank et al., 1997b). Albania managed to obtain good financial support, approximately USD 670 million being promised by international and bilateral donors on that occasion (USD 100 million was also approved to help the state deal with its balance of payments problems).

Moreover, various programmes under the aegis of a number of international organisations were agreed upon, some of which have already entered their implementation phase.

Albania was in this way able to obtain important international aid and funding for its reconstruction. After the generalised chaos of a few months earlier, the involvement of the international community was also crucial if external operators and investors were to be convinced of the viability of the Albanian economy.

3 EUPHORIA ONCE MORE?

This international help gave the Government the impetus it needed to prepare a new economic policy appropriate to the situation, and it is in this spirit that the budget for 1998, prepared in close co-operation with the IMF, was presented to the Albanian Parliament. The general outlines of the budget were clear: address the state budget deficit, reduce inflation, reform the banking sector, and so on. This new budget and the package of reforms were presented on the basis of a range of different forecasts for 1998, prepared together with the IMF, which undoubtedly contrasted strongly with the 1997 figures: 10 per cent GDP growth after a 7 per cent reduction,[1] an inflation rate down from 42 to 10 per cent,[2] and a budget deficit decrease from 14 to 6.5 per cent of GDP.[3] State budget revenues were expected to increase by more than 80 per cent. Only the trade deficit was allowed to increase, from 11.9 to 13.8 per cent of GDP.[4]

1. Continuous growth was also forecast for the years 1999 (7 per cent) and 2000 (7.5 per cent).
2. Also, a 5 per cent inflation rate by the year 2000.
3. It is planned that this shall fall to 3 per cent of GDP by 2001.
4. To USD 650 million.

In a period of deep depression and riven by doubt, the presentation of such favourable figures led to a period of renewed euphoria among experts, marked by a series of optimistic statements from both the Government and international advisers. According to Prime Minister Fatos Nano, "Indicators are looking very positive; they are an expression of the success of the joint efforts of the Albanian economy with the IMF to apply the programme of resuscitation."[5] The IMF stated that it "[has] been impressed by the remarkable progress Albania has made following the crisis last year," and that "[t]he budget plan for 1998 that we have discussed with the authorities provides strong assurance that the government's targets can be achieved".[6]

However, considering the recent past, the great expectations which were never met, and the overoptimistic statements overturned by the most serious political and economic crisis so far encountered by any transition economy in the region, we must question whether this was the right approach. Indeed, a number of Albanian experts have expressed considerable scepticism: "the new government's leaders are euphoric, though the pyramid scheme scandal has yet to be concluded. The first statements of optimism have already started;"[7] and "[t]he most debatable indicator is the predicted increase in GDP. Why do they present a record increase in GDP? There is only one explanation. The budget deficit, one of the main indicators which the IMF agreement is based upon, is calculated in relation to GDP. The higher the GDP, the lower its derivative, the budget deficit."[8]

More fundamentally, the presented forecasts seem to have overlooked the deep crisis faced by the Albanian economy, casting doubt on the Government's ability to reach such ambitious targets, especially since there does not seem to be any global strategy for the reconstruction of Albania's productive forces, particularly in respect of the problem of motivating thousands of enterprises to resume their activities.

According to forecasts produced by the Economist Intelligence Unit, Albania would be one of the "fastest-growing economies in 1998", on the basis of a prediction of GDP growth of 12 per cent in 1998. To underline the absurdity of these figures, the country occupying the first rank was expected to be Bosnia, with a 35 per cent increase in GDP: this in a country ravaged by the worst fighting seen in Europe since the Second World War![9] Ranking two

5. As reported in the *Albanian Observer*, Vol. 3, No. 12 (1997), p. 9, after an initial quotation in the Albanian daily newspaper *Zeri i popullit*.

6. See the *Albanian Observer*, Vol. 3, No. 12 (1997), p. 3.

7. See the *Albanian Observer*, Vol. 4, No. 2 (1998), p. 33.

8. Mitro Ceila, "Budget Numbers Undermine Government's Economic Euphoria", in the *Albanian Observer*, Vol. 4, No. 2 (1998), pp. 20–22.

9. When production starts from a low base, the percentage increase is inevitably high once anything like normal production resumes.

countries starting almost from scratch in first place in terms of economic growth and comparing that growth with that achieved by more consolidated economies, such as Hungary, is probably one of the most misleading arguments issued by economists in recent years on the subject of Central and Eastern Europe. Even worse, it was policies based upon statements of this kind which had led Albania into deep recession in the first place, and, since those who forget history are destined to repeat it, another recession might be inevitable if no serious action is taken to revive Albania's productive forces.

4 ECONOMIC POLICY CONSIDERATIONS

The Albanian budget for 1998 clearly set out the Government's priorities, and took the form of a radical fiscal and monetary policy.

However, we may question whether this was the only possible policy option, and if not, whether there were other alternatives more suitable to the prevailing circumstances. To this end, we must attempt to provide an accurate picture of the Albanian economy in early 1998. It was clearly experiencing stagflation, characterised by a slowdown in economic activity combined with rising inflation. This is particularly problematic for policy-makers (and also for economists) because the economic policies generally utilised to reduce inflation often have the side-effect of dampening production rather than boosting it, while attempts to jump-start the economy carry the risk of increasing inflation. Anti-inflationary action requires a tight monetary policy on the part of the central bank in order to reduce the money in circulation, while squeezing borrowing. The fight against inflation is also vital to preserving the stability of the domestic currency. On the other hand, production cannot be revitalised without providing enterprises with strong incentives, particularly in the form of necessary credit. It also requires boosting demand through higher incomes, which in some circumstances can also lead to higher inflation. The road to macroeconomic stability was therefore far from obvious. The Government chose a radical anti-inflationary fiscal and monetary policy.

Nevertheless, the terrible situation of enterprises, on the brink of bankruptcy, and their increasing difficulties due to the general fall in consumption should have induced the Government to pay more attention to policy options favouring production, or at least to implement a more carefully balanced economic policy. The terrible social situation requires an ambitious programme to progressively increase sources of income (see Chapter 16), one which could have gone a long way towards increasing demand and so enterprise production. Other conditions prevailing at the end of 1997 also pointed in this direction, including the fall in foreign investment, and lower remittances from emigrants, two basic elements of Albania's economic growth hitherto.[10] The Government's chosen policy will starve enterprises of credit, although it is impossible to generate economic growth without capital inputs.

Some economists have argued that it would have been possible to follow a more balanced policy, and in particular that a higher inflation rate could have been tolerated for the sake of boosting production.[11] Others believe that it was the hope of attracting significant international financial aid and funding that led the Government to give preference to fiscal and monetary policy measures: for example, this was apparently the only way it could persuade the IMF to sign the three-year Enhanced Structural Adjustment Facility agreement, a state of affairs grimly summarised by an Albanian: "[t]he dilemma facing the government now is whether to act on the International Monetary Fund's directives, or on the basis of developments in the Albanian economy".[12]

As the Economist Intelligence Unit has indicated, however, "with a government fiscal deficit (domestically financed), the administration, urgently needing outside funding, had a considerable incentive to conform".[13] After a review, the IMF in May 1998 accorded Albania a second three-year USD 47 million Enhanced Structural Adjustment Facility agreement, designated ESAF2.[14]

It is unfortunate that the IMF rarely includes boosting domestic demand and local productive forces among the advice it gives to national governments.[15] This is particularly questionable in the case of a destroyed economy in desperate need of reconstruction. Despite the uprising and the subsequent production crisis, economic policy in Albania remains the same as it was during the first years of reform. According to one Albanian analyst, "[t]he budget approved by the IMF looks like that of 1992."

The IMF agreement was also supposed to serve as a major signal for foreign investors to return to Albania. It was also expected to open the door to more funds from other foreign donors.[16] In the prevailing circumstances,

10. Remittances from emigrants, which amounted at annual USD 558 million in 1996, will be only USD 330 million in 1997. Annual foreign investment in 1997 was also half of that in 1996.

11. See the *Albanian Observer*, Vol. 4, No. 2 (1998), p. 22.

12. See the *Albanian Observer*, Vol. 3, No 12 (1997).

13. See EIU (1998a), p. 14.

14. See the editorial "The Magic Signature", in the *Albanian Observer*, Vol. 4, No. 5 (1998), pp. 1–3.

15. According to Minister of Finance Arben Malaj: "The main conditions that the IMF put on the agreement were: the establishment of a fiscal package; reforms in the banking system; completion of the laws on the Central Bank of Albania; the auditing and administration of the pyramid firms." Interview with the *Albanian Observer*, Vol. 4, No. 1 (1998), pp. 5–6.

16. The Albanian authorities, in a number of interviews, have often repeated the figure of USD 300 million expected from foreign donors in 1998.

however, the achievement of economic growth—not the official GDP growth figure of 10 per cent,[17] but real production growth—appears more than doubtful.

We describe in the following sections some of the main directions that we believe Albania should take in order to ensure long-term economic recovery.

5 THINK LOCAL, NOT ONLY INTERNATIONAL

In the first years of transition, the Albanian Government seemed to believe that most economic growth would be generated by opening the country up to foreign assistance and investment. Unfortunately, as we have seen, these great expectations, easily explicable in terms of years of isolation, have not been met. Foreign investment in particular led only to mixed results. Contrary to expectations, foreign investors did not bring an overall positive trade balance, the growing exports of joint ventures often being accompanied by significant imports of raw materials (for instance, in textiles and shoes). The economic performance of many of these companies, especially in services and in food processing, has been disappointingly poor. In other words, although foreign investment constituted—and will continue to constitute—an important pillar of the Albanian economy, it has also shown its limits, at least in its present form, partly due to overexpectations on the Albanian side, but also partly to the misbehaviour of many foreign firms (see Chapter 9). This calls for a more diversified strategy from the Government. In particular, there is a need to be more selective when choosing foreign investors: for years, policy-makers—and most economists—emphasised that Albania could not afford to refuse a single penny offered by foreign investors, given its low level of development. Past experience has clearly shown that this strategy was fundamentally wrong: in Chapter 9 we mentioned the huge amount of money that the state is now losing after being dragged before the international courts for "divorces" from foreign partners. We have also seen how many joint ventures have ceased operating or are running with continuous deficits, for instance in services and the food industry, not to mention the factories whose workers are still waiting to restart work in the absence of a foreign manager who disappeared without giving notice—this seems to have happened on a significant scale during the crisis.

All this has led to the waste rather than the valorisation of local productive forces. The events of 1997 laid bare the weaknesses of the Albanian economy when starved of foreign capital. Better selection of foreign investors, with preference given to projects beneficial to local development, could only lead

---

17. From the lower level reached in 1997 compared to 1996, and with the restart of more enterprises, this official indicator can only increase.

to higher returns. In the same vein, the privatisation process should be resumed with more transparency: all too often, auctions have been avoided for obvious reasons, while the vouchers option, as elsewhere in the region, has shown its drawbacks and should be replaced by other privatisation forms.

Similarly, the Government has been active in diplomatic circles—and not without success—in order to obtain the financial resources so necessary for their country. The first challenge of the new Government has been to try to get the maximum possible in monetary terms, but also technical co-operation projects and assistance from the international community. However, whatever the amounts and effectiveness of international assistance, they clearly cannot bring about economic recovery on their own, particularly if they are not channelled towards their most productive use and do not form part of a more global national economic strategy. In the absence of such an overall directing strategy, some have become sceptical about the value of international contributions:

> From the financial assistance that has been promised we should see what will really be used for production recovery. According to the Minister of Economic Development and Co-operation, Ermelinda Meksi, foreign assistance per head in 1991–96 was an average of USD 27; out of USD 653 million promised only USD 375 million had been absorbed or disbursed. It seems the same thing is happening with the new government. Some USD 600 million were promised last October at the Brussels donor conference, but very little has come into the different spheres of the economy.
>
> *Albanian Observer*, Vol. 4, No. 2 (1998), p. 33

For others the future still depends exclusively on foreign capital or international assistance. According to the Economist Intelligence Unit: "[t]he restructuring of the economy depends on inflows of foreign capital. In the absence as yet of significant foreign private capital, the government is dependent on support from multilateral agencies and government-led credit."[18] This is precisely the situation from which, in our view, Albania should seek to move away as soon as possible. While opening its economy to the rest of the world, it is important that it develops its own productive capacities and resources.

6 THE LIMITS OF GROWTH DRIVEN ONLY BY AGRICULTURE

In the first years of reform, agriculture was often presented as the only driving force of Albanian economic recovery. Indeed, compared to 1990, agricultural

18. EIU (1998a), p. 14.

production levels have increased consistently as the main contributor to GDP (to 55 per cent). However, this increase is mainly a side-effect of the collapse of industry. Moreover, many clear signs of weakness in agriculture have shown that it is unlikely to remain a pillar of the Albanian economy, at least under present conditions. During 1996, the real increase in agricultural production was lower compared to previous years, and the results for 1997 do not indicate that this sector will soon emerge from stagnation. The continuous increase in food imports also reflects both the decrease in farm production and the crisis in the domestic food processing industry.

It seems that the initial increases in agricultural production could be attributed to rapid privatisation and the initial enthusiasm brought by private ownership. At the same time, the dismantling of co-operatives has also destroyed marketing and market-oriented production, replacing them by a survival economy, the limits of which may be illustrated by the fact that many peasant farmers have emigrated to the cities for the sake of survival. Smallholders typically lack market experience and are condemned by tradition to the utilisation of poor cultivation technology which, combined with the division of land into minuscule parcels, is an almost insuperable obstacle to effective production.[19] Moreover, the seasonal nature of agricultural production—and the weaknesses of food processing enterprises—has made it more and more difficult to satisfy domestic demand, leading to increased food imports. If these problems are not addressed, rural areas will soon be plunged into crisis, with agriculture no longer able to play the role of economic life-jacket.

At present, around 60 per cent of the population is located in rural areas, with 65 per cent of the labour force working in agriculture, on small private plots. Such a high share of the population in the countryside and mostly dependent on agriculture is largely an artificial creation, reflecting the forced settlement of the communist period, and well beyond the capacity of the land to support human life. However, it is also the result of the policy followed during transition, characterised by the distribution of small—one might even say tiny—plots of land and the absence of industrial policy. The share of total employment in agriculture was 22 per cent in 1990 compared to 65 per cent in 1996.

At the same time, industry accounts for a mere 8 per cent of total employment as compared to 34 per cent in 1990. Furthermore, persons considered to be engaged in agriculture cannot be officially counted as unemployed, although most of them are clearly 'underemployed', either on a seasonal or a permanent basis. As might be expected, rapid and significant

19. Most farming is done manually since people cannot afford machinery; the equipment used during the communist years is now outdated or unserviceable.

rural–urban migration has already occurred: over the last five years at least 200,000 people—6 per cent of the population—have migrated from the countryside to the towns. This process suddenly accelerated after the collapse of the pyramid schemes and subsequent crisis.

Under such conditions, far-reaching reforms are urgently needed in agriculture. Some farmers have already spontaneously formed associations or forms of co-operative in order to increase the scale of their operations, transforming subsistence production into production for the market. The co-operative form that may now develop in a capitalist environment,[20] not subject to ideological considerations, on the initiative of the farmers themselves rather than being imposed on them, may be one way of progressively transforming the agricultural system. Sale to other enterprises is another option, advised mainly by international monetary institutions, that could rapidly modernise agriculture, although it would leave most farmers out of the process and any new opportunities that may emerge. In any case, the establishment of a market for the purchase and sale of land is an urgent priority. Needless to say, this should be closely monitored, possibly by the state, to avoid the concentration of land in a few hands and the creation of monopolies which may bring about economic distortions—for example, in price formation—but also serious social problems, with the abandonment of the countryside by former peasant farmers and so increased unemployment.

Agriculture should also be developed as an important pillar of support for industrial development. Many foreigners have understood the importance of Albanian agricultural and fish products for the processing industry, multiplying their investments for instance in the processing of milk, frozen fish, and many other local products. Local enterprises must also be created and developed in this niche of the market, and with the prospect of reinforcing the links between agriculture and industry. If mutually sustained, such links could turn out to be the real pillar of the Albanian economy. In this connection, the food processing industry must be given priority. For this reason, it is important to develop small-scale credit and the financial infrastructure in rural areas.

7 BOOSTING INDUSTRIAL PRODUCTION

For many, industry is dying in Albania and should be allowed to die. We believe, on the contrary, that this would be the surest way to condemn the Albanian economy to a hopeless future. Our enterprise survey results, while

---

20. The agricultural co-operatives in Italy, for instance, have been shown to be performing rather well.

clearly presenting the profound problems encountered in some industries, further aggravated by the recent events, also identify a number of promising sectors. A clear industrial policy should be designed to help the few dynamic, export-oriented industries, such as textiles and clothing, and leather and shoes. During the first years of reform, these two sectors progressed continuously and attained "pole-position" in terms of exports in 1996, showing that Albania was able to export finished products as well as raw materials. We also saw that these were the first sectors to revive after the crisis. The wood and paper industry could also emerge as a major sector exporting processed goods.

There are also promising signs in such traditional sectors as minerals, dominated hitherto by large state-owned enterprises, where new private firms—including joint ventures—are developing. Other traditional industries are also important, such as mining and chemicals, which proved their importance during the crisis, especially in terms of trade, when they partly compensated failing exports from textile or shoe companies. Measures to rehabilitate the mines and ferrochrome smelters have already met with considerable interest from foreign strategic investors.[21]

As already mentioned, the food processing industry requires a particular policy focus. It is a crucial sector in rebalancing the trade deficit—food items represent more than 35 per cent of imports—especially after the crisis which resulted in the collapse of food exports and a new surge of food imports. It is also a sector that can attract much foreign investment. More importantly, food processing is also the essential hinge joining the modernisation of agriculture and the revival of industry, with the potential to transform the current strength of the Albanian economy, agriculture, into a strong industrial force, both at home and abroad.

It is also important to develop suppliers of raw materials for the most promising industries: for example, textiles, shoes, and wood and paper—but also traditional industries—in order to develop an integrated industry in Albania, with different industries sustaining each other at different stages of the production process, from raw materials to final products. By improving the internal market for raw materials, this process would contribute to rebalancing the trade deficit. In 1997, most enterprises in textiles, wood and paper, but also chemicals and metals, mentioned the lack of raw materials as a major determinant of possible future bankruptcy. Small and medium entrepreneurs in particular complained about the absence of fixed contracts with suppliers, which often led to delays and production uncertainties because of the different quality of the raw materials they had to use. Much too often,

21. See "Better Days for Albanian Chrome", in the *Albanian Observer*, Vol. 4, No. 1 (1998).

joint ventures have to import all their basic products, so contributing to trade imbalances. In this context, the Government should take urgent measures to reconstitute the group of suppliers that were destroyed or closed down during the crisis, if it wishes to avoid a gigantic trade deficit and the slow asphyxiation of all major Albanian industries.

More generally, in all the above-mentioned industries, there is a clear need to move towards more value-added products. Albania should not continue to export unprocessed products, which represented nearly 50 per cent of exports in 1997, mainly because a significant part of these raw materials will be used by neighbouring countries to make finished products which will be shipped right back to their country of origin as imports, further worsening the trade deficit, especially over the next few years when Albanian living standards will—it is hoped—start to increase. This is what happened in the first years of transition in the wood industry: foreign operators bought large quantities of unprocessed Albanian wood only to re-sell it to Albanian consumers in the form of finished wooden furniture, before a new law limited exports of unprocessed wood. The same applies to the food industry. Particular emphasis should be placed on processing when signing contracts with foreign companies.

The future of the Albanian economy depends in great part on the reconstruction of its industry, which emerged from the events of 1997 in a miserable state. This requires that the government design—at long last—an overall industrial strategy (not just a privatisation programme) and support it with all the appropriate policy instruments, fiscal, commercial, credit, and others. The elaboration of such an industrial policy could take better advantage of foreign investment, which could then be channelled, within the framework of specific incentives, towards the activities which need it most. As already mentioned, all too often investors were made welcome in Albania even if their operations were entirely antagonistic to the regeneration of local production networks. In many Western European countries, for example, governments try systematically to push foreign investors to deal with local suppliers.[22] It is also important to induce foreign investors to help local enterprises to move towards more value-added products, especially in industries such as textiles and clothing, and leather and shoes, for example, by investing more in research and development activities in Albania.

The emergence of small private enterprises should also be more actively promoted, for example, by relieving them of such burdens as over-taxation, scarce credit, and export difficulties. This is also important in services, which turned out to be particularly vulnerable during the crisis, despite their

---

22. This happened, for instance, in Portugal with the French automobile company Renault, which contributed much to local industrial development.

dynamism in 1995–96, many of them unable to avoid closure. The authorities must also try to promote greater diversification in services, especially by attracting foreign investors not only into tourism and trade, but also into other services important for local communities.

8 REVIVING EXPIRING CONSUMER DEMAND

The mass poverty that emerged in Albania after the crisis not only affects the social sphere, but has large implications for Albanian economic life. Domestic demand is now slowly dying in Albania. Some statistical indicators are particularly telling, such as the consumption of petrol and electricity, but primary food products have also suffered significantly. We have seen that the fall in consumption was, along with the physical damage incurred, the major factor in the imminent bankruptcy reported by enterprises (see Chapter 12). The fall in consumption that occurred after the crisis has thus contributed to block economic activity almost totally. It also has obvious implications for tax revenues. In 1997–98 the Government has suffered considerably from an increase in the number of enterprises operating in the black economy, entailing a huge loss of revenue for the social security system. At the same time, less consumption generates less VAT revenue.

In such a context, it seems clear that the production sector will not survive unless a serious boost is given to domestic demand. The Albanian economy cannot be sustained by exports alone, because the absence of a domestic market will inevitably generate a structural trade imbalance, with imports dominating exports, a scenario that is already stifling the Albanian economy. Moreover, producers in a country like Albania, where product quality is still in great need of improvement, require staged industrial development, the local market representing an unavoidable preliminary stage before production for external markets can really take off.

Stronger domestic demand could also help to attract a different type of foreign investor, one motivated not only by quick profits from export activities, but interested in the long-term development of the Albanian economy. A relatively small number of such investors would do the Albanian economy more good than the many small foreign investors who have so far descended on the economy like a plague of locusts.

A boost in consumption would also help to fight the informal economy, the growth of which is directly related to the fall in incomes and living standards: on the consumption side, low living standards induce households to consume on the black market, where goods are cheaper although of lower quality; on the production side, very low wages in the formal economy, especially in the budget sphere, push an increasing number of people to complement the insufficient income they receive from their first job with incomes from second or third jobs in the informal sector. In the final analysis, this increasingly deprives the state of tax revenues and social contributions. A demand boost is therefore also essential to reinforce the formal economy, and to improve the overall situation of the state budget.

9 CREDIT POLICY AS SUPPORT

In Chapters 4 and 10, we explained how the crisis was provoked mainly by the failure of the banking sector to play its proper role as intermediate financial agent. The pyramid schemes had their roots in the growth of the informal credit sector that emerged by default. This indicates the great importance of developing a suitable credit system. Worryingly, since the recent crisis credit policy has been tightened even further, the Bank of Albania and second-tier banks, on the advice of the IMF, ceasing to issue loans. As a result, almost no credit at all was provided to the production sector in 1997, a process that has continued in 1998: "Albanian banks must be the only ones in the world to have ceased lending. In the last six months, no credit has been given on any terms."[23]

While the absence of credits in 1996 could find justification in the absence of deposits, this was not the case in 1997–98, when deposits increased rapidly after the banks increased interest rates (some to as much as 30 per cent). In particular, time deposits grew by 127 per cent in 1997 compared to 1996, as a direct result of an increase of interest rates, particularly on three-month deposits (the highest since 1993). The restriction of credits was deliberate, a central component of the Government's restrictive supply-side economic policy to buttress inflation targets through "appropriate interest rate policy and judicious application of credit ceilings".[24] The problem is that while "appropriate interest rates" will lead to higher deposits in the banks, "judicious credit ceilings" will simply lead to a total absence of credit, at the very time when enterprises are reporting this as a major factor in their potential bankruptcy (see Chapter 12).

According to some, the deposits have been used to finance the budget deficit: "[t]he credits that state banks give are at the zero level; this process jeopardises the public's deposits and reduces investment capacity in the economy since all the public's savings serve the state budget".[25] According

23. See the *Albanian Observer*, Vol. 4, No. 5 (1998), p. 32.
24. IMF statement, quoted in the *Albanian Observer*, Vol. 4, No. 5 (1998), p. 9.
25. Statement by former Minister of Finance Ridvan Bode, quoted in the *Albanian Observer*, Vol. 3, No. 12 (1997), p. 24.

to others, "second-tier banks have stopped issuing credits to the public following a previous IMF recommendation . . . as a result of the poorly performing loans that had plagued many banks".[26]

Whatever its primary objective, the continuation of this credit policy—or absence of a credit policy—can only lead more enterprises to close down or to prevent others from resuming activities because of a lack of credit. This problem particularly hurts the multitude of small and medium-size enterprises—for instance, in food—that had to close down during the crisis. Should they remain closed, despite the fact that in 1995–96 they were the most dynamic enterprises, giving a substantial boost to the Albanian economy? More generally, should all industrial activity remain blocked because of monetary objectives? Finally, what is the point of controlling inflation if economic activity fails to restart?[27]

Not only economists but bankers have criticised the tight credit policy: "minimal levels of credit and budget expenditure are bringing the country face to face with economic collapse" (*Albanian Observer*, Vol. 3, No. 12 (1997), p. 34). According to the Governor of the Bank of Albania himself, Shkelqim Cani, credit provided to the economy is a crucial element in relaunching the Albanian economy.[28] This is the reason why the Prime Minister made an official request to the IMF to consider "more flexibility with credit matters".[29]

As far as the IMF is concerned, the priority is to carry out the privatisation or liquidation of the second-tier banks. It has been decided that the Agrarian Bank will be merged within the Savings Bank, that will itself be privatised later on. However, if Albanian enterprises have to wait for the privatisation of the state-owned banks, which may take a number of years, before being able to obtain credits, it will be a wonder if any are still in business.

Moreover, beyond the privatisation of state-owned banks, it is important to encourage the creation of new Albanian private banks. In mid-1998, six years after the beginning of the reforms, there are still no native private banks in Albania,[30] while the number of foreign banks has increased rapidly.

26. See the *Albanian Observer*, Vol. 3, No. 12 (1997), p. 21.

27. This situation is reminiscent of the satisfactory statements issued by IMF experts in 1996 in Ukraine when credit had been tightened so far that inflation had been brought down to zero. This took place in an economy in which, for lack of credit, no enterprise could pay wages for months on end, production being reduced to the lowest possible level in almost every enterprise. This was an economy that had ceased to function.

28. In conversation with the author, who is grateful to Mr Cani for the very interesting discussion on banking reform held just before he was appointed Governor.

29. See "Nano to IMF: more tolerant with the banks", in the *Albanian Observer*, Vol. 3, No. 12 (1997), p. 21.

30. In contrast with the situation in other Central and Eastern European countries, where domestic private banks rapidly multiplied.

Criticisms have been raised against foreign banks which have been accused not only of accumulating deficits, but also of dealing exclusively with foreign enterprises. Although this may change in the future, Albanian banks could create greater opportunities for Albanian entrepreneurs, while injecting more competition into the Albanian banking sector. In contrast to state-owned banks, by limiting the risks of linkages with particular political parties or with the Government, they would help to limit the problem of unpaid credits and so re-establish well-functioning credit facilities and financial mediation.

10 DECENTRALISED INCOMES POLICY AS SUPPORT

To bring about an increase in demand requires a progressive improvement in wages and incomes in real terms. By contrast, the Government—and the international monetary institutions advising it—opted again for a strict supply-side policy in which wage controls figure prominently, on the basic assumption that any increase in demand could bring inflationary pressures, through the well-known theoretical wage–price spiral. However, while this theoretical economic relationship has been observed in practice in most industrialised countries, the first years of transition have clearly shown that it does not apply much to Central and Eastern Europe in general, still less to Albania. In fact, while the IMF and the World Bank have been advising restrictive incomes policies all around the region, empirical evidence has progressively shown that wages could not—and did not—constitute a major inflationary factor in these countries.[31] First, because wages at the beginning of the transition were relatively low, and have remained low in most of these countries. Secondly, because wage costs have always represented a minor percentage—generally of less than 20 per cent—of total production costs, so contrasting with the situation prevailing in Western countries where wages constitute a major production cost. In Albania, for instance, wage costs represented less than 15 per cent of total production costs in 1994, 1996, and 1997. Thirdly, because inflation has been fuelled in most of these countries by price liberalisation, so that wages could not represent the major inflationary factor. The same happened in Albania, where wages, far from leading to inflationary pressures, were maintained as the main anchor of inflation, so leading to their out-and-out depreciation in real terms while prices were liberalised.

In such a context, we believe that wages could be progressively increased without adverse effects on prices. Liberalisation of wage controls in Hungary

31. See the comparative volume prepared by the ILO in Central and Eastern Europe— Vaughan-Whitehead (1998a).

and its replacement by a tripartite incomes policy negotiated between the Government, employers, and trade unions did not lead to any inflationary surge, the mythical wage–price spiral notwithstanding. The same applies to the Czech Republic and many other countries in the region. It is the accumulation of empirical evidence of this kind that has motivated almost every country in Central and Eastern Europe to progressively remove restrictive tax-based incomes policies and other central wage regulations.[32] A similar removal of central wage regulations is needed in Albania. In the country's present state, with domestic demand simply drying up, compromising enterprise survival, the continuation of a restrictive incomes policy could hamper any serious attempt to bring about economic take-off. By contrast, increased wages and incomes would represent an important economic instrument for boosting demand, but also for increasing workers' motivation and productivity. Both these elements are essential for reviving Albania's productive forces. This would also help to progressively shift some of the activities currently pursued in the informal economy to the mainstream—and so taxable—sector. Finally, it would help to curb the worrying braindrain taking place, particularly among civil servants and motivated by the higher wages available abroad, so helping to keep the best personnel to assist in local economic recovery. Special action is also needed to adjust low pensions and social assistance benefits (Chapter 16).

Central wage policy is still being implemented by means of four main instruments: (i) the continuation of wage controls for state enterprises; (ii) the irregular adjustment of wages and rigid tariff scales in budget organisations; (iii) the irregular adjustment of the national statutory minimum wage; and (iv) the absence of indexation mechanisms. We have seen the adverse effects that this centralised wage policy had in the first years of reforms in Albania, not only on the social, but also on the economic side (Chapter 6). Nevertheless, some progress has been made in the recent past, within the framework of a UN technical co-operation project carried out together with the Albanian Ministry of Labour.[33] A tripartite wage committee was created in 1996 and commenced operations in 1997 with the important task of reaching agreement on adjustment of the minimum wage. This led to a first increase of the minimum wage negotiated between the Government and the social partners in early 1998. This tripartite group was also put in charge of preparing a draft law for abolishing wage controls in state enterprises, although this had not

32. Only Bulgaria—along with Albania—seems to have maintained a restrictive tax-based incomes policy in 1997 and 1998.

33. Technical co-operation project for "Reforming wage policy in Albania" funded by UNDP and implemented by the ILO in direct co-operation with the Ministry of Labour of Albania. See ILO–UNDP–Ministry of Labour of Albania (1995 and 1997).

been done by mid-1998. Moreover, no indexation mechanism, either automatic or negotiated, had been put in place in 1998 to compensate workers for the 50 per cent fall in their real wages in 1997. More fundamentally, however, the new direction given by the 1998 budget and the IMF agreement did not leave much space for any improvement in wages and incomes (see Chapter 16). It is of course important to continue to implement all the mechanisms necessary to bring about wage decentralisation until it becomes rooted in national economic policy. However, whatever instruments of wage negotiation can be developed, wages and incomes will not increase if the Government is not committed to the process, and the restrictive fiscal and monetary policy of 1998 clearly points in the opposite direction, that is, to the perceived need to keep wages under control to combat inflation. We believe this direction is fundamentally mistaken, since it will contribute only to reduce, rather than increase, living standards and consumption, and so continue to suffocate production forces from every side.

This centralised scheme could be advantageously replaced by a system of tripartite consultations which could issue recommendations on wage increases on the basis of forecasts of inflation, GDP, and other economic developments at the national level, complemented by bilateral collective bargaining that would take place at decentralised levels within this framework of wage increases and would try to promote payment systems related to productivity. In fact, wages can also be kept under control by linking them more closely to economic performance, any wage increase triggered by productivity being non-inflationary by definition. In this regard, the Government could pursue the promotion of profit-sharing schemes and other performance-related payments that started with its new legislation in 1992, and which have proved to be particularly effective with regard to workers' motivation and productivity, even in enterprises facing economic difficulties (see Chapter 6). Such a multi-layered approach—a combination of national tripartite consultations with bilateral collective bargaining and decentralised performance-related payments —has proved to be successful in countries such as Hungary, Italy, and the Republic of Ireland where they have helped not only to relate wages to productivity at the enterprise level, but also to generate non-inflationary wage growth.

11 BUDGET AND FISCAL POLICY AS SUPPORT

Faced by the significant budget deficit recorded in 1997, the Government had to take stringent measures. Amidst the desolation that prevailed after the crisis, government expenditure could hardly be reduced, given the need to rehabilitate critical physical infrastructure both damaged and destroyed, not to mention the need for social security and social assistance on the part of the impoverished population. Priority therefore had to be given to the revenue side: in particular, every means had to be used to resume and improve the collection of revenues that were desperately missed in 1997.[34] In this regard, the strengthening of the authorities' fight against smuggling and general corruption is a major step. Illegal trade not only brings no revenues to the state, but also directly affects productive activity; small and medium-sized enterprises are particularly harmed by the resulting unfair competition, especially for products such as tobacco, beverages, and other food items.

Faced by a weaker tax collection system and increased expenditure, the Government took a series of measures, among which the increase of VAT from 12.5 per cent to 20 per cent figured prominently.[35] However, this measure has only helped to boost inflation, hitting hardest the most basic commodities needed for subsistence. Paradoxically, in 1997 it did not have the desired effect of bringing additional revenues: on the contrary, the consequent lowering of demand has served only to reduce VAT revenues, so contradicting the Prime Minister's initial expectations: "the VAT increase is expected to raise billion of leks over the last quarter of 1997".[36]

Given the Albanian context, characterised by dying demand and inert industrial production, a reduction in VAT—a trend observed in many other European countries—would probably have had exactly the opposite effect, namely, to increase consumption and production,[37] and therefore state revenues. Similar measures are needed in respect of income tax. The Government may consider its general reduction, and also exemption for all those whose wages are below the subsistence level. On the enterprise side, tax reductions could only motivate them to restart and to return to full capacity, while reducing their need to avoid tax payments.[38] In a country where less than 10 per cent of taxes are collected, it makes little sense to increase them further. Only their reduction can motivate enterprises, but also individuals, to pay their profit or income tax.

Reducing taxes must also be considered as an integral piece of the Government's overall strategy to boost industrial production and economic activity. Small and medium-sized enterprises must be given special incentives

34. See "Collecting Revenues: The Government's Achilles Heel", in the *Albanian Observer*, Vol. 3, No. 12 (1997), p. 1.

35. Mentioned by the Minister of Finance as part of the new fiscal package advised by the IMF; see the *Albanian Observer*, Vol. 3, No. 9 (1997), p. 3.

36. See the *Albanian Observer*, Vol. 3, No. 9 (1997), p. 9.

37. The increase in the price of oil and its products, vital to most enterprises, was particularly bad for small firms.

38. According to a manager at the Ajka milk processing factory, they are operating at 20 per cent of their full capacity as a direct consequence of the current VAT regime. Many other food companies reported they would soon have to declare bankruptcy if no steps are taken soon to adjust VAT; see the *Albanian Observer*, Vol. 3, No. 9 (1997), p. 9.

in this regard, to help them to overcome the current crisis and continue operating. Before the crisis, small private entrepreneurs were already finding it difficult to bear the multitude of taxes they had to pay on turnover, profits, income, merely being a small business, and property, as well as impositions for social and health insurance.[39] In the wake of the crisis, most of them will simply buckle beneath this crushing tax burden, a prospect which can only encourage them to continue their activities in the informal sector. The fact that 60 per cent of those employed are now working in the informal sector clearly illustrates the significant impact that a generalised decrease in taxes could have on limiting this process.

12 CONCLUSION

The profundity of the crisis needed a rapid and substantial response. This came first from the international community, with important funds being raised on the occasion of the donors' conference in Brussels in October 1997. The new Government of Albania also took significant action, preparing a package of economic reforms in its 1998 budget. This paved the way for the signature of a second three-year agreement with the IMF aimed at helping the Government to reach fixed targets. All the political and financial conditions seemed to have been put in place to ensure the Albanian economy's progressive recovery.

A closer look at this process, however, shows that the Government's economic programme was based on overoptimistic forecasts, leading to a series of overstatements and generalised euphoria concerning the real prospects of the economy. This could have been dismissed as a normal and even a necessary post-crisis reaction if it were not for the similarly overoptimistic figures presented throughout the first years of reform, which did much to obscure perception of the forthcoming crisis. More fundamentally, the new economic policy, aimed mainly at preventing a high budget deficit and a heightened inflationary rhythm, did not seem to respond adequately to the terrible blow that the recent events had dealt to production forces: by relying exclusively on restrictive fiscal and monetary policies, it limited enterprise access to credit and did not create the necessary conditions for reanimating dying demand, the other basic condition of the revival of local production forces. The resuscitation of industrial production was not made an urgent priority, as it surely should have been. Finally, nothing was proposed to reduce the trade deficit, which was even allowed to increase in the 1998 budget.

---

39. Moreover, there is no tax relief for start-up businesses; see Muço (1997).

In this chapter we have tried to identify a number of alternative policy options that we believe are essential for Albania's long-term recovery. First, we emphasised the need for the Albanian economy to end its apparent reliance on foreign investment and assistance, and to channel them, by means of a more selective policy, towards domestic economic development; it should also de-emphasise—or rather change the emphasis within—agriculture, instead channelling it, through enhanced competition, towards industrial development. The problem of trade deficit was also addressed: although generated in 1997 by exceptional conditions—with industries destroyed, joint ventures closed down, and imported goods of substitution—the trade deficit has become one of the central features of the Albanian economy, observed again in 1998.

In these circumstances, the transformation of Albanian industry is clearly the cornerstone of recovery. It could survive the current crisis and progressively gain strength if it were developed on the basis of two main pillars: (i) reabsorption of the structural trade deficit, for instance supported by such exporting sectors as textiles and shoes, but also the processing industry (especially food) whose trade imbalances are currently the largest; (ii) development of the domestic market, for instance by reconstituting the network of suppliers destroyed during the crisis. From our enterprise surveys, a voluntary policy to revive domestic demand also seemed to be needed in a context in which enterprise operations are stumbling in the face of inert consumption. A policy aimed at progressively increasing wages and incomes in real terms should constitute an integral part of this design, and contribute to increased levels of consumption while raising workers' motivation and productivity, which are particularly low after months of inactivity or non-payment of wages. Budget policy must also be adapted to the conditions put in place by the crisis, mainly tax evasion, that require a reduction rather than an augmentation of the tax burden on enterprises and individuals. Tax incentives are also required to help destroyed or damaged enterprises—especially small and medium-sized enterprises—to resume their activities.

However, in mid-1998 enterprises were still unable to resume production or to avoid bankruptcy in the absence of a strong credit policy and effective financial intermediation on the part of the banking sector. This has rapidly appeared as one of the main drawbacks of the Government's restrictive monetary policy, which has induced banks not to lend to the production sector.

This policy seems to render Albanian economic actors dependent once again, forcing them to rely on foreign aid as the only source of funding for economic reconstruction and development. In this context, the economic growth registered in 1998—and predicted for 1999—would again not reflect the real potentialities of the local economy, so hindering the return of Albanian enterprises to normal activity, again postponing necessary reforms, and delaying further and further real economic recovery.

16. Reviving Life Forces

1 INTRODUCTION

Our description of what we called the "social abyss" in Chapter 14 clearly showed that, once again, ordinary Albanians were the main victims of the recent events. After having had all their savings siphoned off by the pyramid schemes they were then hit directly by the effects of the subsequent economic crisis, with enterprise closures, economic slowdown, non-payment of wages, unemployment, and inflation forming a lethal combination which reduced their sources of income to nil. After having been significantly weakened during the first years of transition, Albanian life forces were thus slowly but surely being exhausted by the crisis and its aftermath. The depth of this social crisis cries out for public action.

Many experts have emphasised the need to revive the economy first: social problems would then be automatically solved by means of economic—mainly macroeconomic—recovery, which should therefore remain the principal objective to be pursued by the Government. For the IMF, "[t]he main objectives of Albania's medium-term strategy are to sustain rapid growth and reduce inflation further, with a view to generating employment and reducing poverty";[1] similarly for the World Bank, "[i]n the medium-term, the main condition for the alleviation of poverty will be achieving high growth on a sustainable basis and driven by private sector development, as it was the case between 1993 and 1996."[2] At the same time, international monetary organisations were launching a number of specific programmes for eradicating poverty, aimed at targeting social assistance on particularly vulnerable groups, the poorest categories of Albanian society.

By contrast, without denying the need for economic reconstruction, we believe that the gravity of the social situation and the extent of poverty in 1998 requires a more ambitious and comprehensive programme, rather than being left once more to still only hypothetical economic growth. The problem

1. See the *Albanian Observer*, Vol. 4, No. 5 (1998), p. 9.
2. See the report prepared after the crisis by the World Bank in co-operation with the EU, EBRD and IMF, July 1997, p. 12.

is especially urgent given that the conditions imposed for the purpose of attaining such economic growth are again demanding heavy sacrifices from the Albanian population and increasing poverty even more in the short term: in the present chapter we discuss how the restrictive fiscal and monetary policy followed by the Government contradicts in many respects the objective of alleviating social difficulties. In this regard, the World Bank's comparison with 1993–96 was also rather hazardous, since that period was also characterised by a fall in living standards, interrupted only for a very short time by the artificial increases in income generated by the fraudulent pyramid schemes. At the same time, while the usefulness of targeted anti-poverty projects is not in doubt, the extent of poverty in Albania after the crisis, involving as it does more than one-third of the population—over one million people—clearly shows the limits of targeted assistance and points to the urgent need for a more global, ambitious programme. This is one aspect of the crisis to which the ILO tried to attract the attention of the international community immediately after the crisis.[3]

We describe in this chapter what the most essential elements of such a strategy might be in terms of employment, incomes, social protection, and poverty alleviation, but also corporate governance and social cohesion.

2 RECOGNISING THE REALITY OF UNEMPLOYMENT

We explained in Chapter 5 why there was much more unemployment in Albania than the registration statistics suggest. This was also true in 1997, when unemployment apparently increased to only 16 per cent from 12 per cent in 1996, as if there had been no economic crisis, but rather only a slight tremor, although, as we have seen, more than half of the country's enterprises had been destroyed, closed down, or interrupted their activities. Our estimates based on our enterprise survey put the number of unemployed well above 50 per cent of the labour force. The failure to recognise this reality has had serious social consequences, the most notable of which has been the low priority given to social policy reform, the marginal number of unemployed entitled to benefits, and the miserably low benefits provided to the few who are entitled to them. This ostrich-like approach must end, since it seems that national and international policy will not focus adequately on the needs of the unemployed until their plight and that of those left at the margins of the labour market are adequately exposed. In this regard, the adoption of new benefit

---

3. See *Albania: Social Dimension of Recovery*, prepared by the ILO for the donors' conference, September 1997.

eligibility criteria in 1994 were misleading. In particular, as we have seen, agricultural land owners were not eligible to register as unemployed, although the small amount of land distributed to families often did not give enough work even to one family member. Other categories of worker were systematically excluded, while national statistics do not take into account a great number of people left out of work, both from the formal and informal sector, rendering the term "unemployment benefit" meaningless. In this regard, only a labour force survey could provide more reliable labour market information, and should therefore be prioritised as an indispensable tool for decision-makers: only trustworthy statistics would finally lead policy-makers and advisers to accept the reality of unemployment.

3 ADAPTING EMPLOYMENT SERVICES TO NEEDS

More accurate registration of the unemployed is urgently required. At the same time, all the obstacles to registration and entitlement should be progressively removed through improving the functioning of local labour offices. Workers without a job for more than a year, classified as long-term unemployed, should also receive some assistance, rather than being suddenly left without protection. The failure of basic protection mechanisms can only lead to the further growth of the informal sector, which would in turn increase Albanian workers' lack of protection. Unemployment benefits are also extremely low, and there is surely scope to raise them towards something like a subsistence income. Some experts have suggested that the fear of an increase in registered unemployment was one factor which persuaded the Government to hold down benefit. Whatever the reason, the fact remains that total expenditure on unemployment benefit comprised less than 1 per cent of GDP in 1996. This means that there was at least significant scope for raising unemployment benefit. In 1998, however, despite growing unemployment after the crisis, the number of people receiving benefits fell, as did the total amount paid out in unemployment benefits.[4]

In 1997–98, considerable pressure was put on the Albanian Government to implement more active labour market policies, focusing more on job saving, labour market training, and employment promotion. However, whatever the

---

4. While the official number of unemployed increased from 203,748 in January 1998 to 219,303 in June, the number of unemployed receiving unemployment benefit fell from 28,914 to 23,121 over the same period; see INSTAT (1998–1 [first quarter]) and (1998–2 [second quarter]). Over the same period, transfers for unemployment benefits also decreased: they reached only 822 million leks for the first half of 1998, compared to 2,204 for the whole of 1997; see IMF (1998).

effectiveness of such policies in Western countries, it is clear that so far this type of policy does not seem to have worked at all in Albania, while devouring a considerable quantity of money. A very low percentage of the unemployed—less than 1 per cent—were placed in jobs with the assistance of labour offices, and those who completed labour market training schemes were not much more successful. Moreover, these programmes involved a rather limited number of unemployed persons because of the tight central control and strict eligibility conditions for participation. This shows that there is considerable scope for improvement, and no one should question the importance of labour market training. At the same time, in the crisis situation that prevailed in Albania in early 1998, it should have been the priority to ensure decent compensation for the growing number of unemployed before committing significant resources to heavy training programmes. In any case, participation in training should be kept separate from entitlement to unemployment benefit.

The notion that so-called "public works" can be used to alleviate the employment crisis is subject to the same criticisms. Much faith has been put in the efficacy of such works for the purpose of combating unemployment, especially by international experts, who also saw in them a way of rebuilding the economy after destruction. The World Bank, for instance, proposed injecting USD 8.0 million to finance 8,000 labour-intensive jobs in the different regions of Albania, chiefly aimed at addressing crisis-related damage (see World Bank, 1997, pp. 4 and 12). However, while this would certainly help to repair the damaged infrastructure, such schemes also have a number of drawbacks. In many countries in Central and Eastern Europe, public works have in practice served as a vehicle for subsidising jobs, in other words, they can replace existing jobs, in addition to pushing down wage levels for the rest of the labour force.[5] Moreover, they do not really create job or production opportunities, a dimension that we insist should be privileged in the current context of reconstruction.[6]

4 REHABILITATING SOCIAL ASSISTANCE

The demands on the social assistance scheme in Albania have risen considerably as a result of the crisis. Between January and April 1997, the number of families applying for cash assistance increased by 20 per cent, representing 100,000 additional people (World Bank et al., 1997a, p. 13). The

5. For instance in Russia; see Standing (1996).

6. As indicated in the same document (World Bank, 1997, p. 4), these schemes would only create "short-term employment".

1997 budget was clearly not adapted to such circumstances. The increase in the number of applicants in a context of budget deficit, together with an increase in inflation of nearly 50 per cent, led in 1997 to a sharp fall in social assistance benefits in real terms. We should remember in this context that social benefits before the crisis were already standing at miserable levels, with a monthly average of USD 18 per family in 1996. Larger families—with five or more members—were receiving 3,200 leks per month, that is, about USD 30. This is also recognised by the World Bank: "[s]ocial assistance was awarded mainly to the poor but its amount was so low that it could lift only a very small segment of the poor out of poverty. High inflation, and loss of jobs and savings have increased both the number of poor and the degree of their poverty" (World Bank, 1997, p. 17).

By early 1998 social assistance had thus clearly lost its primary role, that of providing a subsistence income to the poorest families. Not only the level but the coverage of social assistance was totally inadequate to the social situation. Only corrective budgetary measures and the revaluation of social expenditure could modify this gap and rehabilitate the primary role of social assistance. The 1998 budget, however, did not satisfy this need—social assistance expenditure not being increased significantly despite higher contributions[7]—although the international support targeted on the balance of payments was also aimed at ensuring that "the Albanian last resort social safety net could meet the expected larger needs engendered by the crisis" (World Bank, 1997, p. 6).

It is also important to remember that Albania's social assistance expenditure is very small, amounting to only 1.6 per cent of GDP in 1996. This was about half of what Albania spent for the same purpose in 1994 (3.2 per cent of GDP). Altogether, social protection expenditure—including not only social assistance but also pensions and unemployment benefits—constituted less than 10 per cent of GDP in 1996, the lowest in Central and Eastern Europe.

These figures show the considerable scope that exists to increase expenditure on social assistance and on social protection in general. After all, in the final analysis it is always a question of budgetary allocation choices, even in poor Albania, and the percentage that a country allows to social assistance, even in transition countries, reveals a great deal about public

---

7. In the first six months of 1998, 2,513 million leks were transferred in social assistance, compared to 4,274 for 1997 as a whole, therefore constituting only a slight improvement. All subsidies and transfers—including subsidies, social assistance, and unemployment benefits—reached 6,409 leks compared to 12,017 leks for the 12 months of 1997. At the same time, tax revenues increased, amounting to 27,045 million leks for the first half of 1998, compared to 32,820 million leks for the whole of 1997. See IMF (1998).

choices and priorities. The reality is that, so far, social assistance has been rather neglected in Albania.

According to experts from the Social Assistance Administration, in early 1998 specific action was urgently needed on a number of vulnerable groups whose situation has rapidly deteriorated because of the crisis, such as abandoned and abused children, drug addicts and alcoholics (especially teenagers), and women and girls who are victims of prostitution rackets. The disabled and the elderly living alone have not been able to adapt to the post-crisis conditions either. Social insurance has also provided too low benefits so far, the health insurance system in particular having been brought to the brink of collapse as a result of the crisis.

Given the inability of central government to address the new social abyss, the involvement of local government is crucial, which entails the need to clarify the division of responsibilities between the two levels. Local initiatives from non-governmental organisations must also be developed. A legislative framework should be created in this regard, conducive to the involvement of NGOs in social affairs, and providing advice and training.[8] More generally, civil society as a whole must make every effort to eradicate the problem of poverty in the country.

5 LET THE PENSIONERS SURVIVE

The reform process brought with it tough new conditions for workers entering retirement. While the new pension legislation introduced in 1993 (as part of the new law on social insurance) abolished the former system of "work categories" which enabled some professional categories to retire early and to enjoy a series of privileges, the law on supplementary pensions passed in 1995 to compensate this loss has never been implemented.[9] Pensions were ridiculously low already in 1996, especially in the countryside, and inflation will only further erode them; moreover, pensioners were among those who lost everything because of the collapse of the pyramid schemes (Chapter 14). At the same time, the difficulties of the health insurance system will also directly affect older people. This gives us some idea of the situation in which most pensioners, the poorest category of all, found themselves after the crisis. Nevertheless, expenditure on pensions in 1998 did not increase significantly: they were 9,962 million leks in the first half of 1998 compared to 17,443

8. See ILO project (ILO, 1997, p. 24).

9. Only civil servants will be able to enjoy new supplementary pensions through a separate law implemented in 1996; see ILO (1997), p. 10.

million leks for the whole of 1997 (see IMF, 1998). It is imperative that the budget be adjusted to ensure pensioners' survival, and international assistance must be directed towards ameliorating the current deficiencies of the national system.

According to the World Bank, however, "the proposed support [USD 20 million budget support] is not intended to be used to increase pensions, by far the largest cash transfer in Albania", because "[t]here is a danger that if external funding is used to back pension increases, it will permanently increase the country's already high pension burden" (World Bank, 1997, p. 17). It is true that pensions do constitute a relatively heavy burden, representing 6 per cent of GDP, compared to the 1.6 per cent devoted to social assistance, not because of demographic factors—the Albanian population is young with a ratio of pensioners to persons of working age of only 0.27—but because of insufficient contributions.[10] But is this a good reason to leave pensioners drifting towards total destitution? The alternative proposal to "allow pensioners with very low pensions to qualify instead for means-tested social assistance to provide temporary poverty relief" is not a solution,[11] since it would leave a majority of pensioners—all of them having a "very low pension"—without the necessary assistance.

Beyond emergency budgetary assistance for pensioners, structural reforms are also needed, and changes must be made to the existing pension legislation, particularly with regard to foreseen supplementary pensions, smallholders' pensions, and those of other categories, such as the self-employed.

6 THE POVERTY LINE AS THE NEW SOCIAL PROTECTION THRESHOLD

While a number of other Central and Eastern European countries have defined a methodology for calculating a poverty line, and regularly determine and publish a subsistence minimum figure, so far no official poverty line has been adopted in Albania. As we have seen, however, the current social situation makes the determination of a poverty line even more urgent. Such a poverty line should be adopted as a central element in the formulation of the Government's new incomes policy and, more globally, in the development of anti-poverty programmes and of social policy as a whole. It should have two

10. It is estimated that only 30 per cent of those employed in the non-agricultural sector are insured and pay contributions (ILO, 1997, p. 10). As a result, Albania has a relatively high ratio (1:1.45) between those who contribute and those who do not (World Bank, 1997, p. 17).

11. Ibid., pp. 17–18.

primary functions: (i) to identify the poor and other at-risk groups; and (ii) to provide a reference point for the development of social protection policies. Attitudes have changed in Albania in this regard: while a few years ago the term "poverty line" was still "taboo"[12]—its use was carefully avoided among government officials because a poverty line would have facilitated the identification of those below it, and so suddenly reveal the extent of poverty in the country—the need to calculate such a subsistence level has been progressively accepted in the political arena, to the extent that it was recently embodied in the labour code. There seems, however, to be a gap—and a considerable time lag—between intention and action: in autumn 1998, there was still no sign of any official poverty line and no official instruction had yet been given for determining the methodology to be used for calculating it.[13] We believe that the existence of a tripartite committee on wages within the National Labour Council constitutes the most appropriate forum in which government experts, as well as those of the employer and trade union organisations, could elaborate, in co-operation with INSTAT experts, the required subsistence minimum.[14] Tripartite involvement would ensure that the poverty line reflected the real situation in the Albanian economy and was accepted by all three sides.

The calculation of the poverty line should be accompanied by a revision of the calculation of pensions, social allocations, and the minimum wage. Until now, many social benefits have been calculated on the basis of the minimum wage, which is why the minimum wage—through its irregular adjustment alongside price liberalisation—has been used for years as a policy instrument to limit social expenditure and to keep the state budget under control. It led to a perverse system in which the minimum wage and social allocations remained at a constant level. Disconnection of all social benefits from the minimum wage is an essential measure that has been successfully implemented in many other Central and Eastern European countries.[15] The calculation and foreseen publication of an official poverty line should constitute an excellent opportunity to programme and announce such a change in the basis for calculating social incomes.

12. International officials were kindly advised not to mention the word in front of Ministers.

13. Despite official statements already in 1994 concerning the need to calculate such a poverty line, on the occasion of a tripartite conference organised by the ILO, UNDP, and the Ministry of Labour on "Improving Wage Policy in Albania", in Tirana, 1–3 November 1995, reiterated by the new Government on the occasion of a second tripartite conference on "Tripartism and Negotiated Wage Policy against Crisis in Albania", organised in Tirana, 17–18 November 1997; see the official documents of these two conferences in ILO–UNDP–Ministry of Labour of Albania (1995, 1997).

14. See ILO's project (ILO, 1997, p. 26).

15. Poland was the first country to introduce such a reform, the latest being Bulgaria (1998); see Vaughan-Whitehead (1998a).

In the case of Albania, however, it might be difficult to adapt such incomes to the new poverty line immediately, so that a progressive approach should probably be followed. A precise time schedule could be planned with the social partners for the gradual revaluation of social incomes and the minimum wage in relation to the still-to-be-determined poverty line.

7 THE MINIMUM WAGE AS A NEW ANCHOR AGAINST WORKER DESTITUTION

Protection of low wages is crucial if renewed social conflict is to be avoided in Albania. To this end, a number of measures must be urgently discussed and implemented, since the minimum wage has clearly ceased to function as an anchor against worker destitution (see Chapter 6). In the first instance, it is essential to increase the minimum wage at least to the level of the subsistence minimum or poverty line, in order that it can recover its functions as social protector and minimum guarantee for all workers. As already mentioned, crucial in this regard is the official calculation and publication of a subsistence minimum.

We believe that there is now sufficient room in Albania to manoeuvre to increase the minimum wage without creating inflationary pressures. The fact that employers were paying less than 3 per cent of their workers at the minimum wage level at the end of 1997 is a clear sign that most enterprises are already paying well above the minimum wage in any case, so that the increase in the official level of the minimum wage would not change their wage funds significantly.

The average starting wage reported by employers in our enterprise survey at the end of 1997 was 6,607 leks, that is, well above the official minimum wage prevailing at that time (4,400 leks). In order to avoid worker demotivation, employers do not seem to have any other choice than to increase minimum payments at the enterprise level. This shows that there is considerable scope for increasing the minimum wage, which had ceased to act as a wage floor, even for damaged and only partly functioning Albanian enterprises. A positive first step was taken in April 1998, when the minimum wage, after having remained at the same level for nearly two years, was revalued by 30 per cent. Another positive aspect of this increase is that it was decided, for the first time in Albania, within the framework of tripartite negotiations. Nevertheless, this 30 per cent increase was still well below inflation in 1997, and at 5,800 leks the new minimum wage remained far short of all estimates of the Albanian subsistence minimum, none of which are below 10,000 leks.

A further significant increase in the minimum wage at the present time, while not involving great economic risks, would constitute an important psychological boost and ease social tensions. Within the framework of the Government's programme, a significant increase in the minimum wage of this kind could well be introduced at the same time as publication of an official poverty line. The determination of the minimum wage at the same level as the established poverty line could be done in a progressive way, in accordance with a well-planned schedule laid down by the Government in consultation with trade union and employer representatives. This would represent a symbolic first major step in the implementation of the Government's new incomes policy.

We have seen, however, that within the current social protection framework, any increase in the minimum wage would involve substantial changes for the budget. Disconnecting social assistance from the minimum wage could help the authorities to progressively increase the latter so that it would recover its social and economic functions. In order to avoid the risk of labour fragmentation due to wages generally and the minimum wage in particular following inflation, and social benefits remaining constant, trade unions would have a delicate role to play, negotiating the two issues separately while maintaining the purchasing power not only of the minimum wage but of social benefits.

Similarly, the minimum wage has been used to control the wages of budgetary sector employees. We shall discuss in the next section how disconnecting starting wages in the budgetary sector from the minimum wage could progressively improve the situation of public employees, while reducing the downward pressure on the minimum wage.

8 PULLING PUBLIC EMPLOYEES OUT OF POVERTY

We have seen that the growing gap between wages in the budgetary and the non-budgetary sectors is one of the main problems faced by the current wage policy in Albania. Low wages have hit the whole public administration, especially health and education. Public administration employees and their families have become a major new category of the poor, after pensioners, the disabled, smallholders, and the unemployed. These trends have not only led to a motivational crisis, but also to a "brain-drain", as the best public employees—"life forces" most precious to the state—often leave the administration to join the private sector or to find a job abroad. This has already led to a fall in the degree of professionalism in state administration. The institutional crisis during the recent dramatic events seriously affected public administration. Undoubtedly, this will remain one of the most serious problems confronting the Government and the social partners over the next few years. Restoration of the confidence of the Albanian people in their public administration will constitute one of the basic pillars of the reconstruction and consolidation of social cohesion in Albania.

As part of the 1998 budget, the Government announced two important measures in relation to public employees: (i) a 20 per cent increase in their wages, implemented in April; and (ii) the dismissal of between 10,000 and 15,000 public administration employees. These measures do not seem an adequate response to the problems of Albanian public administration, however. First, the 20 per cent wage increase—which will certainly be the only one in 1998—while going in the right direction, does not compensate for the 42 per cent inflation registered in 1997, nor for the price increases expected in 1998—10 per cent according to the Government's forecasts, although likely to be even higher. As a result, the wages of civil servants continue to fall in real terms. Secondly, although the problem of overstaffing has been addressed in almost all transition countries, Albania included, we may wonder whether it was the right time to implement a new round of dismissals, in a context dominated by mass unemployment and poverty, and the general demotivation of public employees.[16] Moreover, this measure, an integral element of the agreement with the IMF, seems to respond more to the need to ease excessive pressure on the public budget than to reform public administration. These redundancies were not accompanied by specific insurance, training, and mobility programmes for the dismissed workers;[17] nor did the negotiations involve trade union representatives.

Moreover, simply reducing staffing levels will not be sufficient to improve the quality of work in the state administration: deep reform of the wage-fixing system is needed. Not only are public administration wages too low, but they also have structural problems. First, wage levels corresponding to different scales are very compressed, and low wage differentials between grades have a strong demotivating influence. Furthermore, a number of distortions in wage differentials may be observed, that do not reflect differentiated individual or collective performance. At the same time, internal mobility between the various services is seriously restricted by a rigid classification grid and the absence of incentives for mobility, both in terms of career and income.

In several countries in the region, wage tariff systems in the budgetary sector have been radically reformed, generally within the framework of a simplification and unification of grades alongside new wage-fixing criteria, often linking wages more closely to educational background, skills, and

16. We have had the opportunity to witness at first hand the negative effects provoked by this measure within the ministries, particularly fears of dismissal and political purges, at the very time better motivation and functioning were urgently required, particularly in the security forces, as well as labour services, labour inspection, and the ministries.

17. See ILO programme proposed on this aspect (ILO, 1997, p. 16).

individual and/or collective performance. These reforms have frequently led to more motivating wage determination mechanisms, with greater flexibility for rewarding performance and more opportunities for upgrading and mobility. Similar reforms should be implemented in Albania.

One way of improving wages in the budgetary sector would be to disconnect the wage floor of employees in the budgetary sector from the minimum wage. This has allowed, for instance, the lowest wages of civil servants in Hungary, but also in other countries in the region, to increase at a much higher rate than the minimum wage. However, in this case the wage floor should never be fixed at a lower rate than the statutory minimum wage. In Albania, this would address the absence of wage increases in the budgetary sector when the minimum wage is adjusted only irregularly. Other reforms can also contribute to improving the situation. A strong human resources policy would help to develop a more efficient and transparent civil service. Beyond the urgent need to pull public employees out of poverty, it is also crucial to return to them a sense of the dignity of their role and public responsibilities.

9 PROTECTING WORKERS IN THE INFORMAL SECTOR

While some Albanians outside the formal economy are covered by social assistance, they remain a small minority. When we consider that more than 60 per cent of the employed were working without a contract in 1997, the extent of the problem becomes clear. These workers are direct victims of the aftermath of the crisis.

Many employees working in the informal sector before the crisis are likely to have lost their jobs because of it; such workers can expect no relief from the unemployment schemes and are therefore more likely to fall into total destitution. The social assistance scheme which is administered by local government should be extended to cover such categories of worker.

10 COLLECTING DIRECT INFORMATION FROM HOUSEHOLDS

Statistics have always represented an important means for measuring poverty. More specifically, it is essential to conduct regular household surveys in order to better identify the depth and extent of poverty and to improve the coverage of social policies. This makes it possible to evaluate whether social assistance benefits are providing the necessary help to Albanian families but also to identify those left out of the system, without any assistance. It could also help to identify local areas of poverty, and to adjust budget allocations by region accordingly. At the moment, there is a complete lack of information on incomes, living standards, and poverty in Albania. Regular household surveys would also help to identify the structure of consumption and revenues, and so represent the basic instrument for calculating the poverty line. It would also provide direct information on the informal sector: how much revenue it generates and its share of family consumption. More generally, household surveys help to identify the effects of economic reforms or developments—such as an increase in inflation, a fall in real wages, and so on—on the social situation. Up to 1998, only one attempt at a household survey had been made, in 1994, by the National Statistical Institute, covering families in Tirana.[18] Other attempts were aborted because of a lack of funding. Again, it is a question of budgetary, and therefore also political, choices.

11 SOCIAL DIALOGUE IN CORPORATE GOVERNANCE

The systematic avoidance of trade union recognition, signing of collective agreements, and indeed any form of worker participation that we observed in small and medium-sized enterprises, generally private or joint ventures, contributed to the wave of discontent and rebellion that was widespread among workers. No doubt some employers will have learnt a valuable lesson from the unexpected violence that erupted in some types of enterprise; the state must also become more vigilant against particular social developments at the establishment level. Laws similar to those prevailing in some Western countries promoting worker involvement in the life of their enterprise, even in small and medium-sized ones, should be encouraged. Specific guarantees of social protection (for instance, in respect of individual labour contracts and work rates) and social dialogue (collective agreements, trade union recognition) should be required of foreign investors. In other words, the further growth of wild capitalism must be avoided in Albania. We have seen that the presence of trade unions and a favourable social climate may have helped some enterprises to avoid closing down despite the crisis. Trade union influence in negotiating alternatives to lay-offs may also have an important social return for the whole community, in a context in which unemployment is likely to become one of the dominant issues in post-crisis Albania. Benefits can also be drawn from direct forms of worker participation—in decision-making or enterprise profits—to promote labour mobility and polyvalence, or to improve internal work organisation and productivity. Experiences in other Central and Eastern European countries have also shown how employee ownership can lead to good corporate governance with desirable social

18. A new Household Survey was planned for the second half of 1998, funded by EC PHARE.

outcomes.[19] Measures to encourage such property forms, which have been totally rejected so far, may be considered by the Government in the next stage of the privatisation process. This would represent a positive development considering the general lack of economic democracy in Albanian enterprises. At the same time, trade unions should seek to reinforce their position at the enterprise level, especially after the sharp fall in trade union membership that we observed in 1997. National trade unions must also launch a global strategy to become progressively involved in the private sector. Employers must also come to understand, especially after the crisis, that long-term profits cannot be generated in a climate of social tension, bad working conditions, and general worker dissatisfaction.

12 TRIPARTISM TO PREVENT A NEW SOCIAL EXPLOSION

In April 1997, despite the fact that Albania was still in turmoil, the social partners met government representatives within the framework of the newly created tripartite National Labour Council to discuss the implications of the events of early 1997, particularly the destruction of enterprise assets and its social consequences. This crucial step undoubtedly contributed to the calming of the situation and to the re-establishment of social dialogue in the country. It represented a promising sign of the importance of tripartism at such a time. Now that the political and institutional crisis seems to have been solved, further progress in this direction is urgently needed to overcome the terrible economic and social predicament in which Albania is still submerged. Significant steps have already been taken. A number of important public institutions, such as the Health Insurance Institute, have acquired a tripartite nature, with a management board composed of representatives of the Government but also of trade unions and employers' organisations. Furthermore, in September 1996 a tripartite agreement was concluded for the first time between the Government and the social partners on the creation of a tripartite committee on wages and incomes. There can be no doubt that the signing of this document represented a decisive turning point in industrial relations in Albania:[20] first, because it clearly reflected the efforts of the Government to decentralise its policy and to involve the social partners in the economic and social life of Albania; secondly, because it established the first tripartite body in Albania, which was accompanied a few months later by the creation of the tripartite National Labour Council, which plays a consultative

19. See Uvalic and Vaughan-Whitehead (1997), and ILO *Experts' Policy Report* (1998).
20. The text of this agreement is available both in Albanian and English; see the annexes of the volume prepared by ILO–UNDP–Ministry of Labour of Albania (1997).

role on more general economic and social issues; and thirdly, because it represented a clear willingness on the part of the Government to share its decision-making power in the very sensitive area of wage determination. In particular, the three sides have decided to give this wage committee the power to reach a tripartite agreement on the level of the minimum wage. The tripartite wage committee, although interrupted by the recent events, immediately resumed its activities after the crisis had passed: for example, a tripartite working group of wage experts—composed of government, trade union, and employer representatives, and assisted by experts from the National Institute of Statistics—prepared a common assessment of the wage crisis and a number of wage policy proposals were jointly agreed (also for the first time) by the representatives of all three sides.[21] As we have seen, this led to the agreement on the increase of the minimum wage in April 1998. This wage committee was also put in charge of preparing the new law to remove wage controls in state enterprises. This work, involving specialists at the technical level, and supported politically by the leaders of the three sides, is essential and should continue. The same wage committee should be asked to constitute a tripartite working group with the task of defining a methodology for calculating a poverty line and related adjustments, with the direct assistance of the National Statistical Institute, which is best placed to carry out the required household surveys on a regular basis.

Beyond wage policy, tripartite social dialogue should be extended to other essential areas, such as employment, social protection, and privatisation issues. In Hungary, where the tripartite National Council for the Reconciliation of Interests has created such a variety of committees—the most recent is concerned with Hungary's prospective EU membership and related issues—this process has ensured a relatively peaceful social climate despite severe economic reforms which have hurt the general population. There is no doubt that such tripartite dialogue should be further strengthened in Albania, where it could serve as an invaluable tool for implementing the new economic and social policy, without risking further social explosions and disruption of economic growth. This is particularly the case if such unpopular measures as employment cuts in public administration, restrictive budgetary policies, strict controls on social expenditure, and a severe incomes policy continue to be implemented.

---

21. The common assessment and recommendations were presented at the International tripartite conference "Tripartism and Negotiated Wage Policy against Crisis in Albania", held in Tirana, 17–18 November 1997. See ILO–UNDP–Ministry of Labour of Albania (1997).

13 CONCLUSION

The present volume, chiefly on the basis of comprehensive enterprise survey results but also a wide range of other sources, has presented strong evidence that the recent wave of discontent was generated not only by the collapse of the pyramid schemes and the consequent revulsion directed against the powers that be, but also by numerous other important factors. These include the social problems accumulated during the first years of reform: increased unemployment, miserable social incomes, impoverishment wages, and deplorable working conditions. The active participation of workers in the conflict and the high number of enterprises destroyed or seriously damaged, as well as the type of enterprise generally targeted, constitute clear evidence of popular discontent with the reform thereto. Evidently, the social problems, far from being solved, only became worse after the crisis, due to the arrival of a new series of impoverishment factors: life savings lost in the pyramid schemes, a new surge of unemployment, rising inflation, and a fall in wages and incomes in real terms. The poorest people in Europe had become poorer, a process which has yet to be halted.

This dramatic situation should have led the Government and the various international organisations concerned to prioritise social development, with a comprehensive programme for progressively increasing living standards and eradicating poverty, the main features of which we have outlined in this chapter. Unfortunately, the main objectives of controlling inflation and reducing the state budget continue to exert downward pressure on social expenditure. Official unemployment rates continue to under-report the reality of mass unemployment; and while the number of unemployed increased, those receiving unemployment benefits decreased in 1998. Social budgets were not substantially raised, as there was no emergency in this area. As in 1993–96, a restrictive fiscal and monetary policy was implemented to stabilise the economy, with the expectation that it would somehow automatically bring about higher living standards.

No account was taken of the boost required by the devastated economy from the social sphere, in a climate characterised by constant social tension, economic slowdown, and a serious decline in domestic demand. No doubt an improvement of living standards would help consumption to recover, and so help enterprises in their attempt to resume their activities; the subsequent increase in production would then help to generate more state revenues, through higher tax incomes and social contributions from enterprises, and higher VAT returns from enhanced consumption. Conversely, an economic recovery—a real one, based on greater productive activity rather than illusory economic indicators—would improve living standards through increased social contributions and assistance, wage increases based on productivity, and more job opportunities. It is in this sense that the policy recommendations presented in this chapter and in Chapter 15 should be seen: as a coherent package of policy reforms aimed at reaching the same objective, the recovery of Albania. We do not advise the neglect of financial and monetary indicators, which inevitably occupy a privileged place in the light of rising inflation and depreciation of the domestic currency experienced in 1997. At the same time, it is important to learn from past mistakes. In 1993–96, Albanian enterprises, in order to remain in operation, had to rely on informal credit, a direct stimulus to the growth of the pyramid schemes. The development of the informal sector and the spectacular growth of illegal traffic of all kinds were also the direct result of the need to survive, a fact well illustrated by the sudden intensive cultivation of cannabis by Albanian farmers in the poorest rural areas of the country. After the pyramid schemes collapsed, and as the Government seeks energetically to wipe out illegal trafficking, what sources of income are left to the Albanian population?[22] For ordinary people, the restrictive monetary policy renders participation in the formal economy non-viable, while enterprises receive less credit than before the crisis. In order to ensure their survival, what will Albanians have to turn to next?

First results (mid-1998) were promising. No doubt the Government will be able to curb inflation.[23] What it will not manage to do is to combat poverty, unless it devotes more time and resources to the problem. Nor will it be able to promote real economic growth without giving more credit and more leeway to the production sector. Albanian life-forces do not seem capable of surviving the current prioritisation of economic indicators, just as Albanian production does not seem capable of surviving the prioritisation of macroeconomic considerations.

All this leaves Albania with an uncertain future. After years of statism and oppression, the well-being of the Albanian people should finally emerge as the main focus of reform. Let them produce, let them consume. And, as the Albanian writer Ismail Kadare said recently, let them simply "have—and believe that they can have—a normal life".[24]

---

22. The police have burned out entire areas of cannabis cultivation.

23. Inflation fell below 10 per cent in the first half of 1998 (INSTAT, 1998b).

24. "After the recent storms and . . . passionate violence that have swept Albania, what I am concerned with as an Albanian citizen and writer is my country's fate, my people's fate. [The] majority [of citizens] must have a clear national vision, the vision that [they] deserve . . . a normal life just like . . . other countries. That vision [would be] enough to make them . . . come to their senses, to have a clear [view of] things, to make the right choice, not to be cheated by the speculations, slogans, [or] deceptions of one . . . grouping [or another]. If a large part of the Albanian people think like that, I believe Albania w[ill make] progress . . ."; interview given to the BBC's Albanian Service, published in the *Albanian Observer*, Vol. 3, No. 3–4 (1997), p. 27.

Bibliography

Albanian Center for Foreign Investment Promotion (1998), *Total Support for Doing Business in Albania*, Tirana.

Ceni, Ahmet (1997), "The Role of the Minimum Wage in Establishing Social Equilibrium," in ILO–UNDP–Ministry of Labour of Albania (1997).

Economist Intelligence Unit (1994), *Country Profile Albania, 1994–95*.

Economist Intelligence Unit (1996), *Country Report Albania, 4th Quarter 1996*.

Economist Intelligence Unit (1998a), *Country Profile Albania, 1998–99*.

Economist Intelligence Unit (1998b), *Country Report Albania, 1st Quarter 1998*.

Economist Intelligence Unit (1998c), *Country Report Albania, 3rd Quarter 1998*.

European Bank for Reconstruction and Development (1995), *Transition Report*, London.

European Training Foundation (1997), *The Vocational Education and Training System in Albania—Recent Changes, Challenges and Reform Needs*, Tirana.

Hashi, Iraj and Lindita Xhillari (1998), "Privatisation and Transition in Albania", mimeo, Staffordshire University (January).

Hobdari, Bersant (1998), "Labor Market and Regional Differences in Unemployment in Albania", *East European Series* No. 53 (January).

Ikonomi, Milva (1997), "Measurement of the Subsistence Minimum in Albania", in ILO–UNDP–Ministry of Labour of Albania (1997).

INSTAT (1997), *Statistika 1996–4* (October–December).

INSTAT (1998a), *Statistika 1998–1* (January–March).

INSTAT (1998b), *Statistika 1998–2* (April–June).

International Labour Office (1997), *Albania: Social Dimension of Recovery: Assessment and Proposals for Action*, ILO (September).

International Labour Office (1998), *Employee Ownership in Privatization—Lessons from Central and Eastern Europe, Experts' Policy Report*, ILO–CEET, Budapest.

ILO–UNDP–Ministry of Labour of Albania (1995), *Reforming Wage Policy in Albania*, prepared for the Tripartite Conference "Improving Wage Policy in Albania", held in Tirana, 1–3 November 1995.

ILO–UNDP–Ministry of Labour of Albania (1997), *Tripartism against Crisis—New Incomes Policy as a Driving Force in Albania*, presented at the Tripartite Conference "Tripartism and Negotiated Wage Policy against Crisis in Albania", held in Tirana, 17–18 November 1997.

International Monetary Fund (1994), *IMF Economic Reviews 1994*, IMF, Washington, DC (July).

International Monetary Fund (1997a), *World Economic Outlook*, IMF, Washington, DC.

International Monetary Fund (1997b), *Albania—Recent Economic Developments*, IMF Staff Country Report No. 97/21, IMF, Washington, DC (April).

International Monetary Fund (1998), *Albania—Monthly Economic Statistics* (June).

Jackson, Marvin (1997), "Restructuring or Structural Change in Industry in Transition Countries: A Review of Issues", Working Paper 63/1997, The Leuven Institute for Central and East European Studies, Katholieke Universiteit Leuven.

Jackson, Marvin and Alexander Repkin (1997), "A Comparison of Structural Changes among the Branches of Industry in Seven Transition Countries", Working Paper 64/1997, The Leuven Institute for Central and East European Studies, Katholieke Universiteit Leuven.

Kadare, Ismail (1992), *La pyramide*, Editions Artheme Fayard, Paris. English translation first published in Great Britain in 1996: *The Pyramid*, Harvill Press, London. (Albanian title: *Pluhuri mbretëror*.)

Kodra, Filloreta (1997), "Enhancing the Role of the Minimum Wage in Albania", in ILO–UNDP–Ministry of Labour of Albania (1997).

Kodra, Filloreta (1998), "Wage Dynamics in Albania during Transition", in Vaughan-Whitehead (1998a), pp. 81–100.

Liko, Stavri (1997), "The Collective Agreement as a Crucial Factor in Labour Relations", in ILO–UNDP–Ministry of Labour of Albania (1997).

Llubani, Xhevdet (1997), "Minimum Wages and Living Standards", in ILO–UNDP–Ministry of Labour of Albania (1997).

Mancellari, Ahmet, Harry Papapanagos, and Peter Sanfey (1996), "Job Creation and Temporary Emigration: The Albanian Experience", in *Economics of Transition*, 4 (2).

Metohu, Diana (1997), "The Wage System in the Budgetary Sector: Improvements and Developments", in ILO–UNDP–Ministry of Labour of Albania (1997).

Monck, Charles (1995), *Future Investment—Prospects in Albania*, Harrogate: Charles Monck and Associates (June).

Muço, Marta (1994), "Economic Transition in Albania: Progress and Problems", Working Paper 94–11, Department of Economics, University of Delaware, USA.

Muço, Marta (1995), "The Ongoing Privatisation and Some Preliminary Outcomes in the Transition Economy in Albania: Social and Economic Evidence", presented at the Fifth Trento Workshop "Privatization and Distribution", organised by the European Association for Comparative Economic Studies, 3–4 March, University of Trento.

Muço, Marta (1997), "The Impact of the Informal Financial Sector in the Albanian Crisis 1996–97", presented at the Workshop "Is There a 'Southern Tier' of Transition Economies?", organised by the OSI/CEU, Institute on Southeastern Europe, Budapest, 4–5 July.

Muço, Marta, and Drini Salko (1996), "Some Issues concerning the Development of the Informal Financial Sector in Albania", presented at the Seminar "Hidden Barriers to Economic Growth in the Balkan Peninsula", organised by the Balkan Network, 14 April, at the Annual Meeting of the EBRD, Sofia.

Muço, Marta, Luljeta Minxhozi, and Zana Rusi (1996), "Issues concerning Employment Creation and SME Policy during the Transition in Albania", presented at the International Conference on SME Development and Policy, 24–25 October, SPS University of Bristol.

OECD–CCET (1995), *Agricultural Policies, Markets and Trade in the Central and Eastern European Countries, Selected New Independent States, Mongolia and China—Monitoring and Outlook 1995*, Paris.

Pipes, Richard (1990), *The Russian Revolution*, London: Fontana.

Progri, Vojsava (1997), "Measuring Labour Costs in Industry: Results of the 1996 Enterprise Survey", in ILO–UNDP–Ministry of Labour of Albania (1997).

Standing, Guy (1996), *Russian Unemployment and Enterprise Restructuring—Reviving Dead Souls*, ILO Studies Series, Macmillan.

UNDP (1996), *Albanian Human Development Report 1996*, Tirana.

UNDP (1998), *Albanian Human Development Report 1998*, Tirana.

Uvalic, Milica and Daniel Vaughan-Whitehead (eds) (1997), *Privatization Surprises in Transition Economies—Employee Ownership in Central and Eastern Europe*, Cheltenham: Edward Elgar.

Vaughan-Whitehead, Daniel (1995), "Wage Dynamics in Albanian Industry: Results of the Albanian Enterprise Survey", in ILO–UNDP–Ministry of Labour of Albania (1995).

Vaughan-Whitehead, Daniel (1997), "What Prospects for Albanian Enterprises? Survey Results on Production, Employment and Wages", in ILO–UNDP–Ministry of Labour of Albania (1997).

Vaughan-Whitehead, Daniel (ed.) (1998a), *Paying the Price—The Wage Crisis in Central and Eastern Europe*, ILO Studies Series, Macmillan.

Vaughan-Whitehead, Daniel (1998b), "Profit-sharing in Albania: Boosting Performance in a Crisis Economy", in *Advances in the Economic Analysis of Participatory and Labor-Managed Firms*, Vol. 6, pp. 91–114, JAI Press Inc.

Wood Alan (1997), "The Meaning of the Albanian Revolution", 16 March, mimeo, London.

World Bank (1994), *Albania and The World Bank—Building the Future*, Washington, DC (July).

World Bank (1996a), *Albania—National Road Project*, Report No. 15464–ALB (20 May).

World Bank (1996b), *Albania: Growing Out of Poverty*, Report No. 15698 (August).

World Bank (1996c), *From Plan to Market—World Development Report 1996*, The World Bank, Washington, DC.

World Bank (1997), *Albania—Quick Impact Program for Economic Recovery* (July).

World Bank–European Commission–EBRD (1997a), *Albania—Directions for Recovery and Growth: An Initial Assessment* (July).

World Bank–European Commission–EBRD (1997b), *Albania Donors' Conference—Sector Investment and Technical Assistance Programs for Recovery*, presented at the Donors' Conference, Brussels, 22 October.

Wortman, Miles (1994), "The Private Sector in Albania", Private sector studies: small and medium-sized enterprises, prepared for International Finance Corporation, Washington, DC (June).

Wortman, Miles (1995), "Update: The Private Sector in Albania", Private sector studies: small and medium-sized enterprises, prepared for International Finance Corporation, Washington, DC (June).

Index